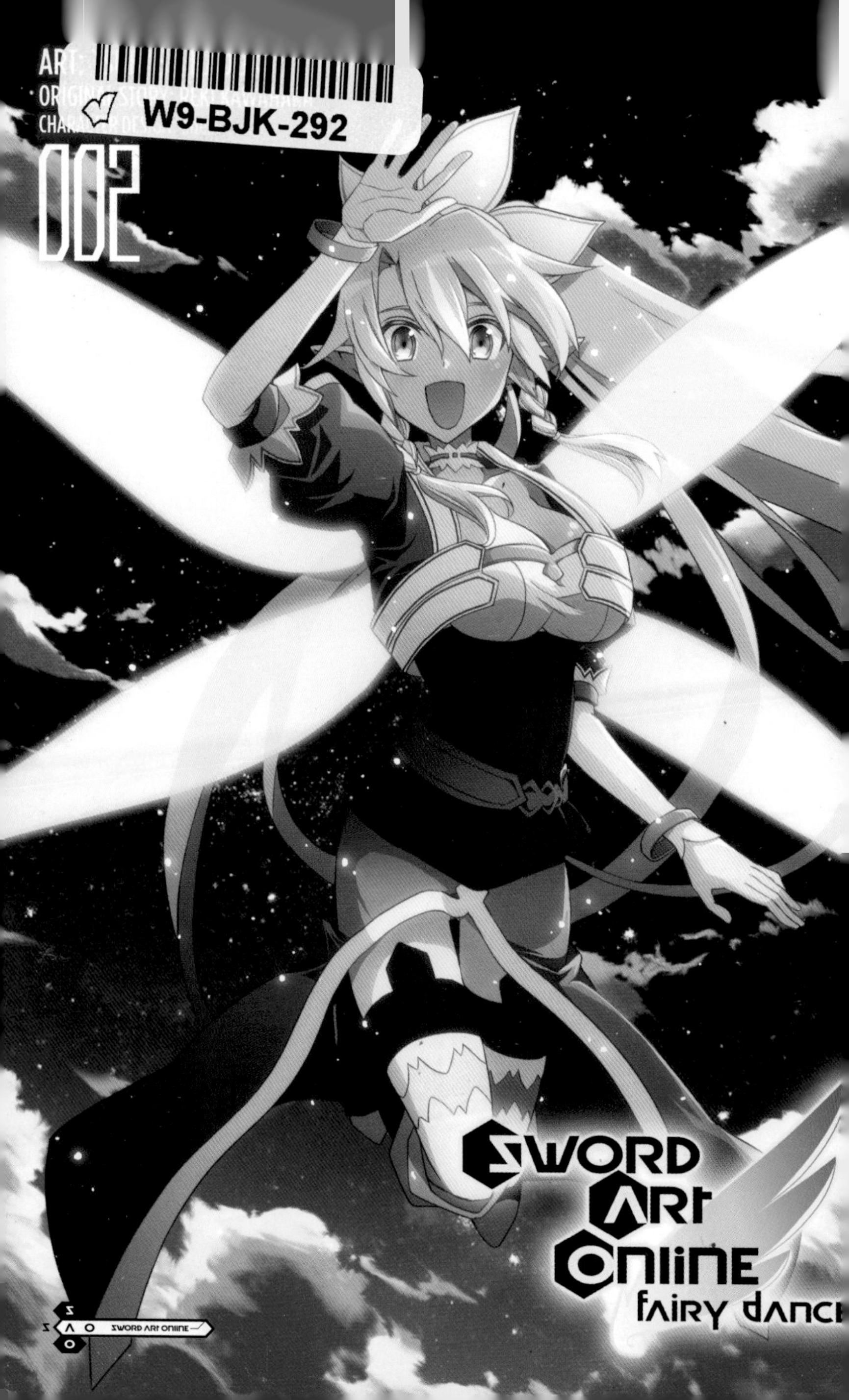
002
SWORD ART ONLINE
fairy dance
SWORD ART ONLINE

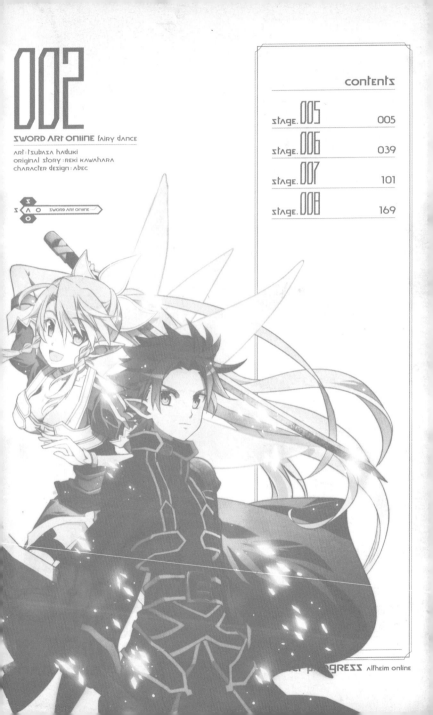

002

SWORD ART ONLINE fairy dance

art: tsubasa haduki
original story: reki kawahara
character design: abec

contents

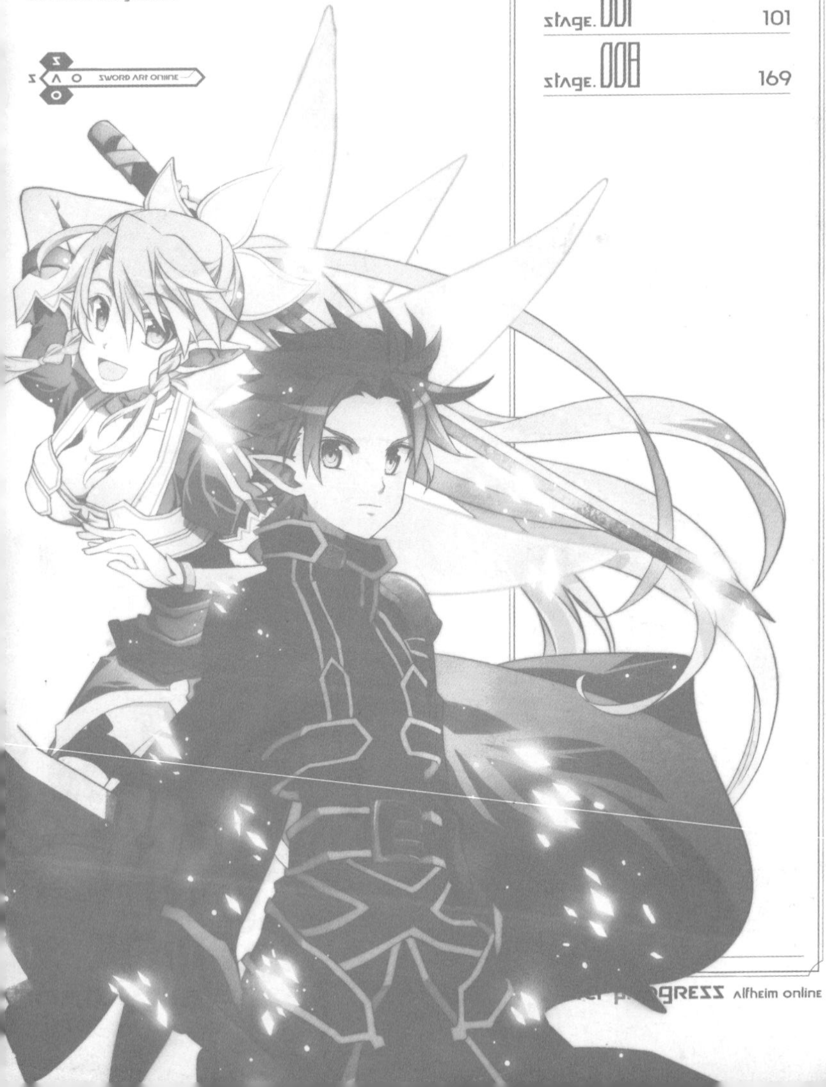

GRESS alfheim online

SWORD ART ONLINE fairy dance

002

SWORD ART ONLINE fairy dance

art: tsubasa haduki
original story: reki kawahara
character design: abec

stage.005

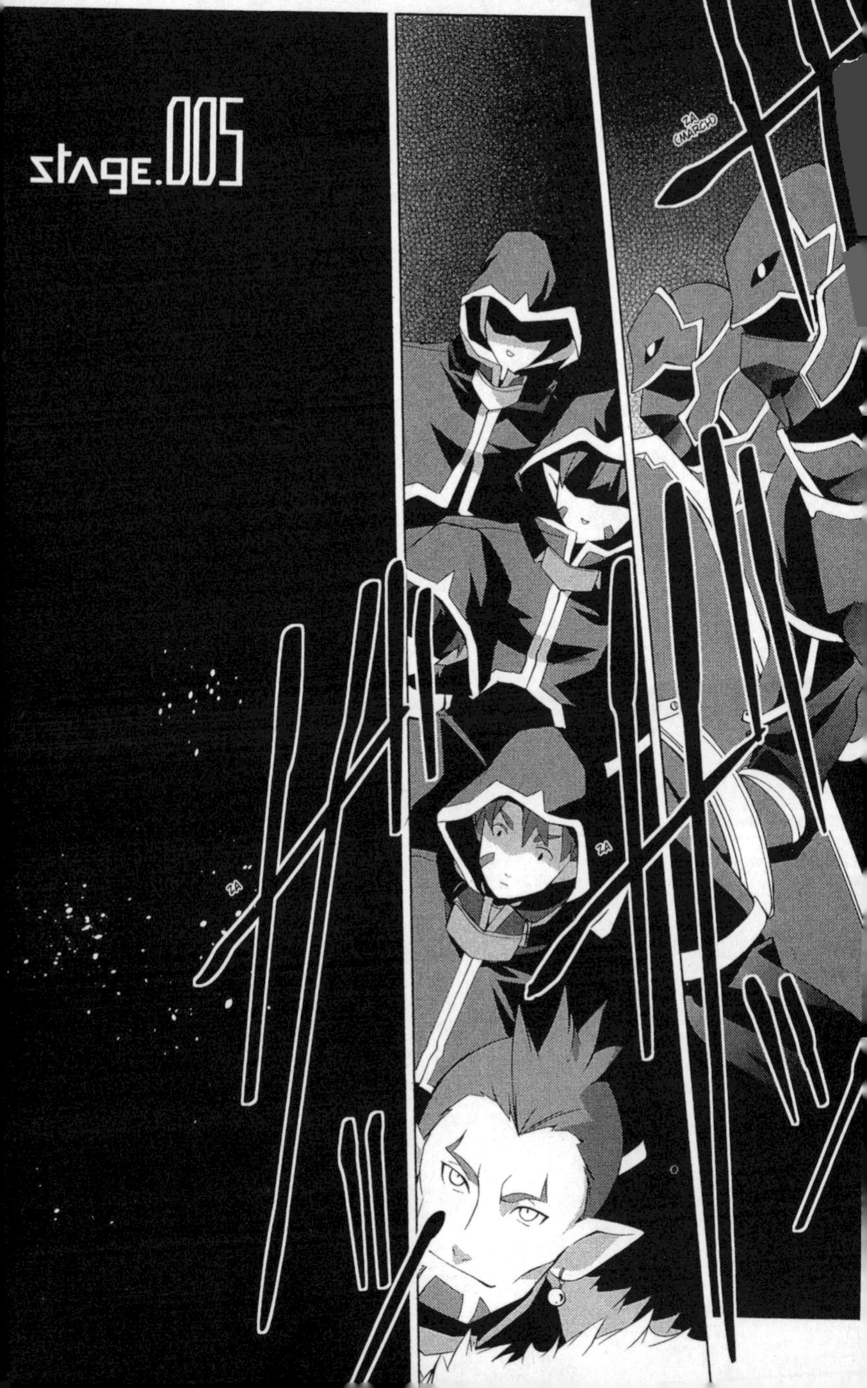
ZA (MARCH)
ZA
ZA

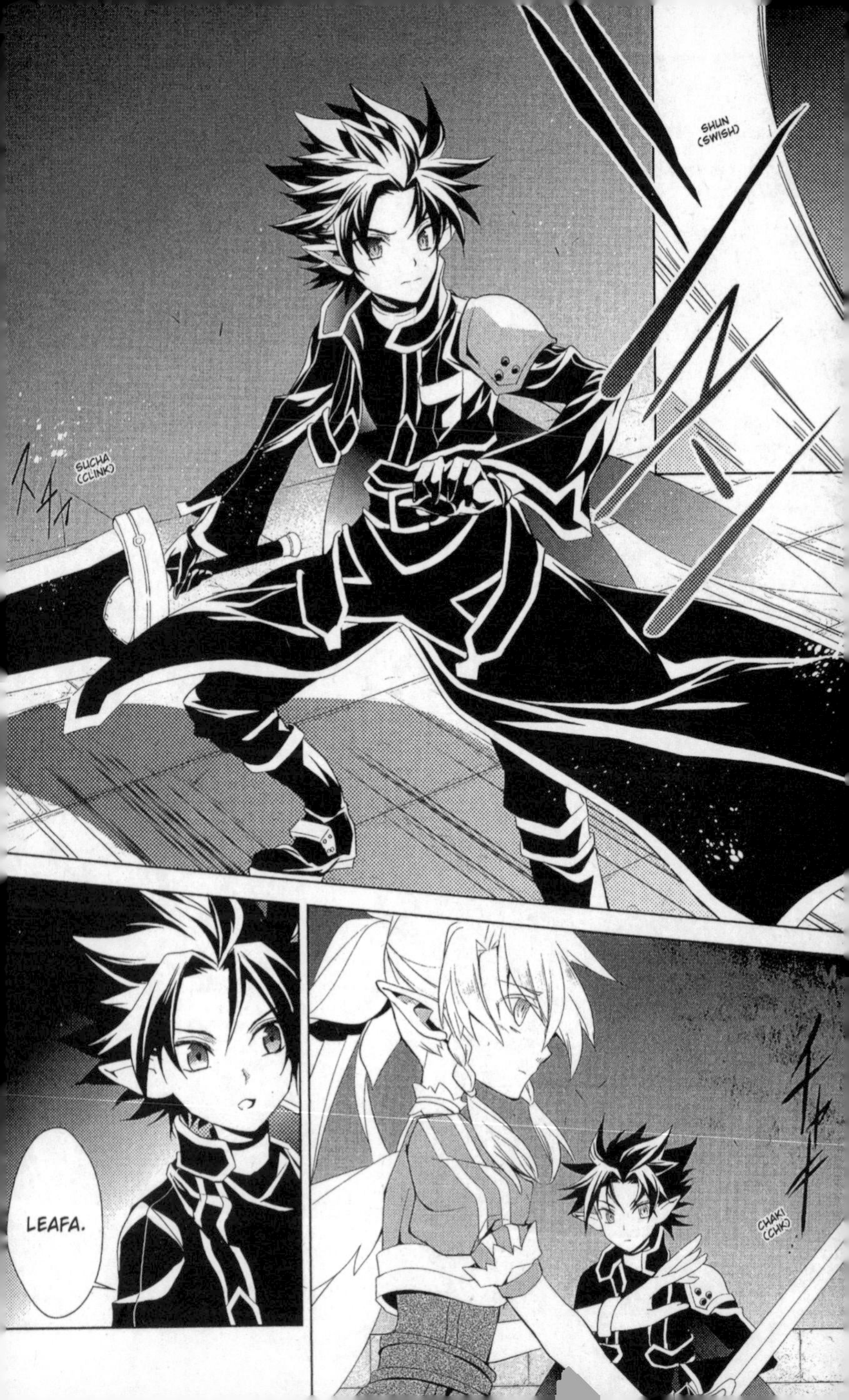
SHUN (SWISH)
SUCHA (CLINK)
CHAKI (CHK)
LEAFA.

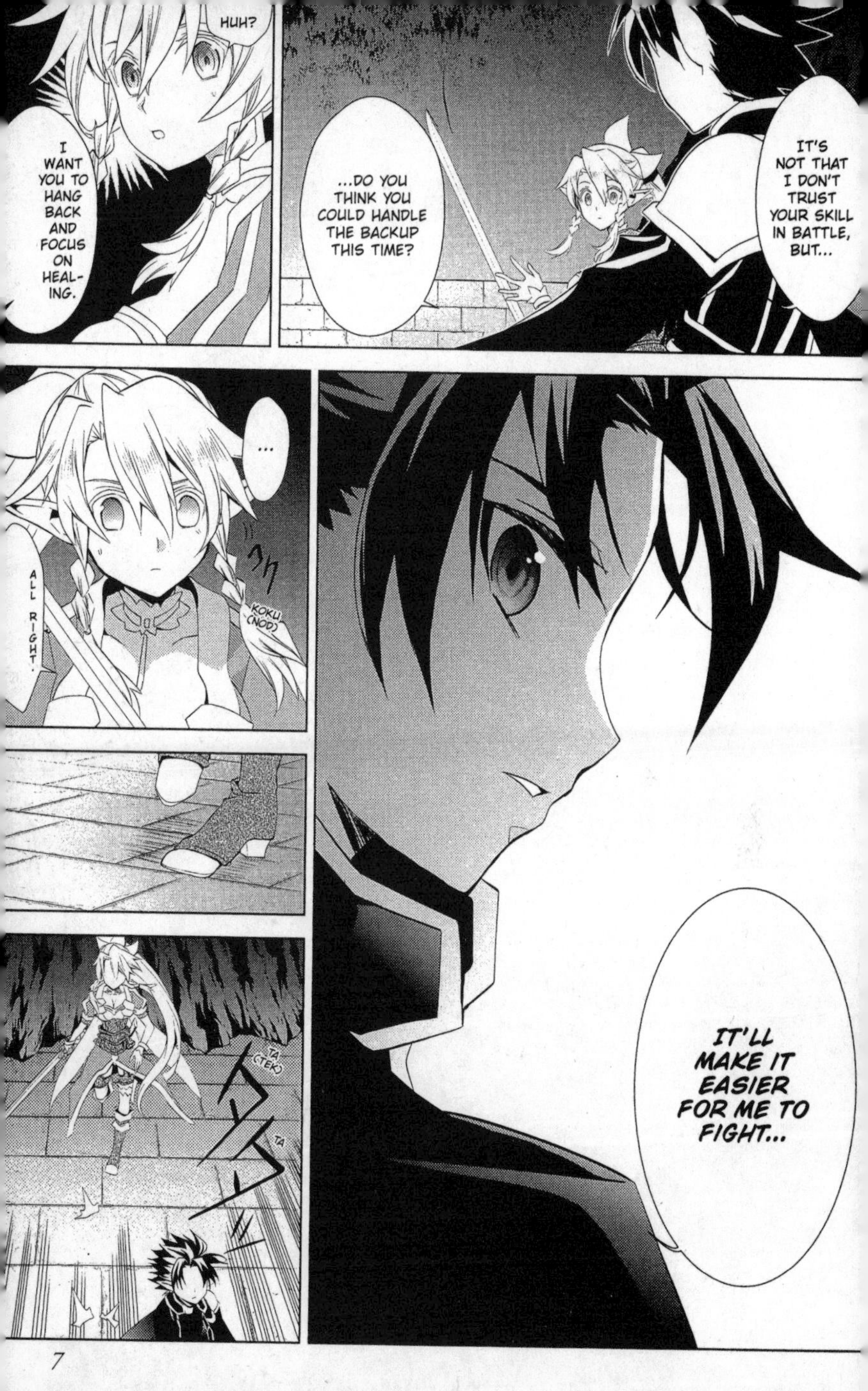
IT'S NOT THAT I DON'T TRUST YOUR SKILL IN BATTLE, BUT...
...DO YOU THINK YOU COULD HANDLE THE BACKUP THIS TIME?
HUH?
I WANT YOU TO HANG BACK AND FOCUS ON HEALING.
IT'LL MAKE IT EASIER FOR ME TO FIGHT...
...
KOKU (NOD)
ALL RIGHT.
TA (TEK)
TA

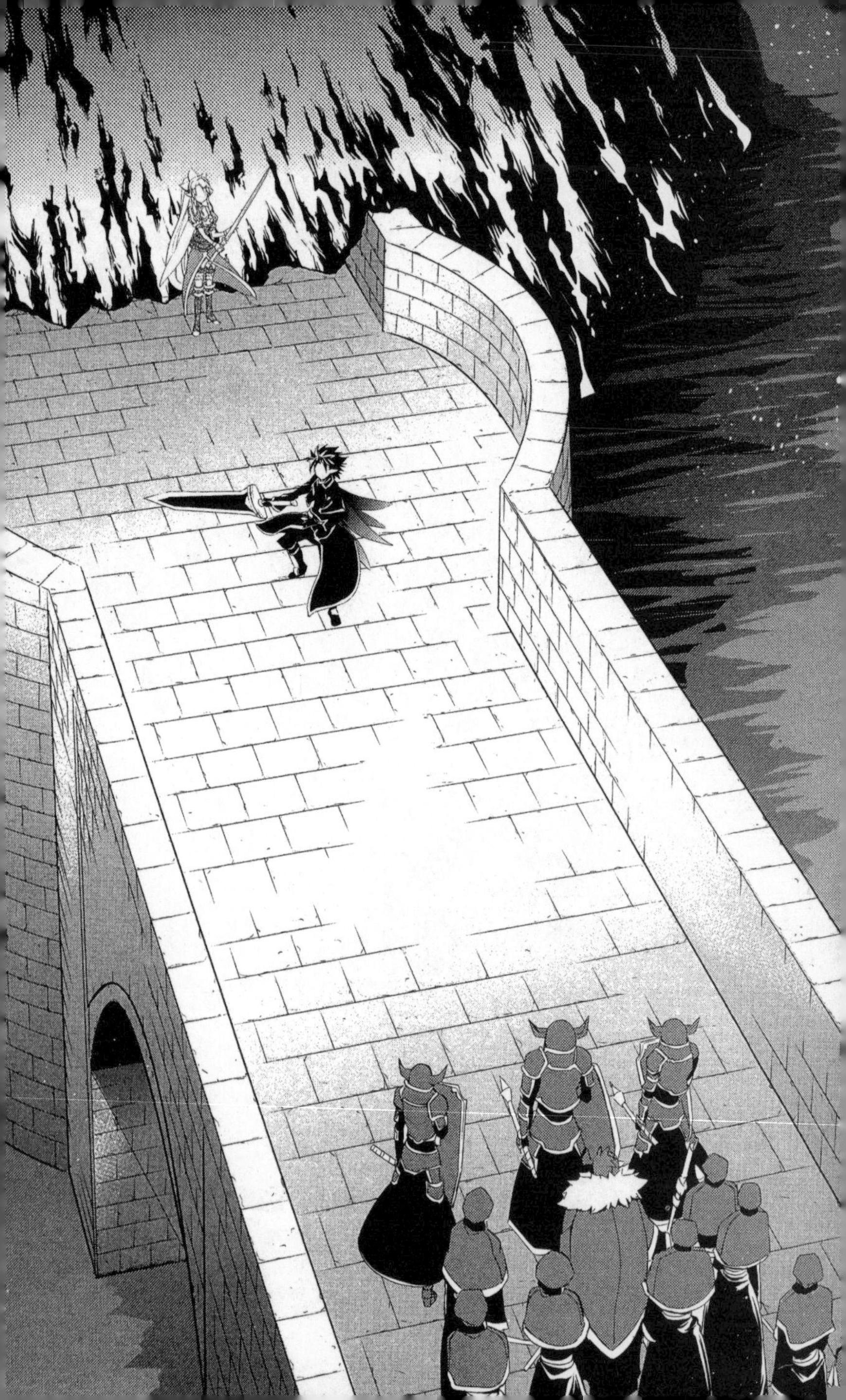

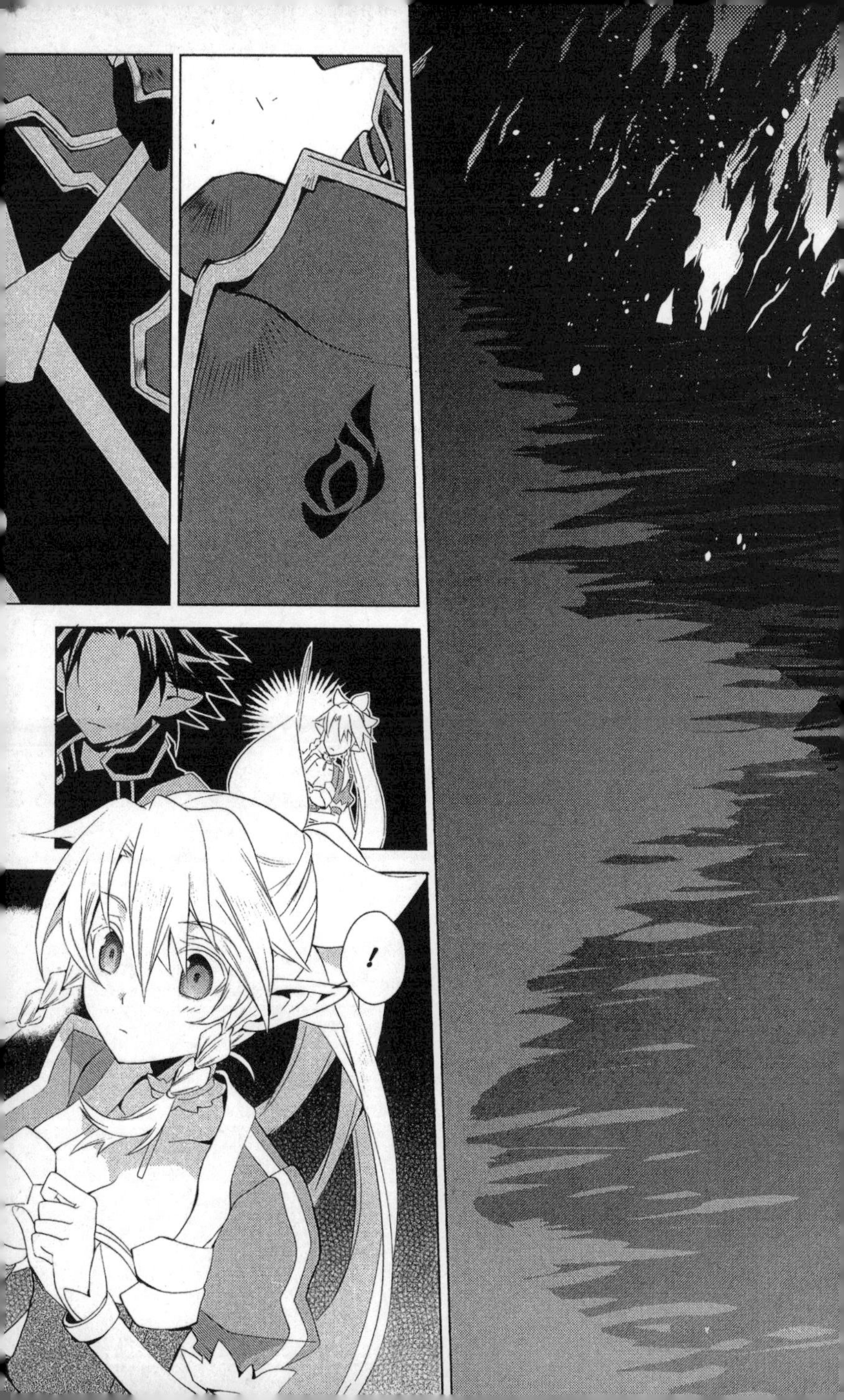
!

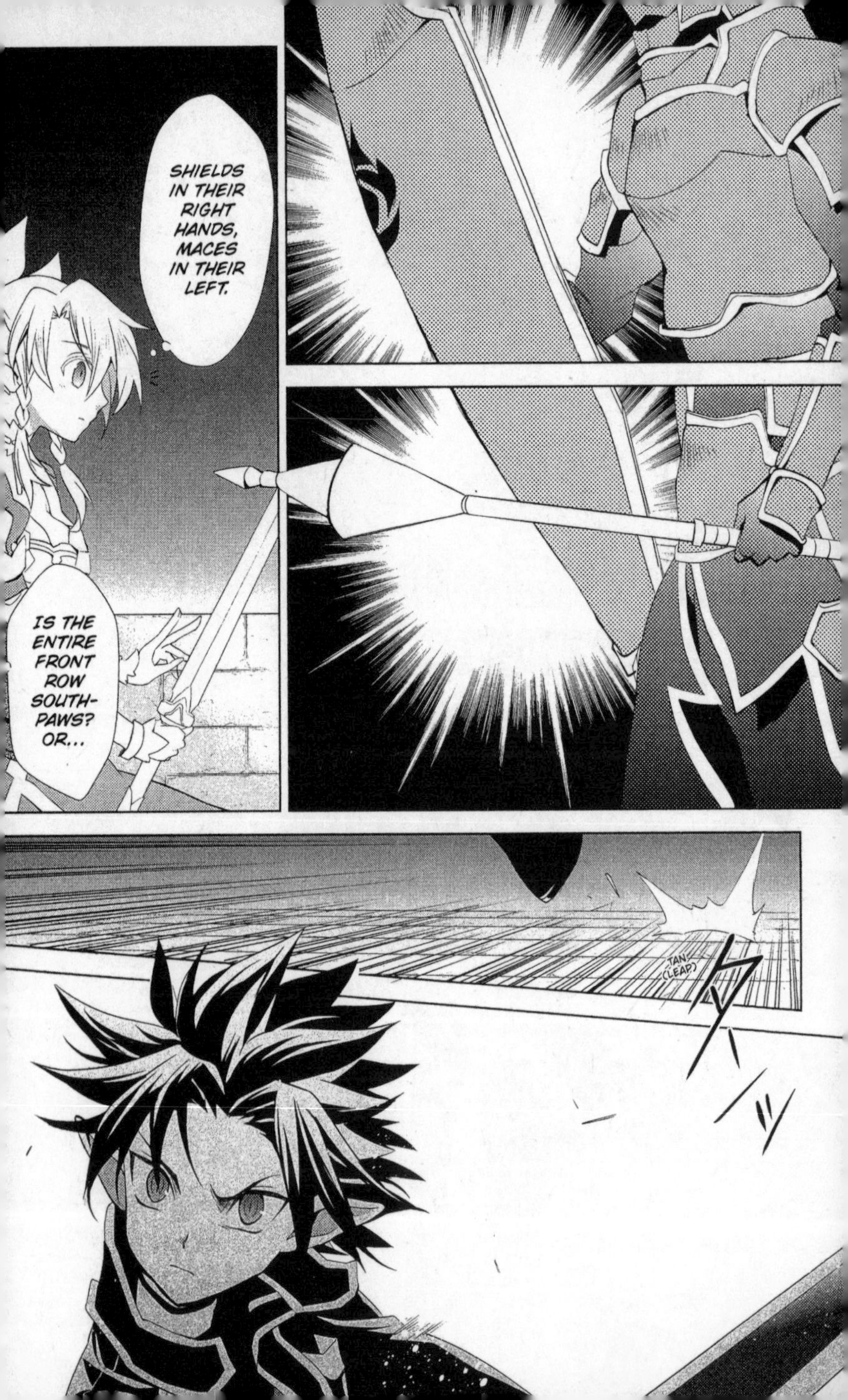
SHIELDS IN THEIR RIGHT HANDS, MACES IN THEIR LEFT.
IS THE ENTIRE FRONT ROW SOUTH-PAWS? OR...
TAN (LEAP)

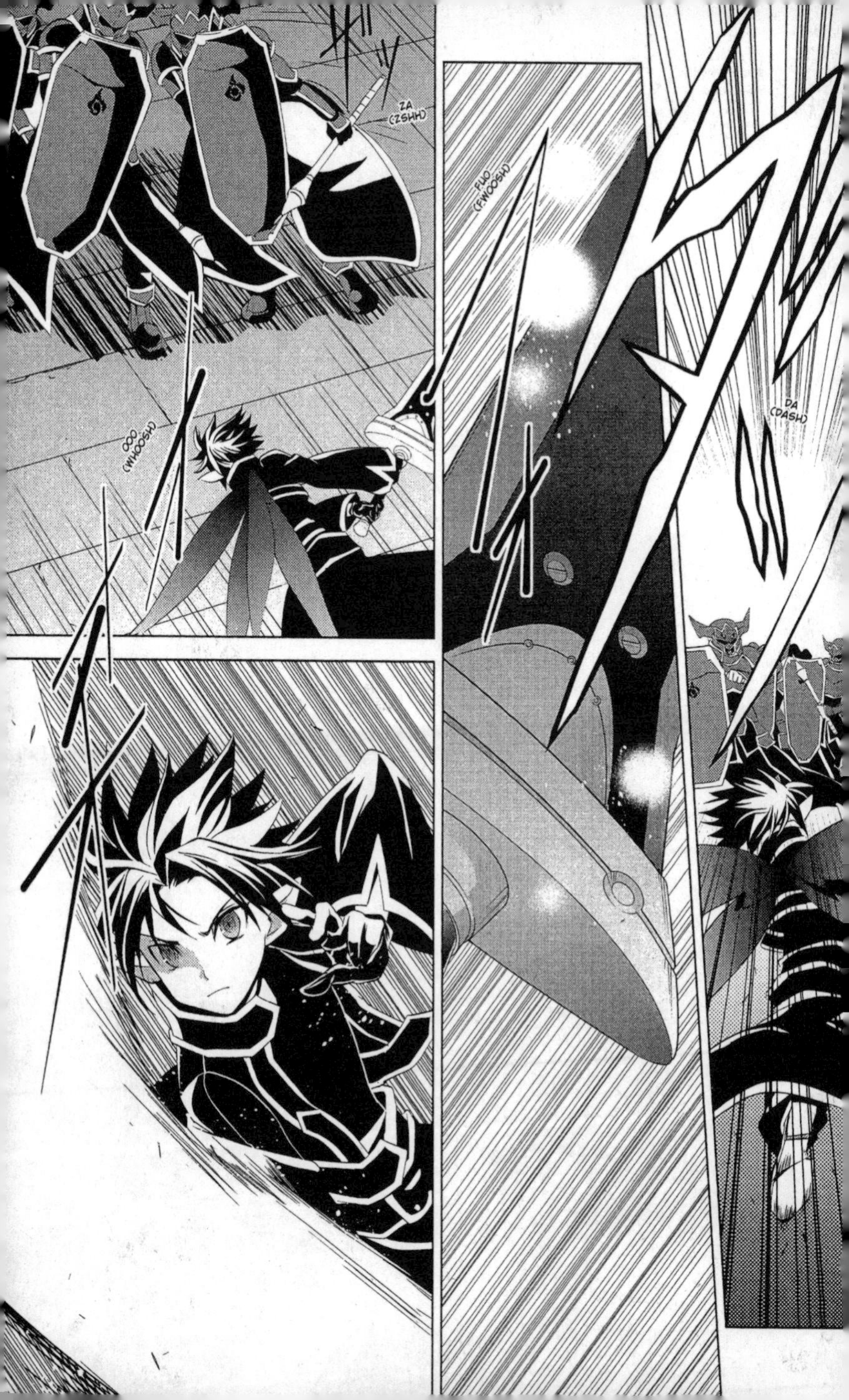
DA (DASH)
FUO (FWOOSH)
ZA (ZSHH)
OOO (WHOOSH)

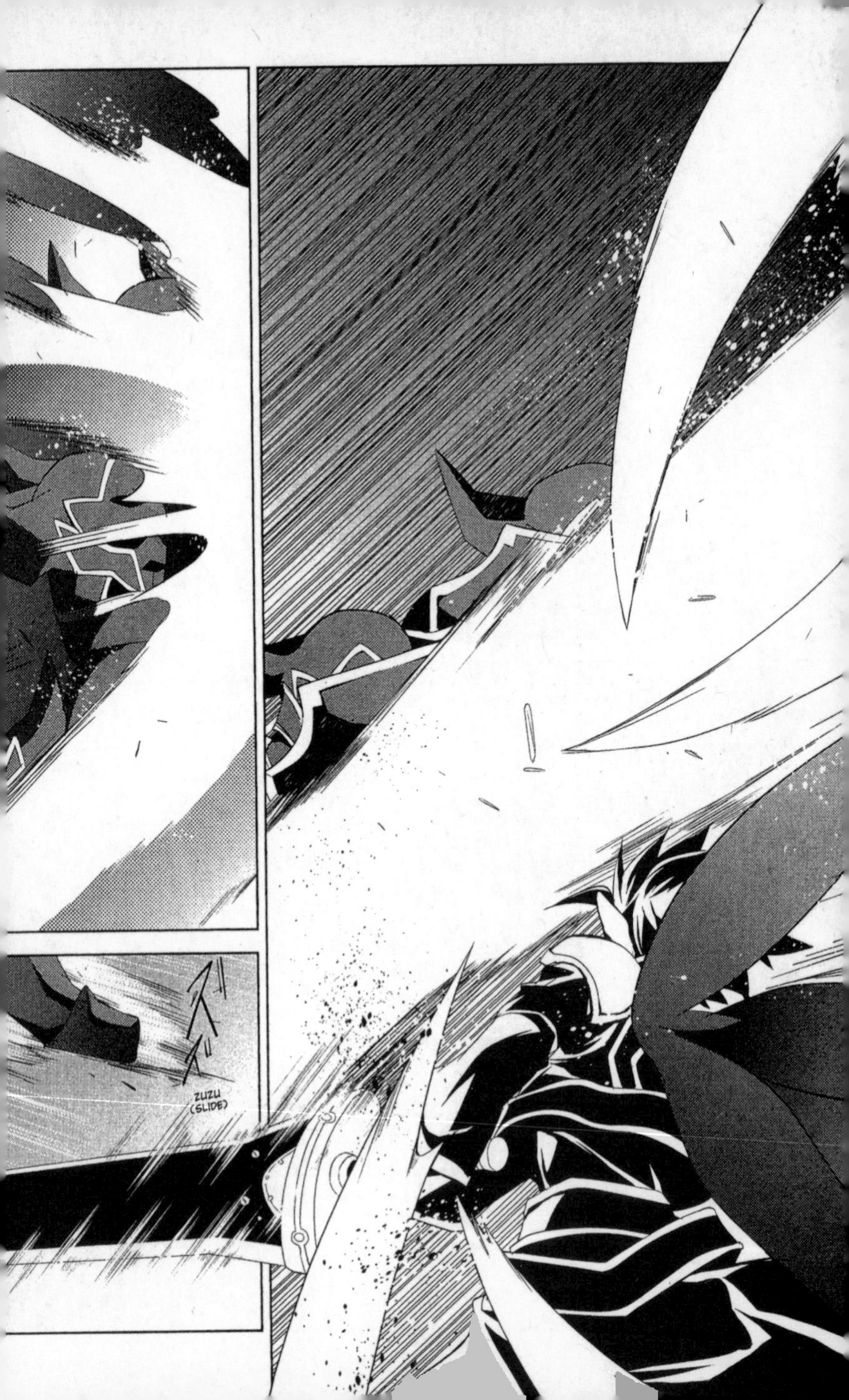
ZUZU
(SLIDE)

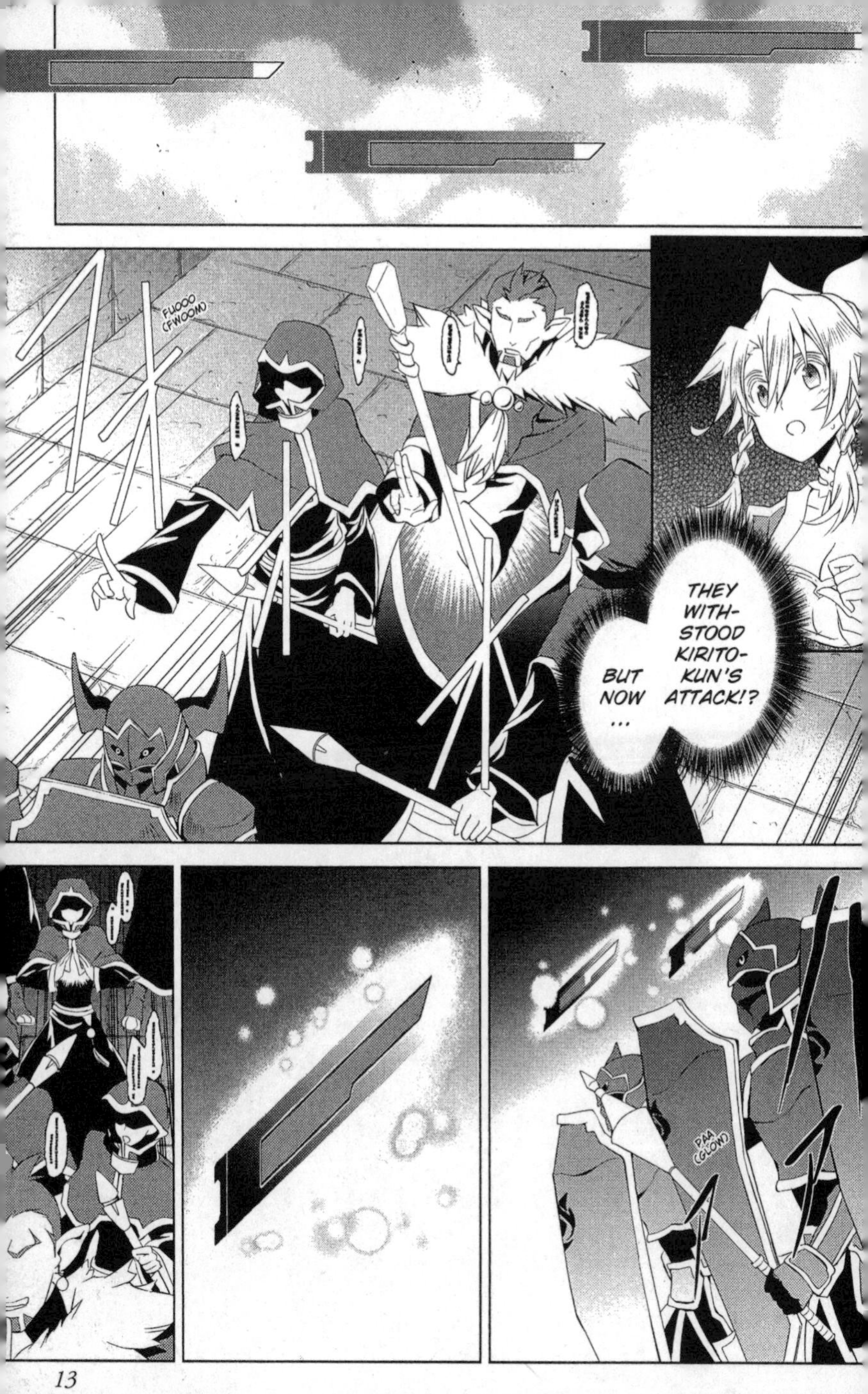
FUOOO (FWOOM)
THEY WITH-STOOD KIRITO-KUN'S ATTACK!?
BUT NOW ...
PAA (GLOW)

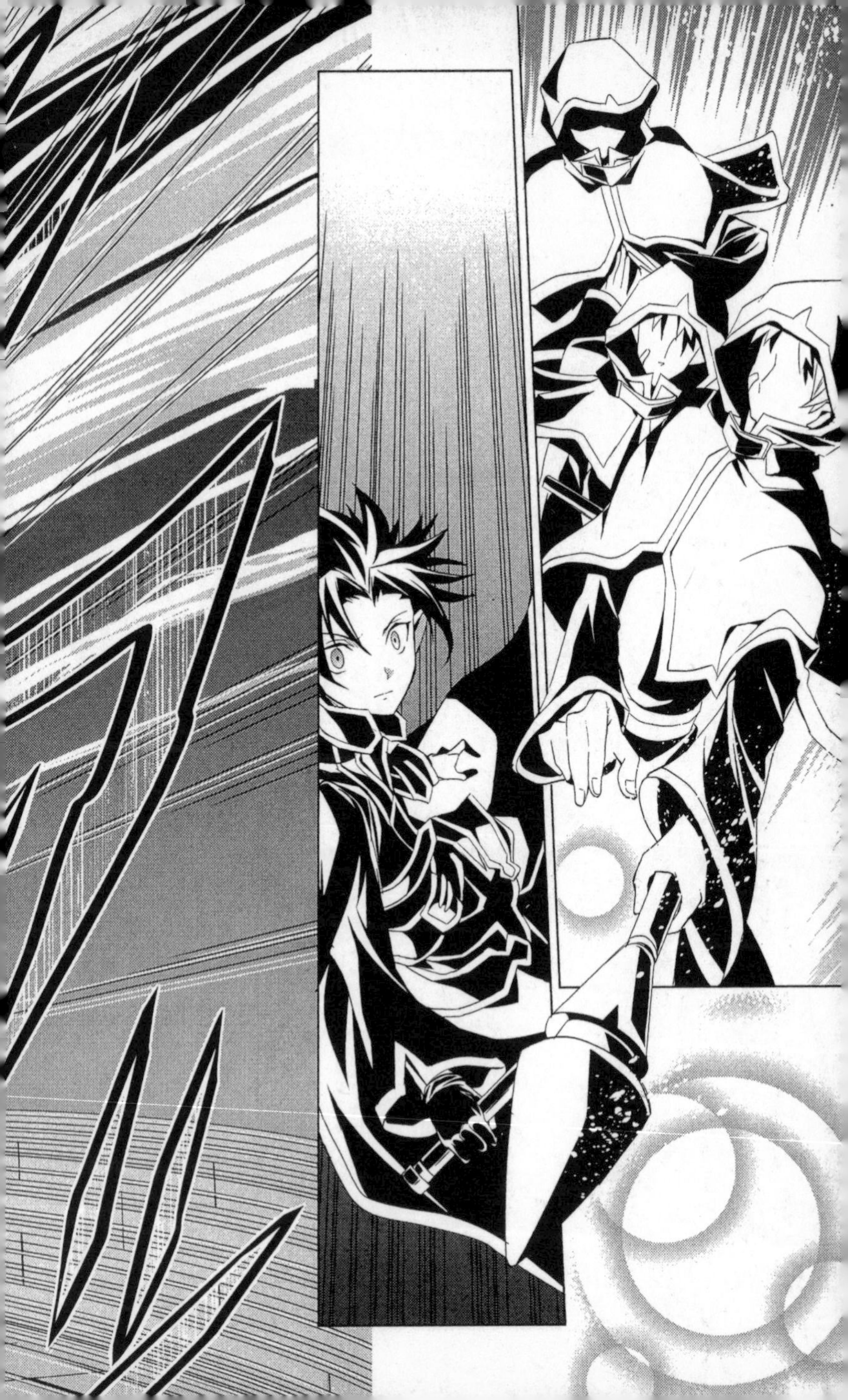

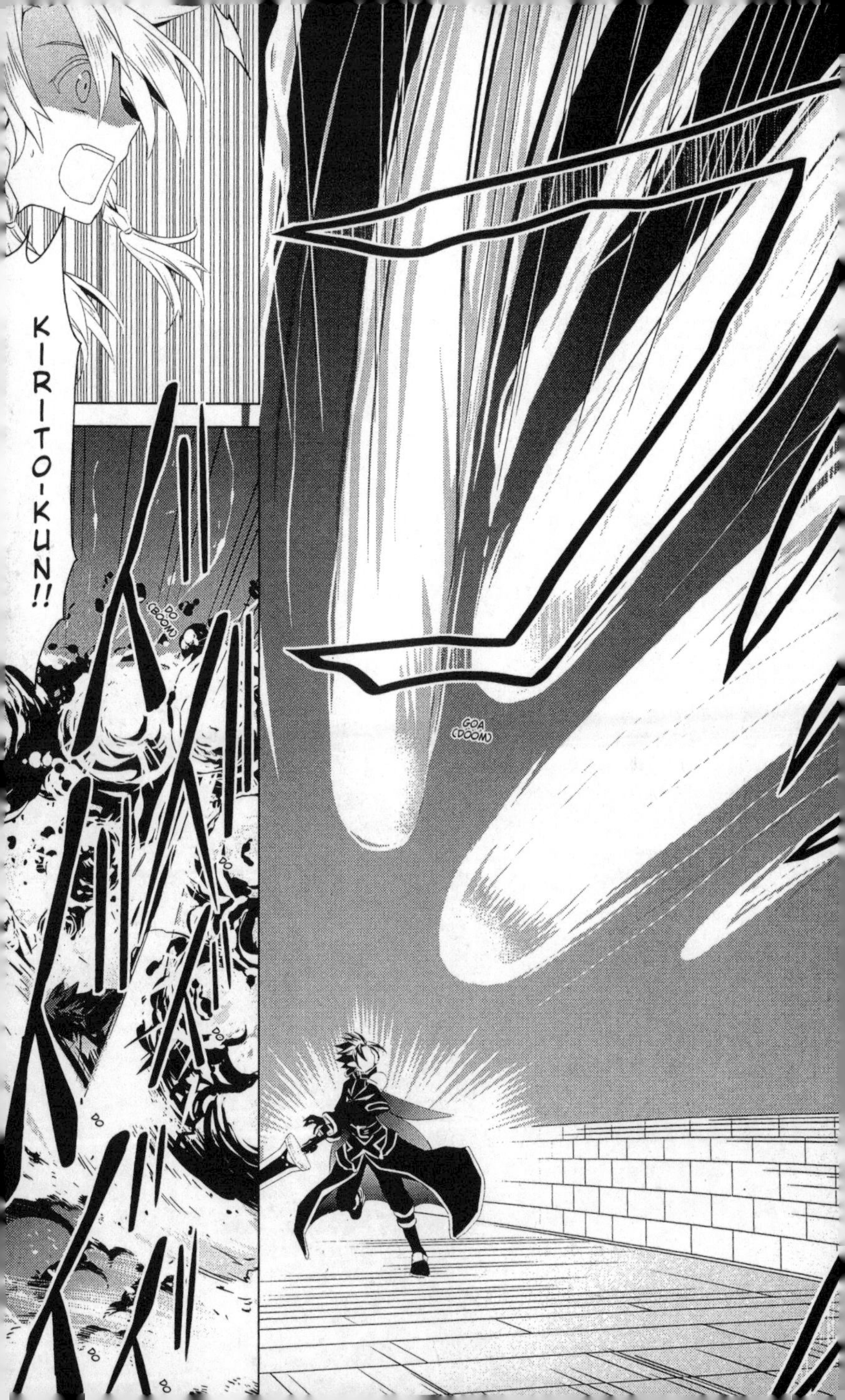
GOA (DOOM)
KIRITO-KUN!!
DO (BOOM)
DO
DO
DO
DO
DO

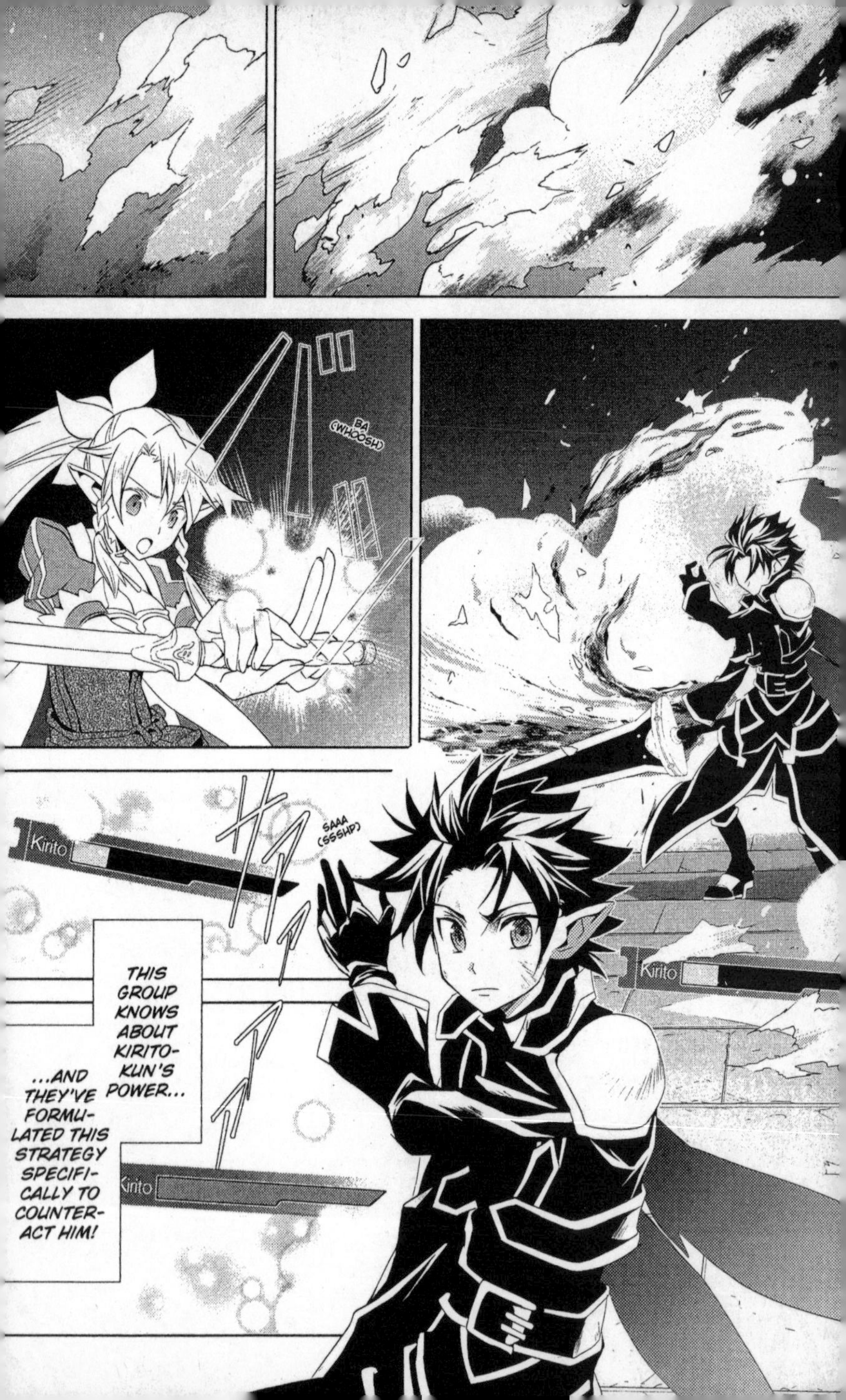
BA (WHOOSH)
SAAA (SSSHP)
Kirito
Kirito
Kirito
THIS GROUP KNOWS ABOUT KIRITO-KUN'S POWER...
...AND THEY'VE FORMULATED THIS STRATEGY SPECIFICALLY TO COUNTERACT HIM!

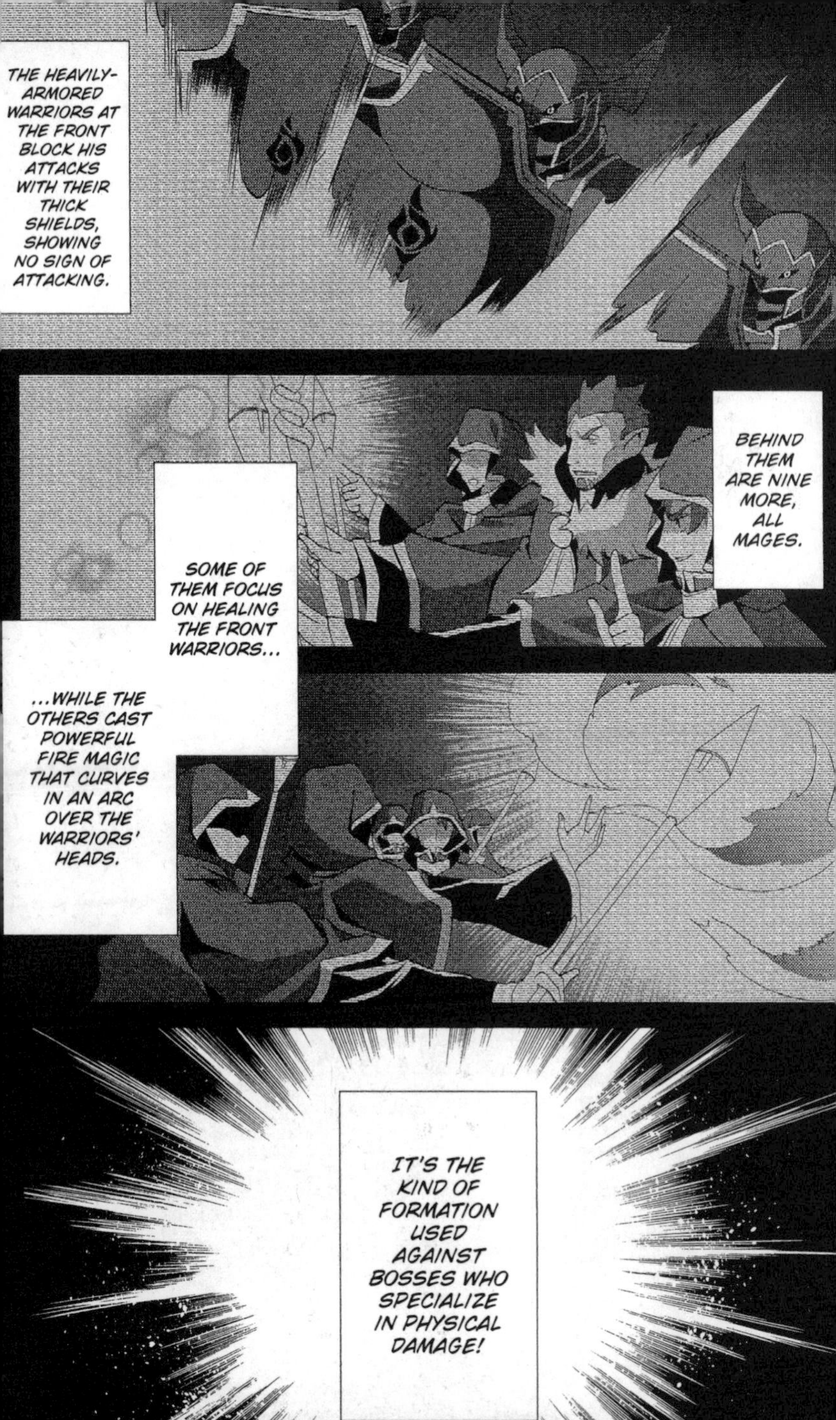
THE HEAVILY-ARMORED WARRIORS AT THE FRONT BLOCK HIS ATTACKS WITH THEIR THICK SHIELDS, SHOWING NO SIGN OF ATTACKING.
BEHIND THEM ARE NINE MORE, ALL MAGES.
SOME OF THEM FOCUS ON HEALING THE FRONT WARRIORS...
...WHILE THE OTHERS CAST POWERFUL FIRE MAGIC THAT CURVES IN AN ARC OVER THE WARRIORS' HEADS.
IT'S THE KIND OF FORMATION USED AGAINST BOSSES WHO SPECIALIZE IN PHYSICAL DAMAGE!

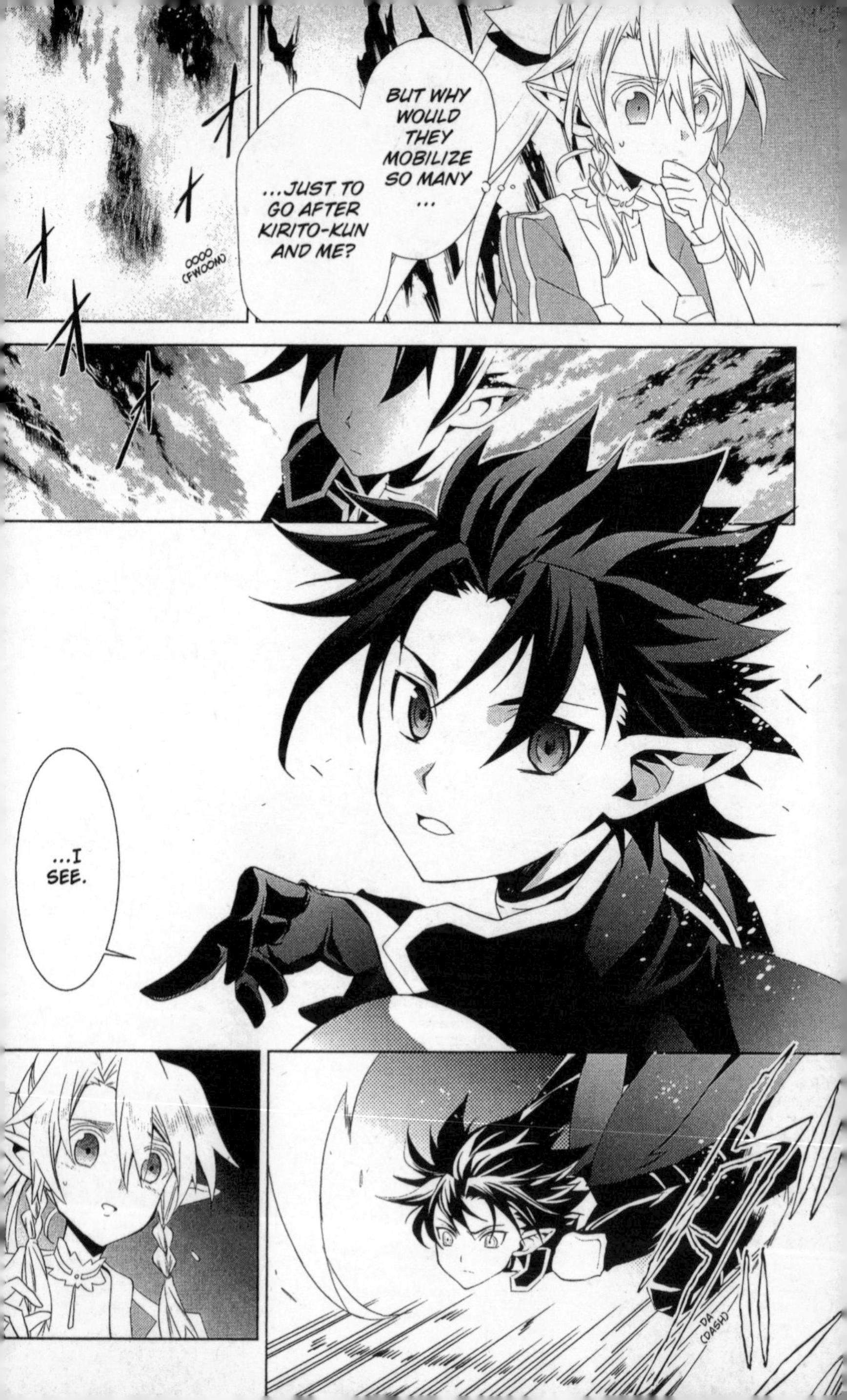
BUT WHY WOULD THEY MOBILIZE SO MANY ...
...JUST TO GO AFTER KIRITO-KUN AND ME?
OOOO (FWOOM)
...I SEE.
DA (DASH)

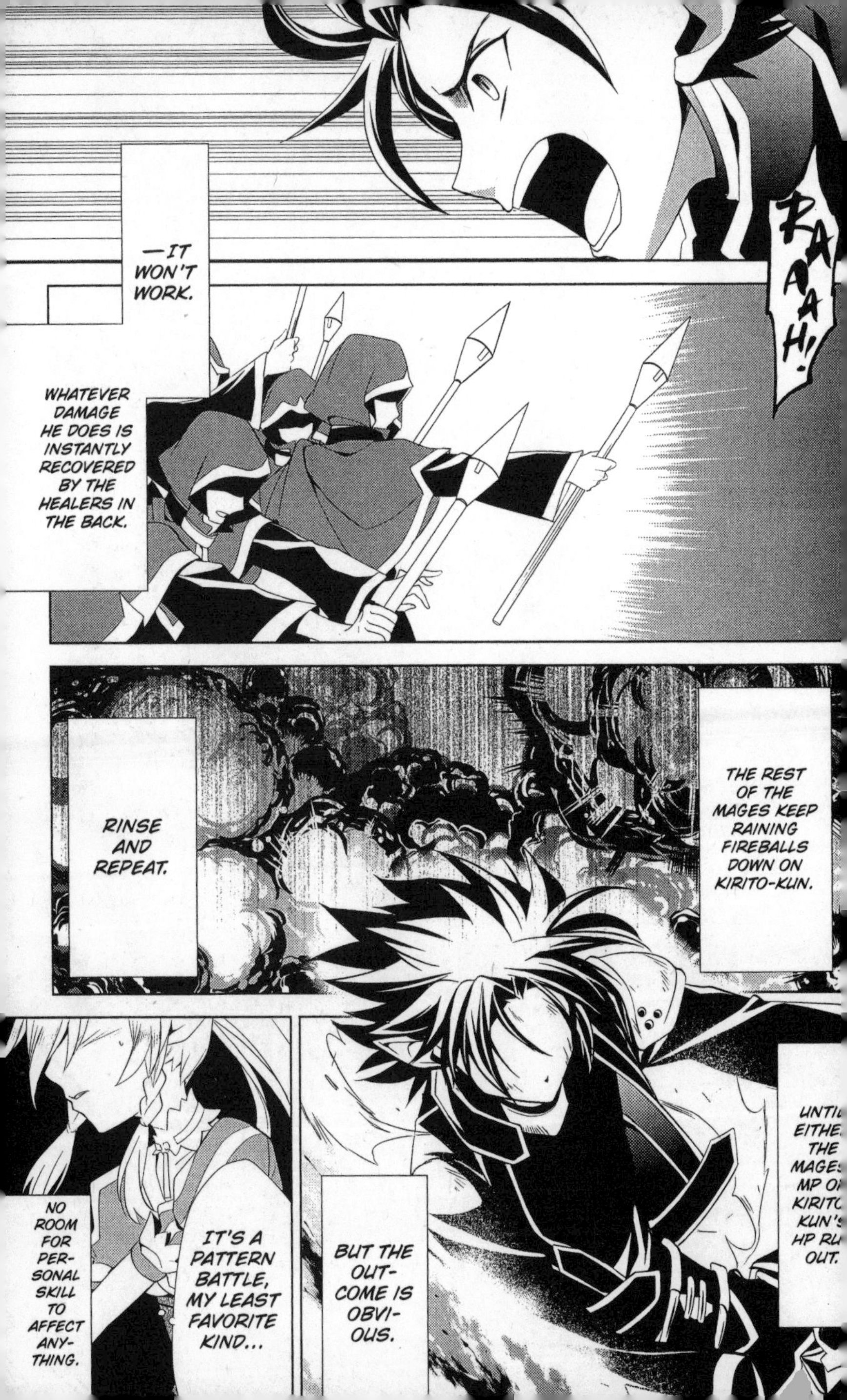
RAAAH!
—IT WON'T WORK.
WHATEVER DAMAGE HE DOES IS INSTANTLY RECOVERED BY THE HEALERS IN THE BACK.
THE REST OF THE MAGES KEEP RAINING FIREBALLS DOWN ON KIRITO-KUN.
RINSE AND REPEAT.
UNTIL EITHE THE MAGES MP O KIRITO KUN'S HP RU OUT.
BUT THE OUTCOME IS OBVIOUS.
IT'S A PATTERN BATTLE, MY LEAST FAVORITE KIND...
NO ROOM FOR PERSONAL SKILL TO AFFECT ANYTHING.

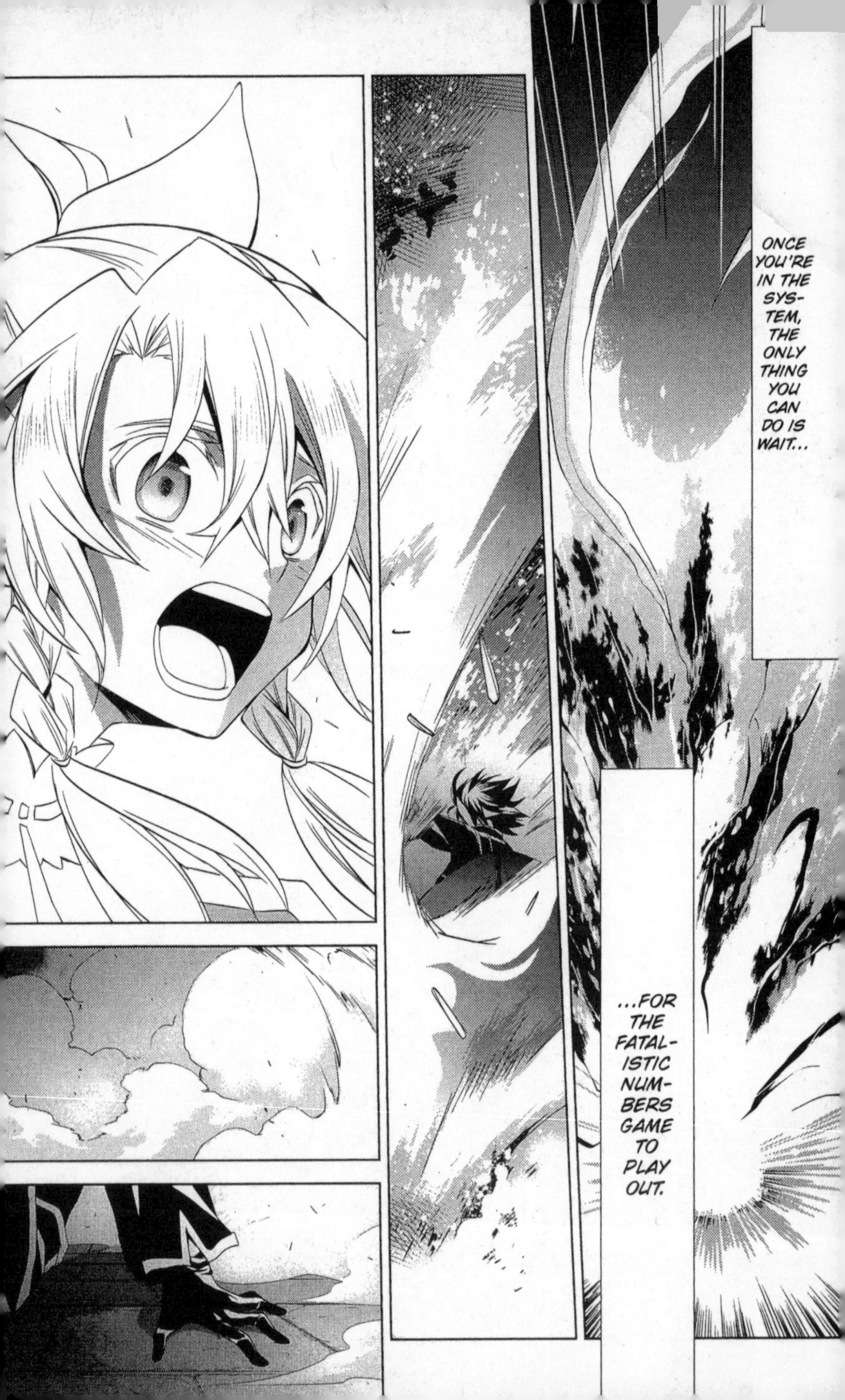
ONCE YOU'RE IN THE SYS-TEM, THE ONLY THING YOU CAN DO IS WAIT...
...FOR THE FATAL-ISTIC NUM-BERS GAME TO PLAY OUT.

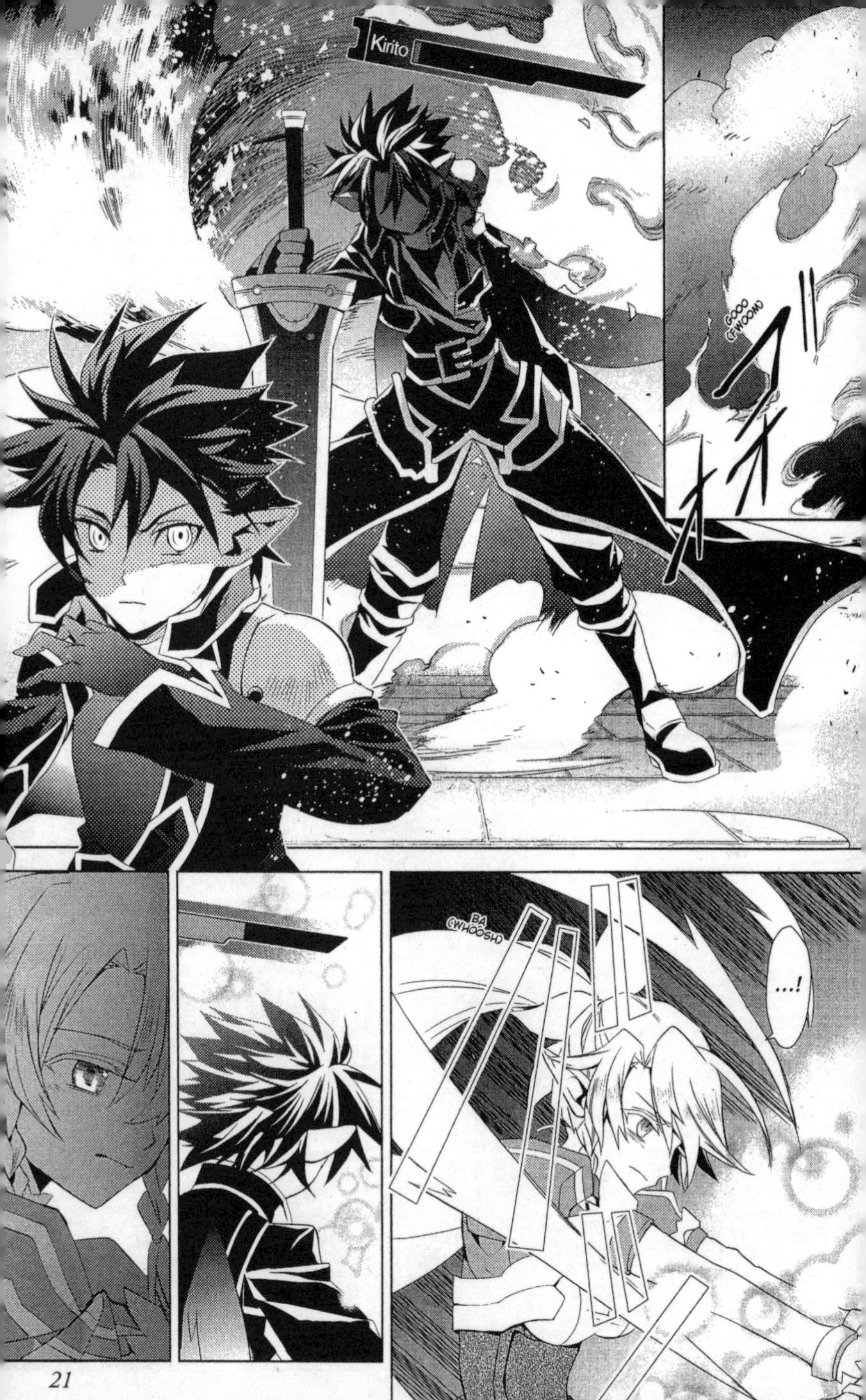
GOOO
(FWOOM)
Kirito
BA
(WHOOSH)
...!

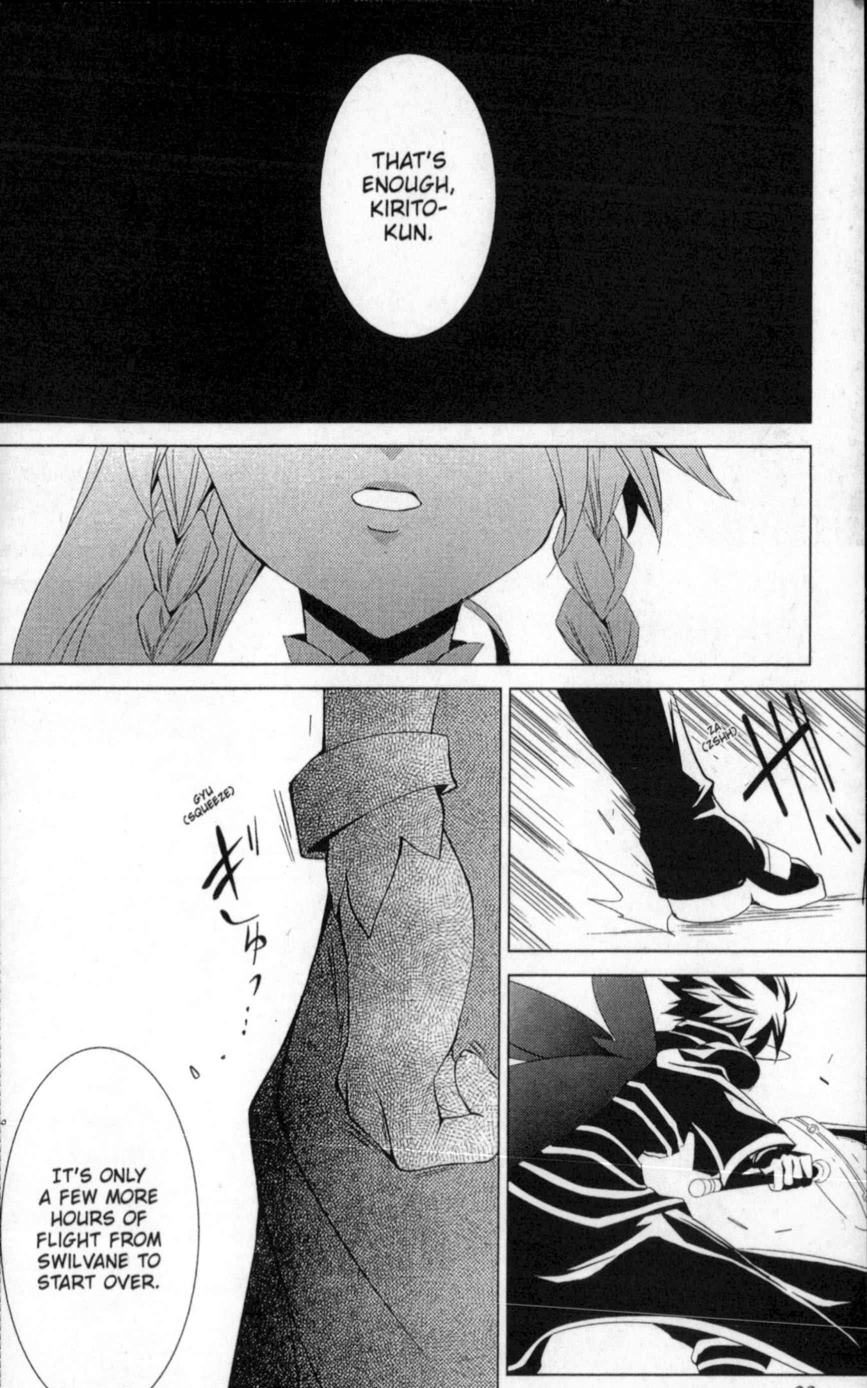
THAT'S ENOUGH, KIRITO-KUN.
ZA (ZSHH)
GYU (SQUEEZE)
IT'S ONLY A FEW MORE HOURS OF FLIGHT FROM SWILVANE TO START OVER.

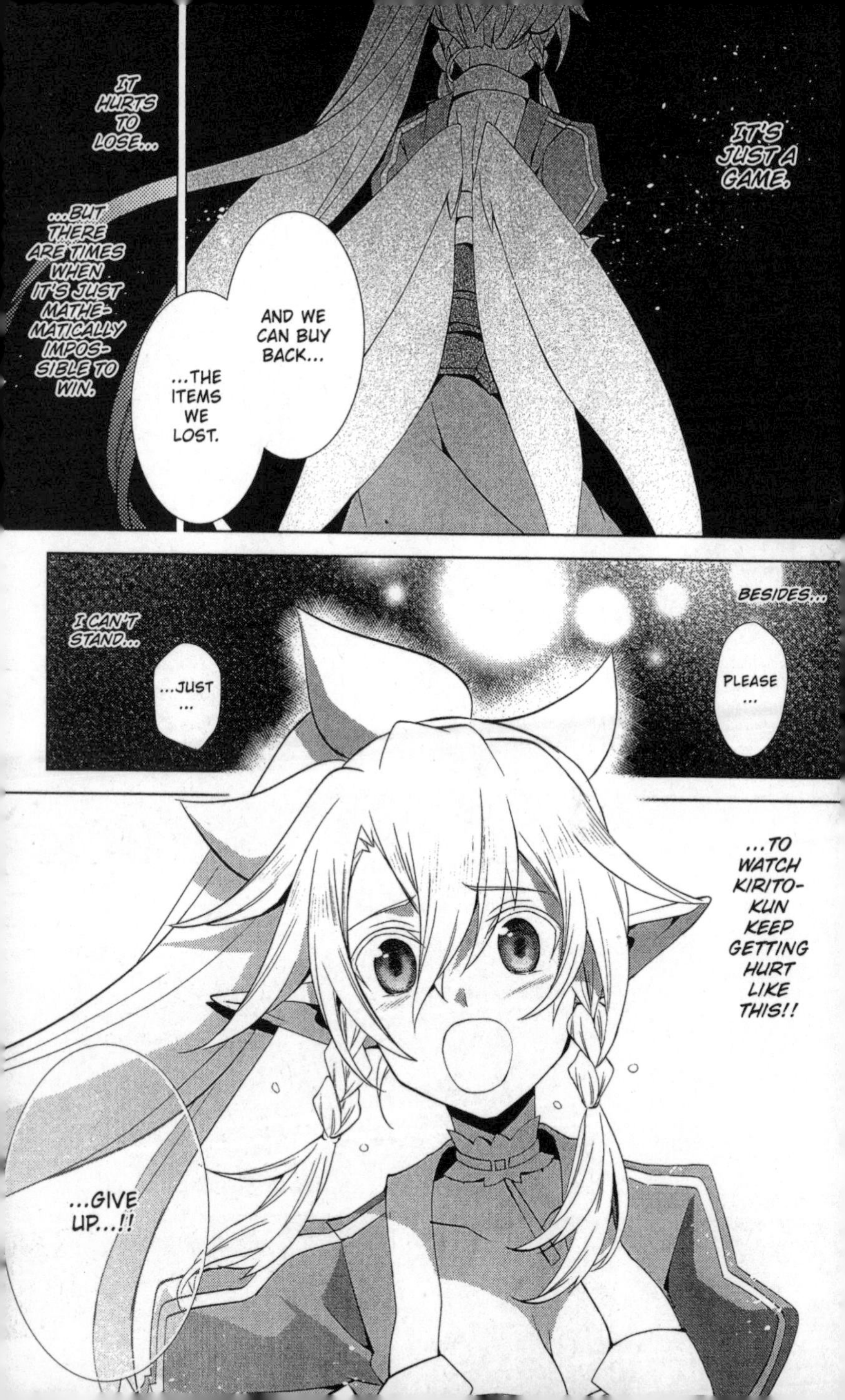
IT'S JUST A GAME.
AND WE CAN BUY BACK...
...THE ITEMS WE LOST.
IT HURTS TO LOSE...
...BUT THERE ARE TIMES WHEN IT'S JUST MATHE-MATICALLY IMPOS-SIBLE TO WIN.
BESIDES...
PLEASE ...
I CAN'T STAND...
...JUST ...
...TO WATCH KIRITO-KUN KEEP GETTING HURT LIKE THIS!!
...GIVE UP...!!

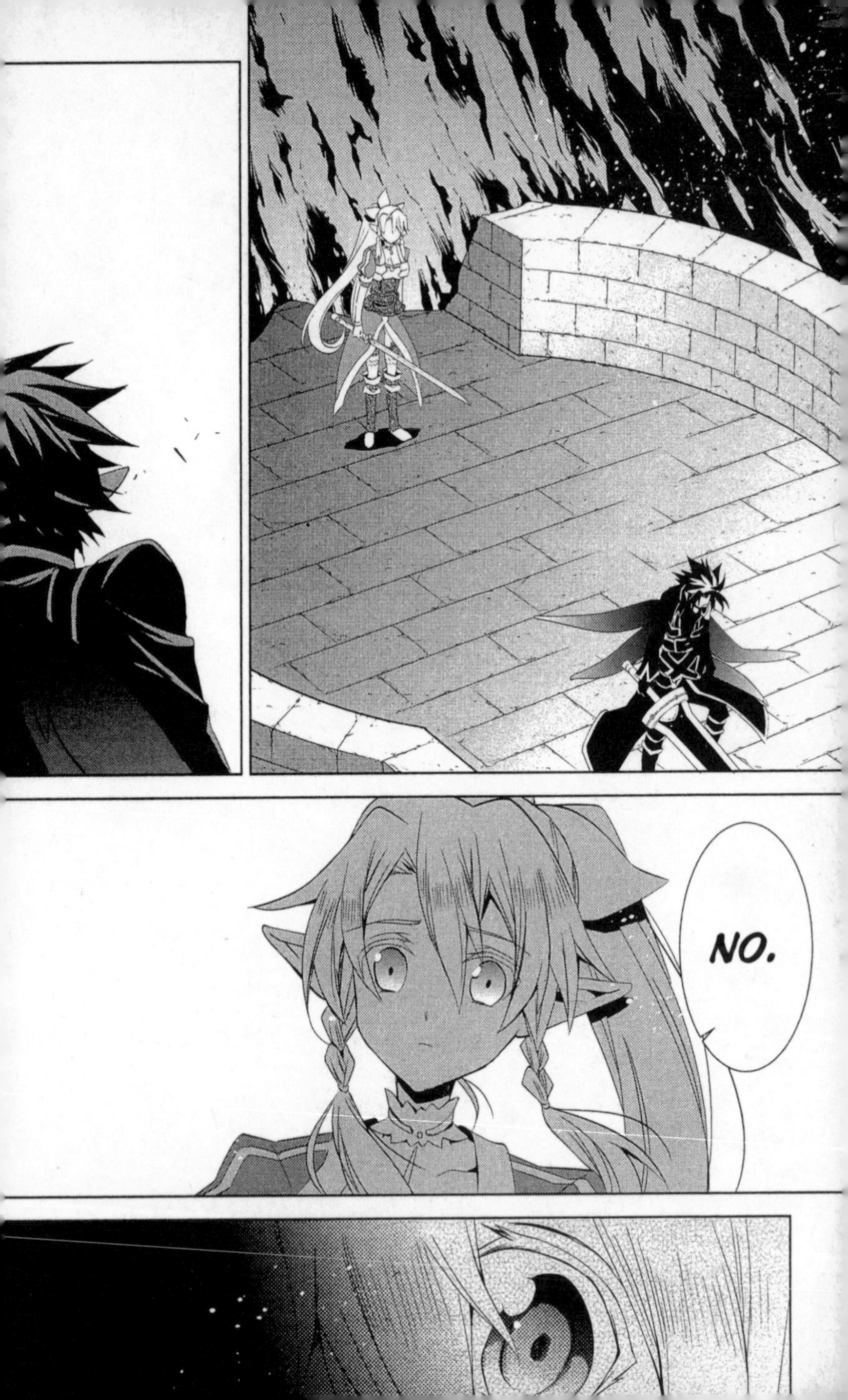
NO.

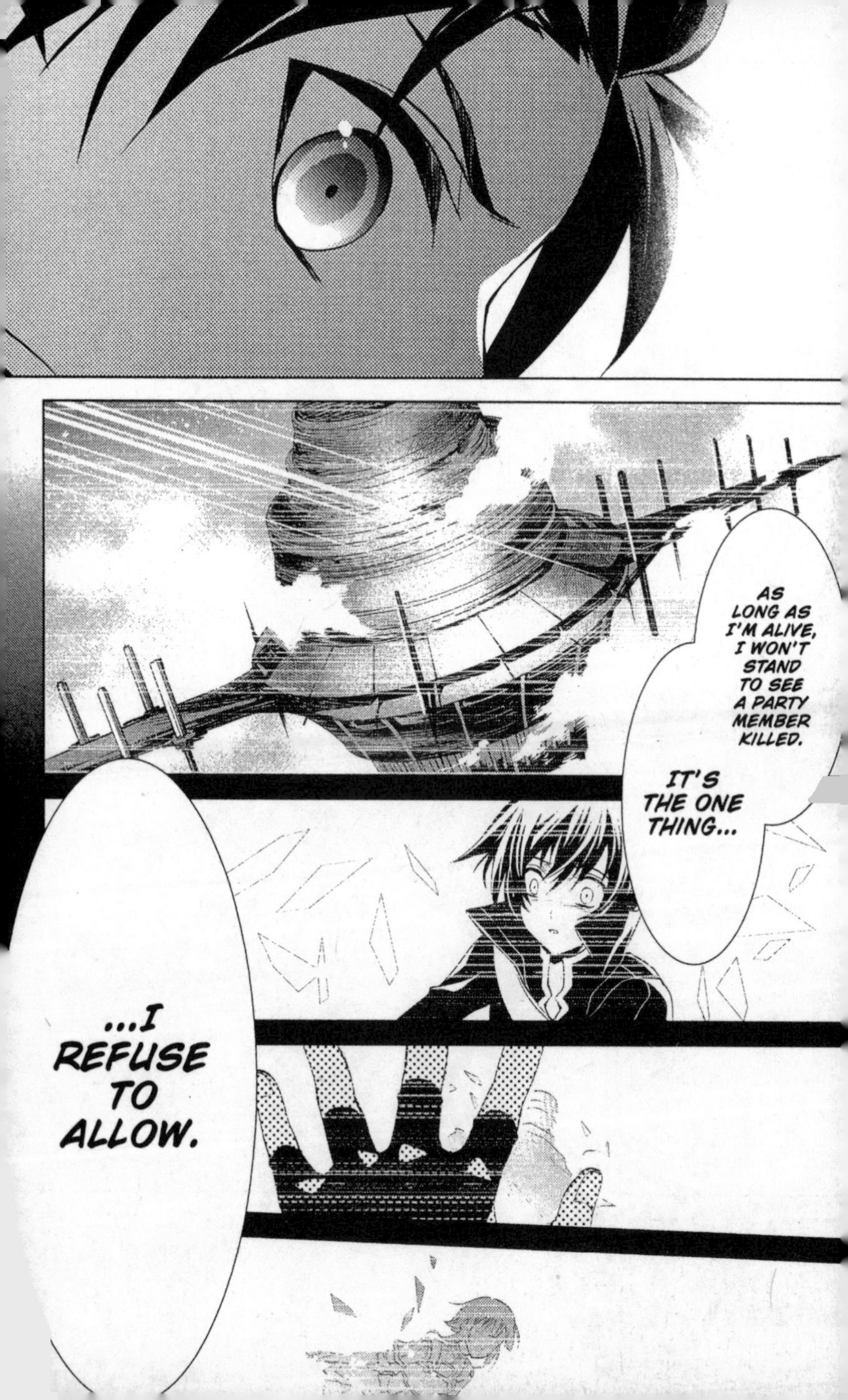

AS LONG AS I'M ALIVE, I WON'T STAND TO SEE A PARTY MEMBER KILLED.
IT'S THE ONE THING...
...I REFUSE TO ALLOW.

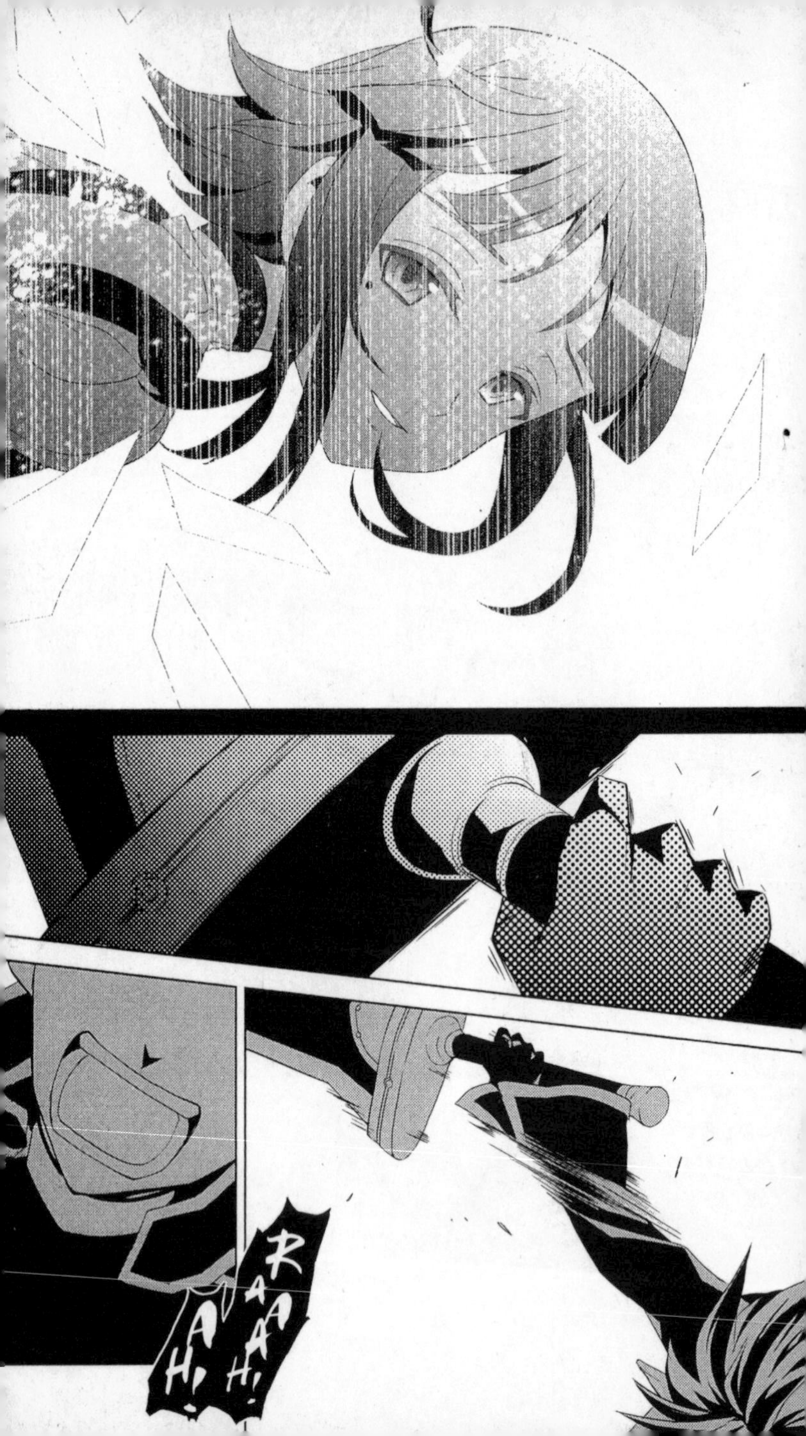
RAAAAH!
AAH!

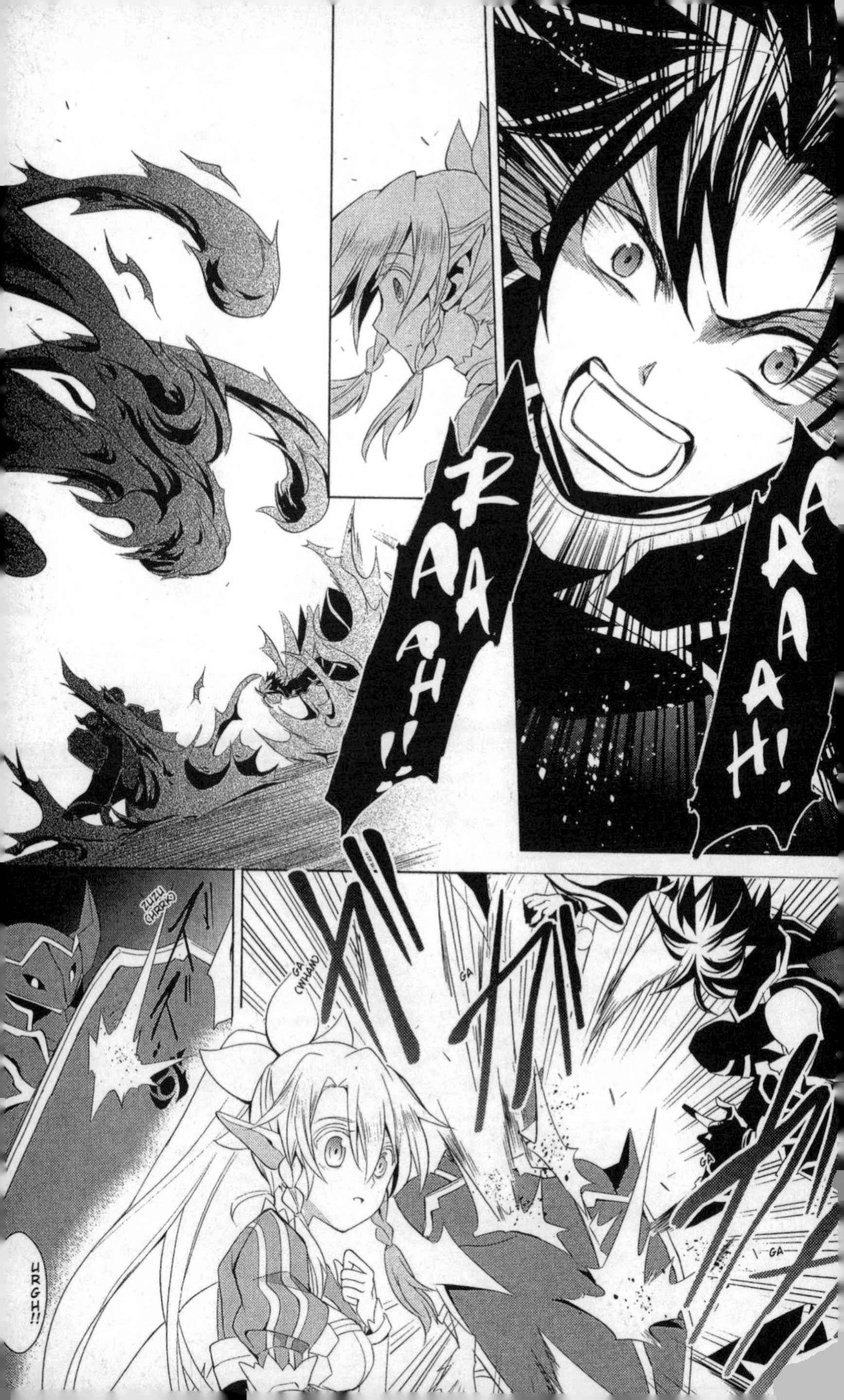
AAAAH!
RAAAH!!
GA
GA
GA
GA (WHAM)
ZUZU (HRRK)
URGH!!

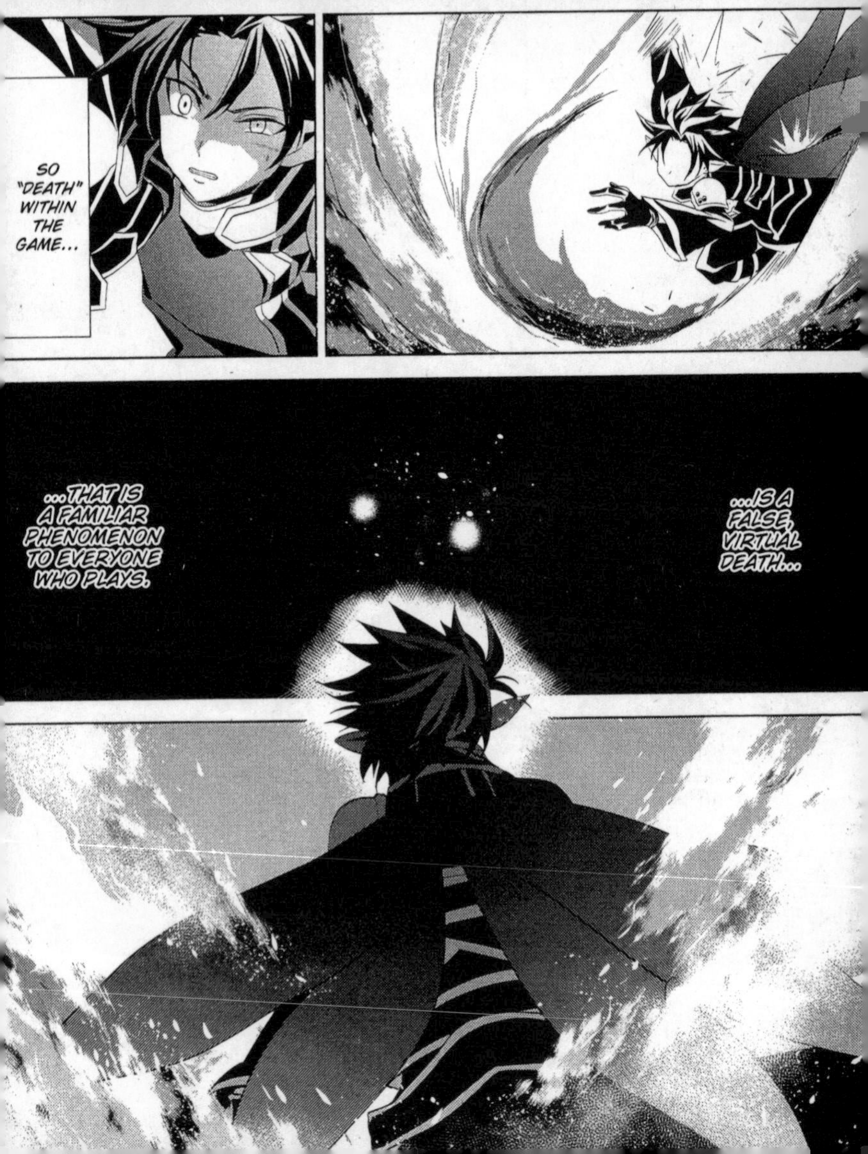
SO "DEATH" WITHIN THE GAME...
...IS A FALSE, VIRTUAL DEATH...
...THAT IS A FAMILIAR PHENOMENON TO EVERYONE WHO PLAYS.

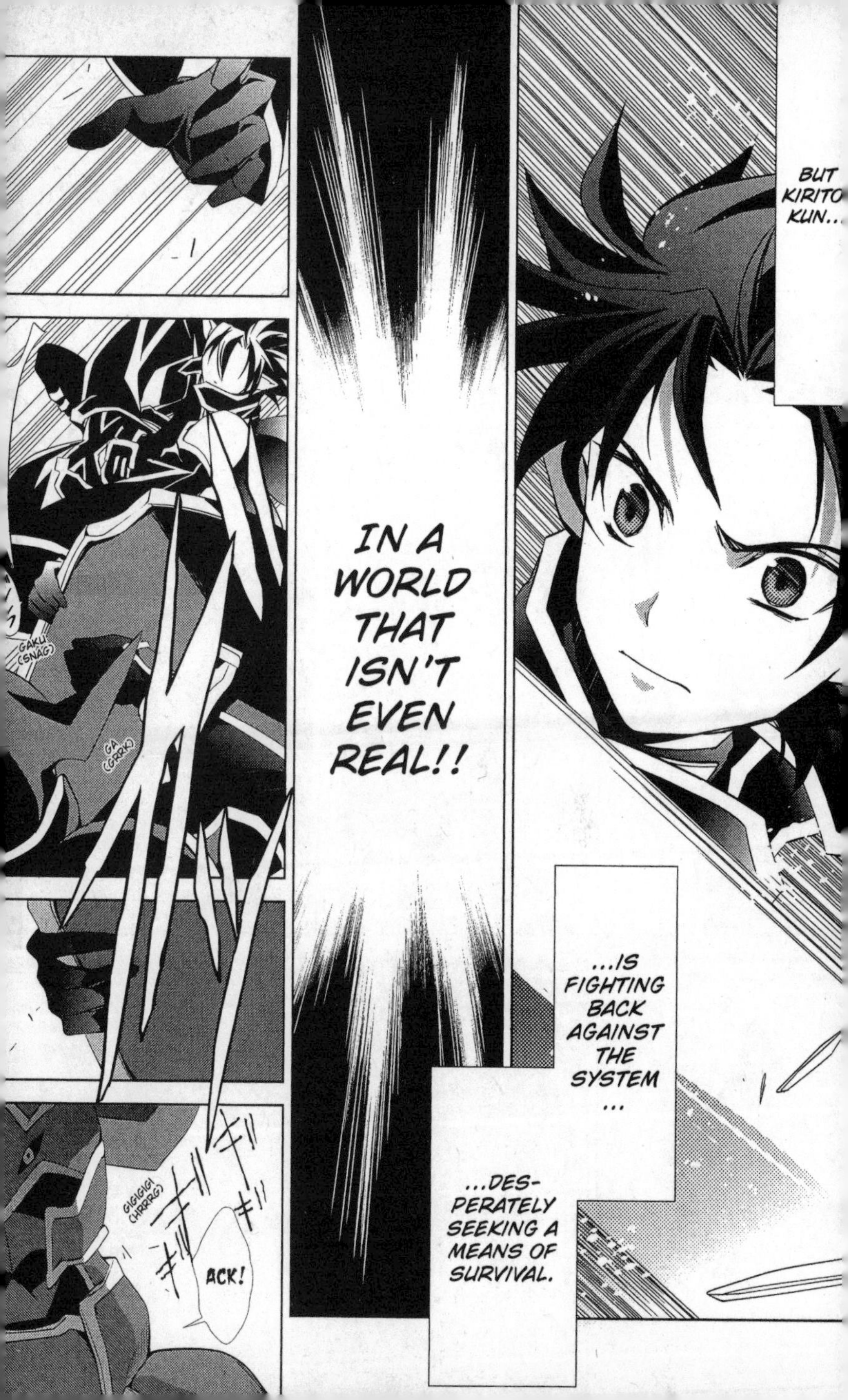
BUT KIRITO KUN...
IN A WORLD THAT ISN'T EVEN REAL!!
...IS FIGHTING BACK AGAINST THE SYSTEM...
...DES-PERATELY SEEKING A MEANS OF SURVIVAL.
GAKU (SNAG)
GA (GRRK)
GIGIGIGI (HRRRG)
ACK!

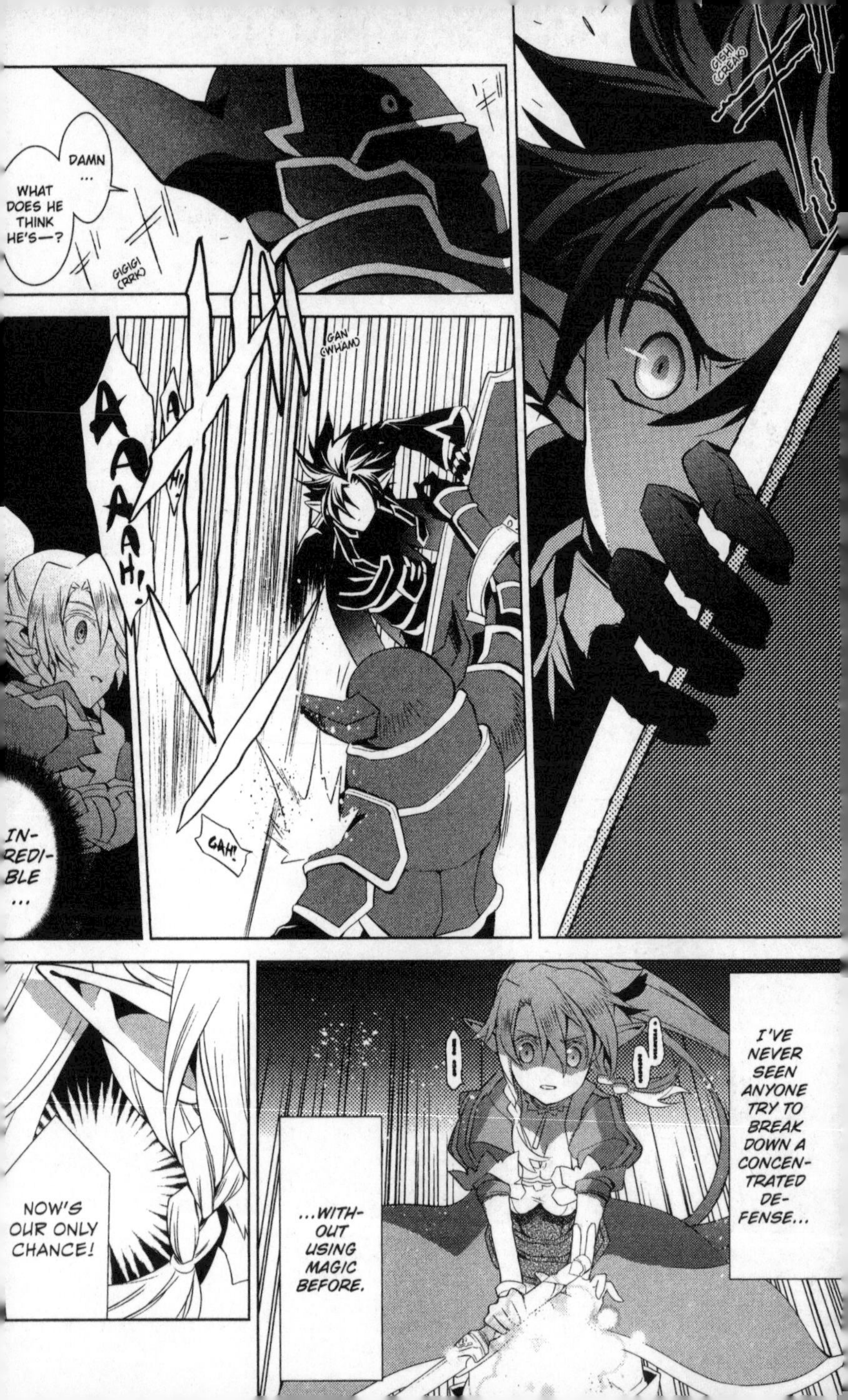
GISHI (CREAK)
DAMN... WHAT DOES HE THINK HE'S—?
GIGIGI (RRK)
GAN (WHAM)
AAAAAH!
GAH!
IN-CREDI-BLE...
I'VE NEVER SEEN ANYONE TRY TO BREAK DOWN A CONCEN-TRATED DE-FENSE...
...WITH-OUT USING MAGIC BEFORE.
NOW'S OUR ONLY CHANCE!

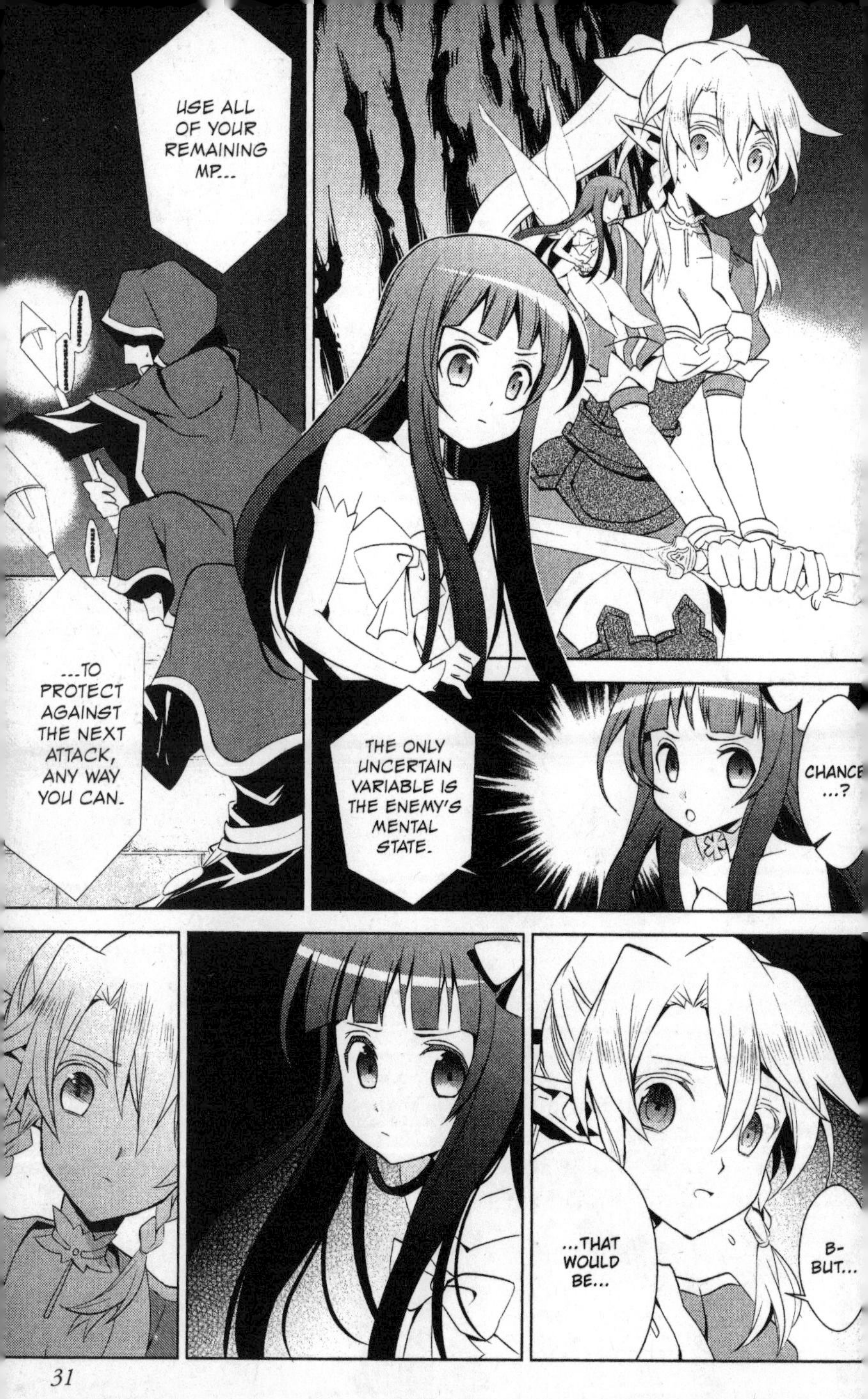
THE ONLY UNCERTAIN VARIABLE IS THE ENEMY'S MENTAL STATE.
CHANCE ...?
USE ALL OF YOUR REMAINING MP...
...TO PROTECT AGAINST THE NEXT ATTACK, ANY WAY YOU CAN.
B-BUT...
...THAT WOULD BE...

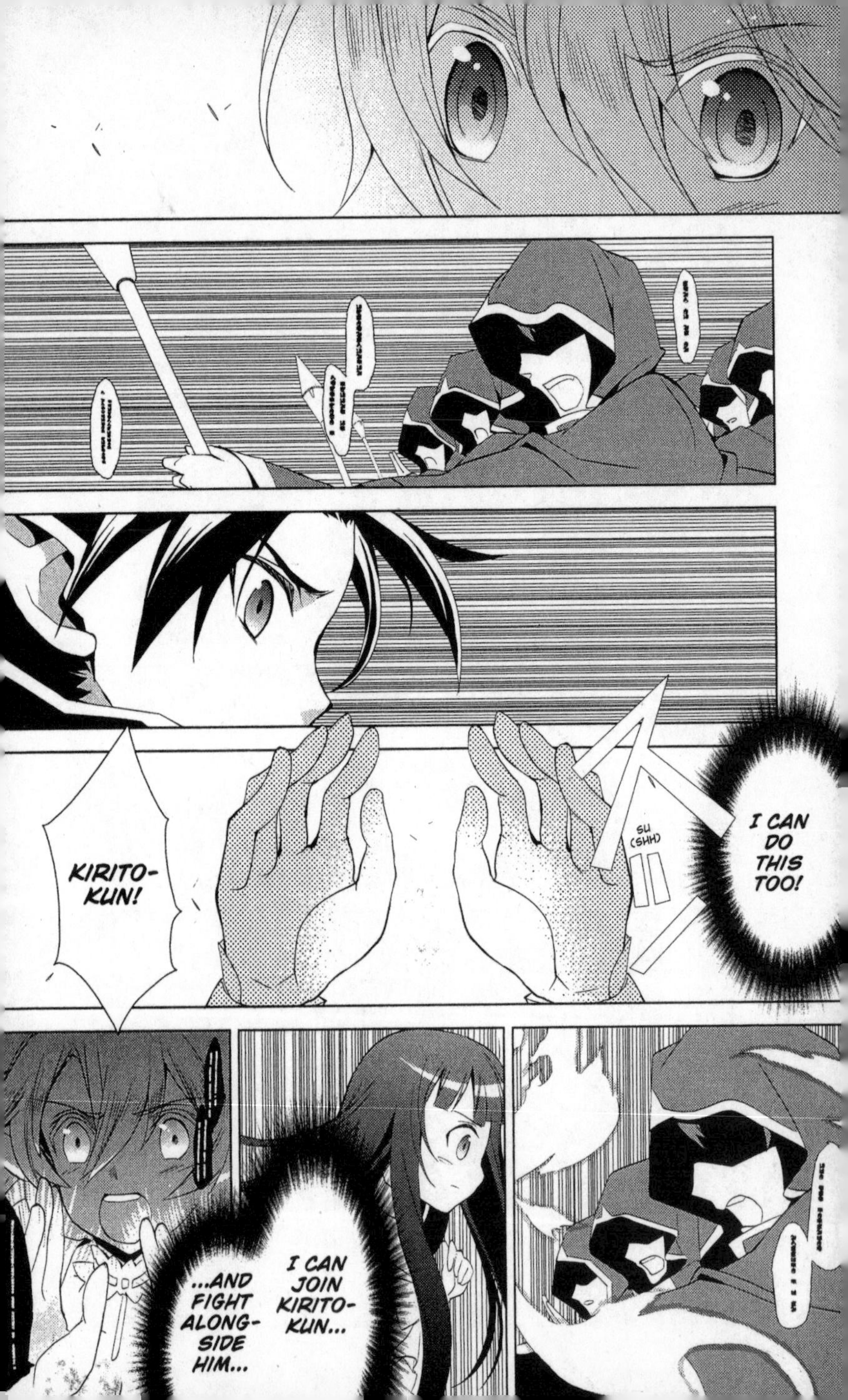
I CAN DO THIS TOO!
SU (SHH)
KIRITO-KUN!
I CAN JOIN KIRITO-KUN...
...AND FIGHT ALONG-SIDE HIM...

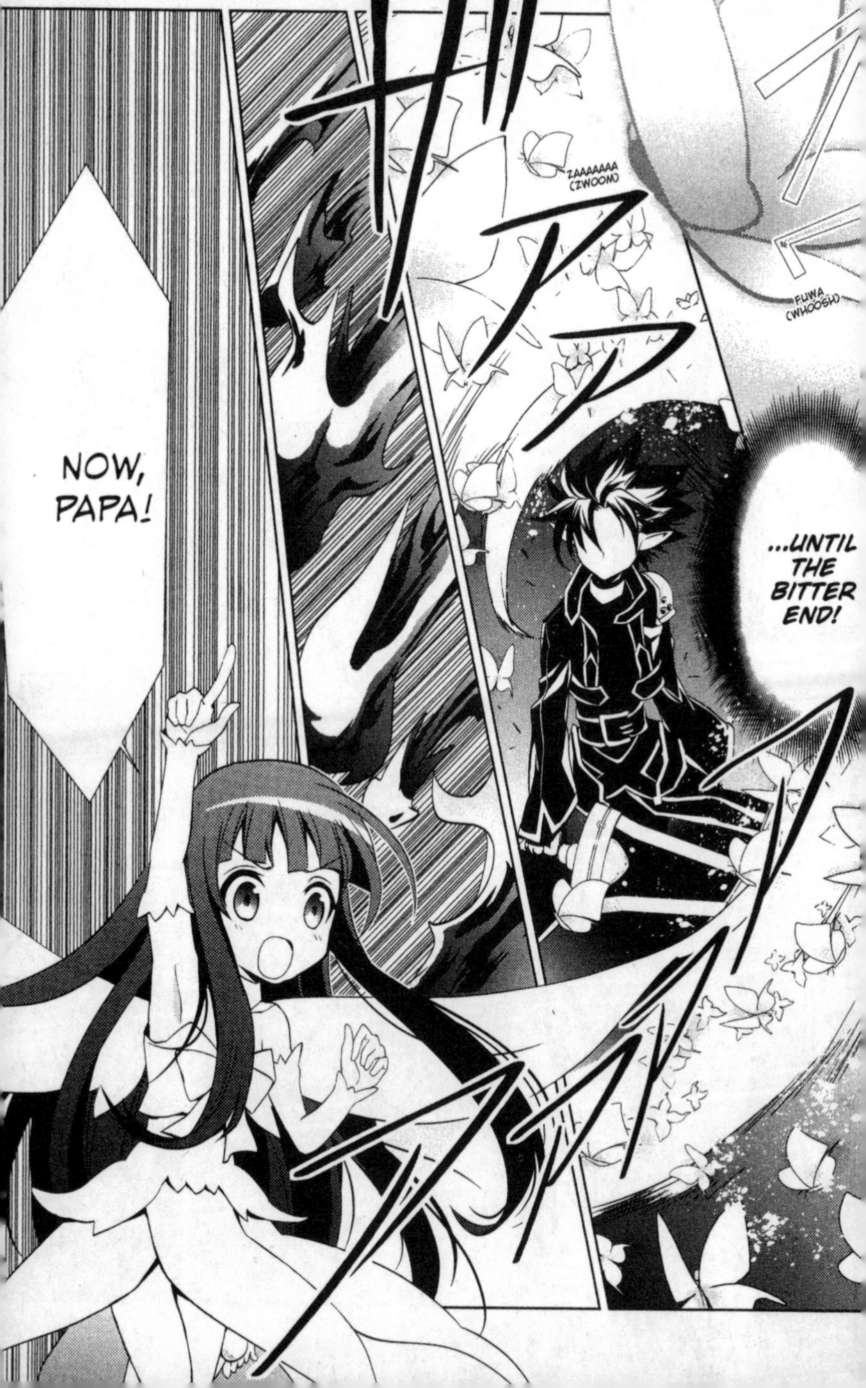
FUWA
(WHOOSH)
ZAAAAAAA
(ZWOOM)
...UNTIL THE BITTER END!
NOW, PAPA!

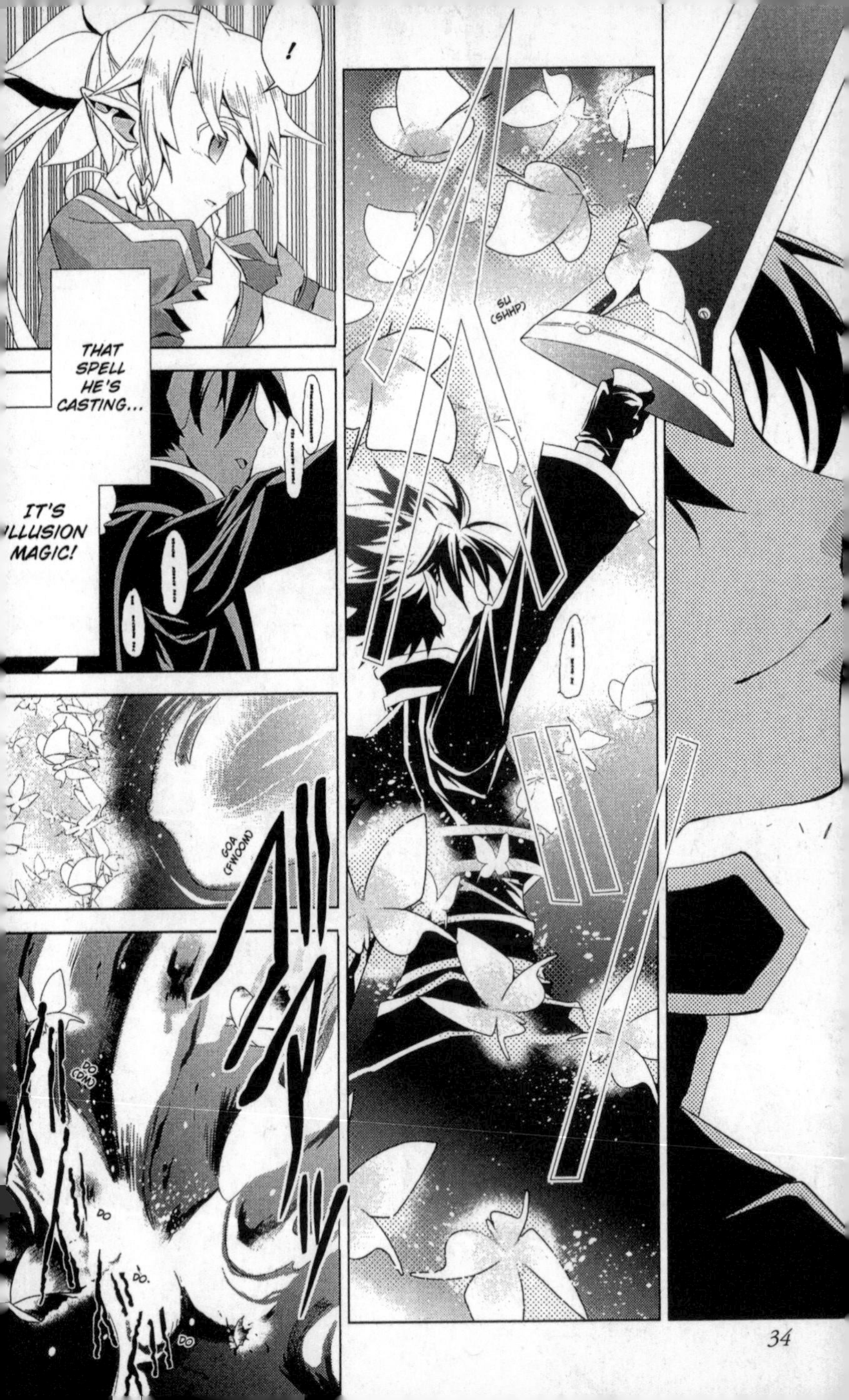
SU
(SHHP)
!
THAT SPELL HE'S CASTING...
IT'S ILLUSION MAGIC!
GOA
(FWOOM)
DO
(DM)
DO
DO.
DO

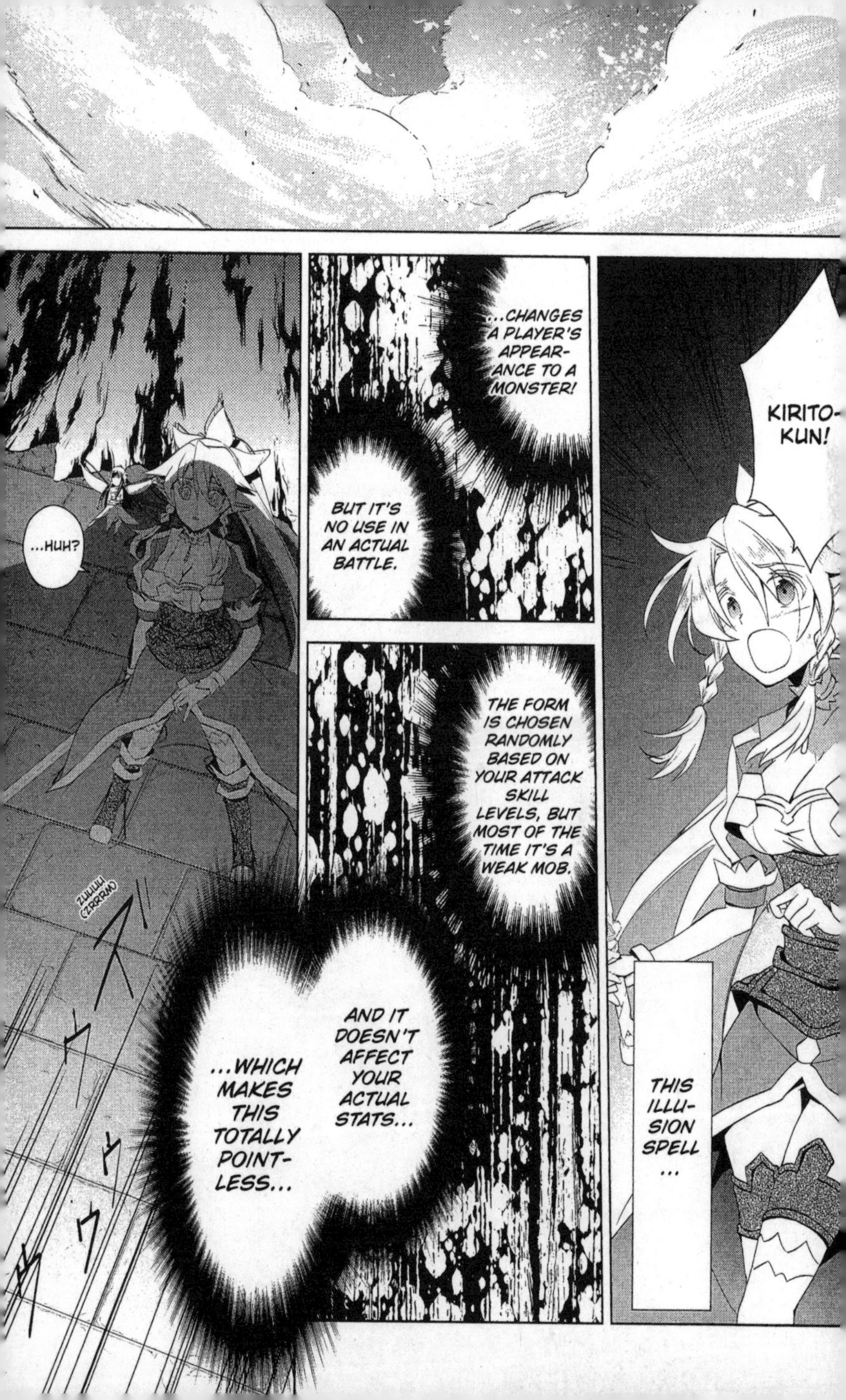
KIRITO-KUN!
THIS ILLUSION SPELL...
...CHANGES A PLAYER'S APPEARANCE TO A MONSTER!
BUT IT'S NO USE IN AN ACTUAL BATTLE.
THE FORM IS CHOSEN RANDOMLY BASED ON YOUR ATTACK SKILL LEVELS, BUT MOST OF THE TIME IT'S A WEAK MOB.
AND IT DOESN'T AFFECT YOUR ACTUAL STATS...
...WHICH MAKES THIS TOTALLY POINTLESS...
...HUH?
ZULULU (ZRRRM)

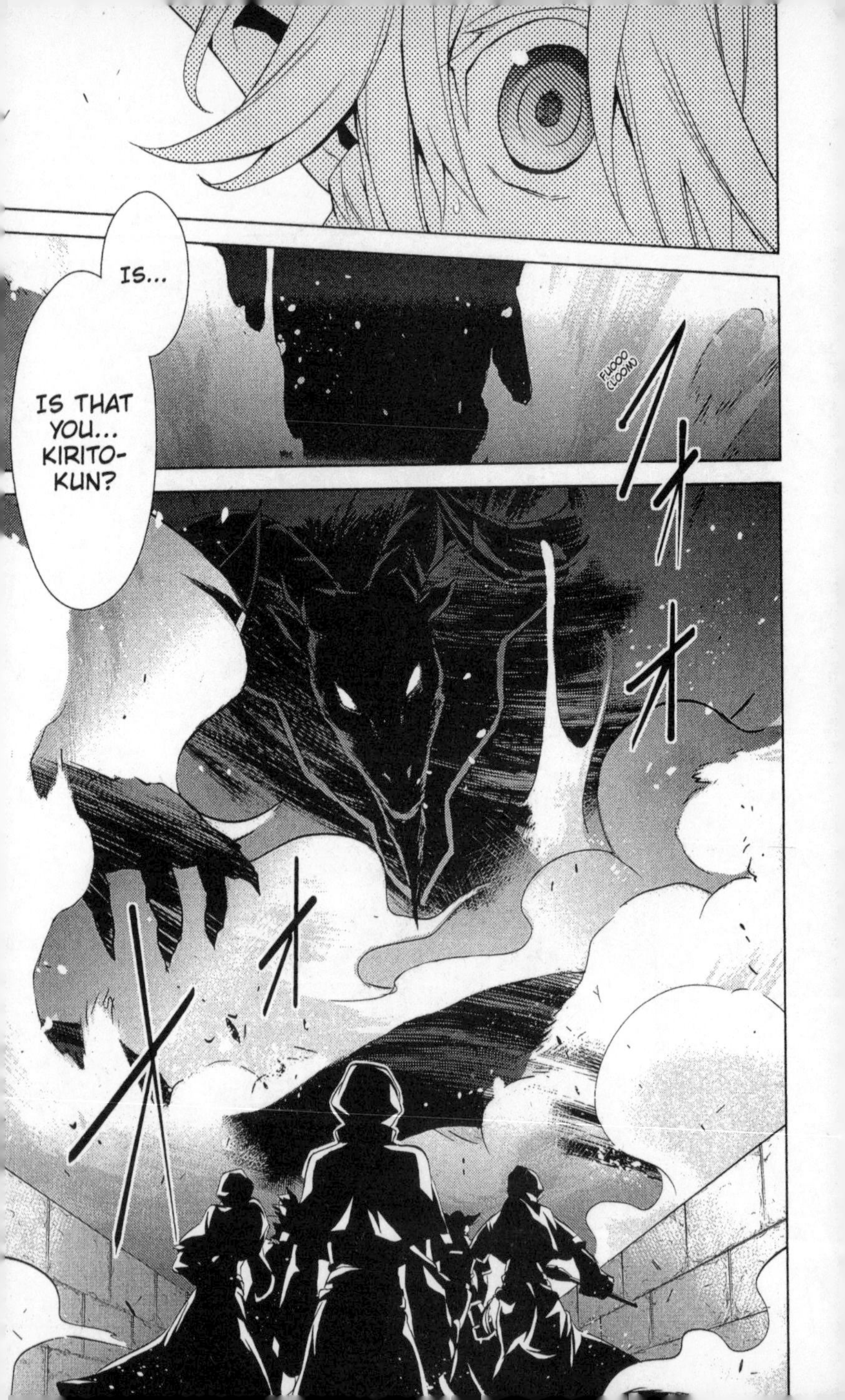
IS...
IS THAT YOU... KIRITO-KUN?
FUOOO (LOOM)

SWORD ART ONLINE
FAIRY DANCE

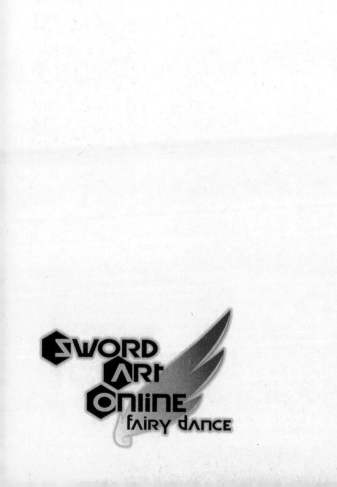

SWORD ART ONLINE fairy dance
BACKGROUND GUIDE 01

KIRITO'S ILLUSION MAGIC

YOU MIGHT HAVE NOTICED THAT KIRITO'S TRANSFORMATION IS NEARLY IDENTICAL TO THE "GLEAMEYES," A MONSTROUS DEMON THAT REQUIRED THE USE OF KIRITO'S DUAL BLADES TO DEFEAT IN AINCRAD AFTER IT DECIMATED AN ARMY SQUADRON. WAS IT PART OF THE "SAO KIRITO" BUGGED DATA THAT CARRIED OVER, OR DID KIRITO'S DESIRE TO UNNERVE THE ENEMY HAVE AN EFFECT ON THE RANDOM TRANSFORMATION...?

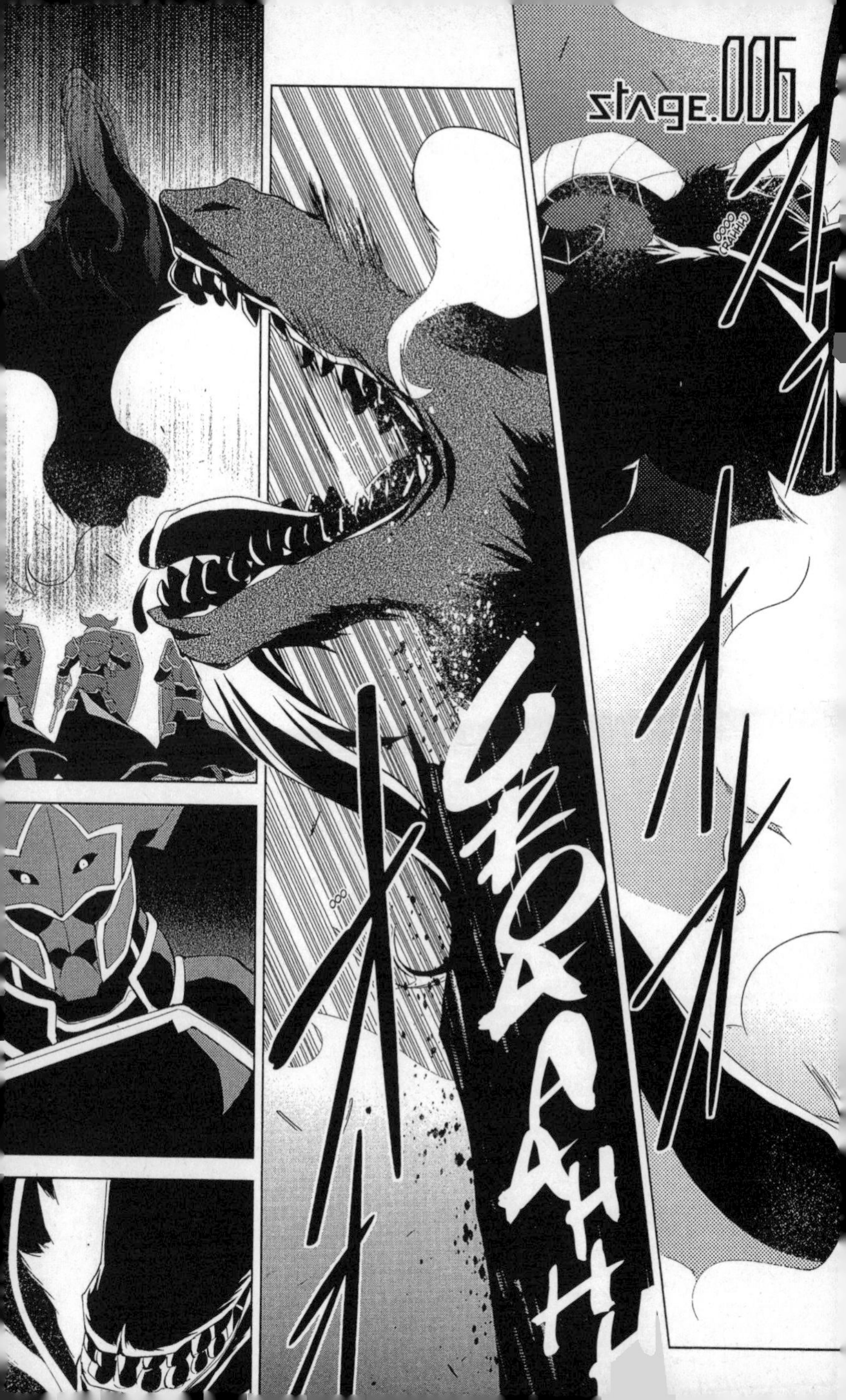
stage.006
UROAAHH

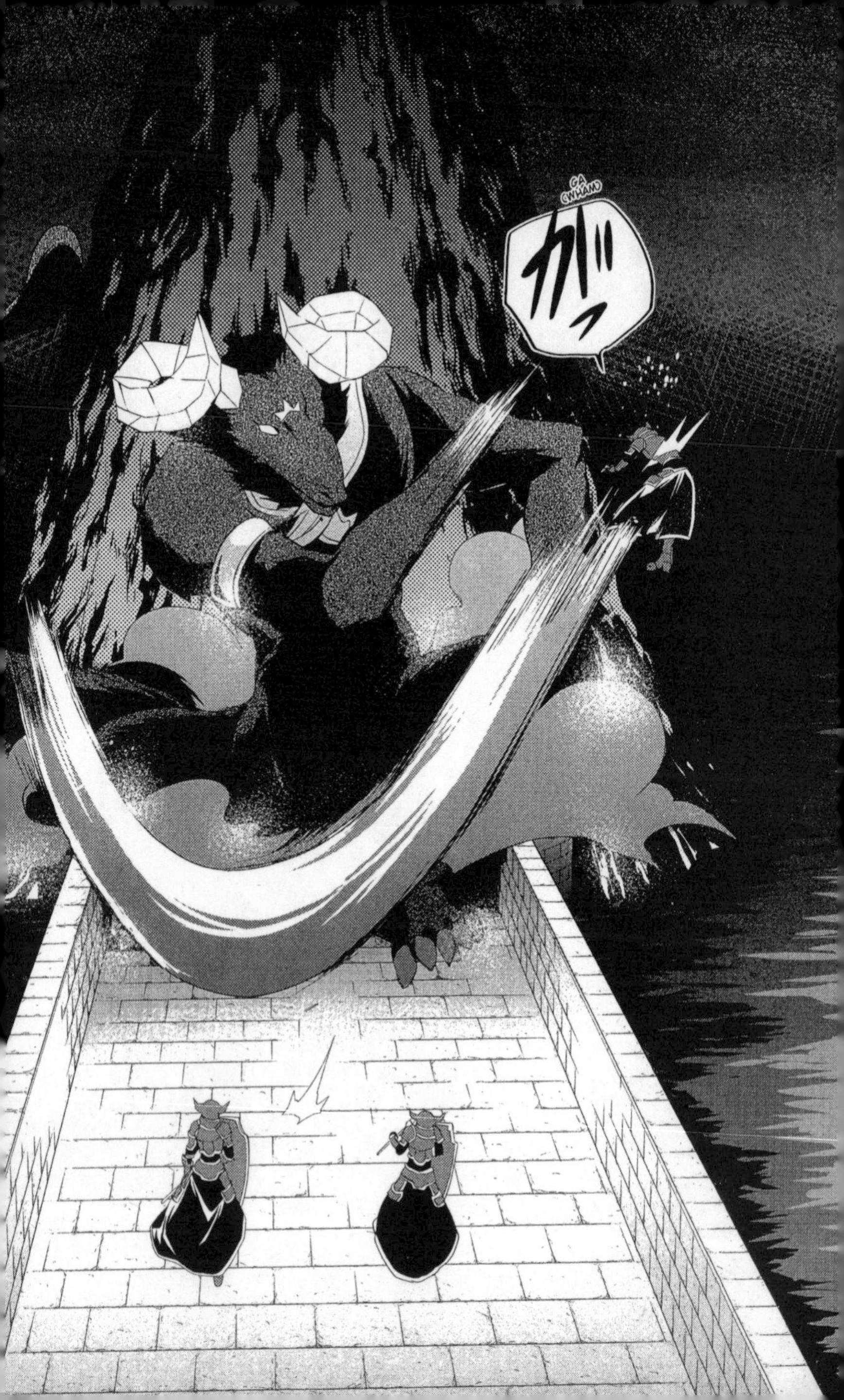
ガッ
GA (WHAM)

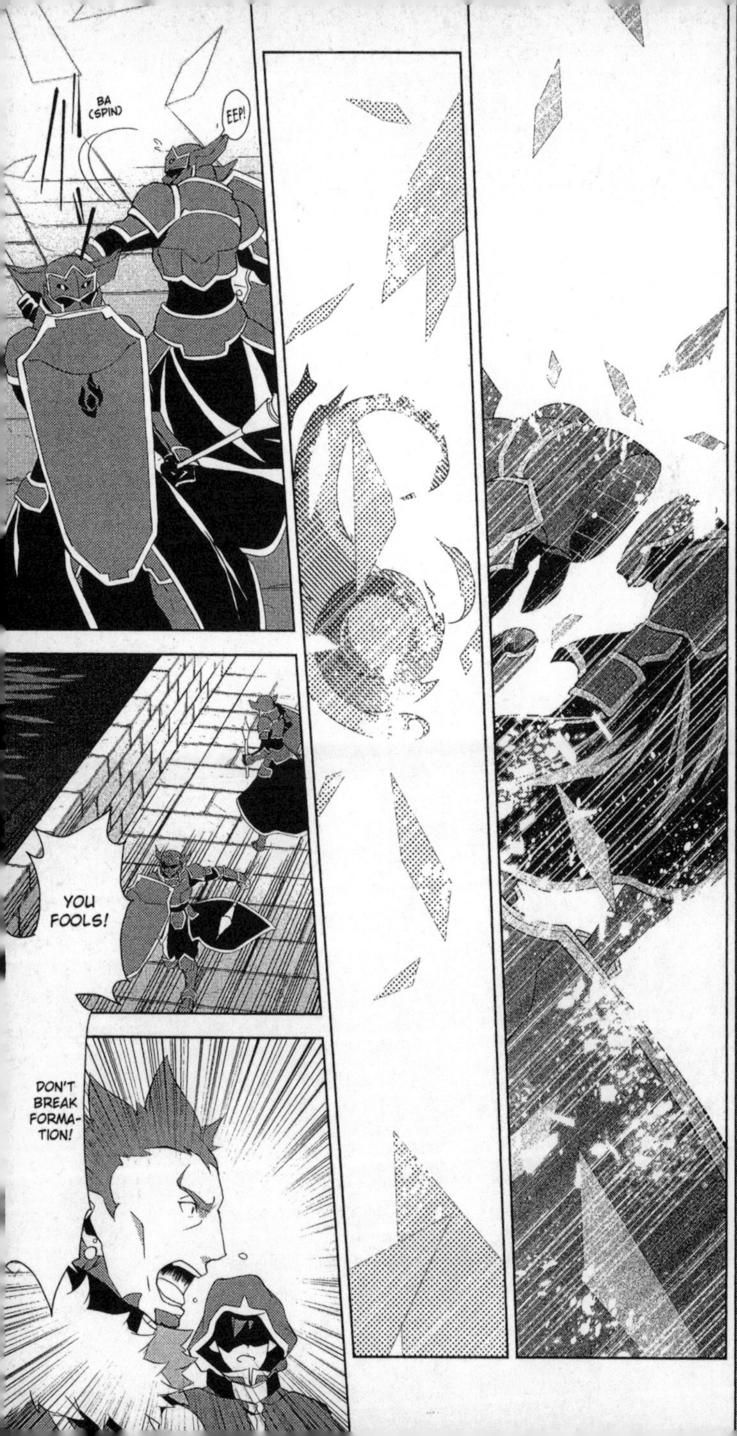
EEP!
BA (SPIN)
YOU FOOLS!
DON'T BREAK FORMA-TION!

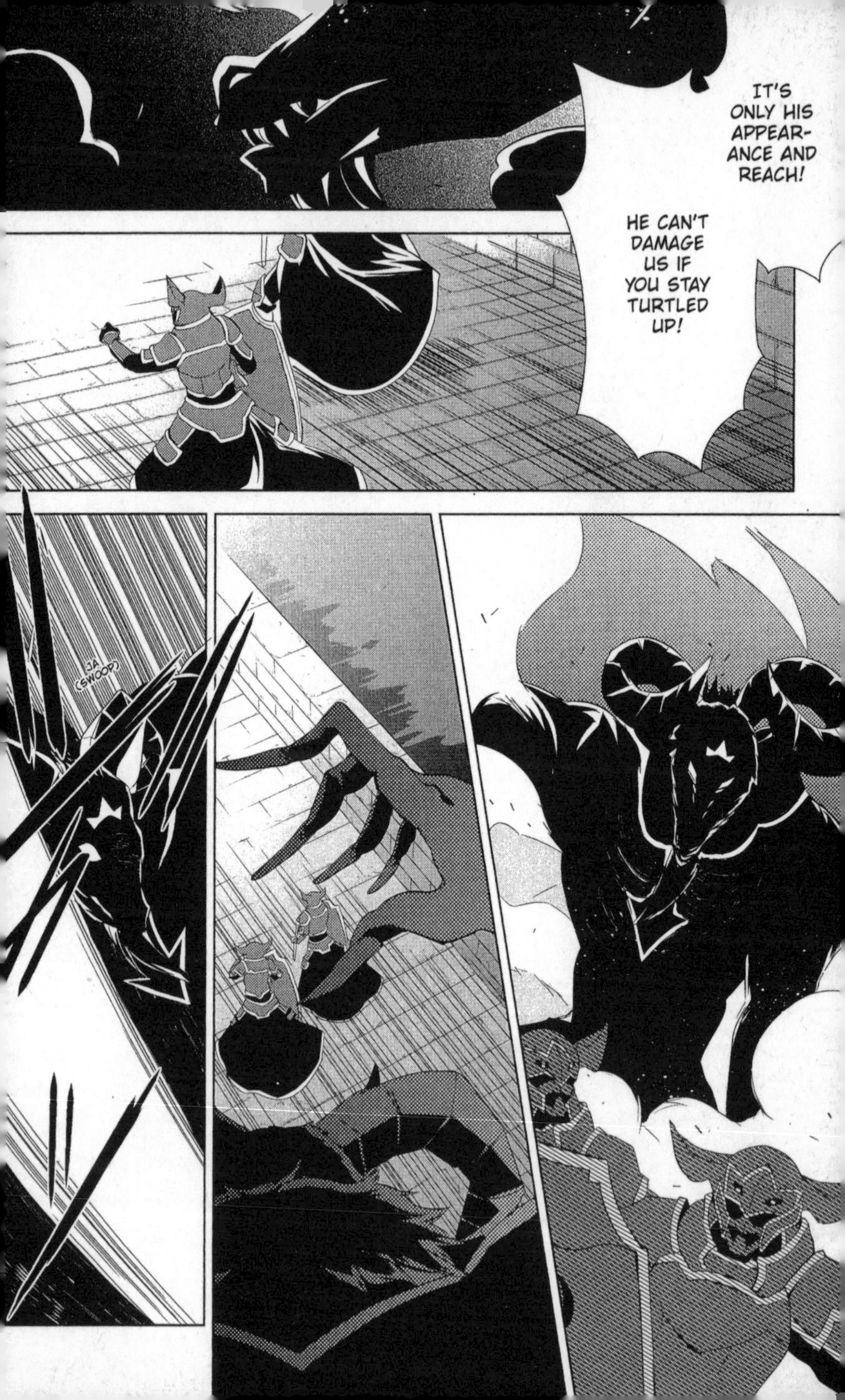
IT'S ONLY HIS APPEAR-ANCE AND REACH!
HE CAN'T DAMAGE US IF YOU STAY TURTLED UP!
JA (SWOOP)

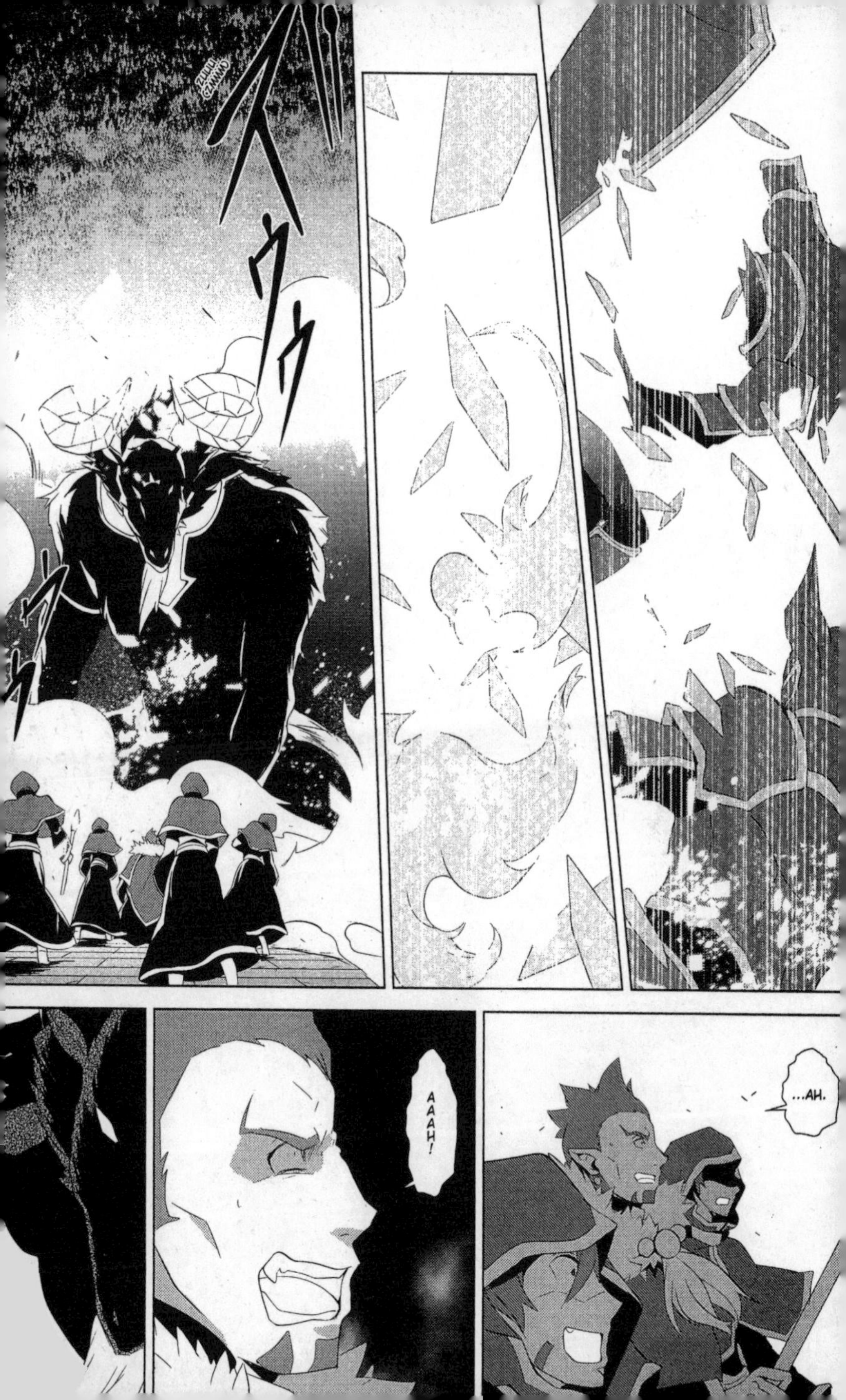
...AH.
AAAH!

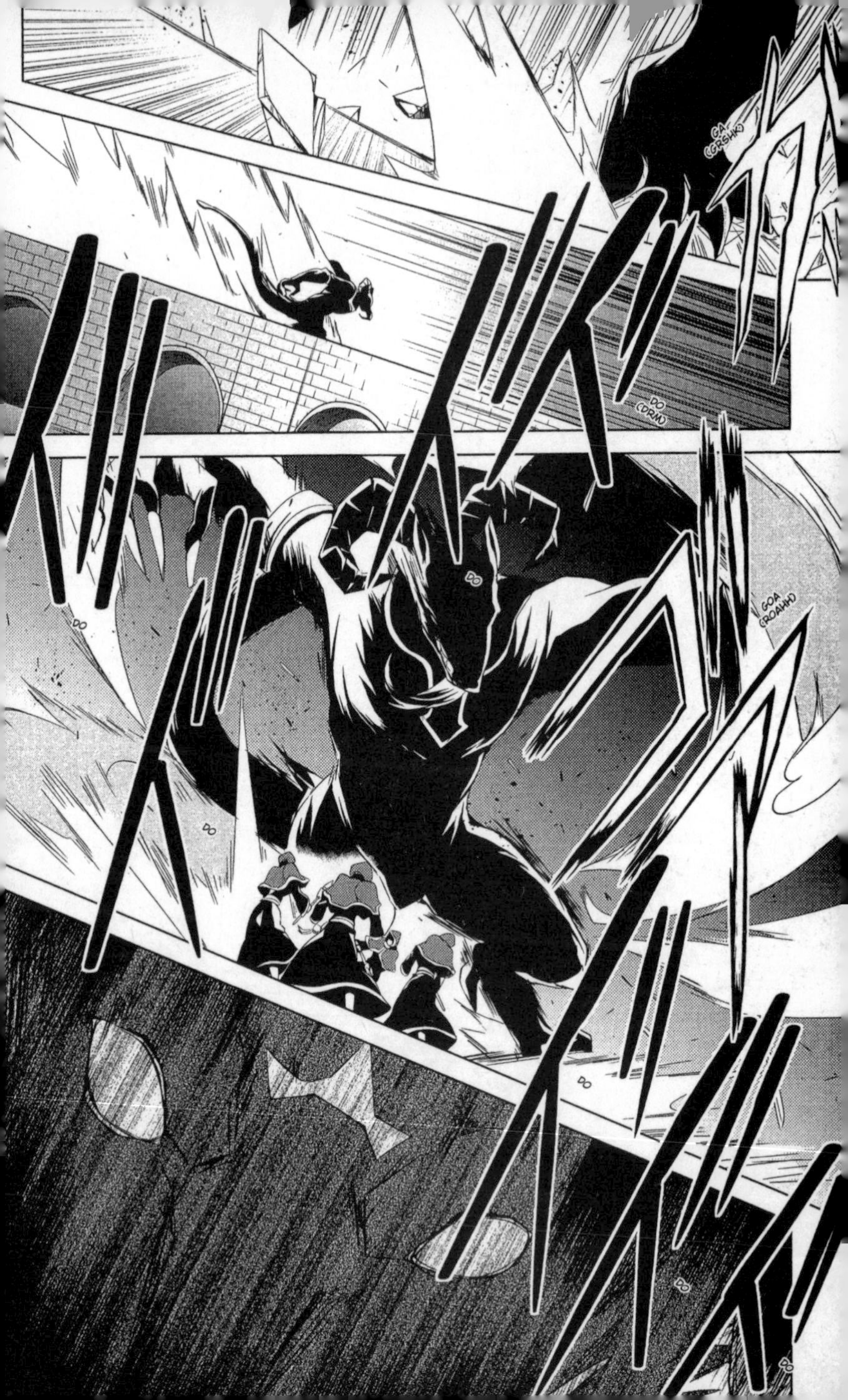
GA (GRSHK)
DO (DRM)
GOA (ROAHH)
DO
DO
DO
DO
DO
DO

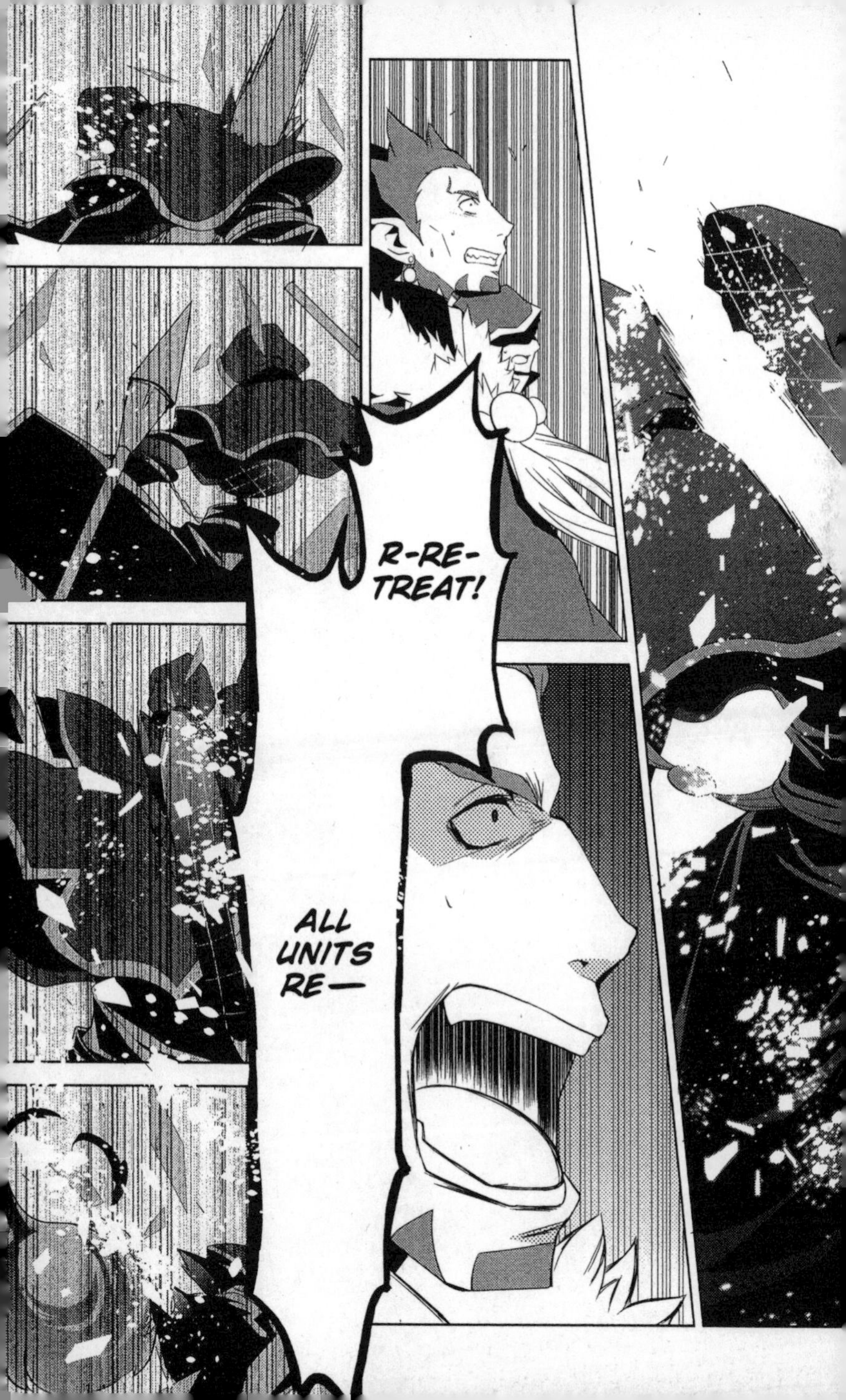
R-RE-TREAT!
ALL UNITS RE—

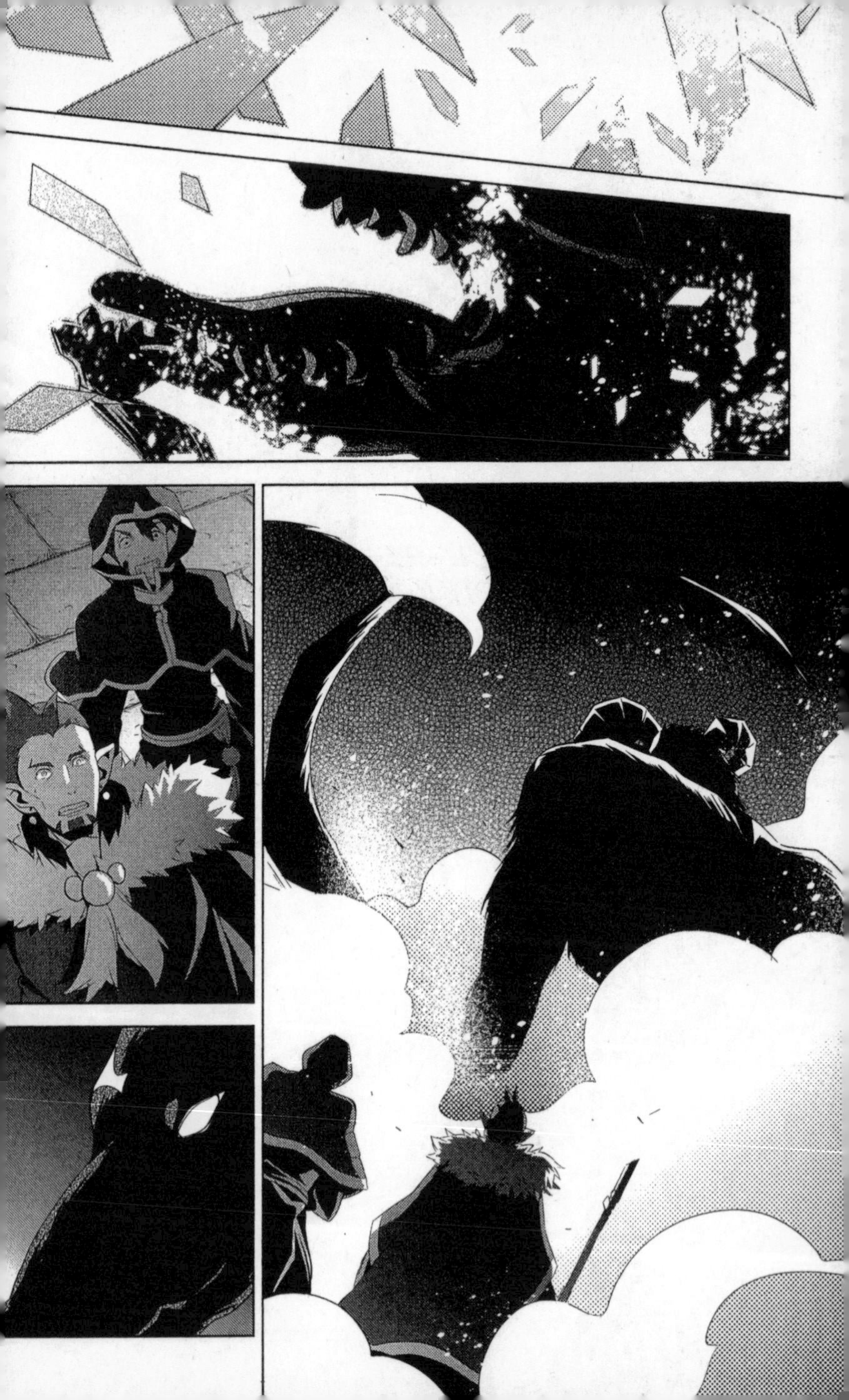

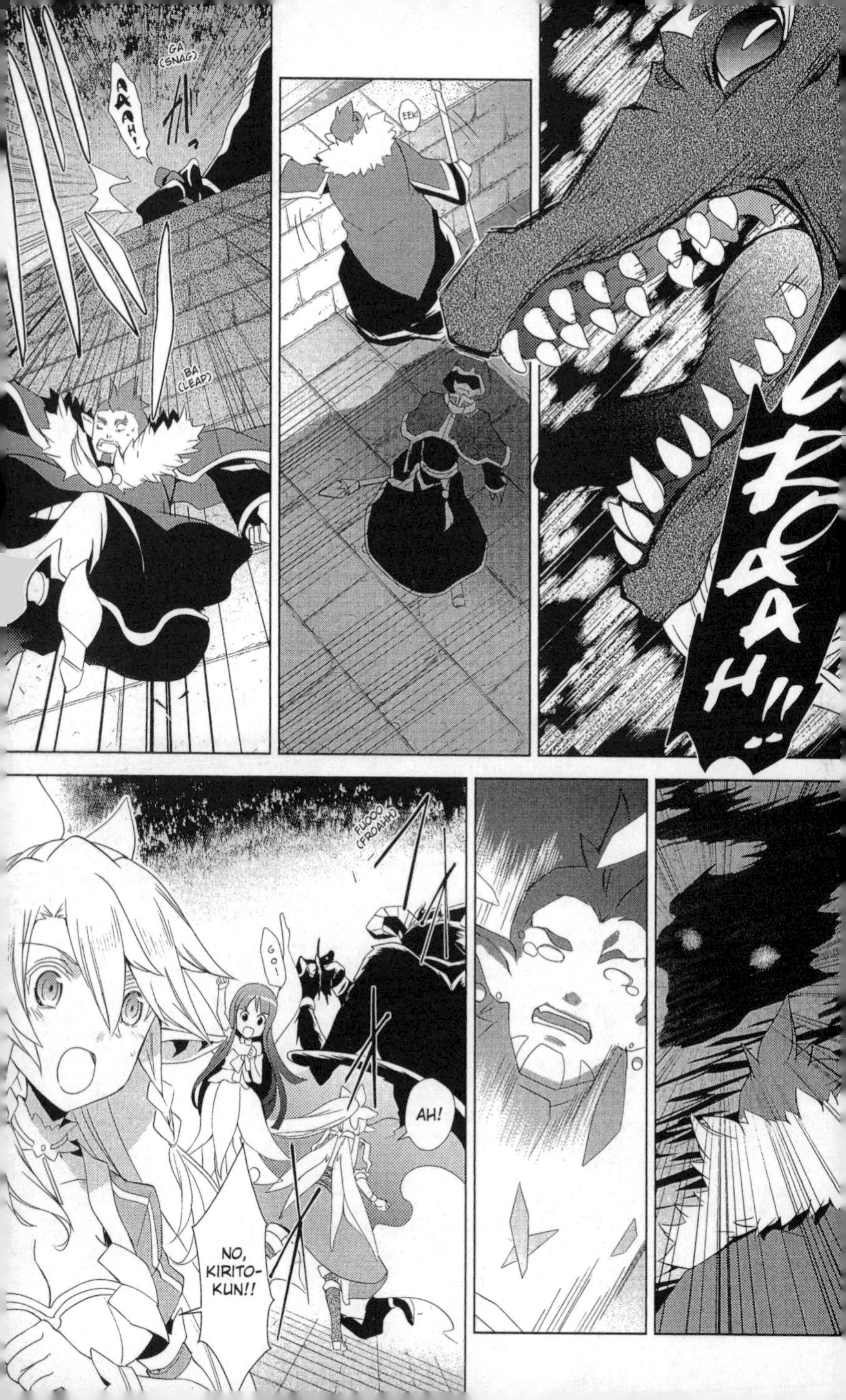
ROAAH!!
EEK!
GA (SNAG)
AAAH!
BA (LEAP)
FUOOO (FROAHH)
GO!
AH!
NO, KIRITO-KUN!!

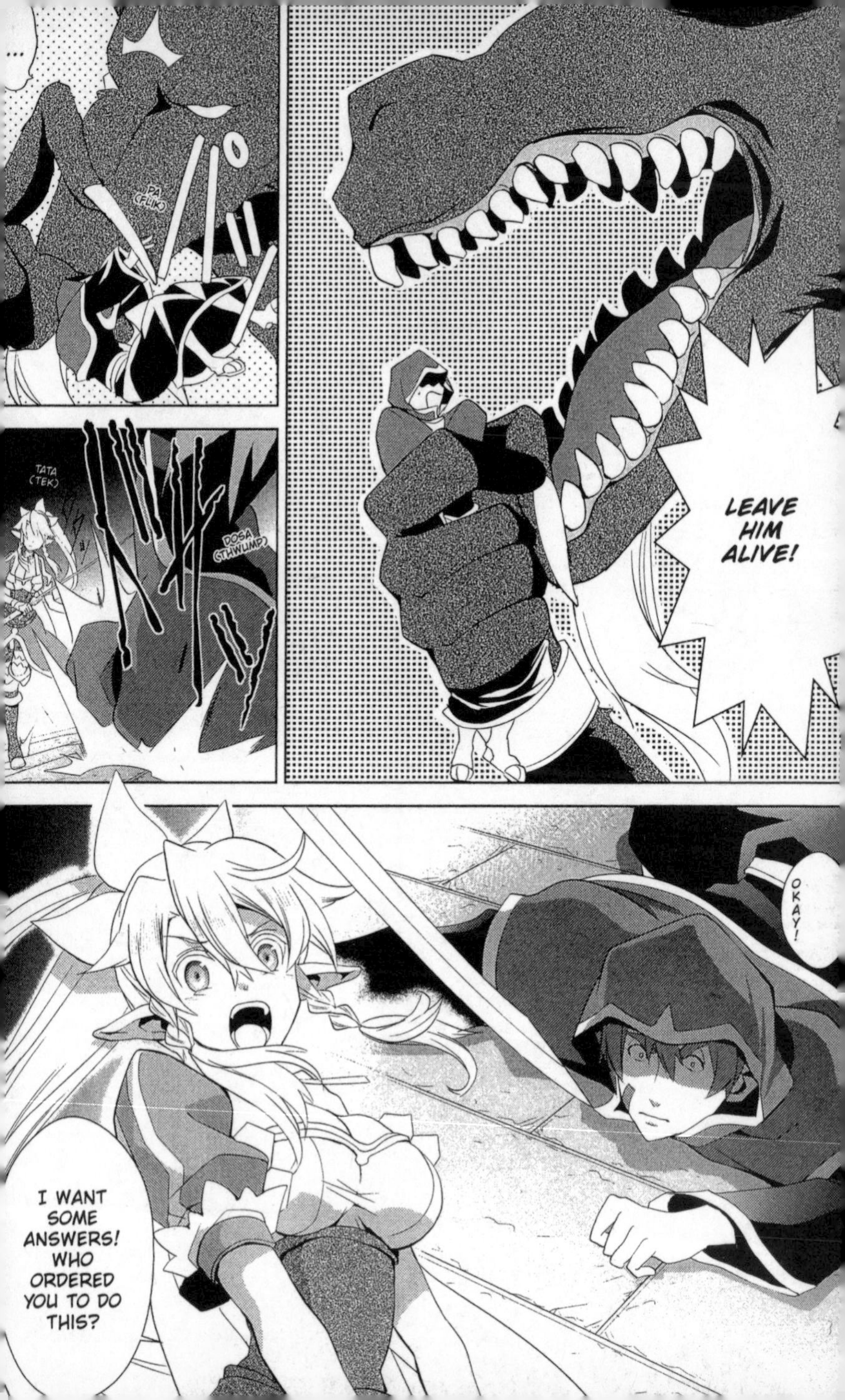
LEAVE HIM ALIVE!
...
PA (FLIK)
TATA (TEK)
DOSA (THWUMP)
OKAY!
I WANT SOME ANSWERS! WHO ORDERED YOU TO DO THIS?

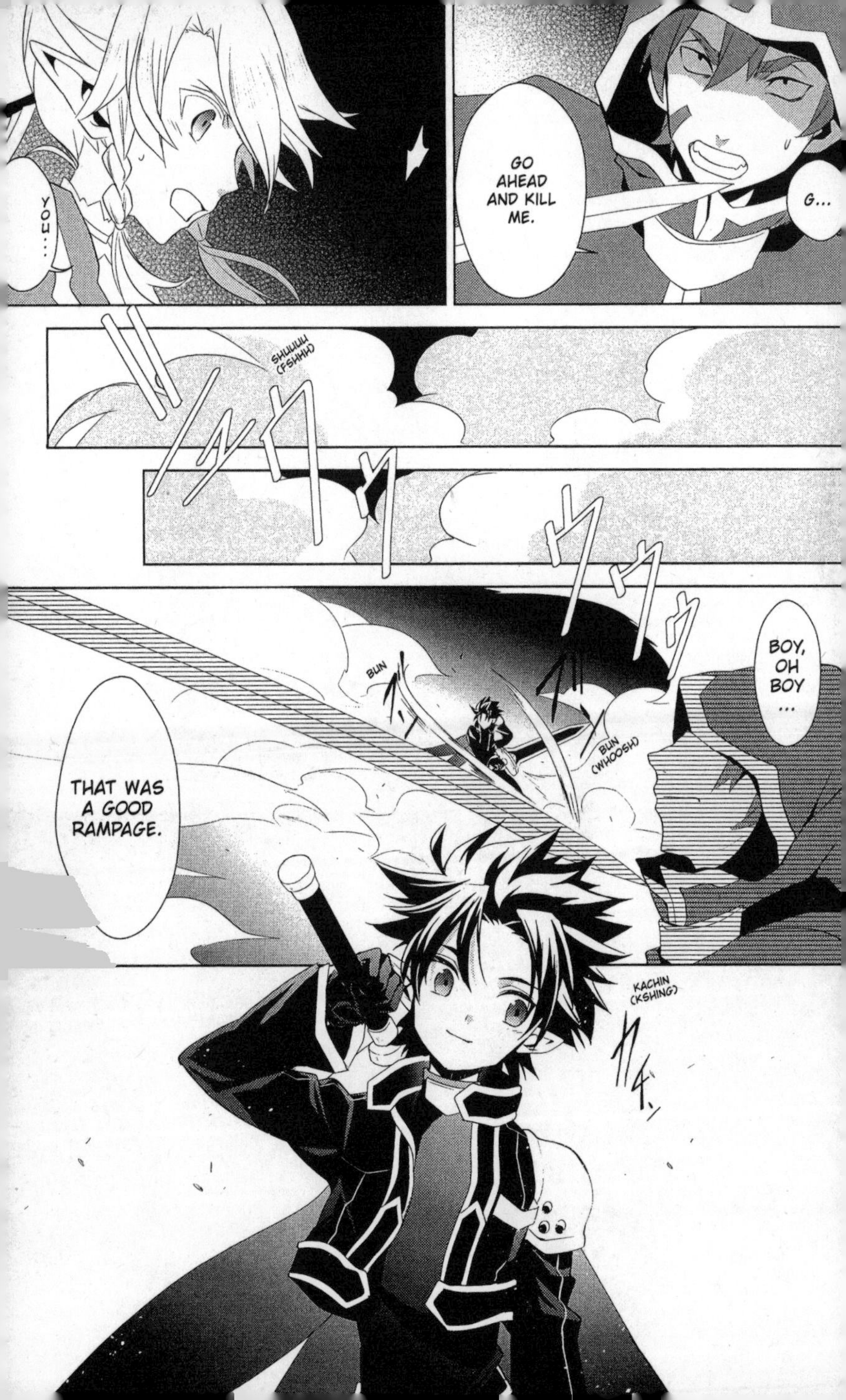
G...
GO AHEAD AND KILL ME.
YOU...
SHUUUU (FSHHH)
BOY, OH BOY...
BUN (WHOOSH)
BUN
THAT WAS A GOOD RAMPAGE.
KACHIN (KSHING)

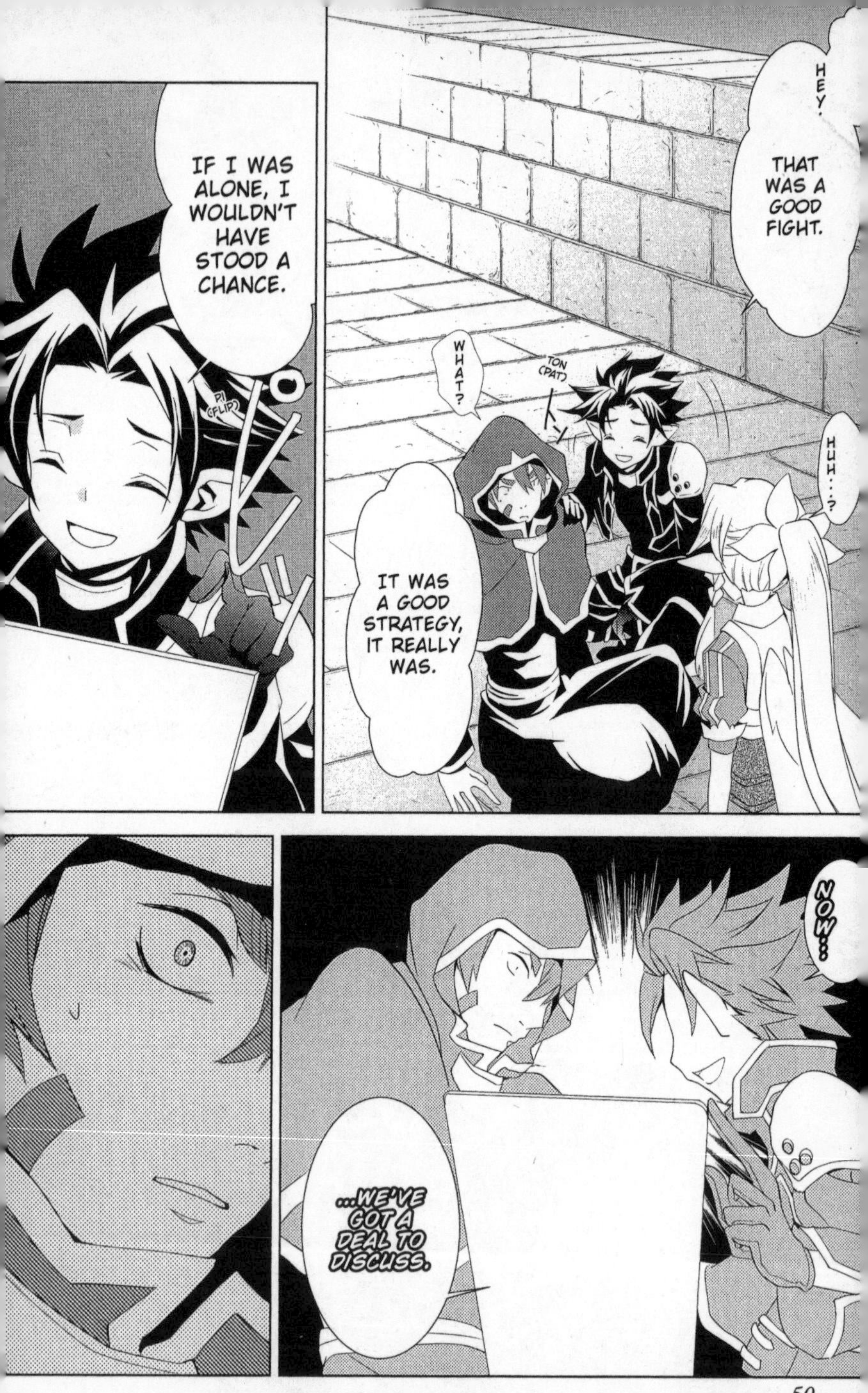
HEY.
THAT WAS A GOOD FIGHT.
WHAT?
TON (PAT)
HUH...?
IT WAS A GOOD STRATEGY, IT REALLY WAS.
IF I WAS ALONE, I WOULDN'T HAVE STOOD A CHANCE.
PI (FLIP)
NOW...
...WE'VE GOT A DEAL TO DISCUSS.

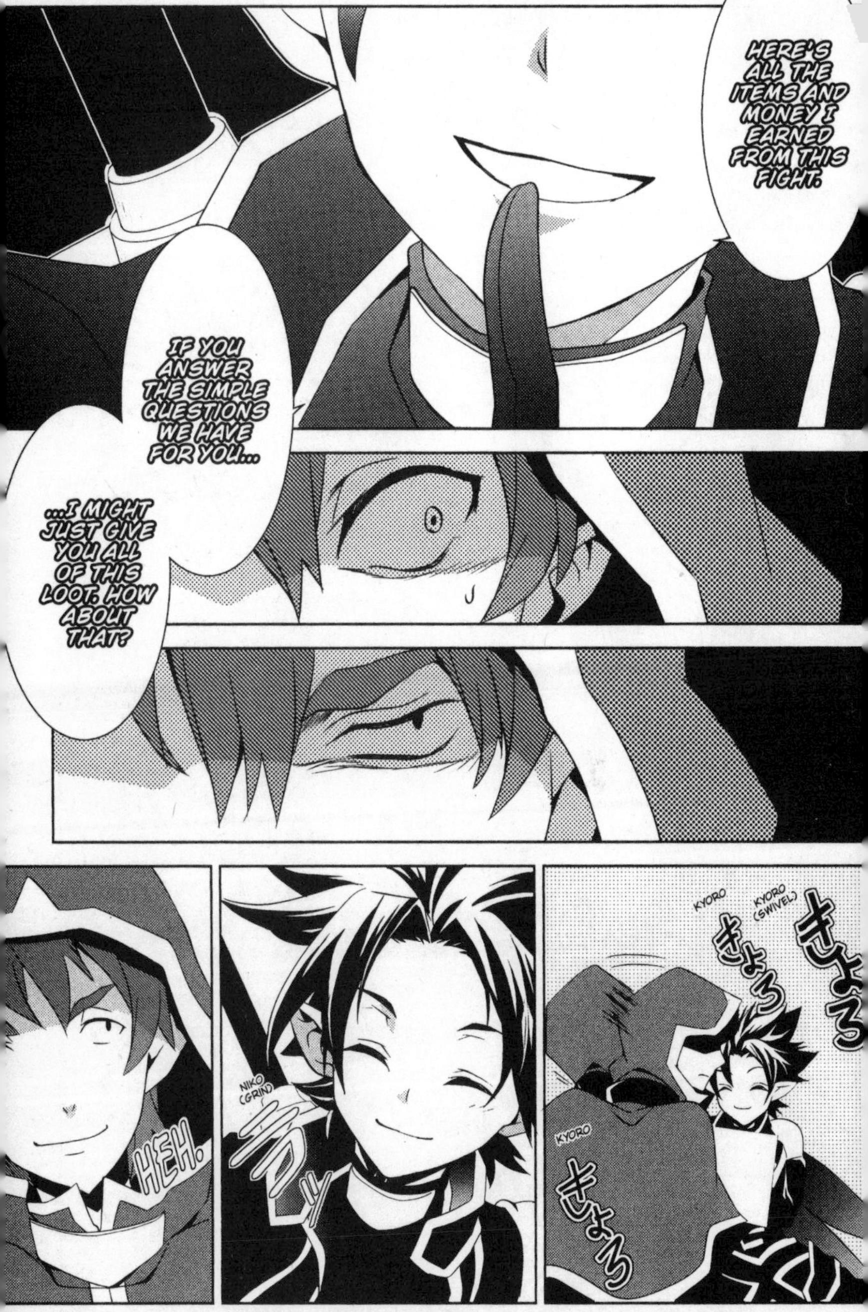
HERE'S ALL THE ITEMS AND MONEY I EARNED FROM THIS FIGHT.
IF YOU ANSWER THE SIMPLE QUESTIONS WE HAVE FOR YOU...
...I MIGHT JUST GIVE YOU ALL OF THIS LOOT. HOW ABOUT THAT?
KYORO
KYORO (SWIVEL)
きょろきょろ
KYORO
きょろ
NIKO (GRIN)
にこッ
HEH.

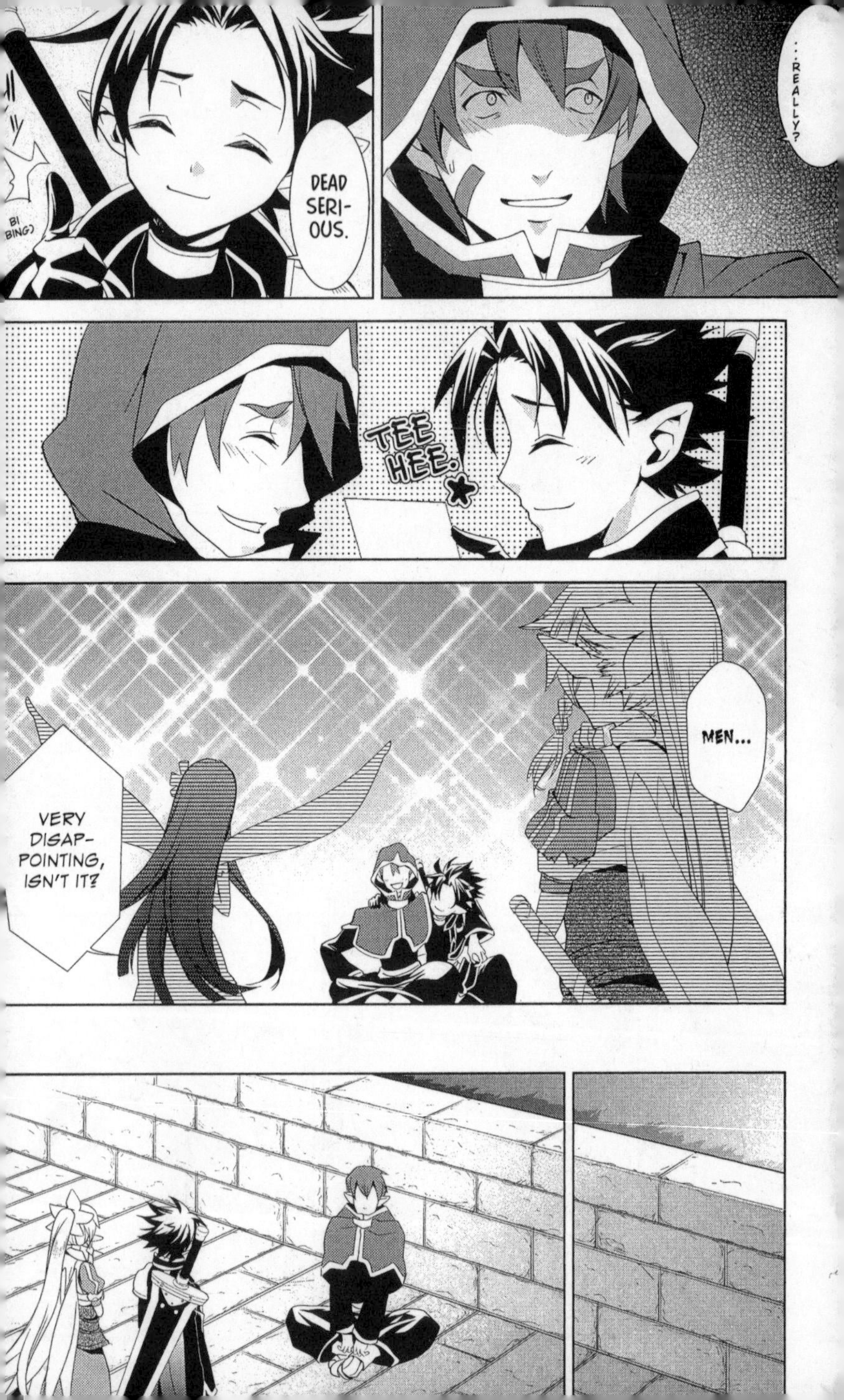
...REALLY?
DEAD SERI-OUS.
BI BING)
TEE HEE.
MEN...
VERY DISAP-POINTING, ISN'T IT?

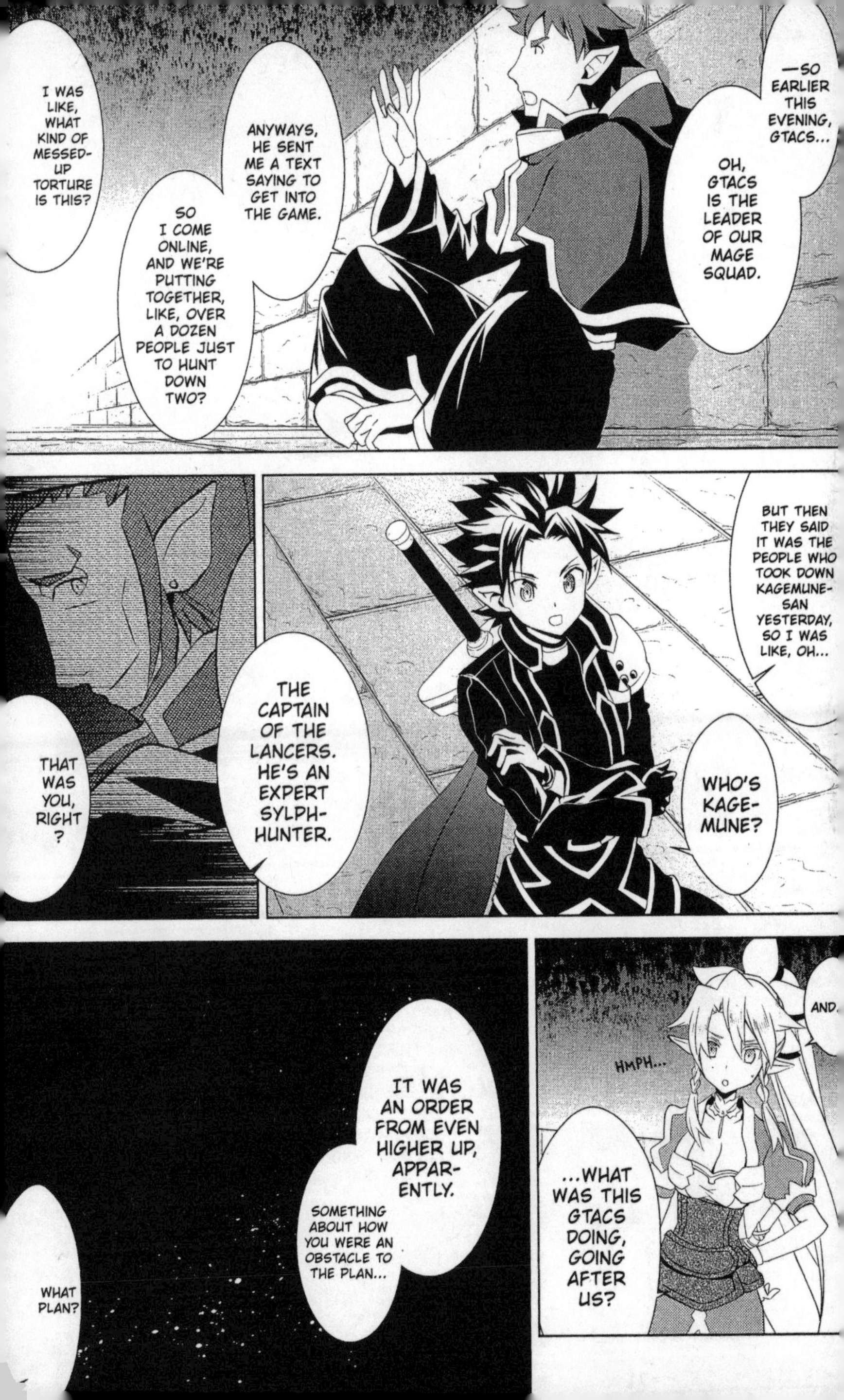
—SO EARLIER THIS EVENING, GTACS...
OH, GTACS IS THE LEADER OF OUR MAGE SQUAD.
ANYWAYS, HE SENT ME A TEXT SAYING TO GET INTO THE GAME.
SO I COME ONLINE, AND WE'RE PUTTING TOGETHER, LIKE, OVER A DOZEN PEOPLE JUST TO HUNT DOWN TWO?
I WAS LIKE, WHAT KIND OF MESSED-UP TORTURE IS THIS?
BUT THEN THEY SAID IT WAS THE PEOPLE WHO TOOK DOWN KAGEMUNE-SAN YESTERDAY, SO I WAS LIKE, OH...
WHO'S KAGE-MUNE?
THE CAPTAIN OF THE LANCERS. HE'S AN EXPERT SYLPH-HUNTER.
THAT WAS YOU, RIGHT?
AND.
HMPH...
...WHAT WAS THIS GTACS DOING, GOING AFTER US?
IT WAS AN ORDER FROM EVEN HIGHER UP, APPAR-ENTLY.
SOMETHING ABOUT HOW YOU WERE AN OBSTACLE TO THE PLAN...
WHAT PLAN?

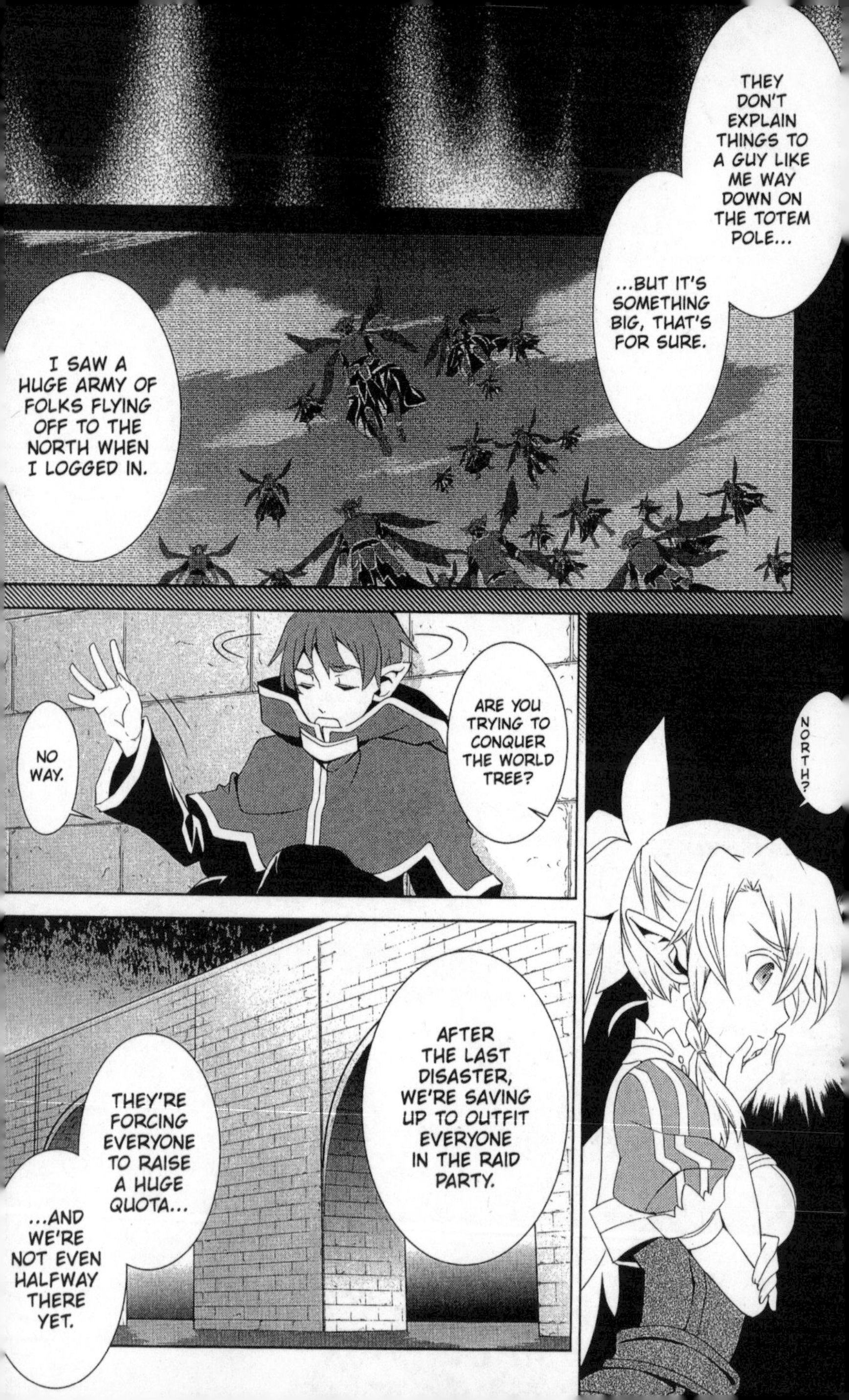
THEY DON'T EXPLAIN THINGS TO A GUY LIKE ME WAY DOWN ON THE TOTEM POLE...
...BUT IT'S SOMETHING BIG, THAT'S FOR SURE.
I SAW A HUGE ARMY OF FOLKS FLYING OFF TO THE NORTH WHEN I LOGGED IN.
NORTH?
ARE YOU TRYING TO CONQUER THE WORLD TREE?
NO WAY.
AFTER THE LAST DISASTER, WE'RE SAVING UP TO OUTFIT EVERYONE IN THE RAID PARTY.
THEY'RE FORCING EVERYONE TO RAISE A HUGE QUOTA...
...AND WE'RE NOT EVEN HALFWAY THERE YET.

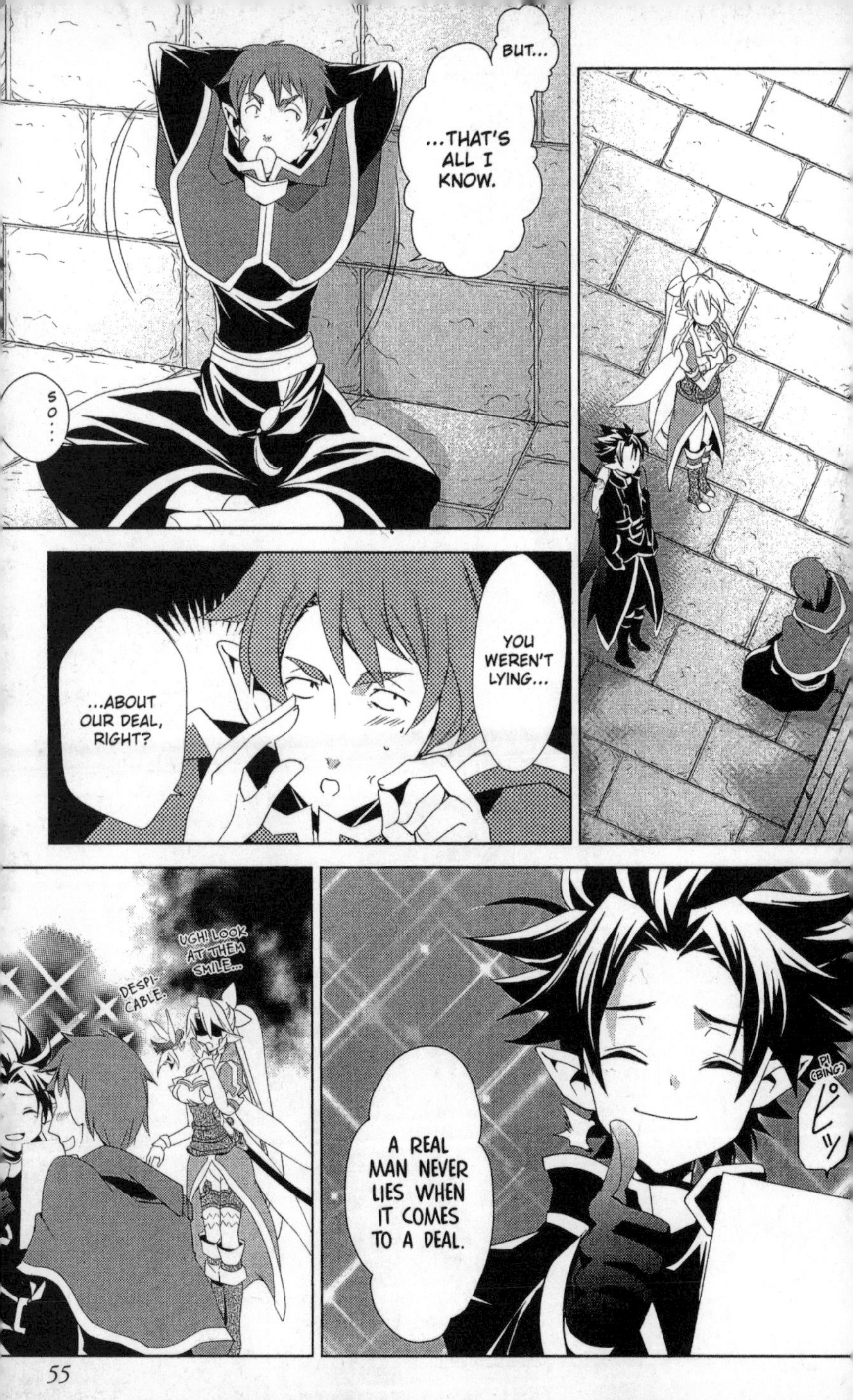
BUT...
...THAT'S ALL I KNOW.
SO...
YOU WEREN'T LYING...
...ABOUT OUR DEAL, RIGHT?
PI (BING)
A REAL MAN NEVER LIES WHEN IT COMES TO A DEAL.
UGH! LOOK AT THEM SMILE...
DESPI-CABLE.

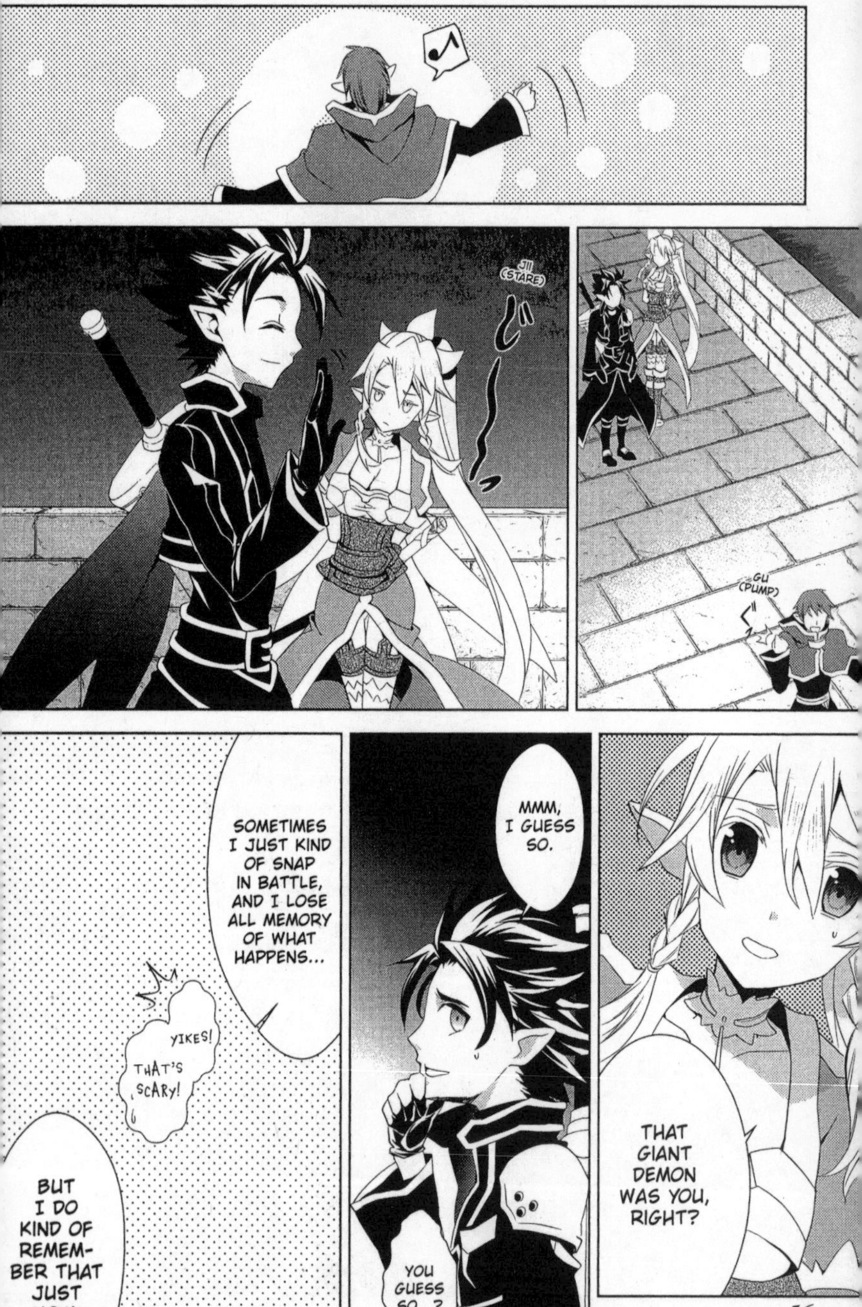
♪
GU (PUMP)
JII (STARE)
THAT GIANT DEMON WAS YOU, RIGHT?
MMM, I GUESS SO.
YOU GUESS SO...?
SOMETIMES I JUST KIND OF SNAP IN BATTLE, AND I LOSE ALL MEMORY OF WHAT HAPPENS...
YIKES! THAT'S SCARY!
BUT I DO KIND OF REMEMBER THAT JUST NOW.

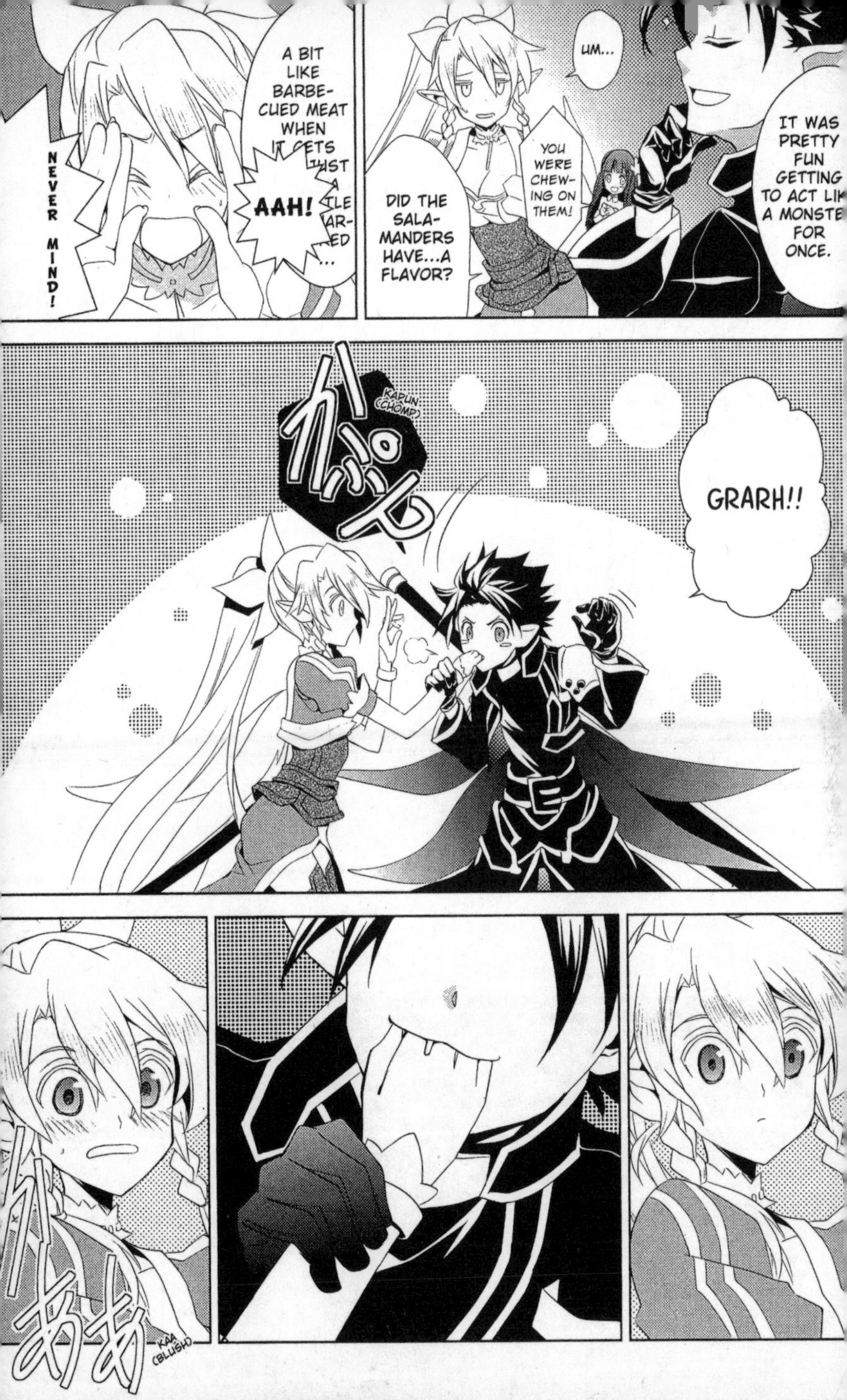
IT WAS PRETTY FUN GETTING TO ACT LIK A MONSTE FOR ONCE.
UM...
YOU WERE CHEW-ING ON THEM!
DID THE SALA-MANDERS HAVE...A FLAVOR?
A BIT LIKE BARBE-CUED MEAT WHEN IT GETS
AAH!
NEVER MIND!
GRARH!!
KAPUN (CHOMP)
KAA (BLUSH)

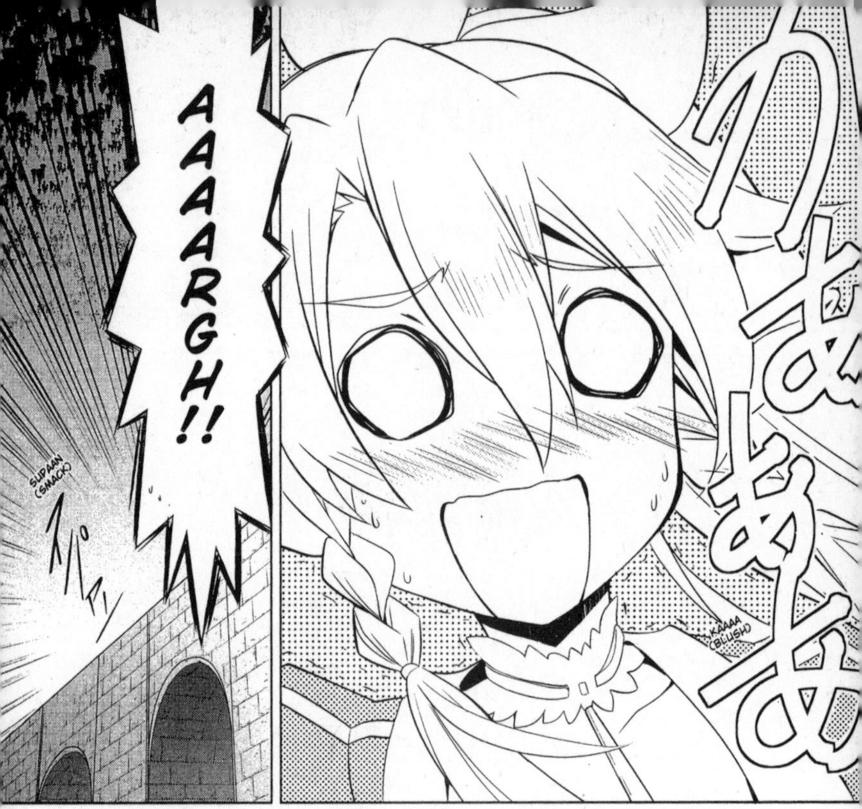
わぁぁぁ
KAAAA (BLUSH)
AAAARGH!!
スパァン
SUPAAN (SMACK)

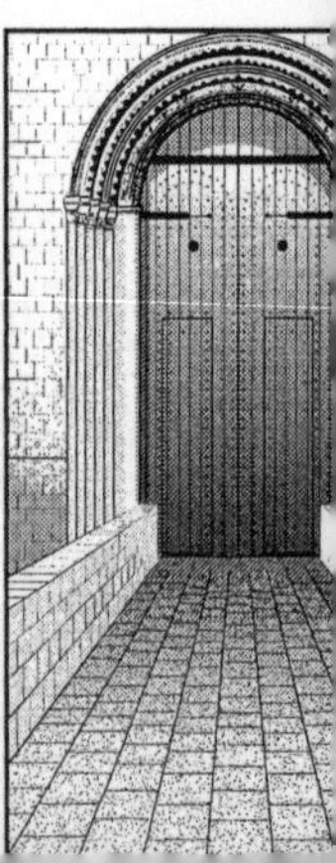

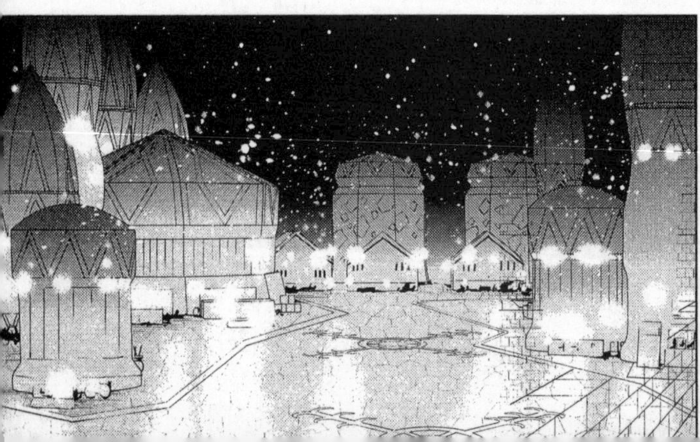

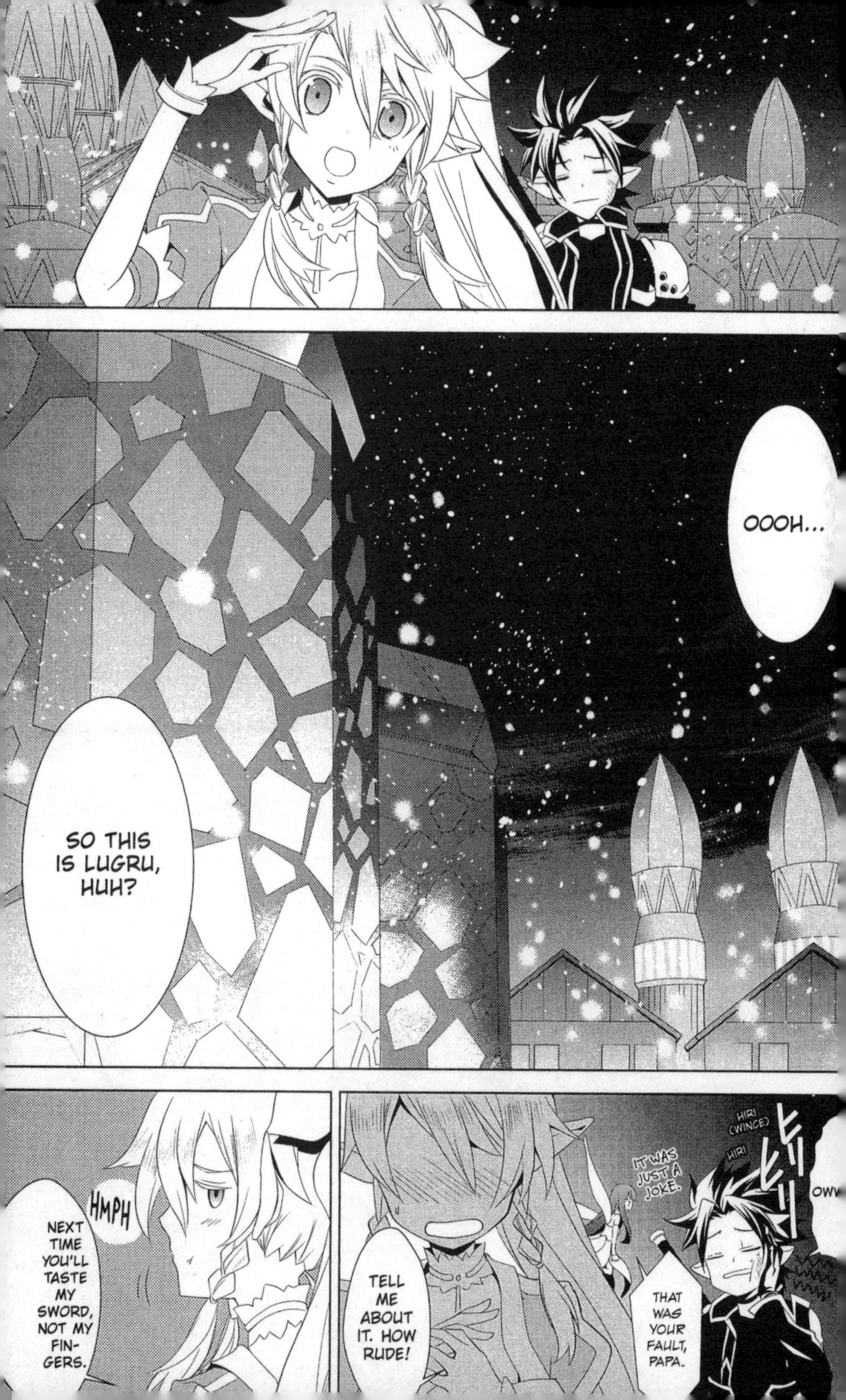
OOOH...
SO THIS IS LUGRU, HUH?
HIRI (WINCE)
HIRI
OWW
IT WAS JUST A JOKE.
THAT WAS YOUR FAULT, PAPA.
TELL ME ABOUT IT. HOW RUDE!
HMPH
NEXT TIME YOU'LL TASTE MY SWORD, NOT MY FIN-GERS.

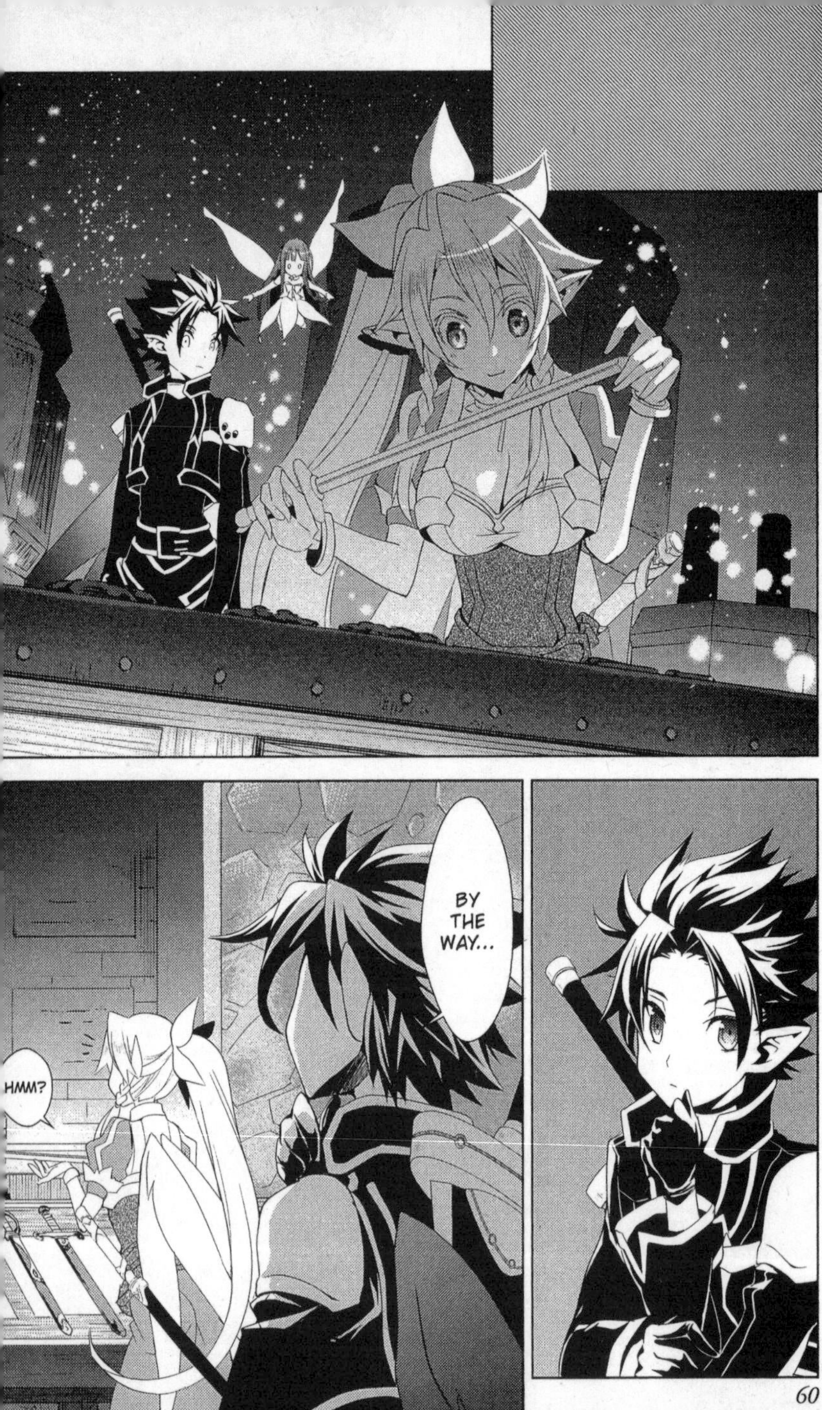
BY THE WAY...
HMM?

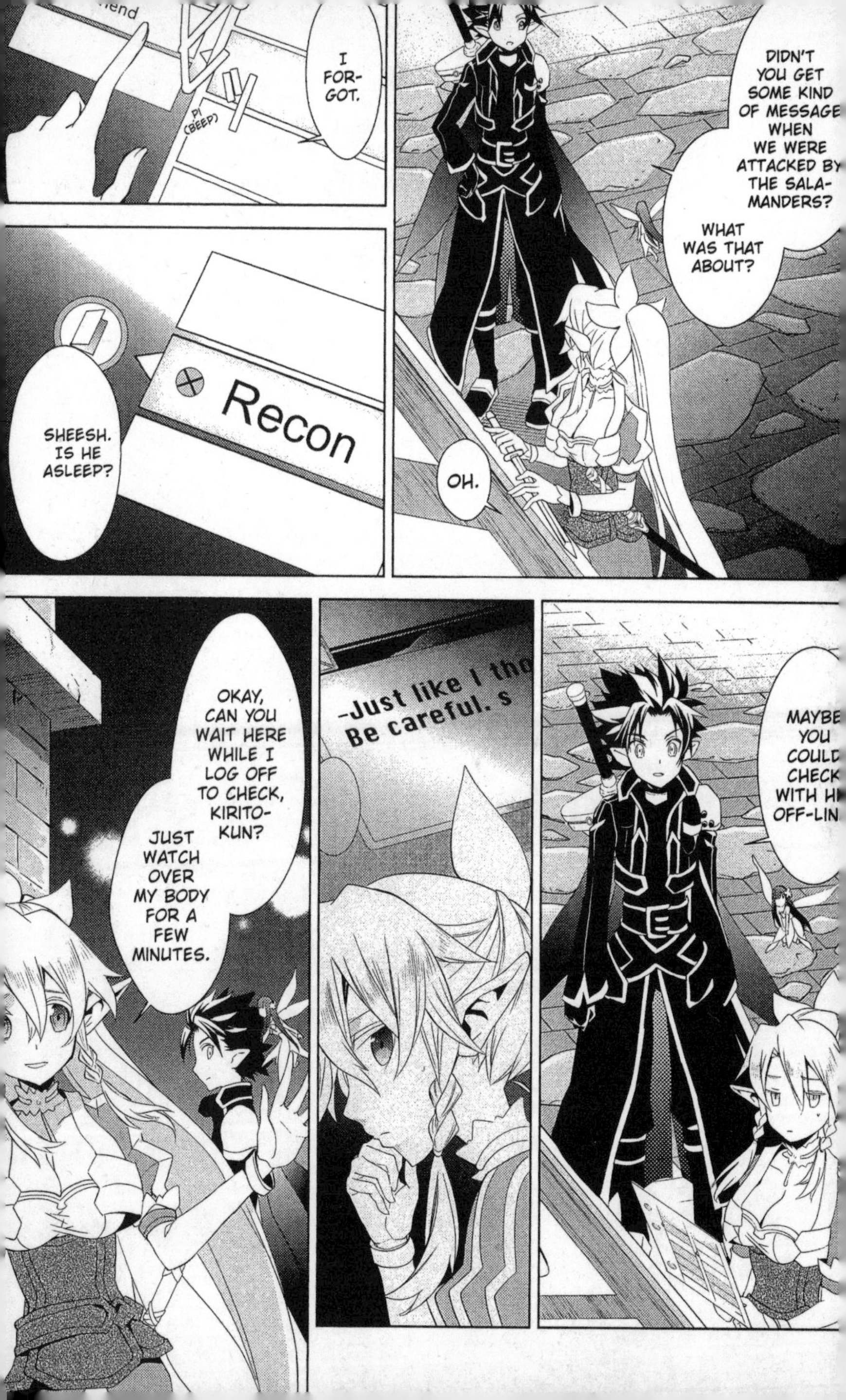
DIDN'T YOU GET SOME KIND OF MESSAGE WHEN WE WERE ATTACKED BY THE SALAMANDERS?
WHAT WAS THAT ABOUT?
OH.
I FOR-GOT.
PI (BEEP)
Recon
SHEESH. IS HE ASLEEP?
MAYBE YOU COULD CHECK WITH HI OFF-LIN
-Just like I tho
Be careful. s
OKAY, CAN YOU WAIT HERE WHILE I LOG OFF TO CHECK, KIRITO-KUN?
JUST WATCH OVER MY BODY FOR A FEW MINUTES.

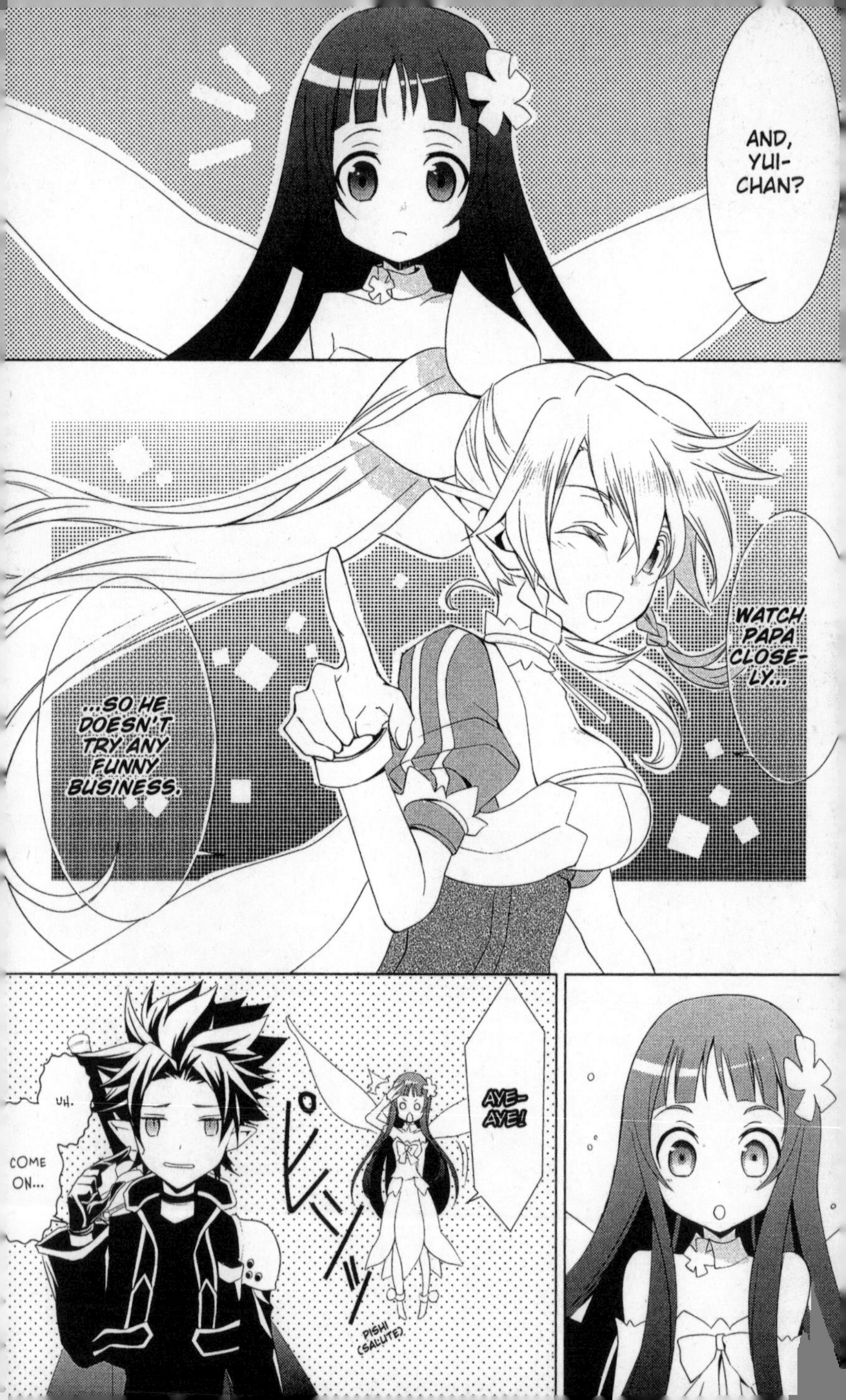
AND, YUI-CHAN?
WATCH PAPA CLOSE-LY...
...SO HE DOESN'T TRY ANY FUNNY BUSINESS.
AYE-AYE!
UH.
COME ON...
PISHI (SALUTE)

LOG OUT

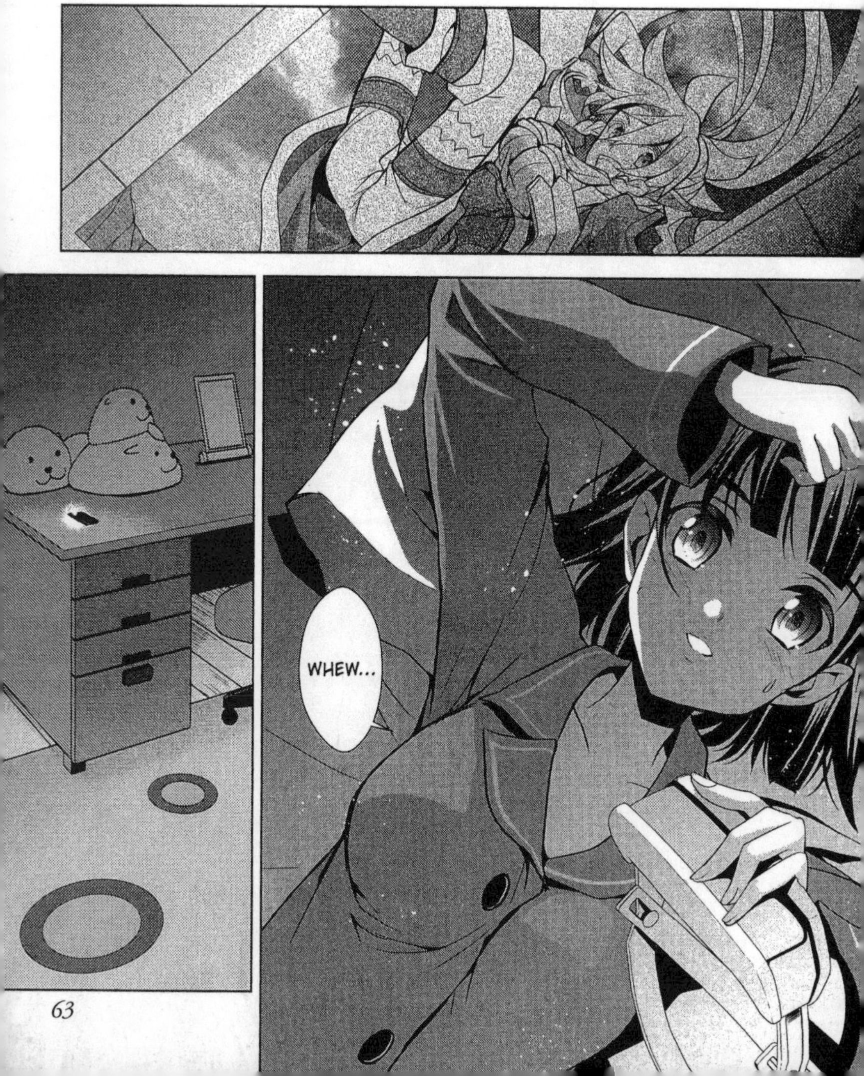
WHEW...

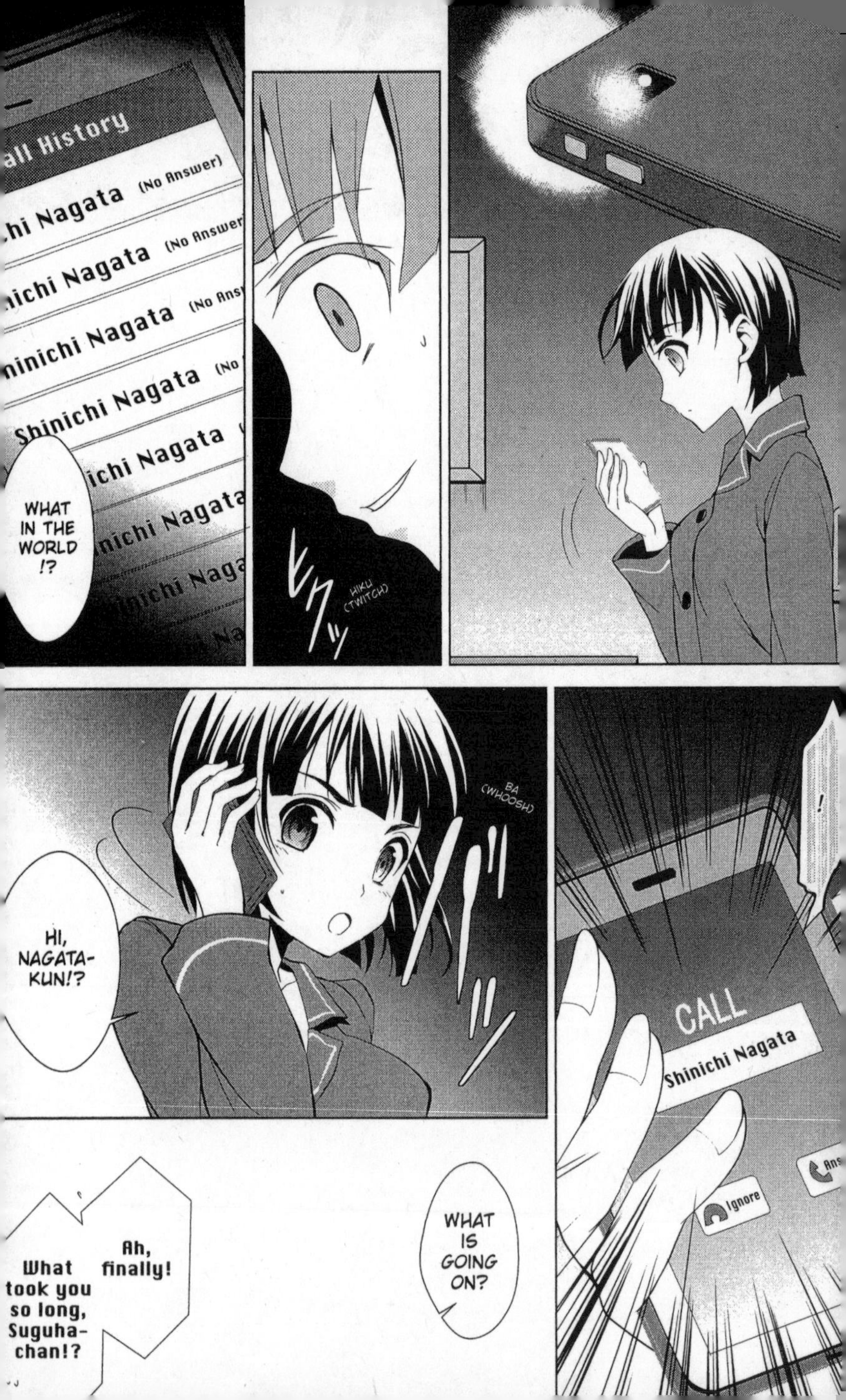
HIKU (TWITCH)
all History
hi Nagata (No Answer)
inichi Nagata (No Answer
ninichi Nagata (No Answ
Shinichi Nagata
ichi Nagata
nichi Nagata
WHAT IN THE WORLD !?
!
CALL
Shinichi Nagata
Ignore
BA (WHOOSH)
HI, NAGATA-KUN!?
WHAT IS GOING ON?
Ah, finally! What took you so long, Suguha-chan!?

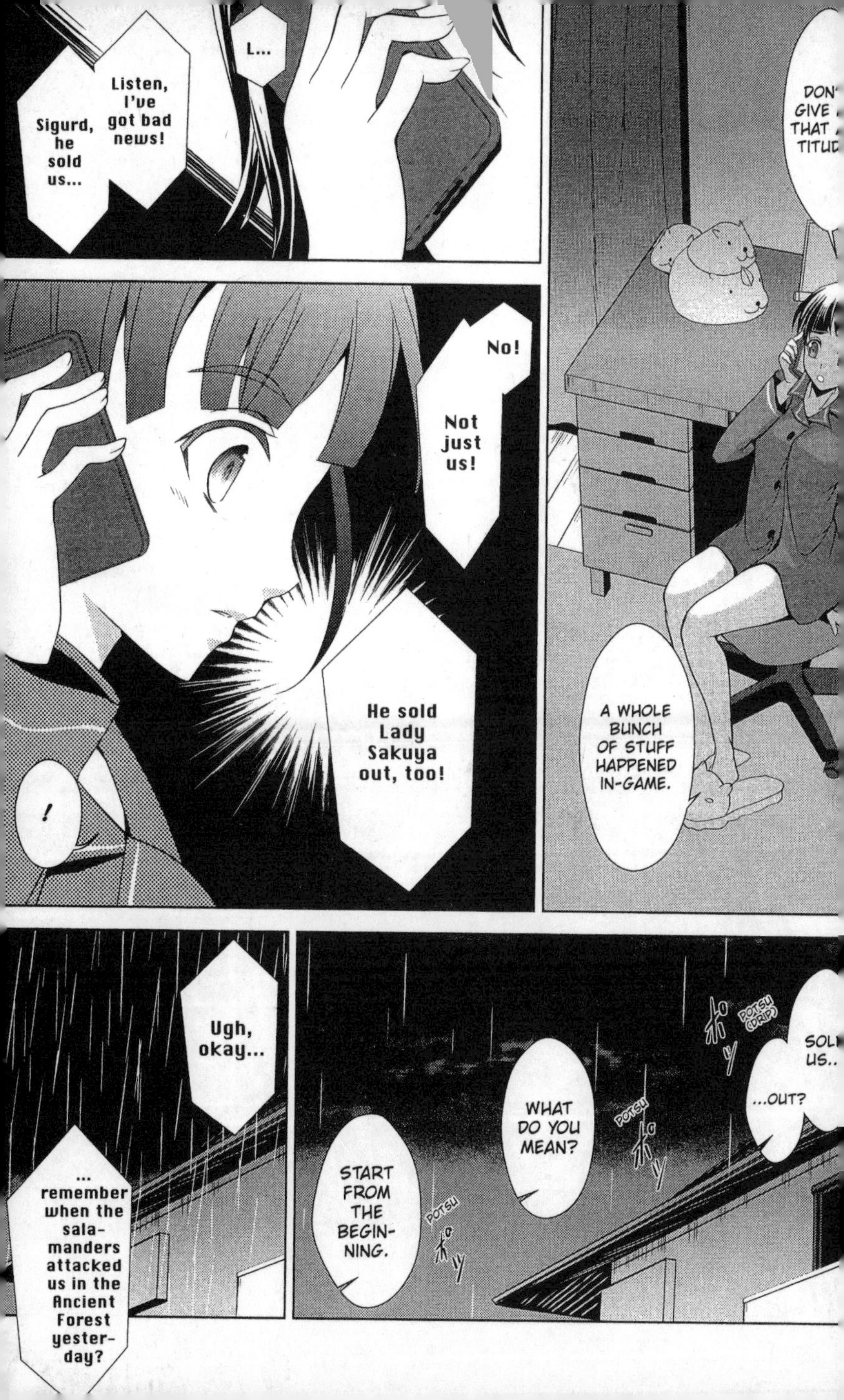
DON' GIVE THAT TITUD
A WHOLE BUNCH OF STUFF HAPPENED IN-GAME.
L...
Listen, I've got bad news!
Sigurd, he sold us...
No!
Not just us!
He sold Lady Sakuya out, too!
!
SOL US..
...OUT?
POTSU (DRIP)
WHAT DO YOU MEAN?
POTSU
START FROM THE BEGIN-NING.
POTSU
Ugh, okay...
...remember when the sala-manders attacked us in the Ancient Forest yester-day?

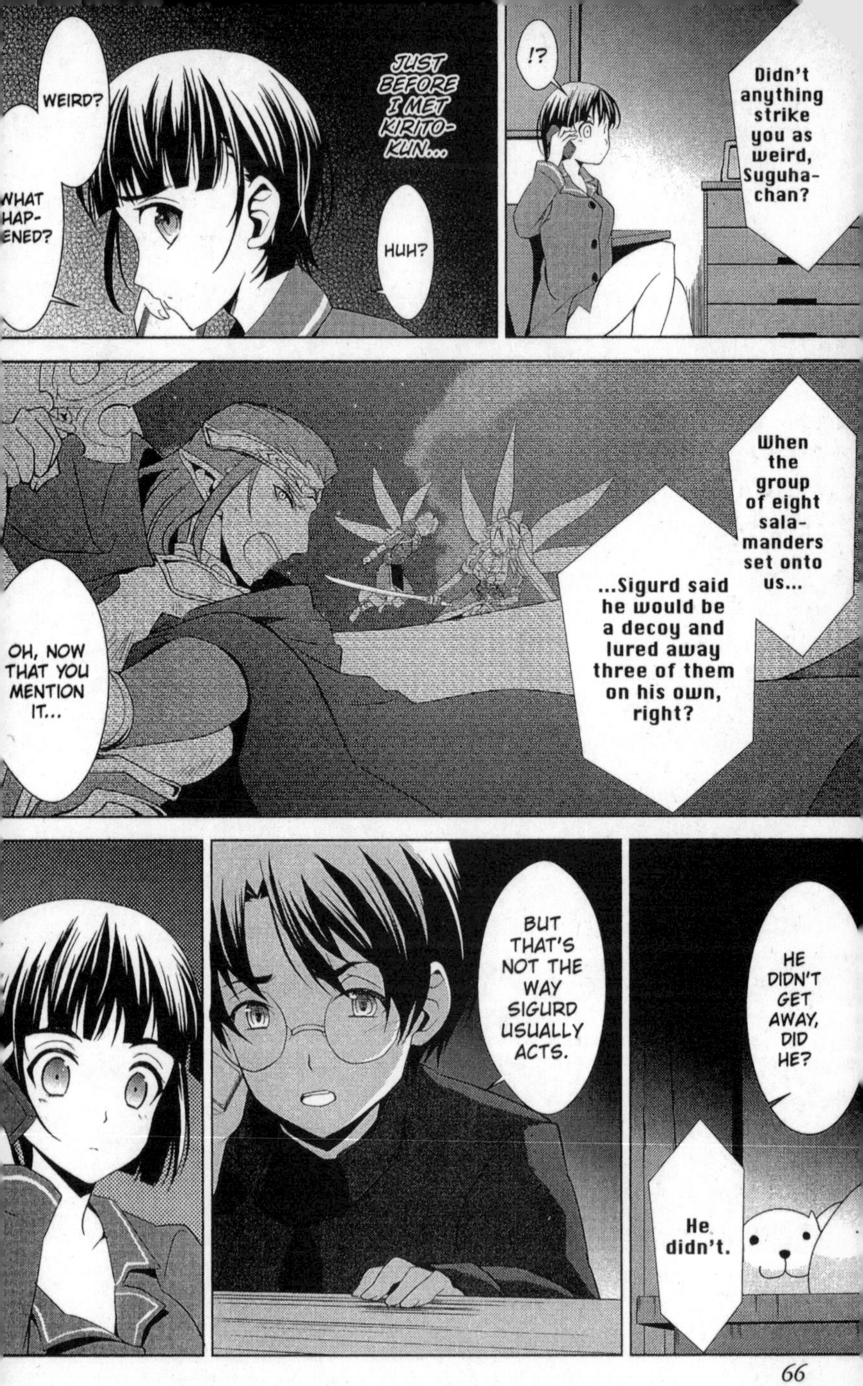
Didn't anything strike you as weird, Suguha-chan?
!?
JUST BEFORE I MET KIRITO-KUN...
HUH?
WEIRD?
WHAT HAP-PENED?
When the group of eight sala-manders set onto us...
...Sigurd said he would be a decoy and lured away three of them on his own, right?
OH, NOW THAT YOU MENTION IT...
HE DIDN'T GET AWAY, DID HE?
He didn't.
BUT THAT'S NOT THE WAY SIGURD USUALLY ACTS.

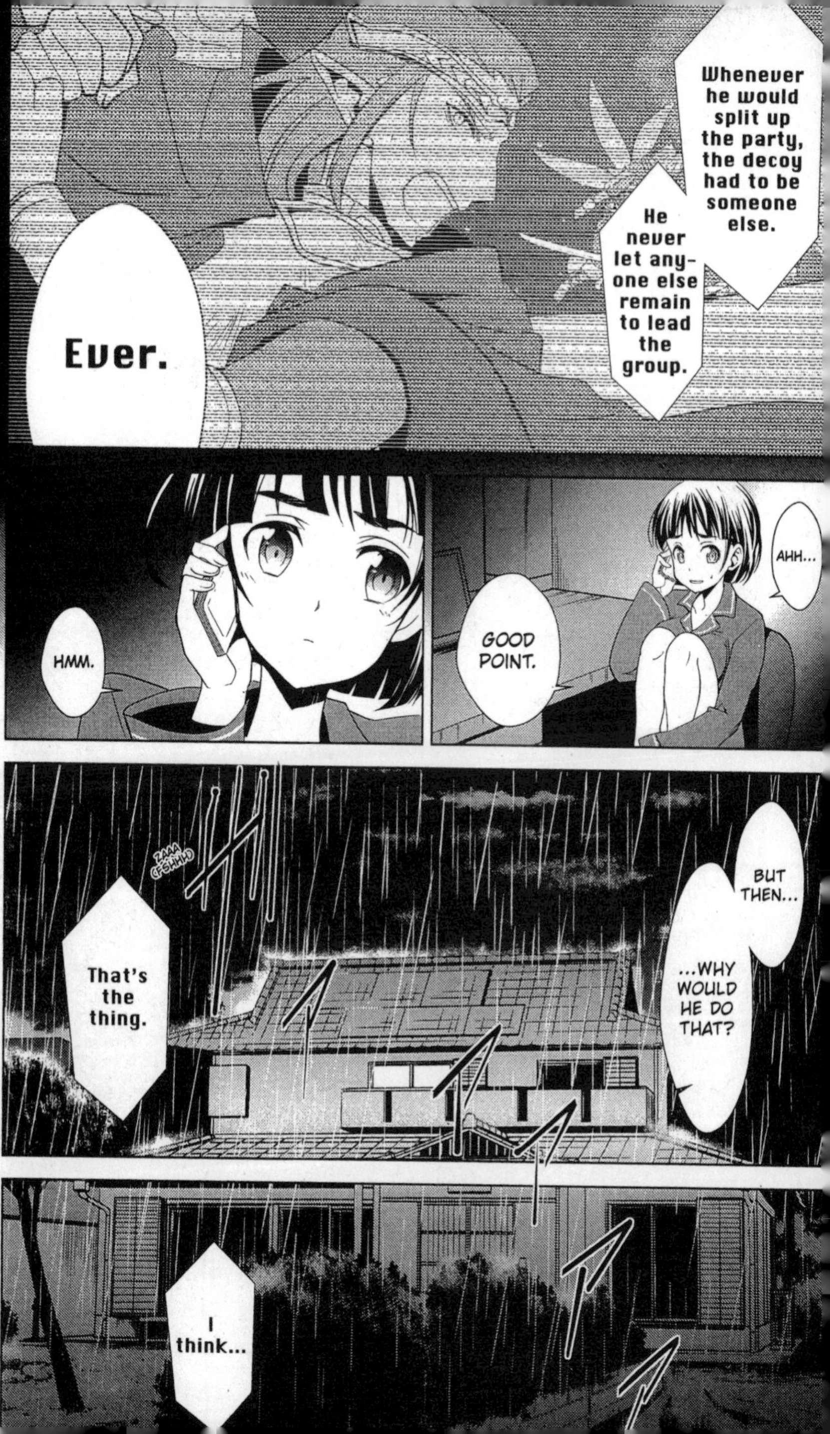
Whenever he would split up the party, the decoy had to be someone else.
He never let any-one else remain to lead the group.
Ever.
AHH...
GOOD POINT.
HMM.
ZAAA (FSHHH)
BUT THEN...
...WHY WOULD HE DO THAT?
That's the thing.
I think...

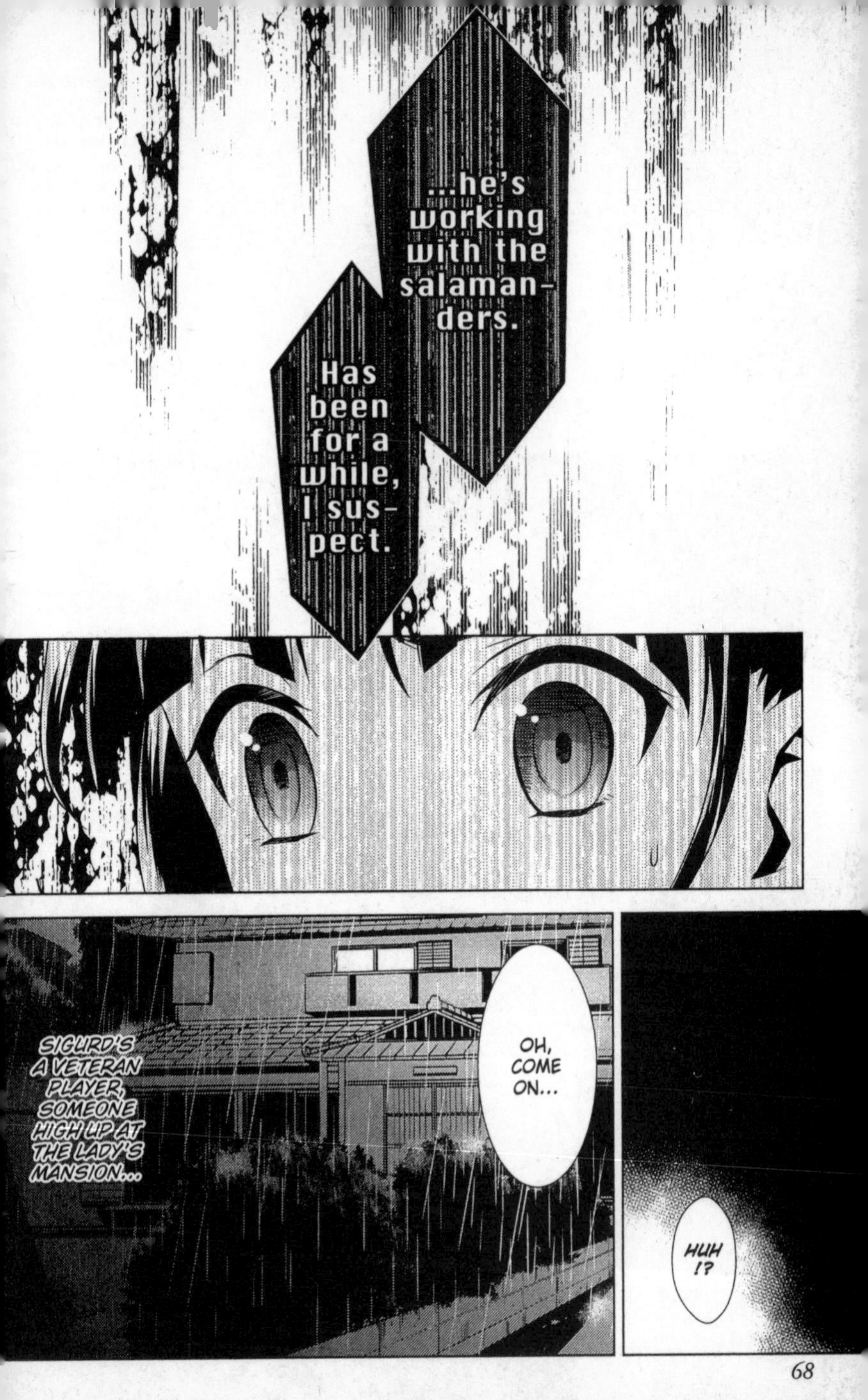
...he's working with the salamanders.
Has been for a while, I suspect.
HUH!?
OH, COME ON...
SIGURD'S A VETERAN PLAYER, SOMEONE HIGH UP AT THE LADY'S MANSION...

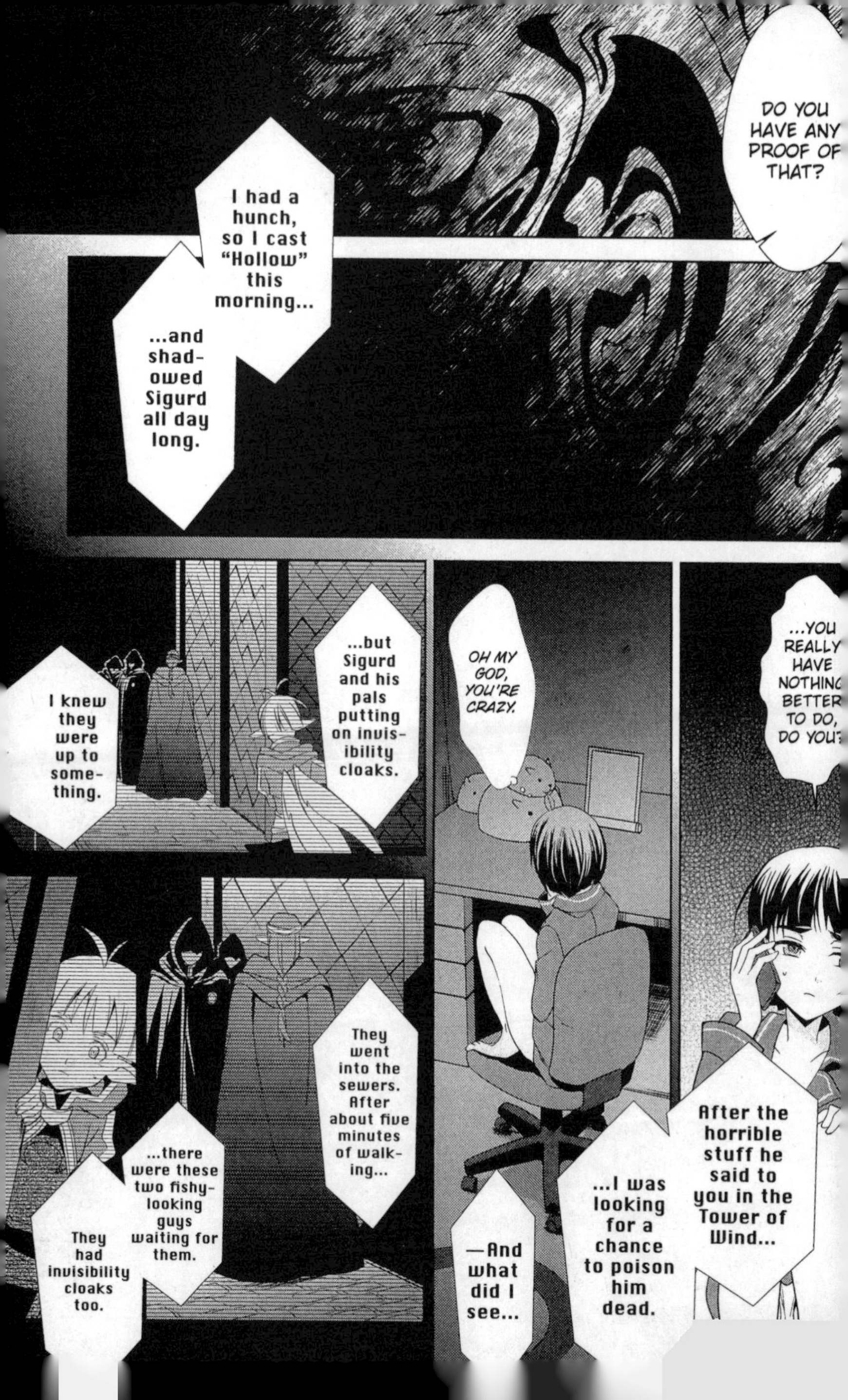
DO YOU HAVE ANY PROOF OF THAT?
I had a hunch, so I cast "Hollow" this morning...
...and shad-owed Sigurd all day long.
...YOU REALLY HAVE NOTHING BETTER TO DO, DO YOU?
After the horrible stuff he said to you in the Tower of Wind...
...I was looking for a chance to poison him dead.
OH MY GOD, YOU'RE CRAZY.
—And what did I see...
...but Sigurd and his pals putting on invis-ibility cloaks.
I knew they were up to some-thing.
They went into the sewers. After about five minutes of walk-ing...
...there were these two fishy-looking guys waiting for them.
They had invisibility cloaks too.

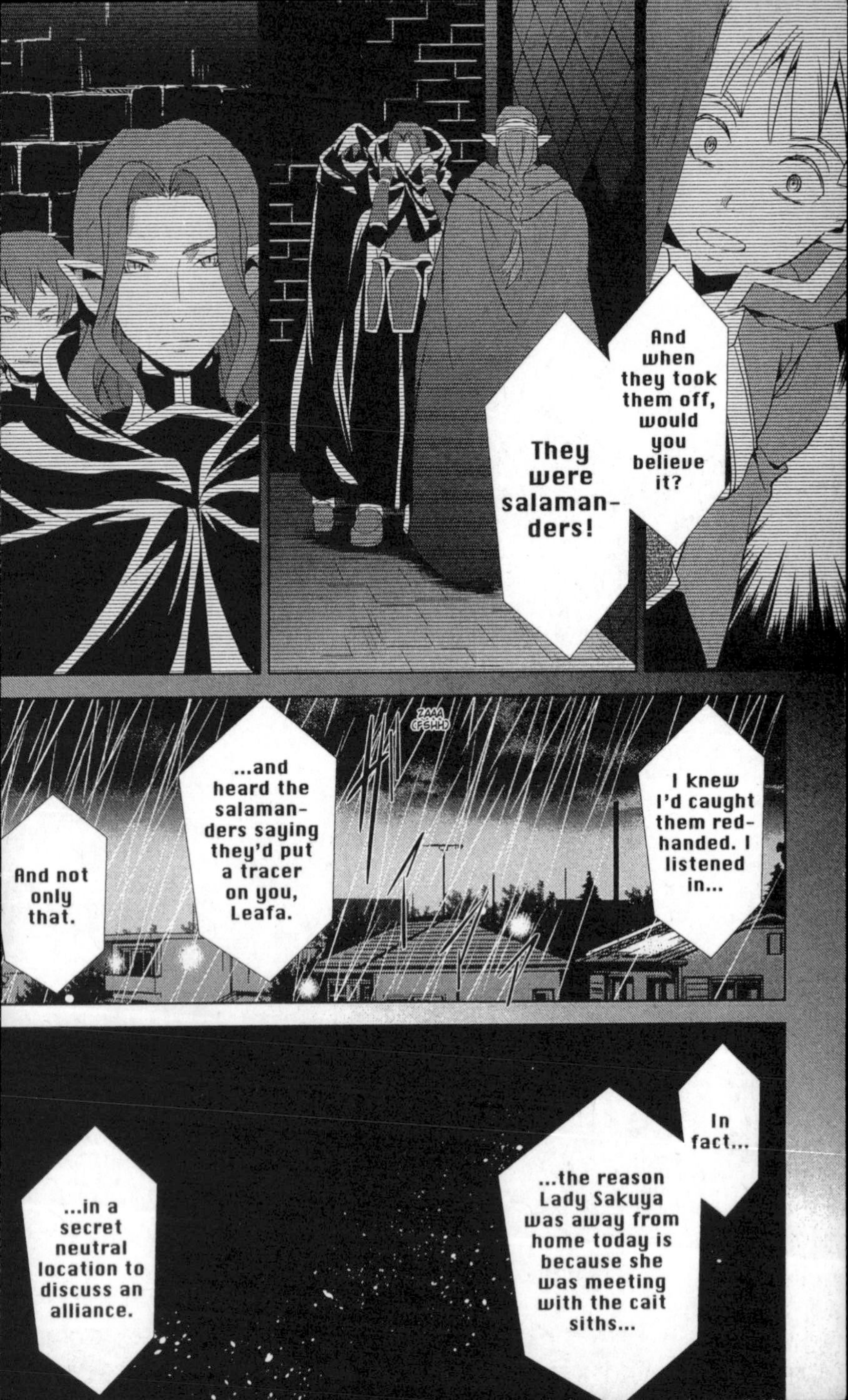
And when they took them off, would you believe it?
They were salamanders!
I knew I'd caught them red-handed. I listened in...
ZAAA (FSHH)
...and heard the salamanders saying they'd put a tracer on you, Leafa.
And not only that.
In fact...
...the reason Lady Sakuya was away from home today is because she was meeting with the cait siths...
...in a secret neutral location to discuss an alliance.

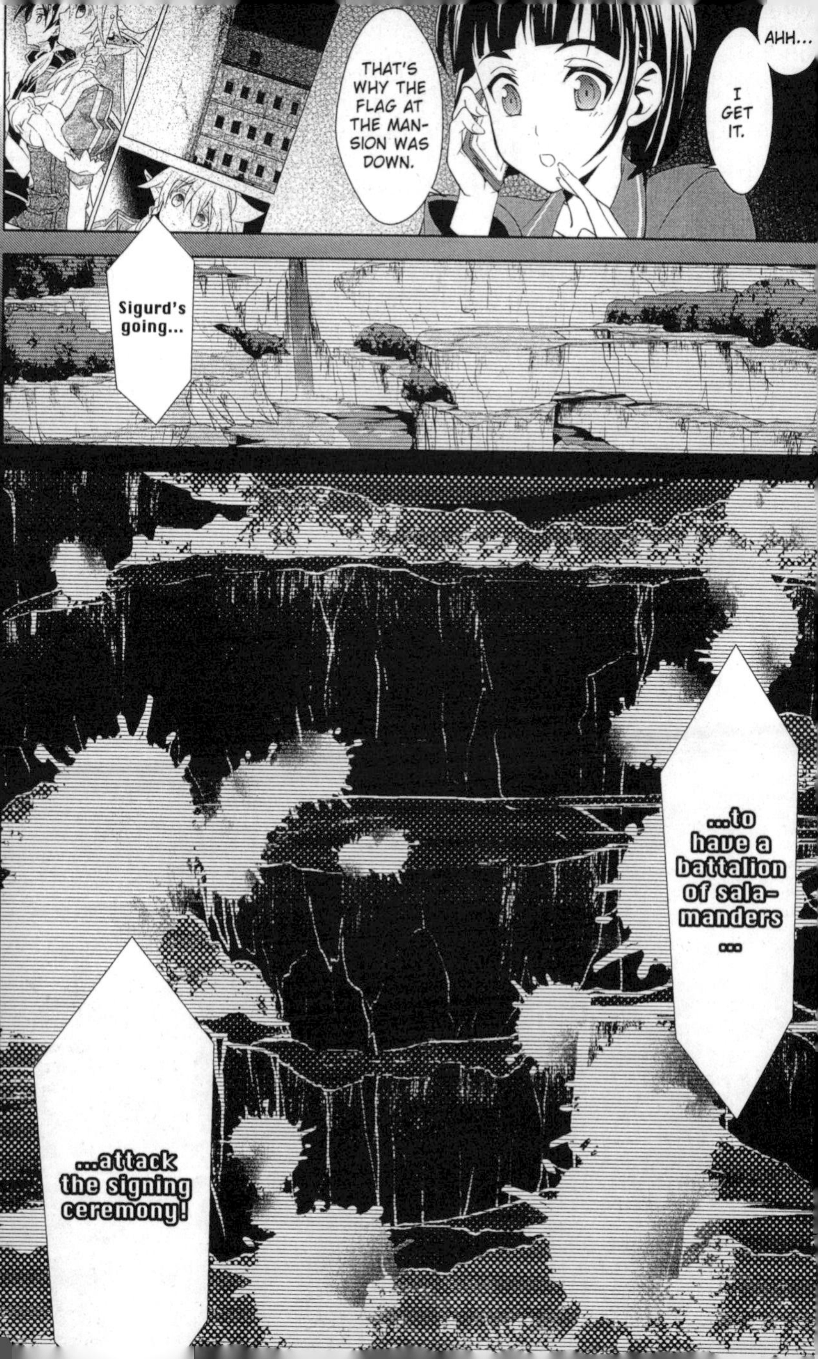
AHH... I GET IT.
THAT'S WHY THE FLAG AT THE MAN-SION WAS DOWN.
Sigurd's going...
...to have a battalion of sala-manders ...
...attack the signing ceremony!

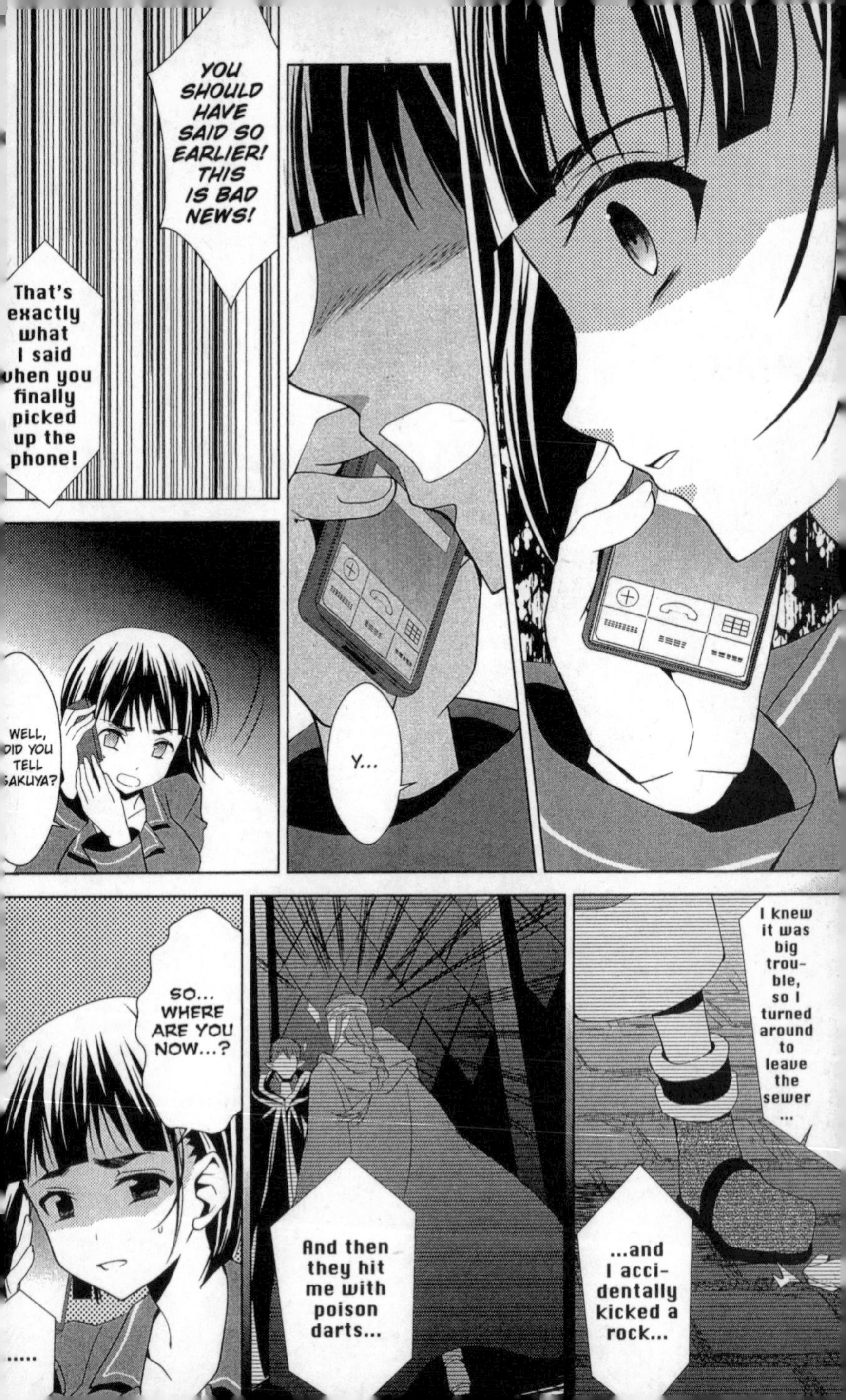

Y...
YOU SHOULD HAVE SAID SO EARLIER! THIS IS BAD NEWS!
That's exactly what I said when you finally picked up the phone!
WELL, DID YOU TELL SAKUYA?
I knew it was big trou-ble, so I turned around to leave the sewer...
...and I acci-dentally kicked a rock...
And then they hit me with poison darts...
SO... WHERE ARE YOU NOW...?
.....

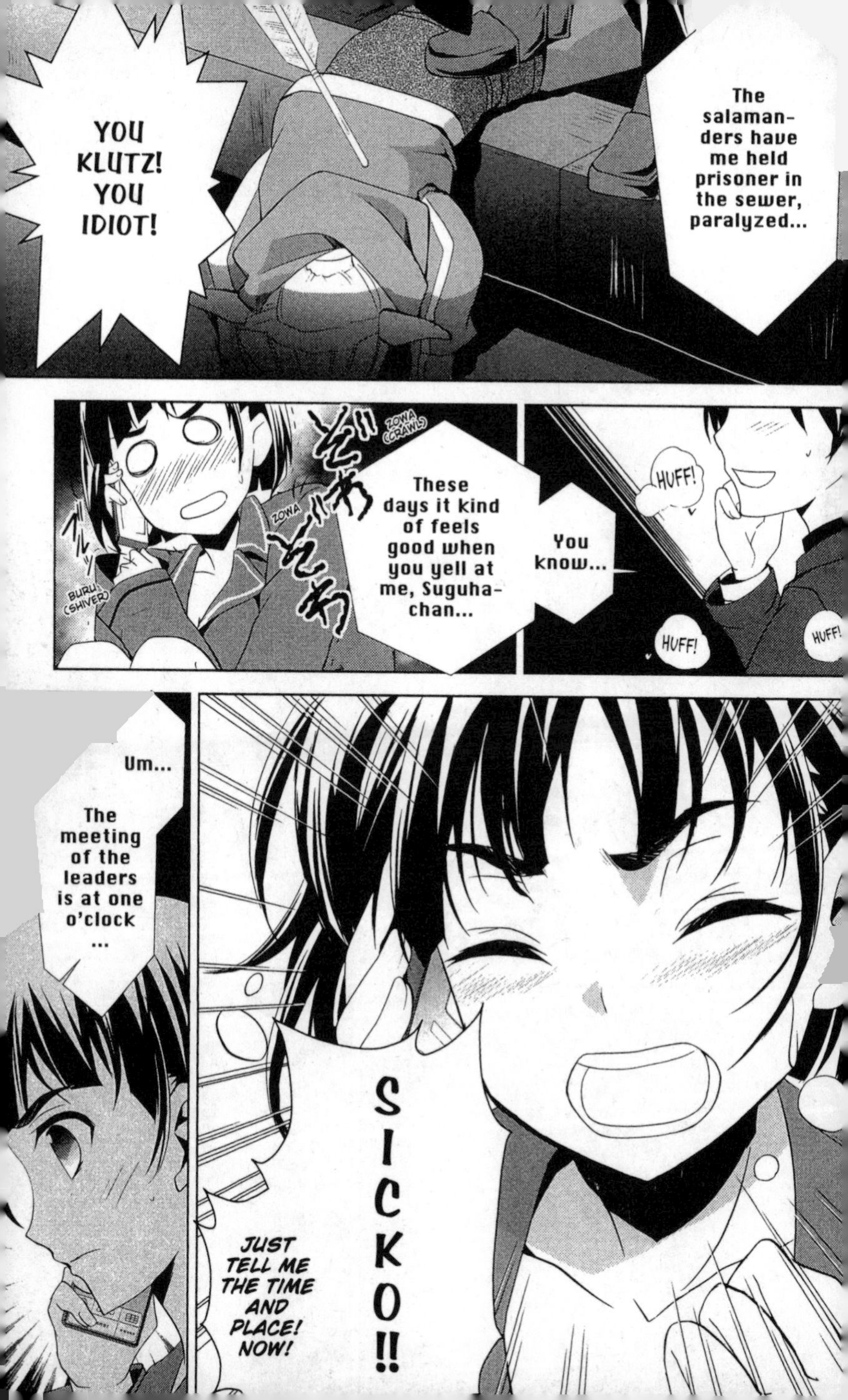

The salamanders have me held prisoner in the sewer, paralyzed...
YOU KLUTZ! YOU IDIOT!
HUFF!
You know...
HUFF!
HUFF!
ZOWA (CRAWL)
These days it kind of feels good when you yell at me, Suguha-chan...
ZOWA
BURU (SHIVER)
SICKO!!
JUST TELL ME THE TIME AND PLACE! NOW!
Um...
The meeting of the leaders is at one o'clock ...

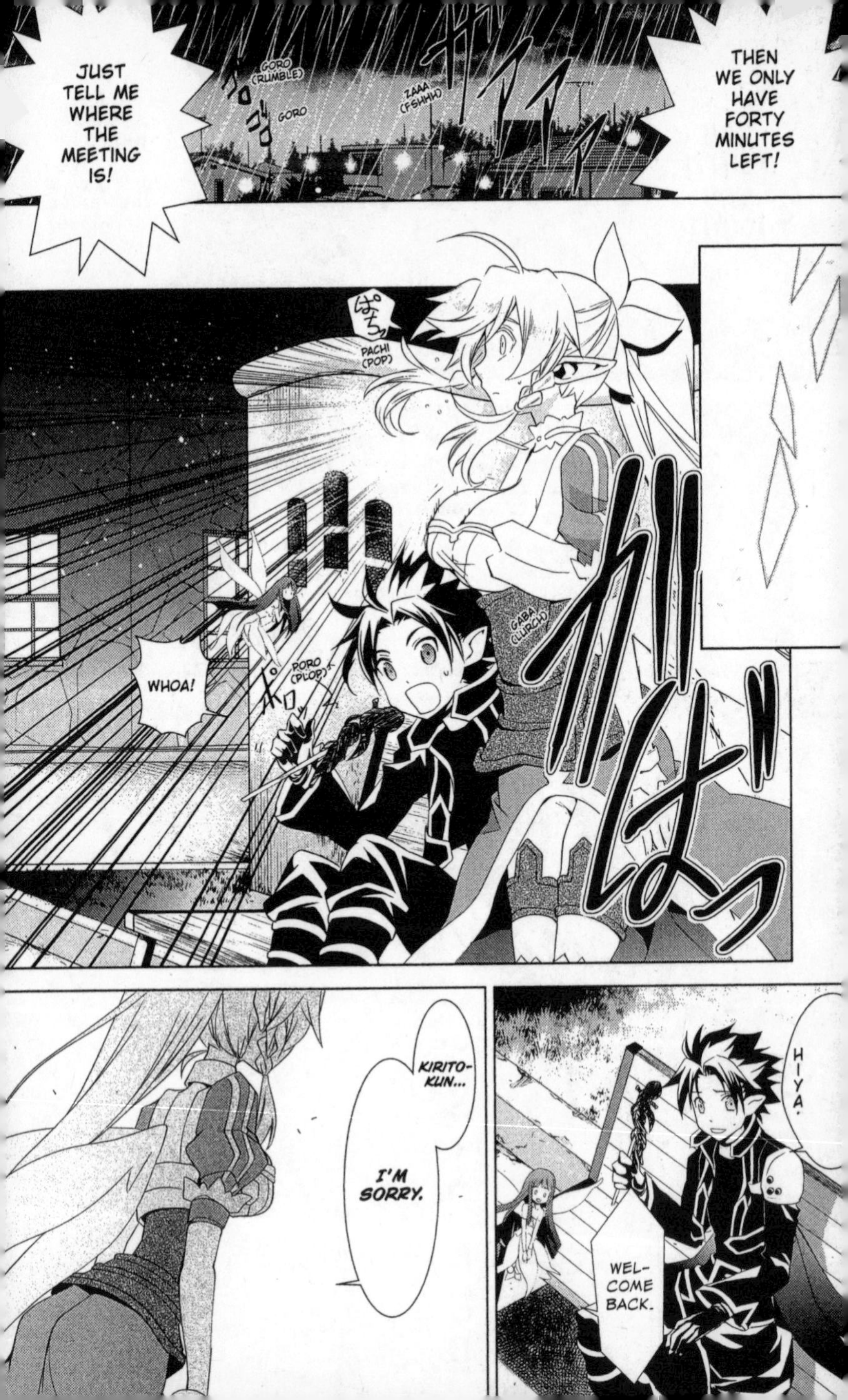
THEN WE ONLY HAVE FORTY MINUTES LEFT!
ZAAA (FSHHH)
GORO (RUMBLE)
GORO
JUST TELL ME WHERE THE MEETING IS!
ぱちっ
PACHI (POP)
GABA (LURCH)
PORO (PLOP)
WHOA!
HIYA.
WEL-COME BACK.
KIRITO-KUN...
I'M SORRY.

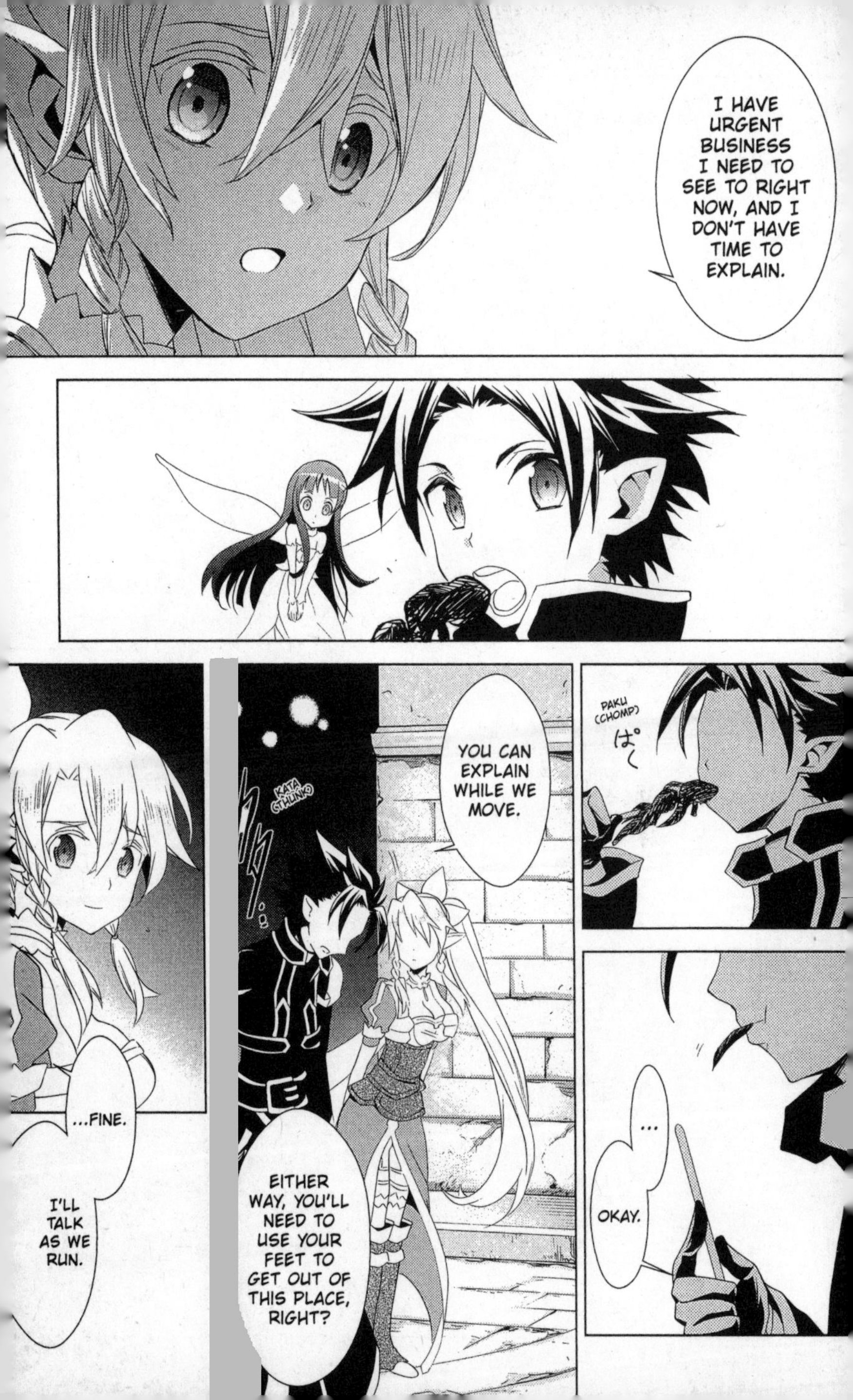
I HAVE URGENT BUSINESS I NEED TO SEE TO RIGHT NOW, AND I DON'T HAVE TIME TO EXPLAIN.
PAKU (CHOMP)
ぱく
...
OKAY.
YOU CAN EXPLAIN WHILE WE MOVE.
KATA (THUNK)
EITHER WAY, YOU'LL NEED TO USE YOUR FEET TO GET OUT OF THIS PLACE, RIGHT?
...FINE.
I'LL TALK AS WE RUN.

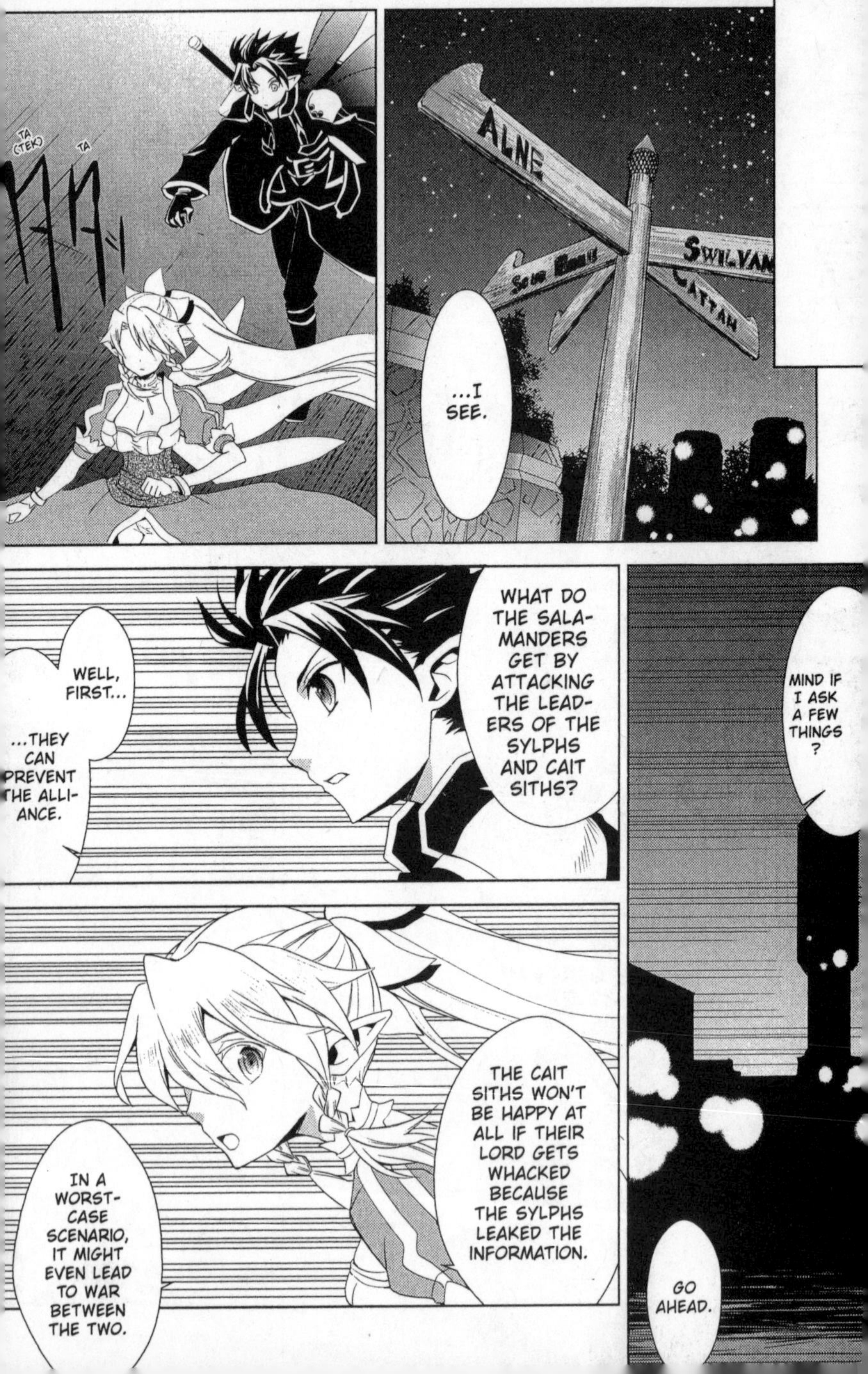
ALNE
SWILVAN
...I SEE.
TA (TEK) TA
MIND IF I ASK A FEW THINGS?
GO AHEAD.
WHAT DO THE SALAMANDERS GET BY ATTACKING THE LEADERS OF THE SYLPHS AND CAIT SITHS?
WELL, FIRST...
...THEY CAN PREVENT THE ALLIANCE.
THE CAIT SITHS WON'T BE HAPPY AT ALL IF THEIR LORD GETS WHACKED BECAUSE THE SYLPHS LEAKED THE INFORMATION.
IN A WORST-CASE SCENARIO, IT MIGHT EVEN LEAD TO WAR BETWEEN THE TWO.

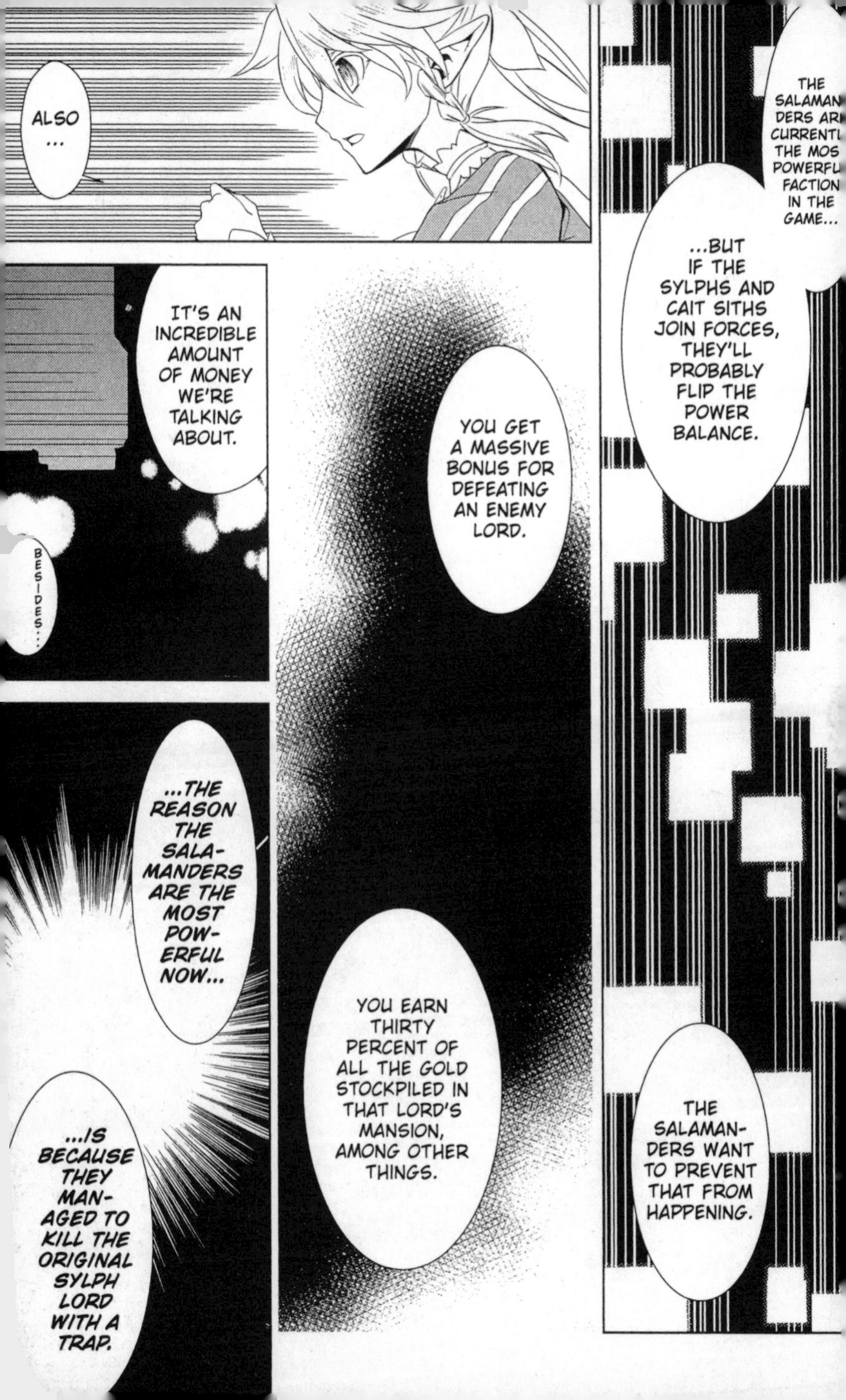
THE SALAMAN DERS AR CURRENTL THE MOS POWERFU FACTION IN THE GAME...
...BUT IF THE SYLPHS AND CAIT SITHS JOIN FORCES, THEY'LL PROBABLY FLIP THE POWER BALANCE.
THE SALAMANDERS WANT TO PREVENT THAT FROM HAPPENING.
ALSO...
YOU GET A MASSIVE BONUS FOR DEFEATING AN ENEMY LORD.
YOU EARN THIRTY PERCENT OF ALL THE GOLD STOCKPILED IN THAT LORD'S MANSION, AMONG OTHER THINGS.
IT'S AN INCREDIBLE AMOUNT OF MONEY WE'RE TALKING ABOUT.
BESIDES...
...THE REASON THE SALAMANDERS ARE THE MOST POWERFUL NOW...
...IS BECAUSE THEY MANAGED TO KILL THE ORIGINAL SYLPH LORD WITH A TRAP.

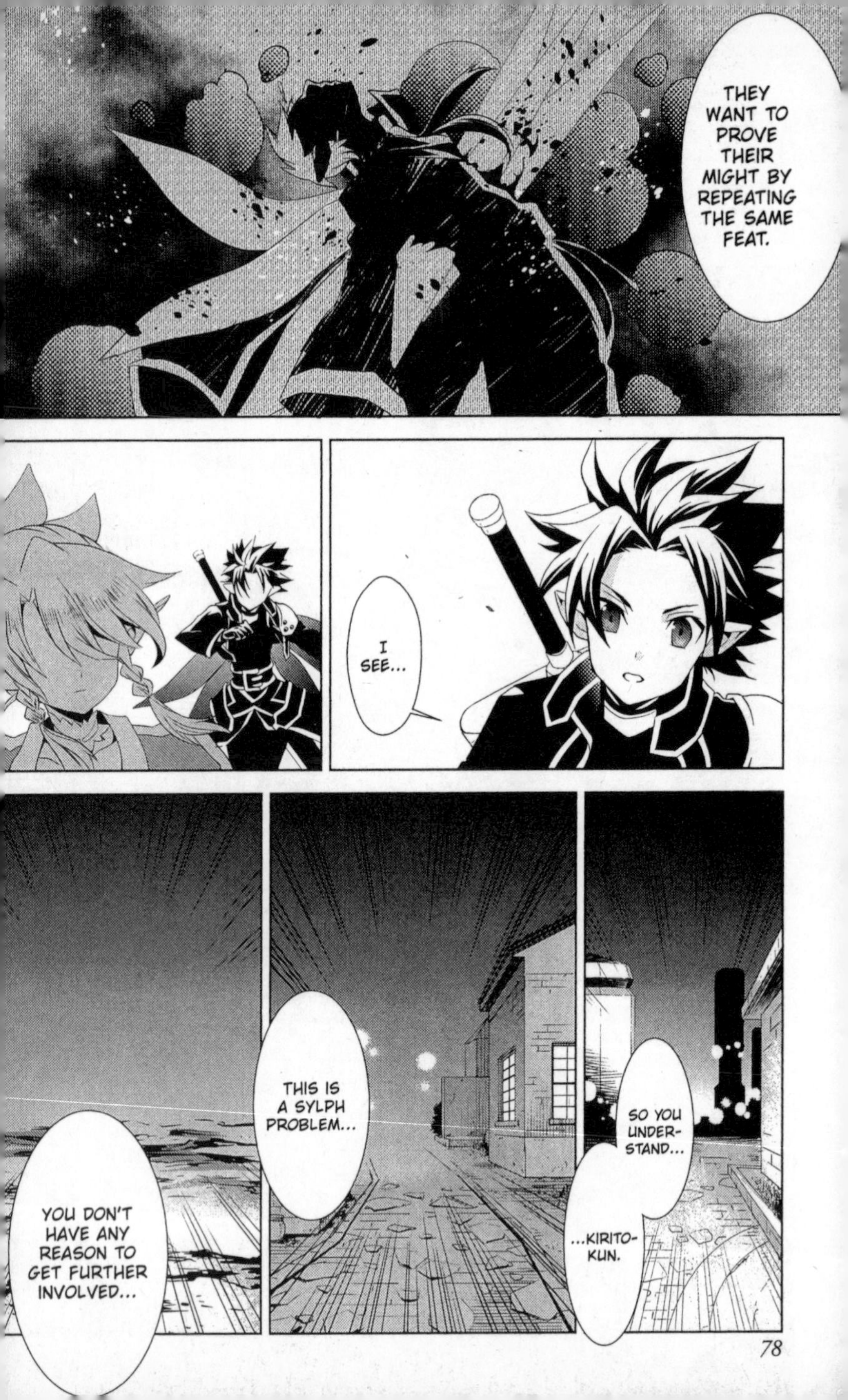
THEY WANT TO PROVE THEIR MIGHT BY REPEATING THE SAME FEAT.
I SEE...
SO YOU UNDERSTAND...
...KIRITO-KUN.
THIS IS A SYLPH PROBLEM...
YOU DON'T HAVE ANY REASON TO GET FURTHER INVOLVED...

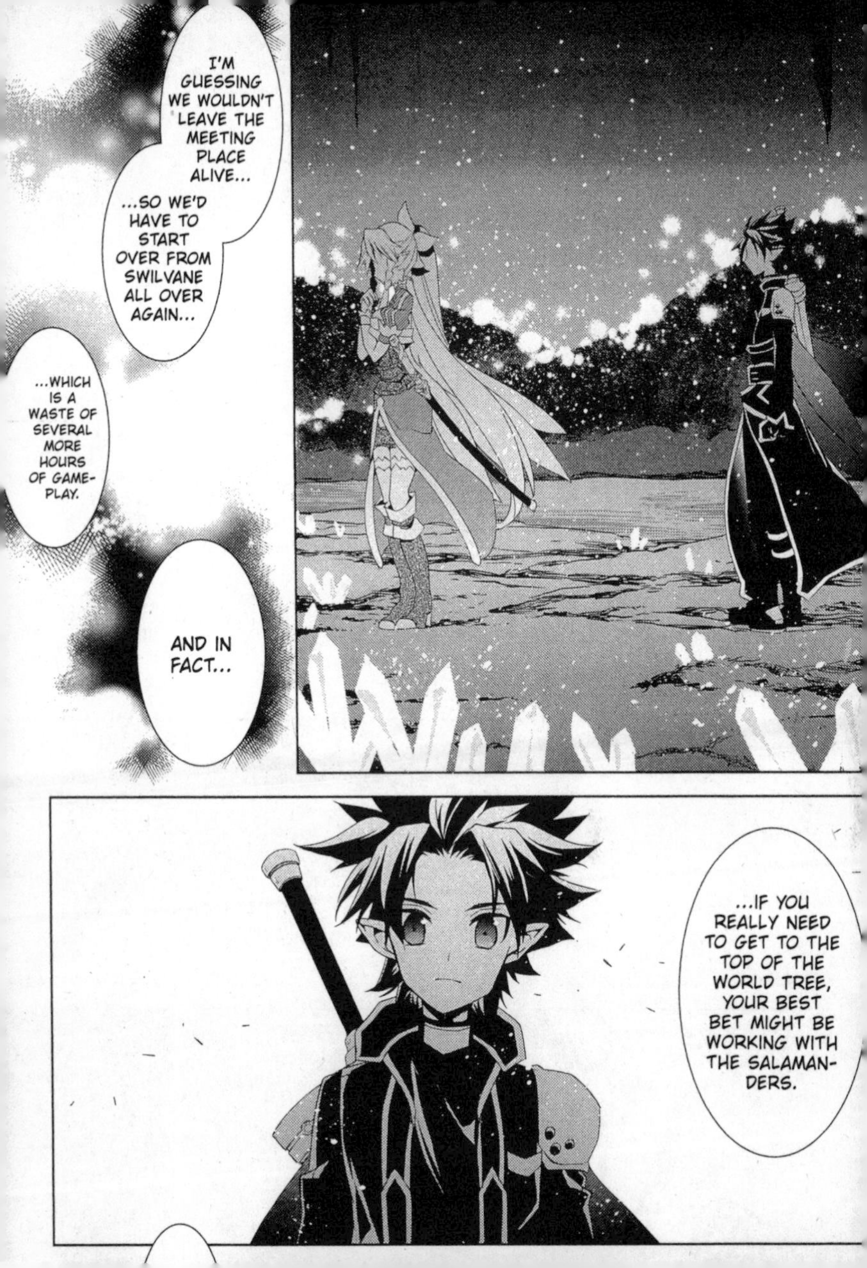
I'M GUESSING WE WOULDN'T LEAVE THE MEETING PLACE ALIVE...
...SO WE'D HAVE TO START OVER FROM SWILVANE ALL OVER AGAIN...
...WHICH IS A WASTE OF SEVERAL MORE HOURS OF GAME-PLAY.
AND IN FACT...
...IF YOU REALLY NEED TO GET TO THE TOP OF THE WORLD TREE, YOUR BEST BET MIGHT BE WORKING WITH THE SALAMAN-DERS.

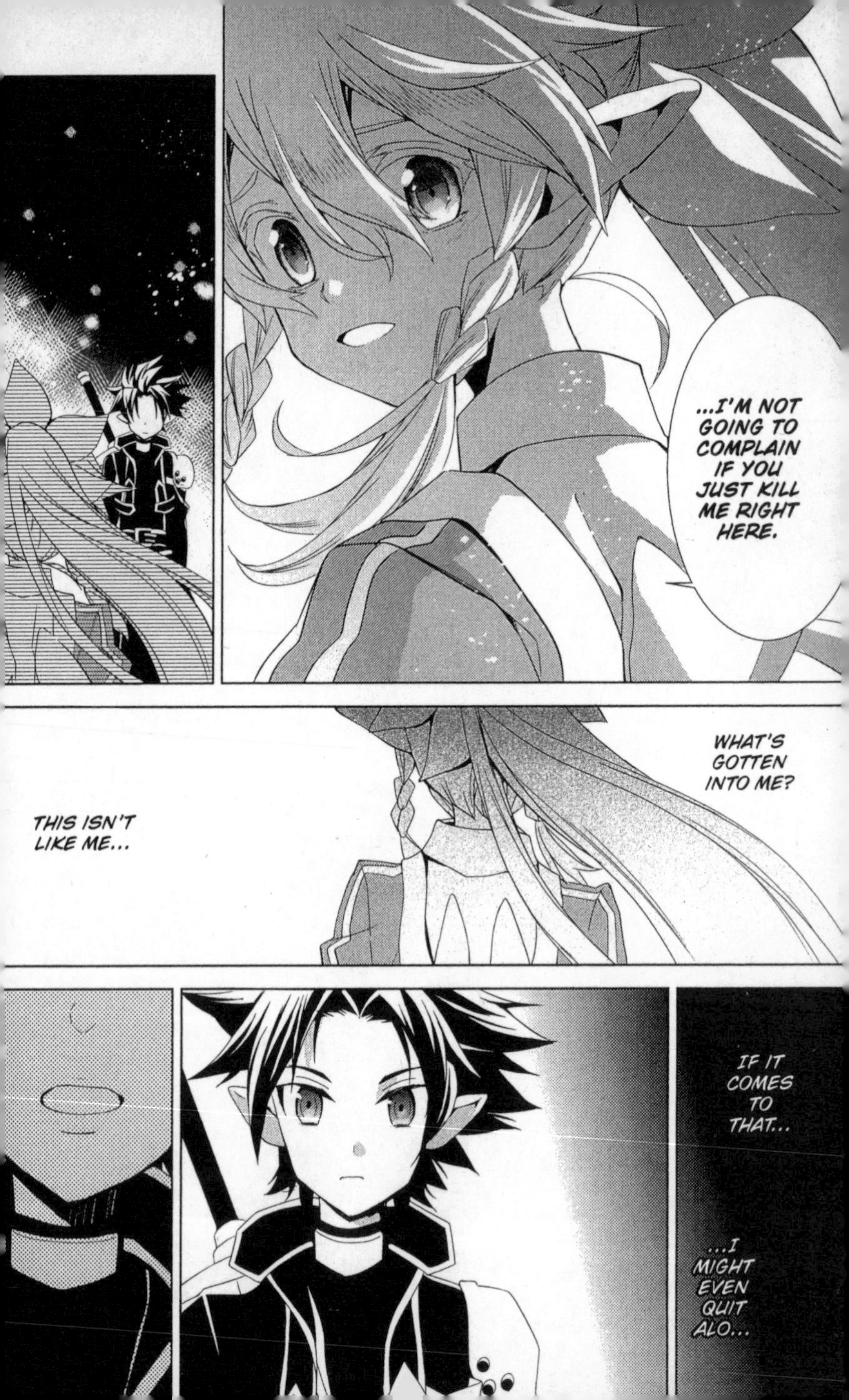
...I'M NOT GOING TO COMPLAIN IF YOU JUST KILL ME RIGHT HERE.
WHAT'S GOTTEN INTO ME?
THIS ISN'T LIKE ME...
IF IT COMES TO THAT...
...I MIGHT EVEN QUIT ALO...

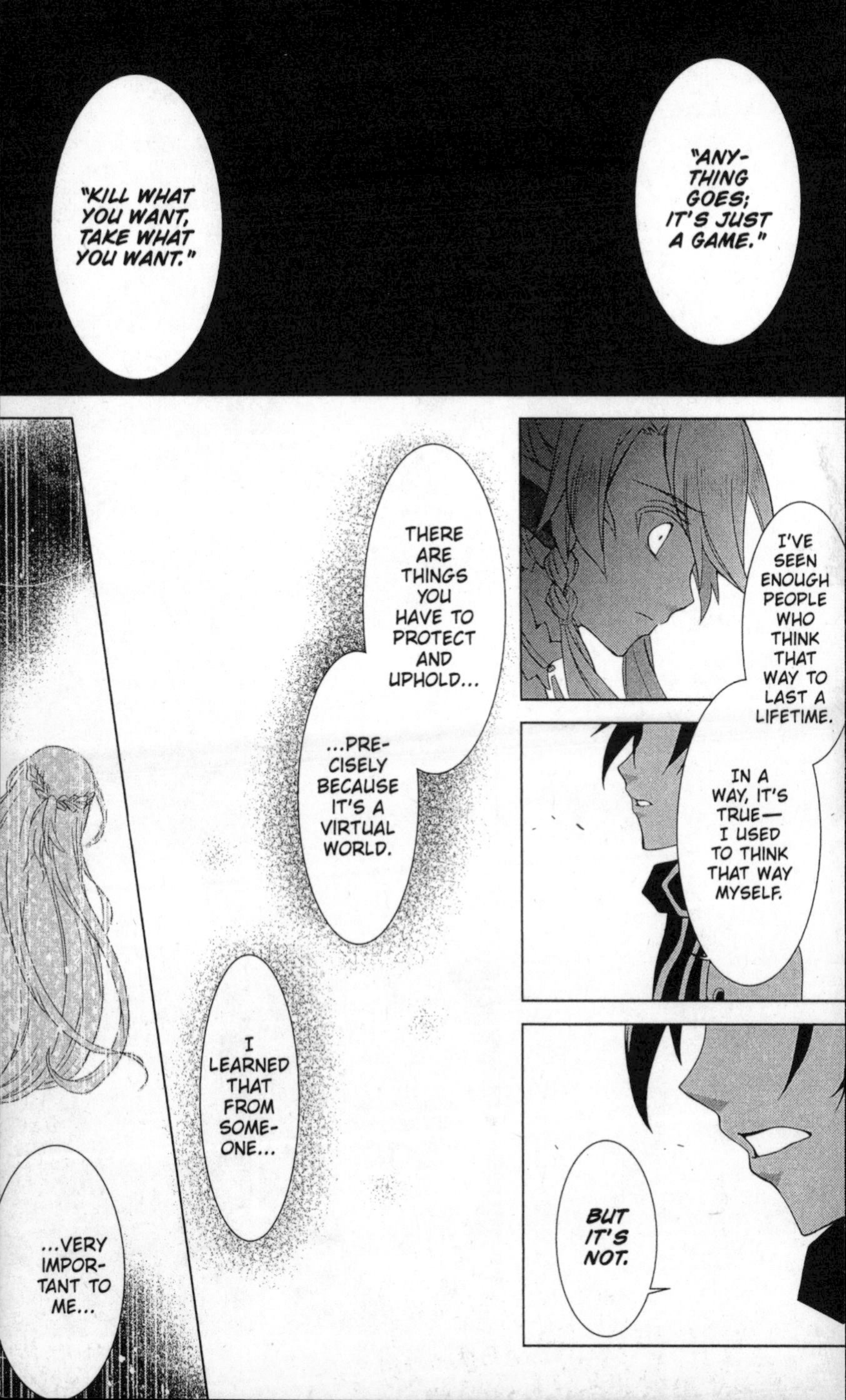
"ANY-THING GOES; IT'S JUST A GAME."
"KILL WHAT YOU WANT, TAKE WHAT YOU WANT."
I'VE SEEN ENOUGH PEOPLE WHO THINK THAT WAY TO LAST A LIFETIME.
IN A WAY, IT'S TRUE— I USED TO THINK THAT WAY MYSELF.
BUT IT'S NOT.
THERE ARE THINGS YOU HAVE TO PROTECT AND UPHOLD...
...PRE-CISELY BECAUSE IT'S A VIRTUAL WORLD.
I LEARNED THAT FROM SOME-ONE...
...VERY IMPOR-TANT TO ME...

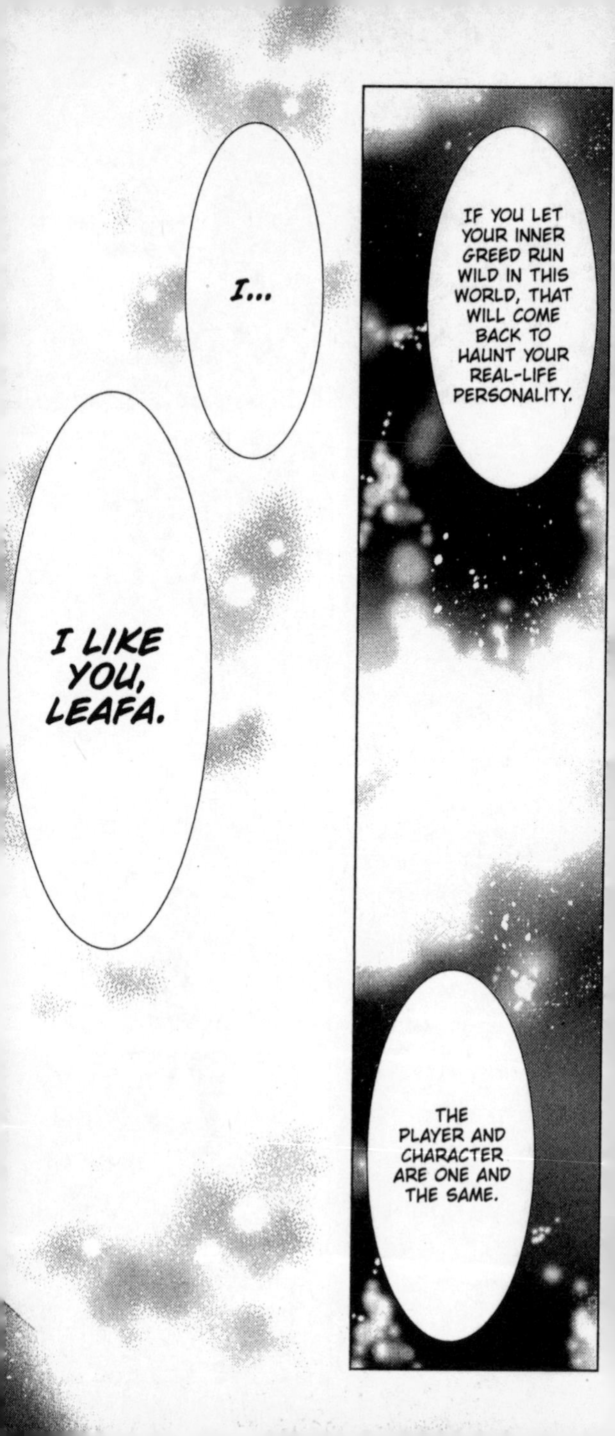
IF YOU LET YOUR INNER GREED RUN WILD IN THIS WORLD, THAT WILL COME BACK TO HAUNT YOUR REAL-LIFE PERSONALITY.
THE PLAYER AND CHARACTER ARE ONE AND THE SAME.
I...
I LIKE YOU, LEAFA.

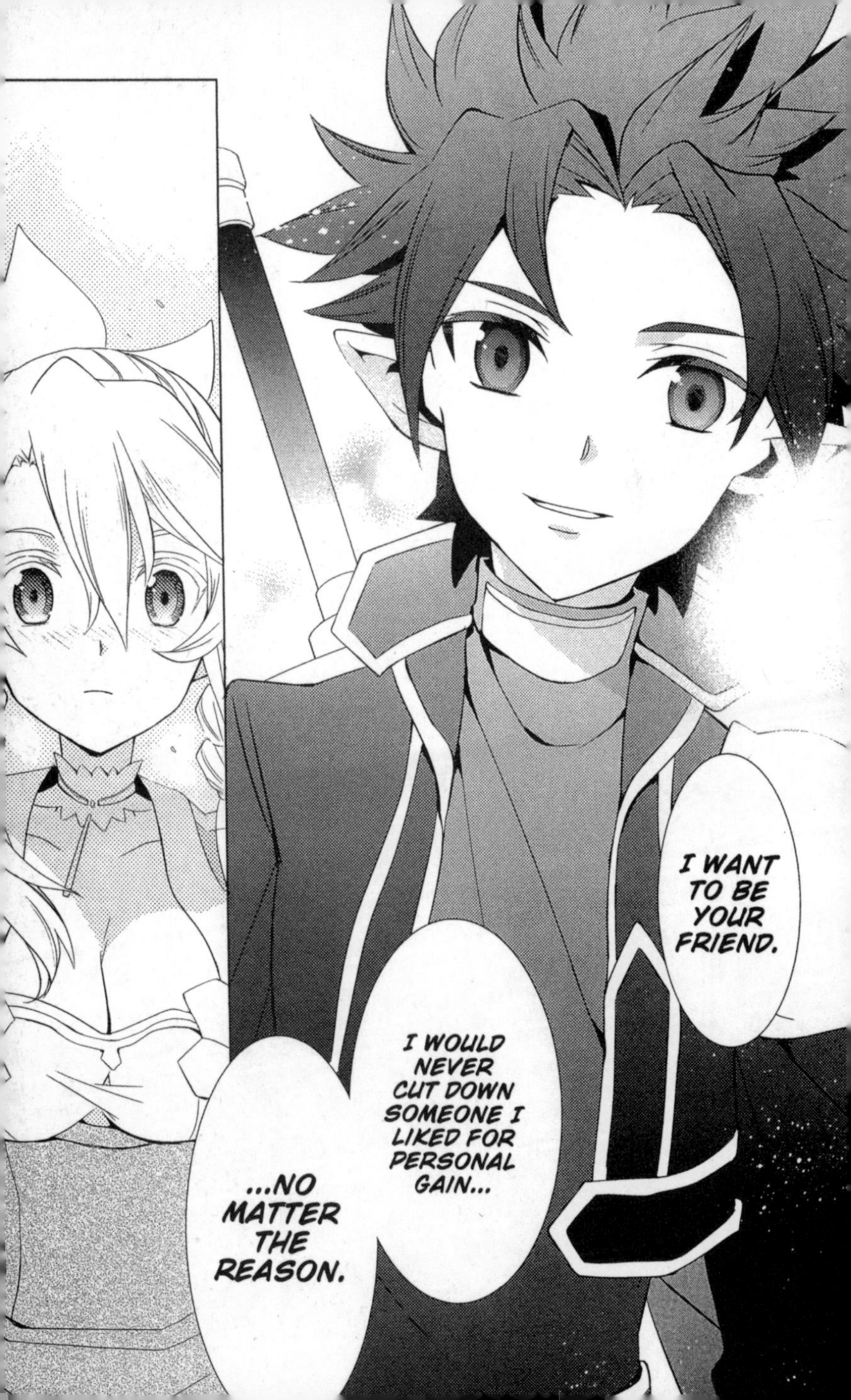
I WANT TO BE YOUR FRIEND.
I WOULD NEVER CUT DOWN SOMEONE I LIKED FOR PERSONAL GAIN...
...NO MATTER THE REASON.

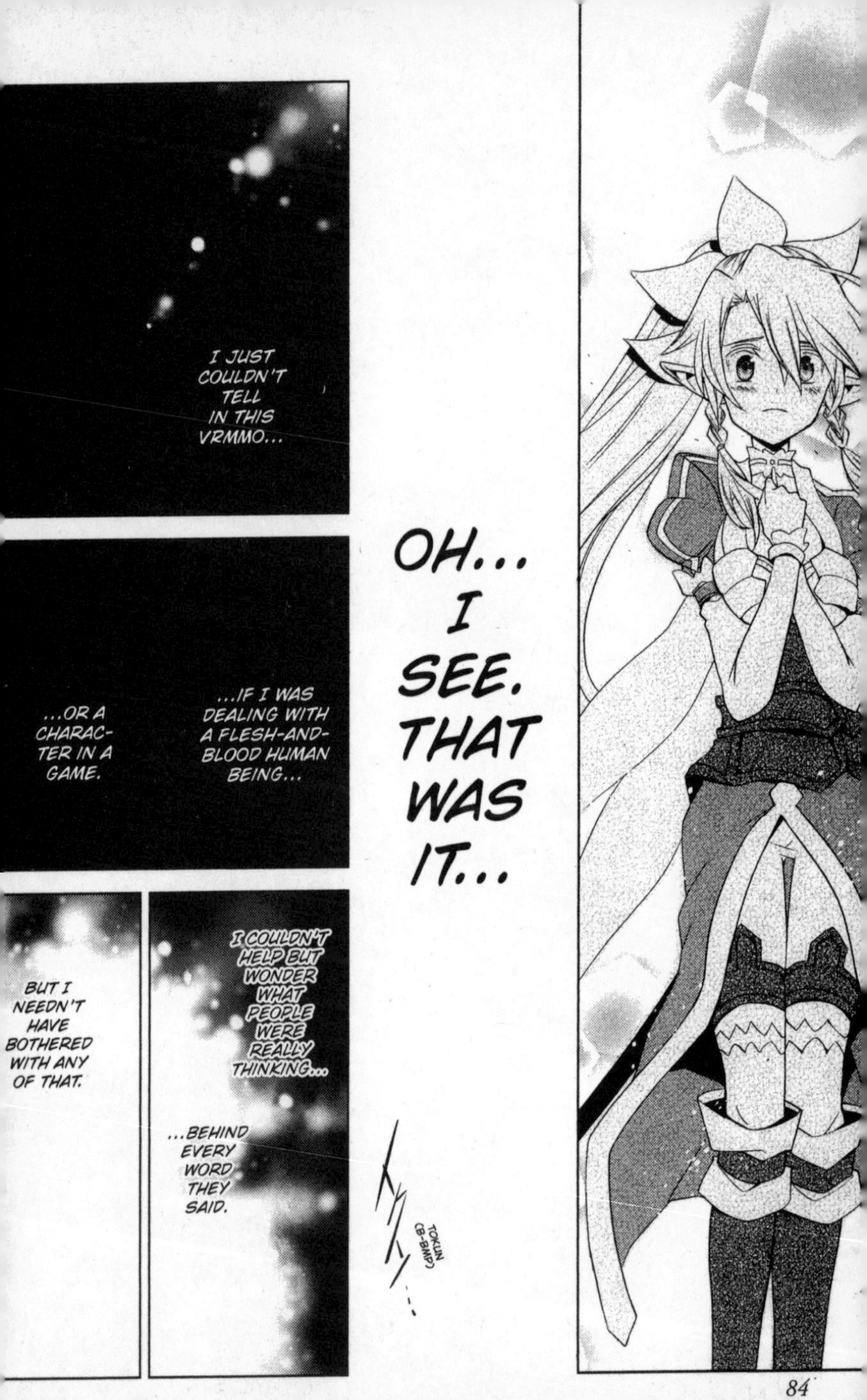
OH... I SEE. THAT WAS IT...
TOKUN (B-BMP)
I JUST COULDN'T TELL IN THIS VRMMO...
...IF I WAS DEALING WITH A FLESH-AND-BLOOD HUMAN BEING...
...OR A CHARACTER IN A GAME.
I COULDN'T HELP BUT WONDER WHAT PEOPLE WERE REALLY THINKING...
...BEHIND EVERY WORD THEY SAID.
BUT I NEEDN'T HAVE BOTHERED WITH ANY OF THAT.

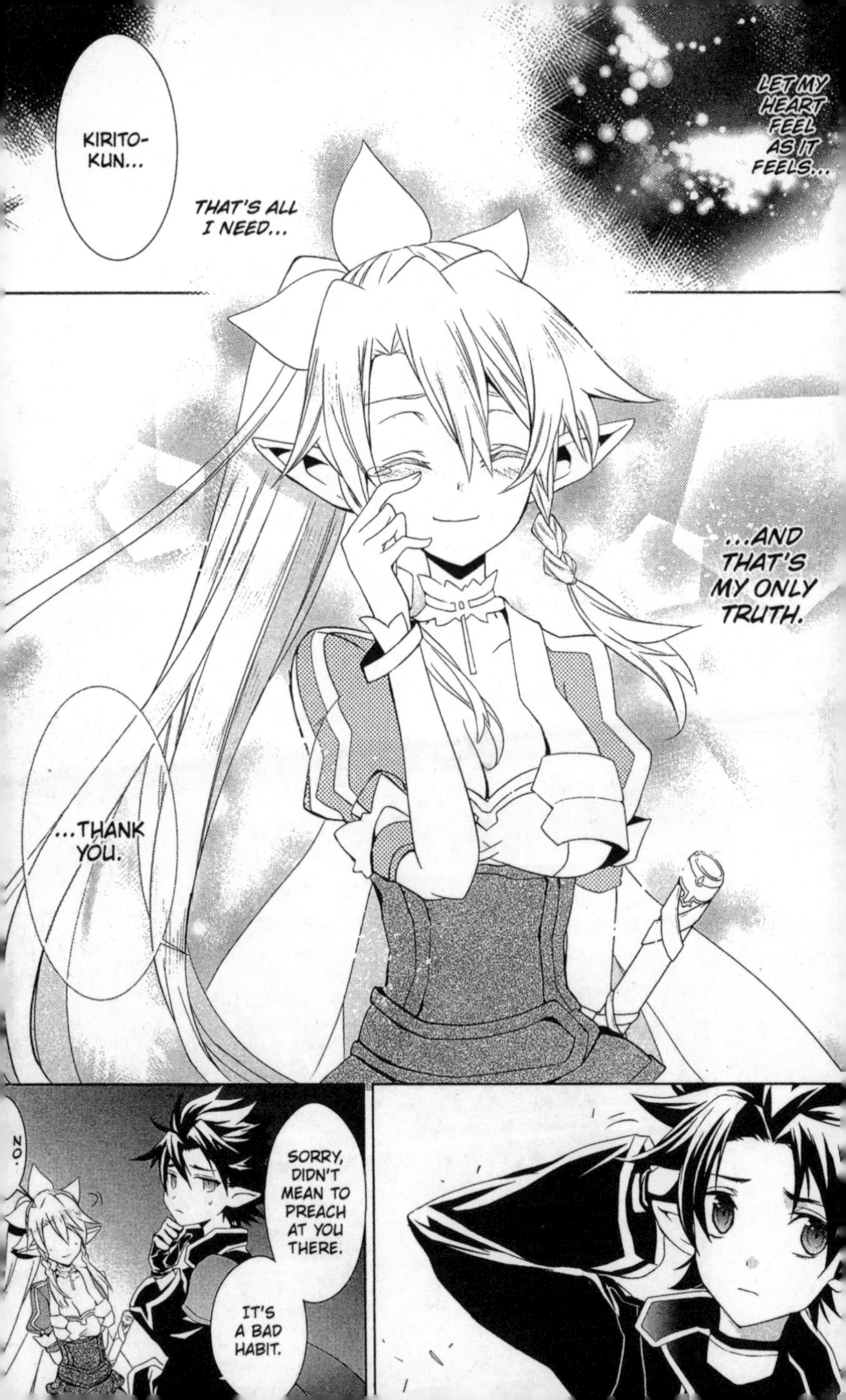
LET MY HEART FEEL AS IT FEELS...
THAT'S ALL I NEED...
KIRITO-KUN...
...AND THAT'S MY ONLY TRUTH.
...THANK YOU.
SORRY, DIDN'T MEAN TO PREACH AT YOU THERE.
IT'S A BAD HABIT.
NO.

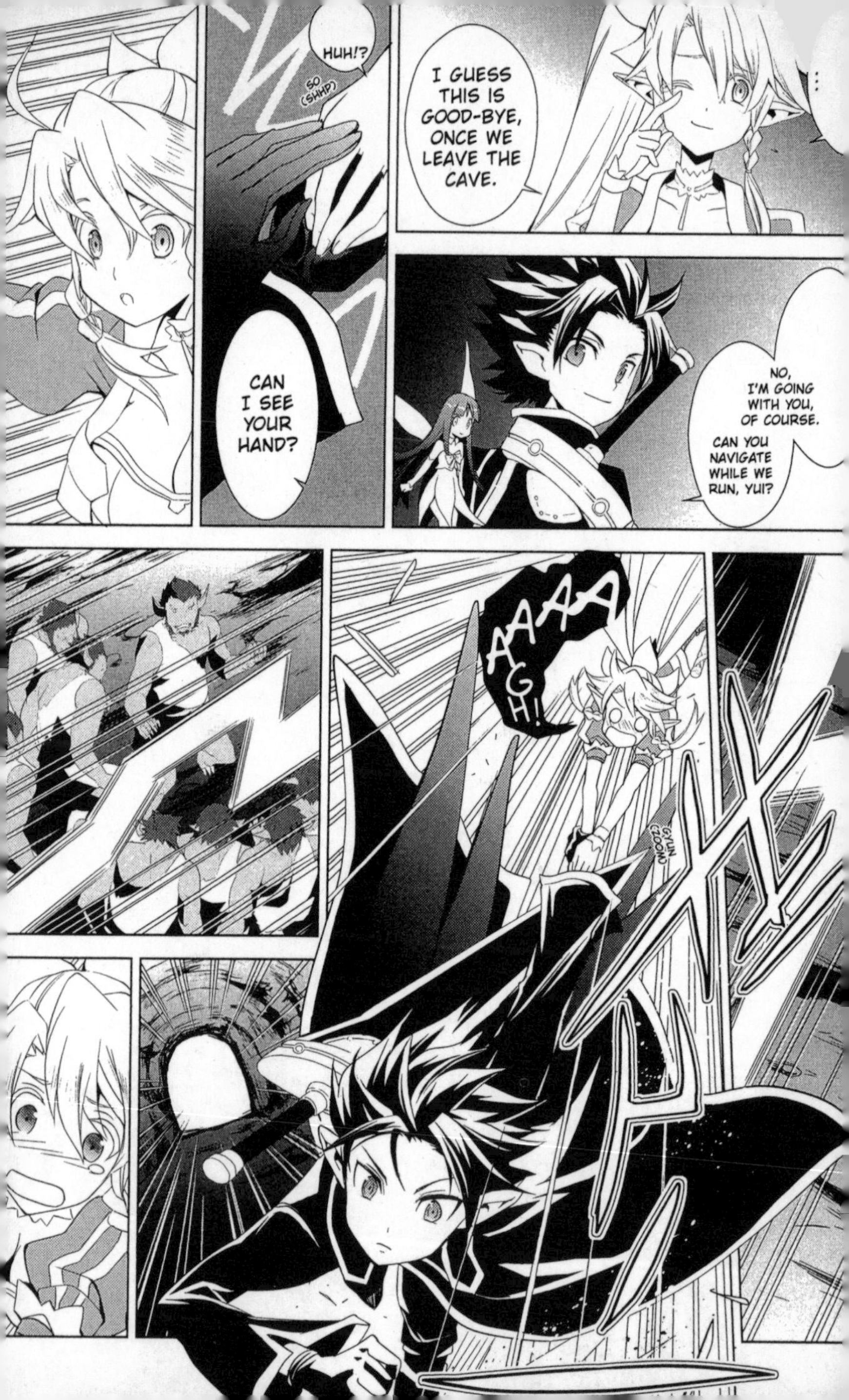
...
I GUESS THIS IS GOOD-BYE, ONCE WE LEAVE THE CAVE.
NO, I'M GOING WITH YOU, OF COURSE.
CAN YOU NAVIGATE WHILE WE RUN, YUI?
HUH!?
SO (SHHP)
CAN I SEE YOUR HAND?
AAAAAAGH!
GYUN (ZOOM)

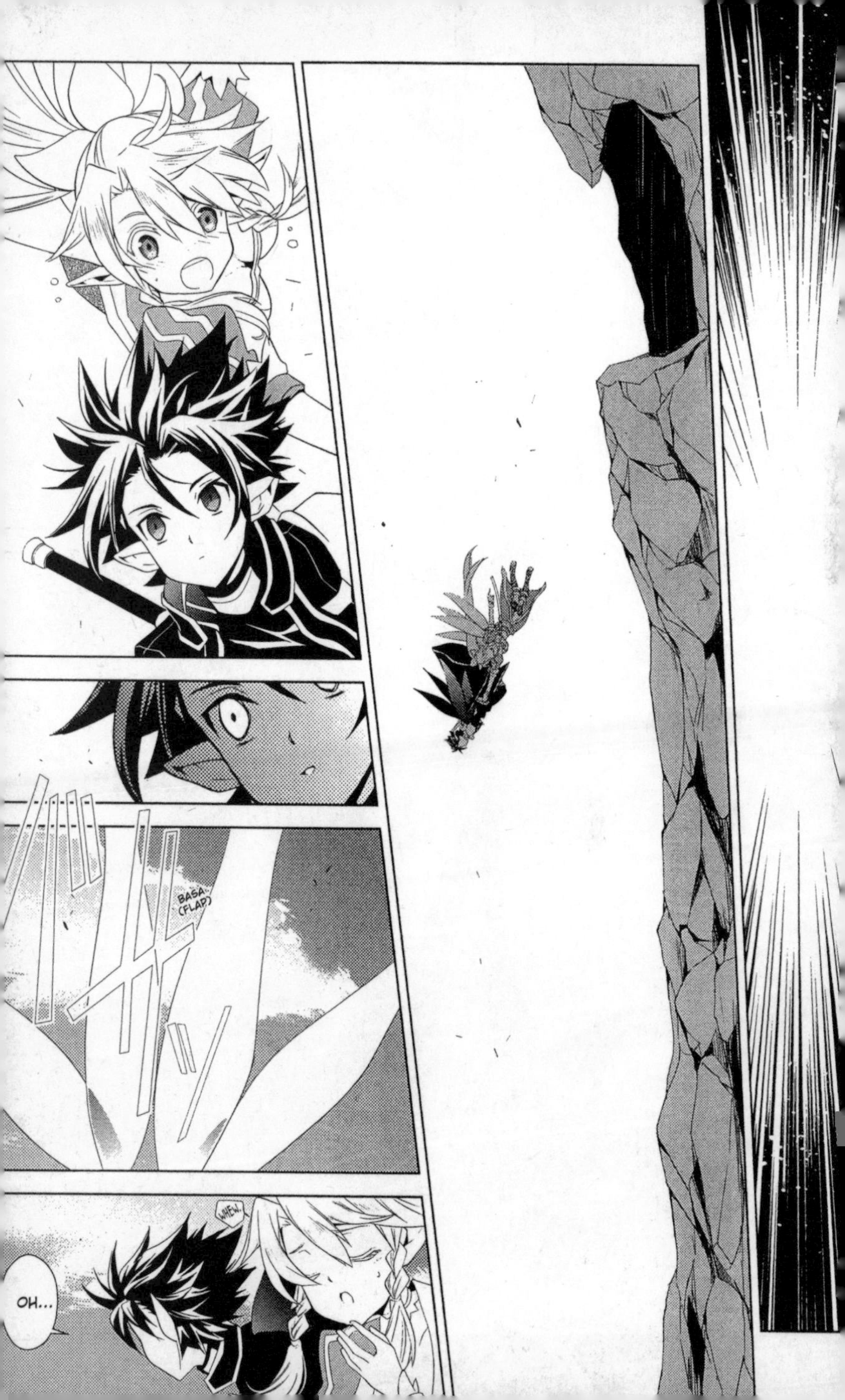
BASA (FLAP)
WHEW.
OH...

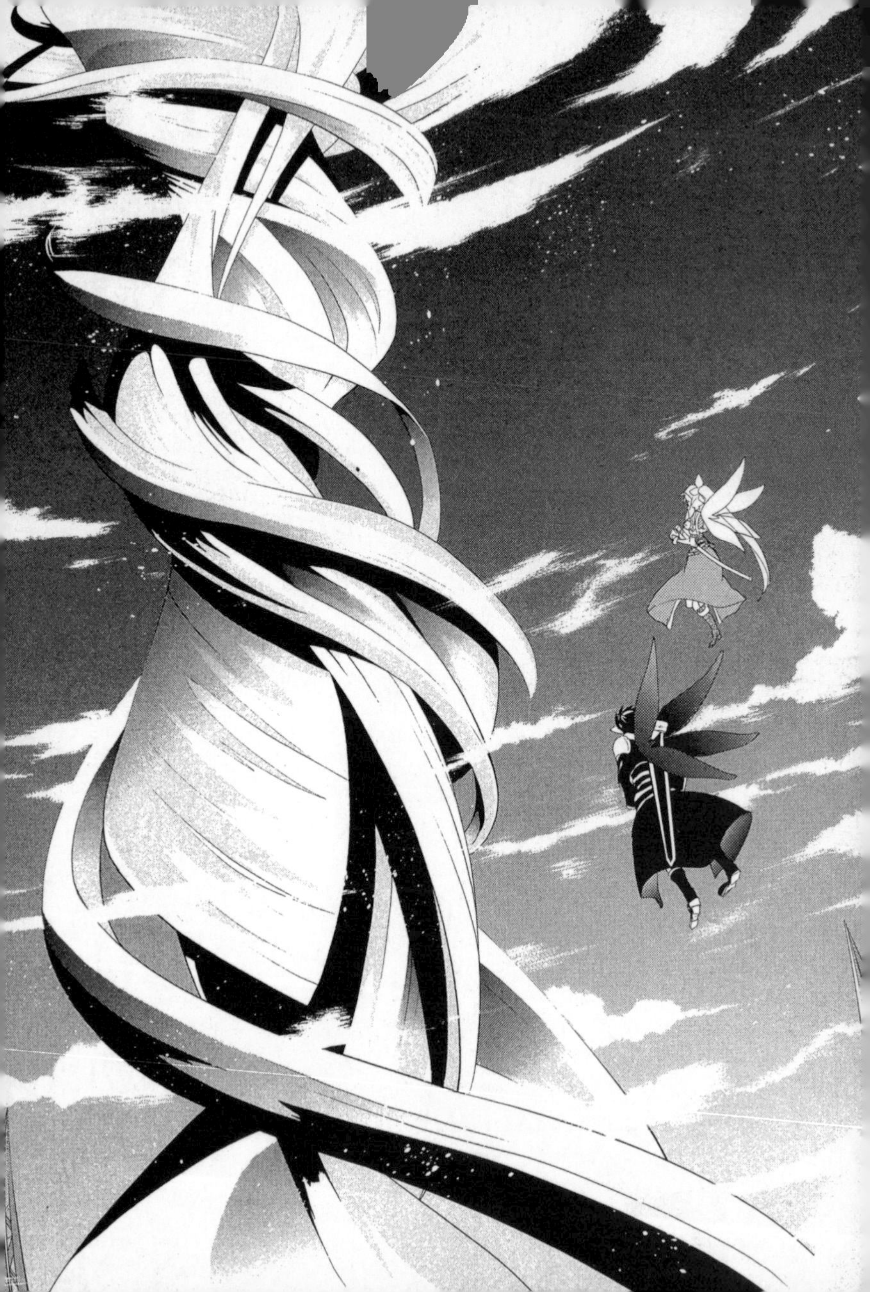

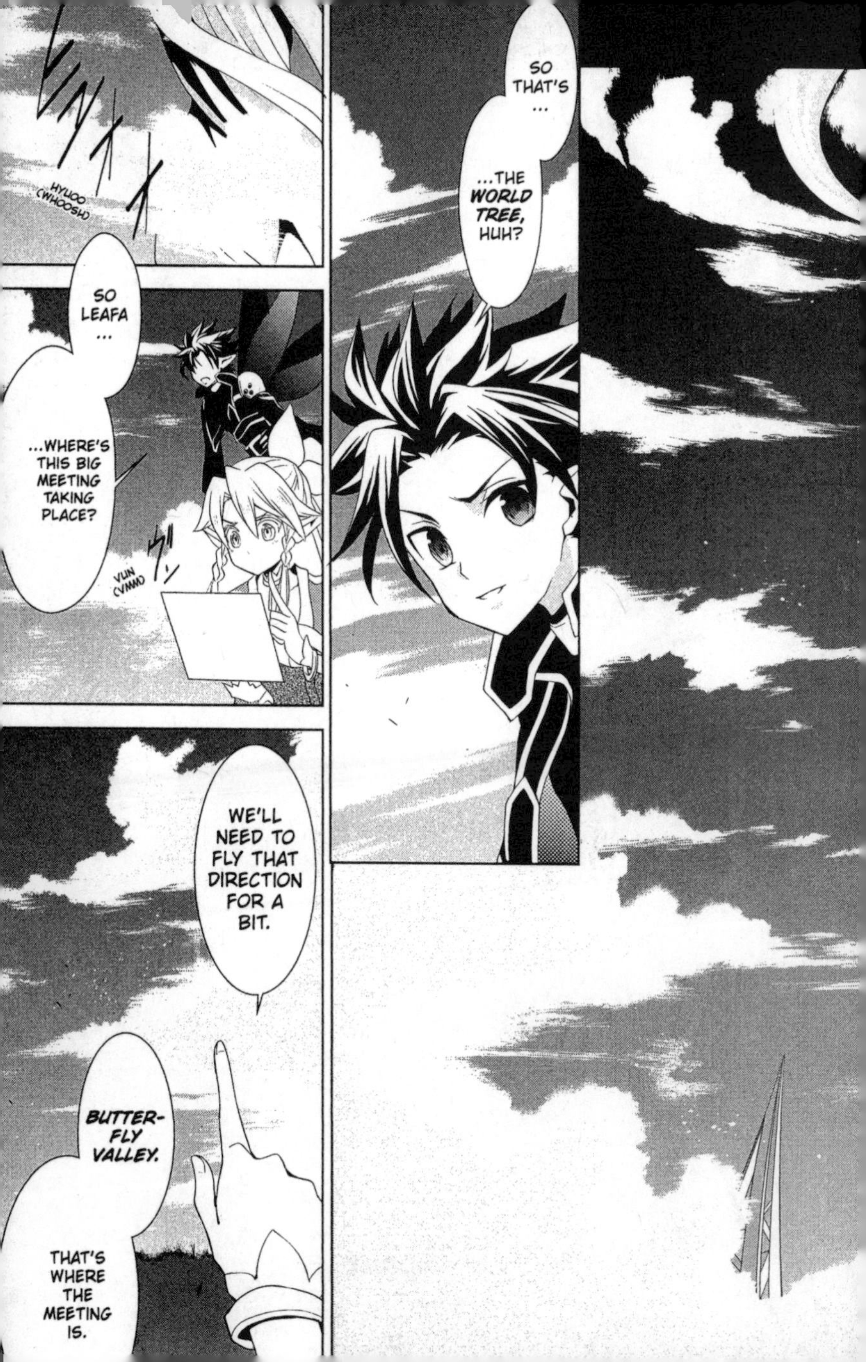
SO THAT'S...
...THE WORLD TREE, HUH?
HYUOO (WHOOSH)
SO LEAFA...
...WHERE'S THIS BIG MEETING TAKING PLACE?
VUN (VMMM)
WE'LL NEED TO FLY THAT DIRECTION FOR A BIT.
BUTTER-FLY VALLEY.
THAT'S WHERE THE MEETING IS.

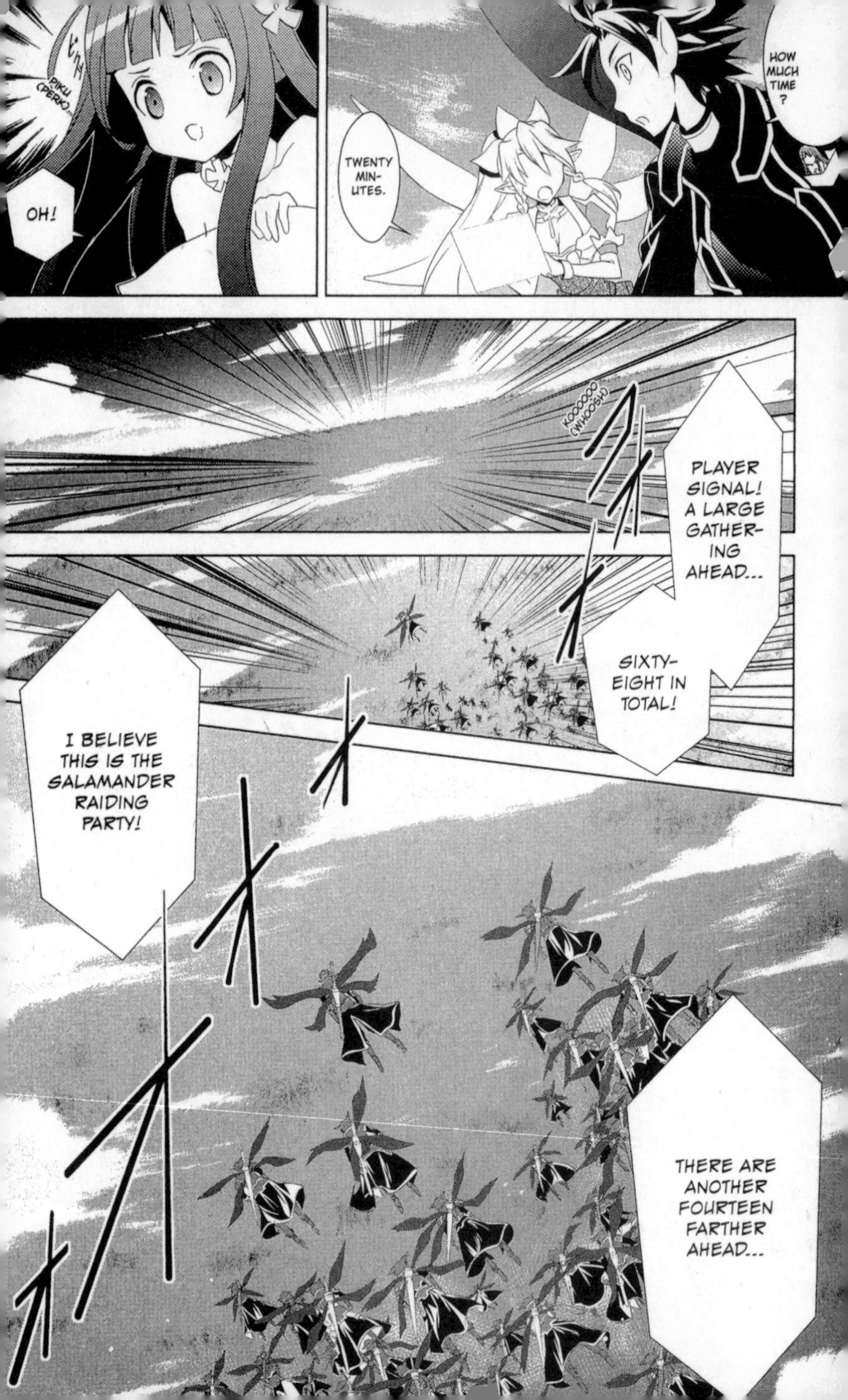
HOW MUCH TIME?
TWENTY MIN-UTES.
PIKU (PERK)
OH!
KOOOOOO (WHOOSH)
PLAYER SIGNAL! A LARGE GATHER-ING AHEAD...
SIXTY-EIGHT IN TOTAL!
I BELIEVE THIS IS THE SALAMANDER RAIDING PARTY!
THERE ARE ANOTHER FOURTEEN FARTHER AHEAD...

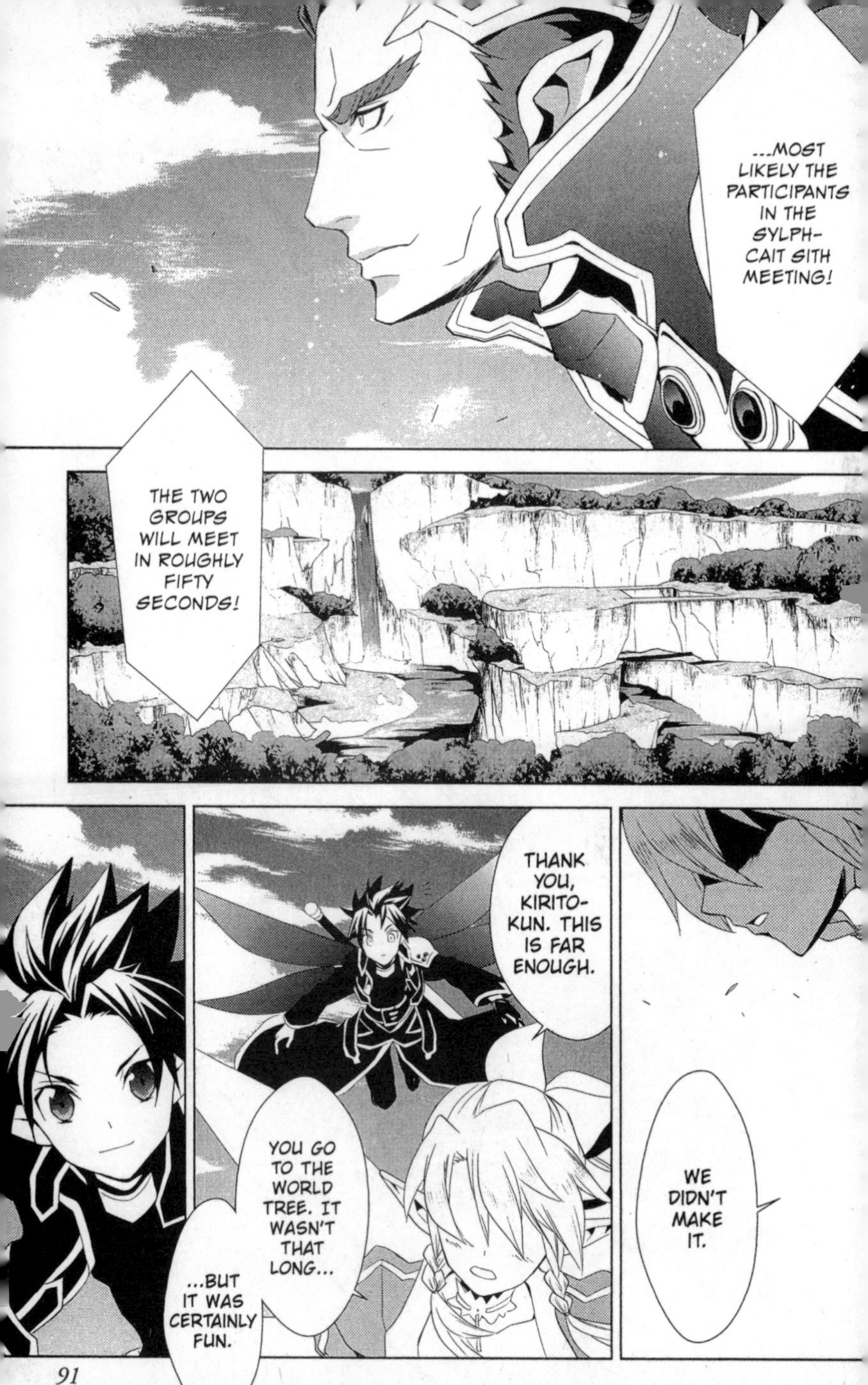
...MOST LIKELY THE PARTICIPANTS IN THE SYLPH-CAIT SITH MEETING!
THE TWO GROUPS WILL MEET IN ROUGHLY FIFTY SECONDS!
WE DIDN'T MAKE IT.
THANK YOU, KIRITO-KUN. THIS IS FAR ENOUGH.
YOU GO TO THE WORLD TREE. IT WASN'T THAT LONG...
...BUT IT WAS CERTAINLY FUN.

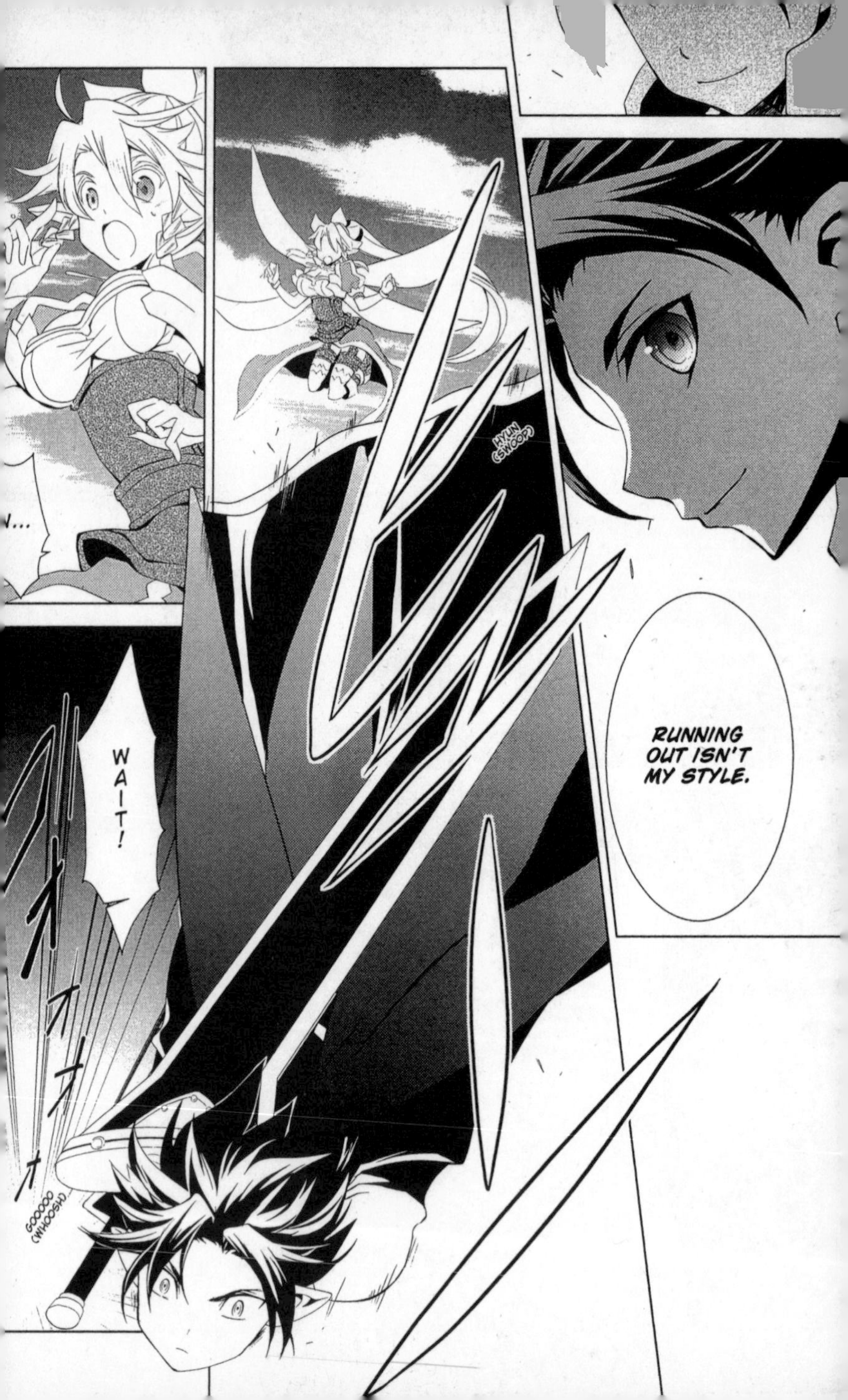
RUNNING OUT ISN'T MY STYLE.
HYUN (SWOOP)
N...
WAIT!
GOOOOO (WHOOSH)

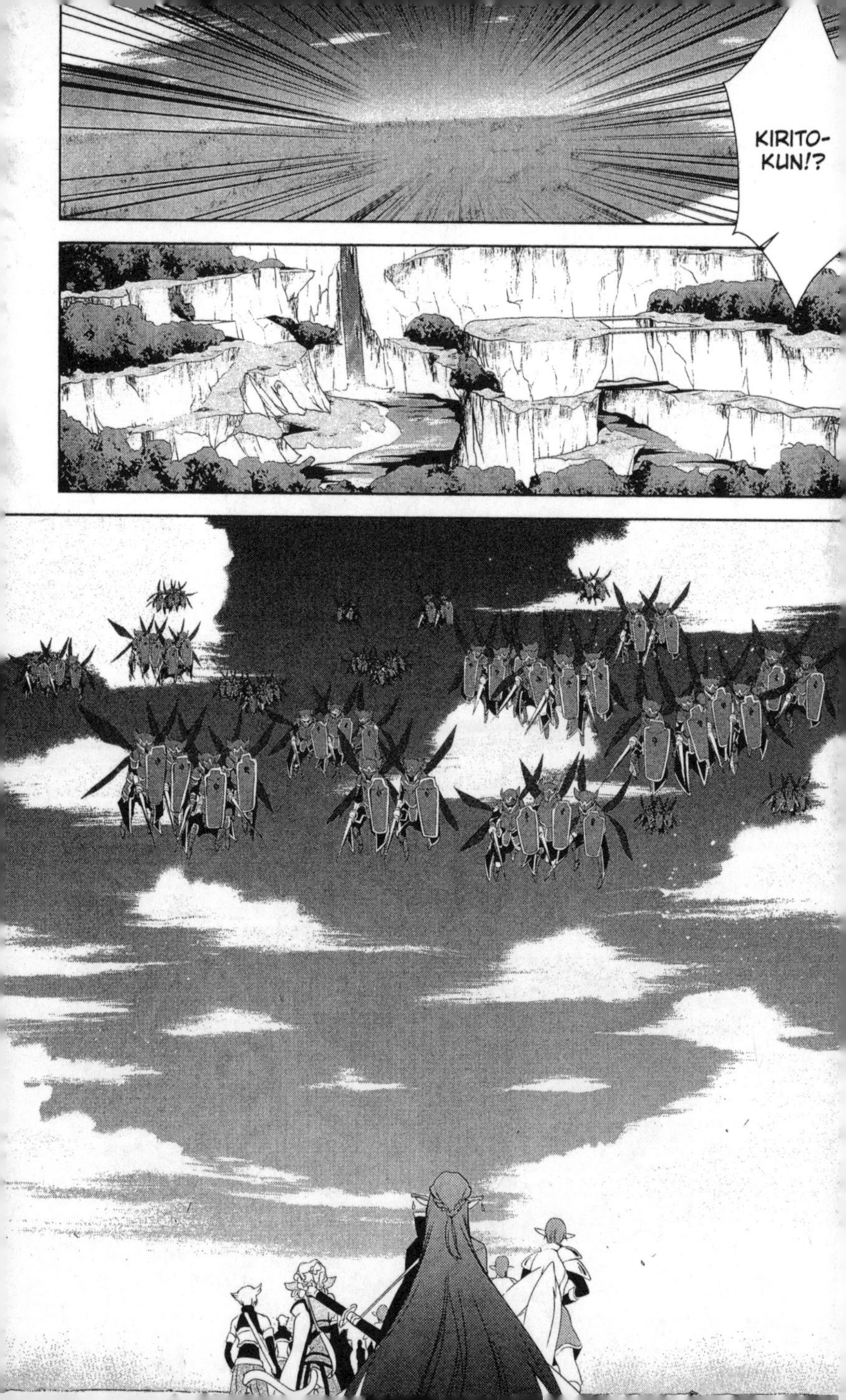
KIRITO-
KUN!?

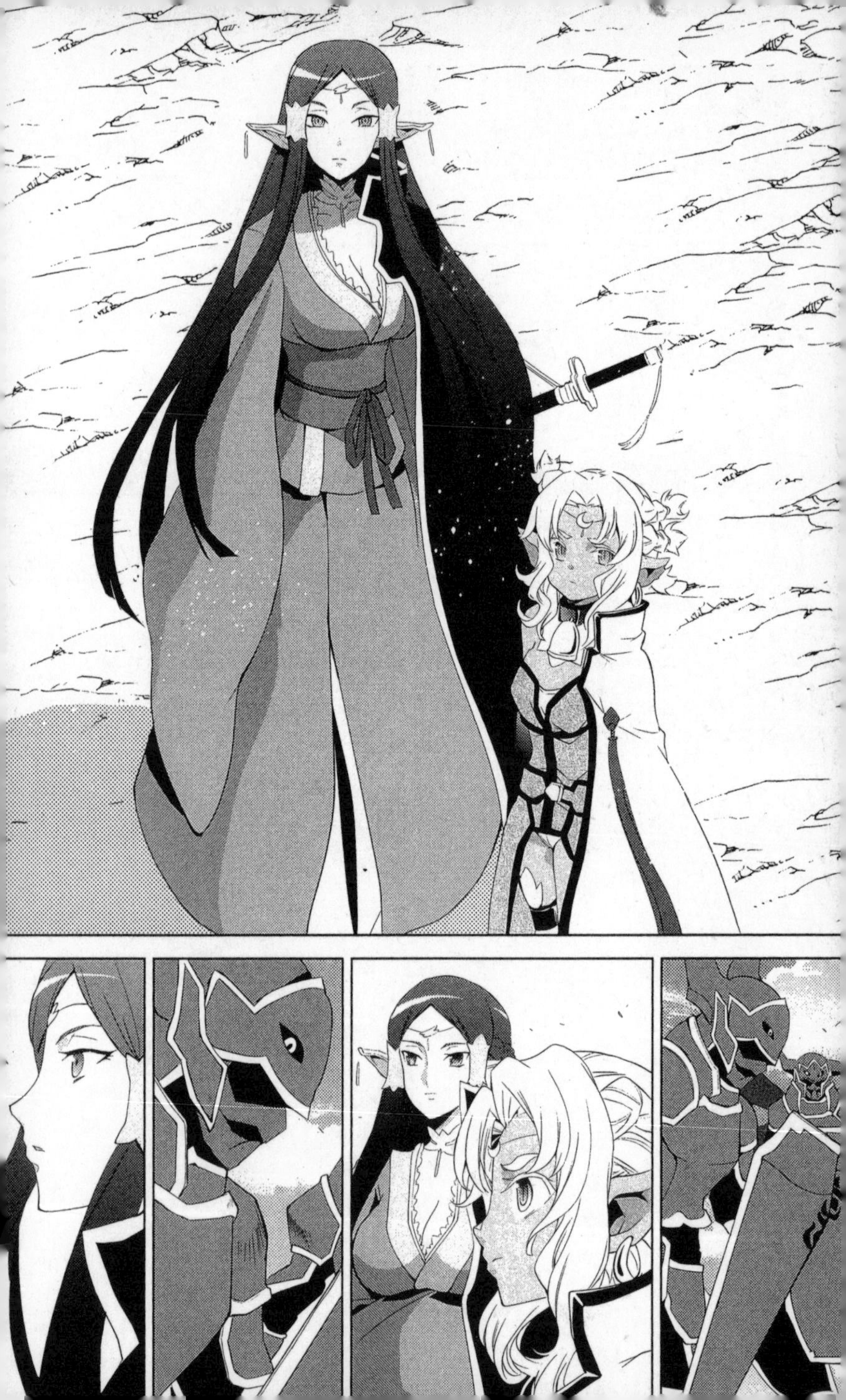

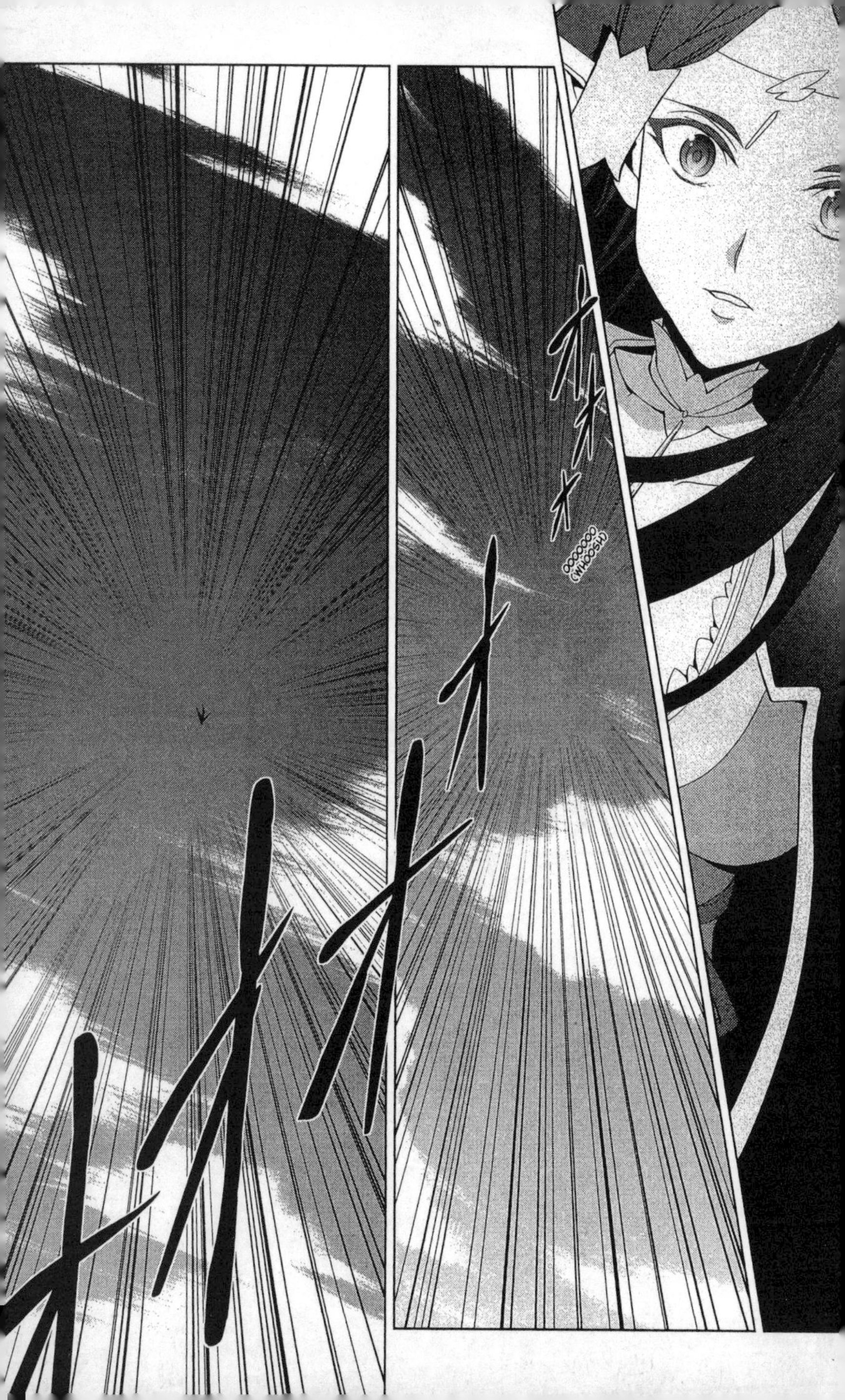
OOOOOOO
(WHOOSH)

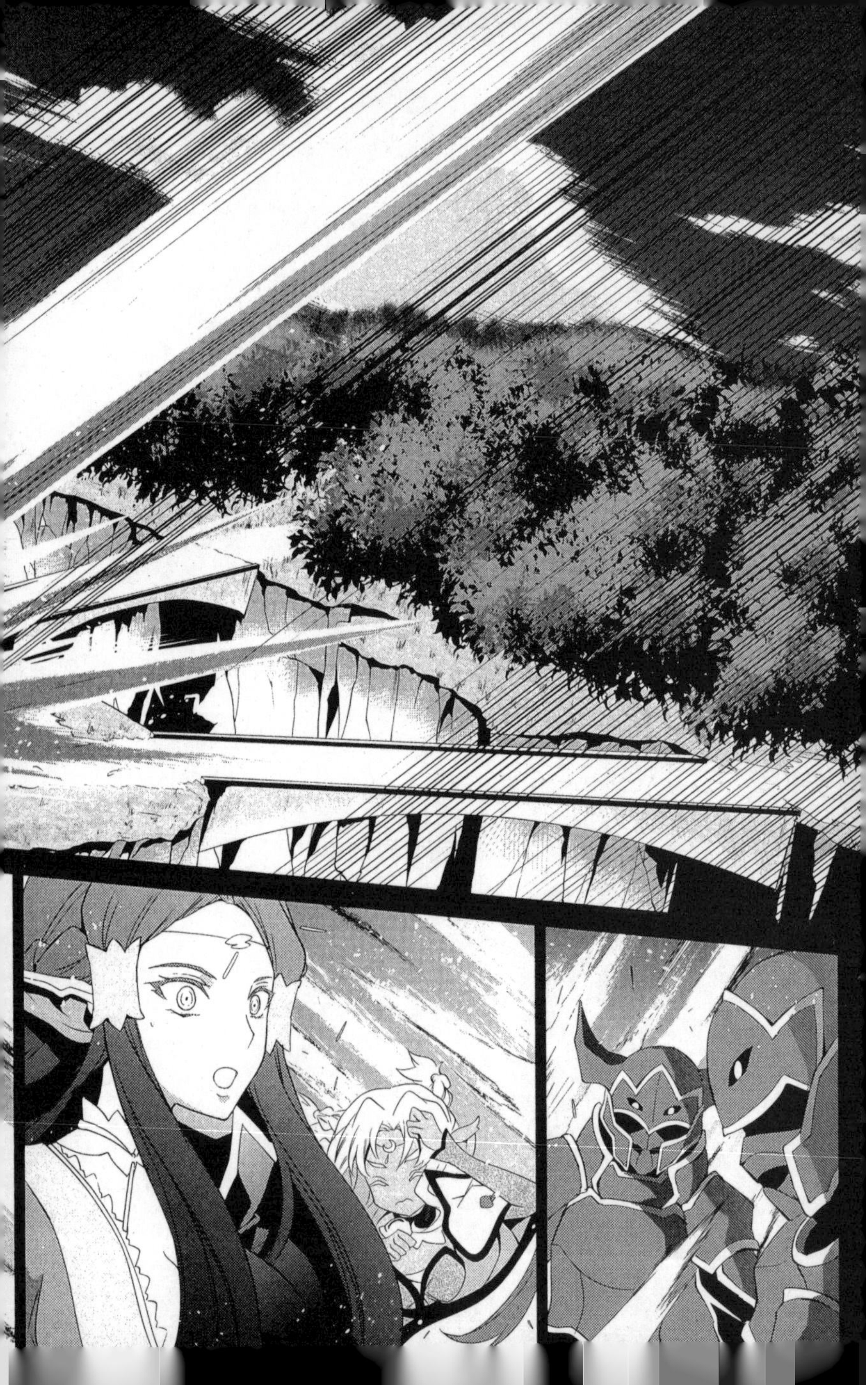

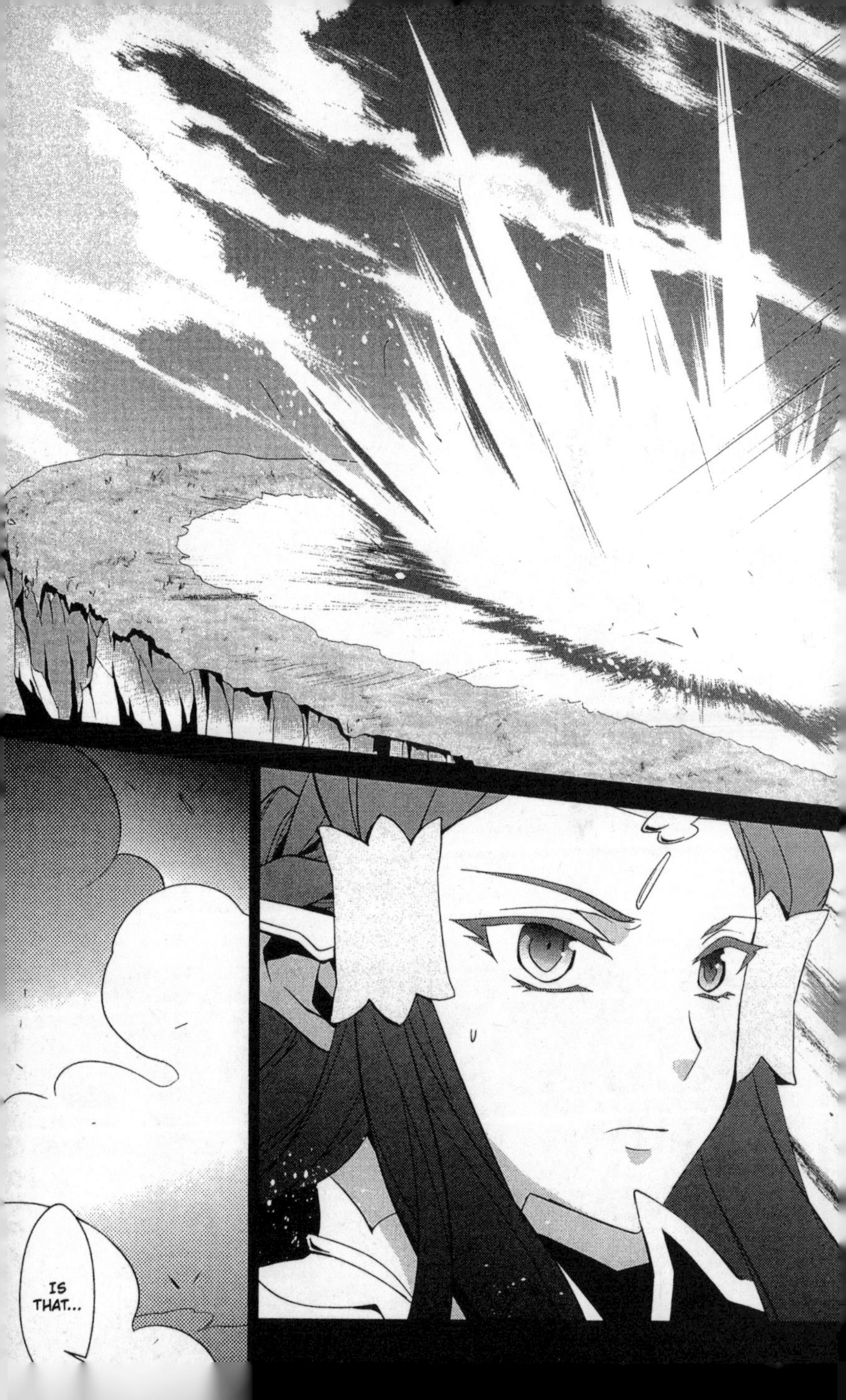
IS THAT...

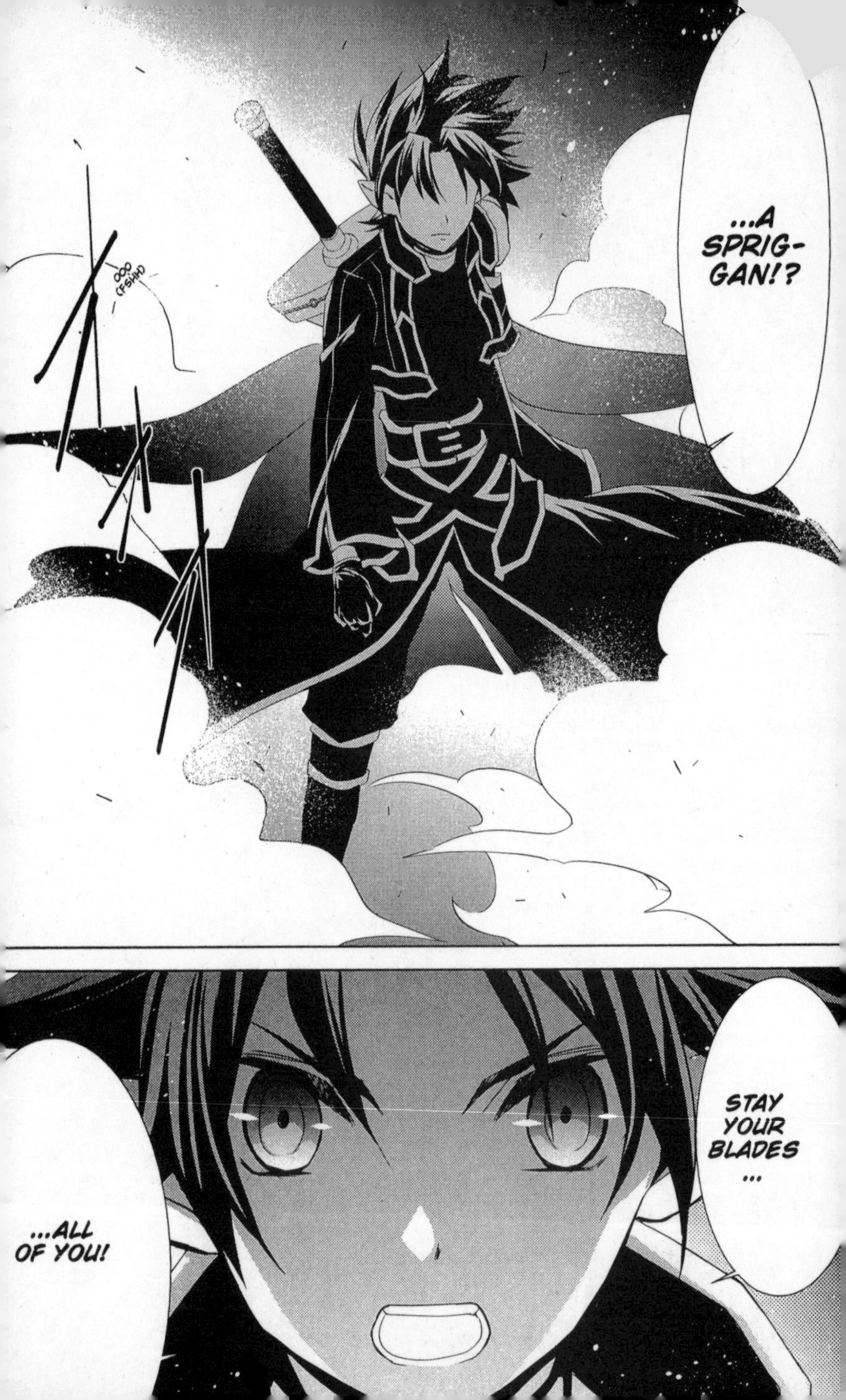
...A SPRIG-GAN!?
OOO (FSHH)
STAY YOUR BLADES ...
...ALL OF YOU!

SWORD ART ONLINE
fairy dance

SWORD ART ONLINE fairy dance
BACKGROUND GUIDE 02

RECON

SHINICHI NAGATA, AKA "RECON," THE
PERVERTED GENTLEMAN WHO LIKES
IT WHEN SUGUHA YELLS AT HIM.
HIS CHARACTER NAME COMES FROM
THE ENGLISH MILITARY NICKNAME
FOR "RECONNAISSANCE." LIKE HIS
NAME, HE'S GOOD AT TRACKING AND
SPYING. HE SUPPOSEDLY ONCE USED
HIS SKILLS TO SNEAK INTO LEAFA'S
INN ROOM, WHICH GOT HIM BEATEN
HALF TO DEATH. HE CLAIMS IT WAS
SO HE COULD "GIVE HER A SURPRISE
BIRTHDAY PRESENT."

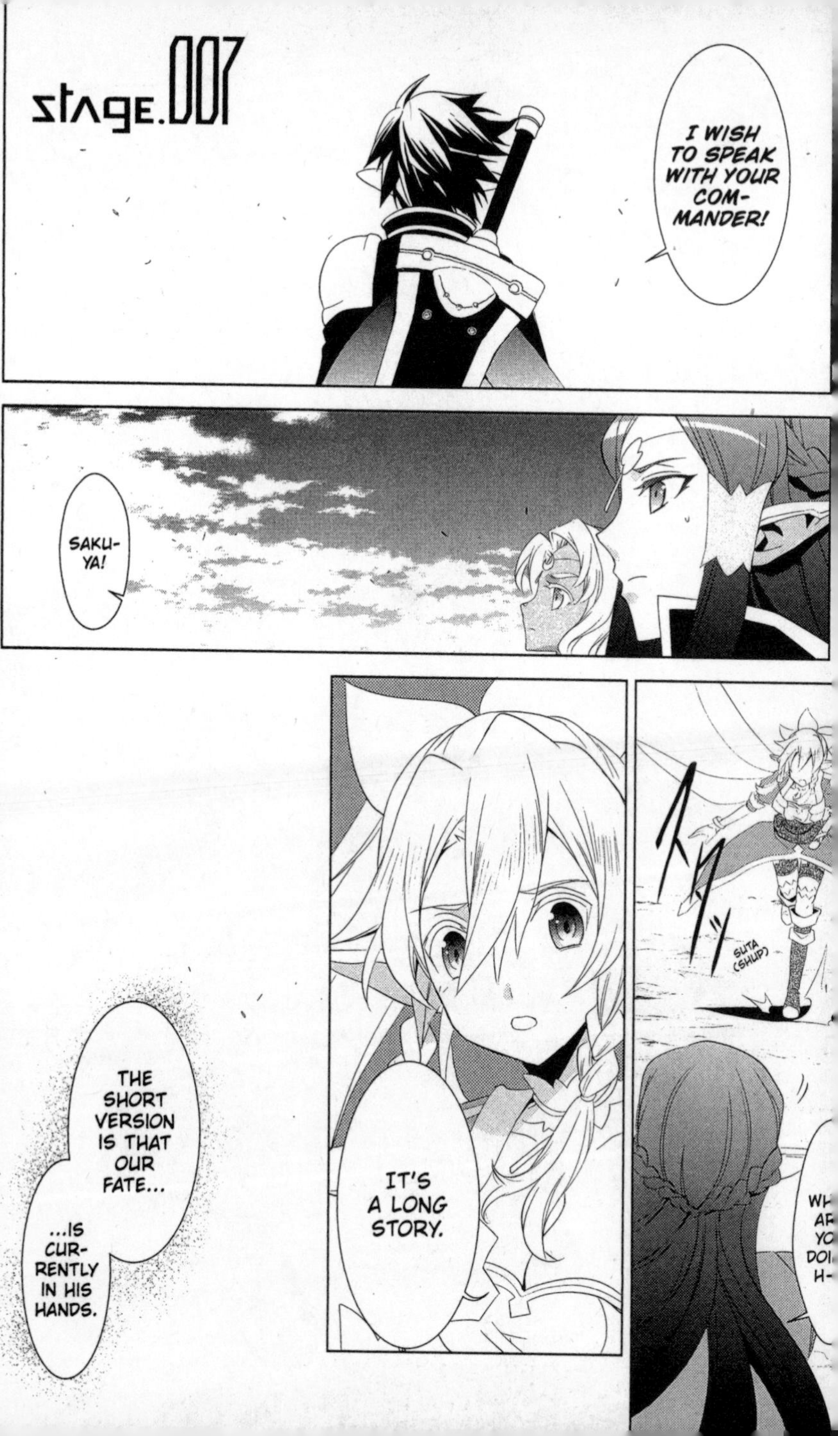
stage.007
I WISH TO SPEAK WITH YOUR COM-MANDER!
SAKU-YA!
SUTA (SHUP)
WH AR YO DOI H-
IT'S A LONG STORY.
THE SHORT VERSION IS THAT OUR FATE...
...IS CUR-RENTLY IN HIS HANDS.

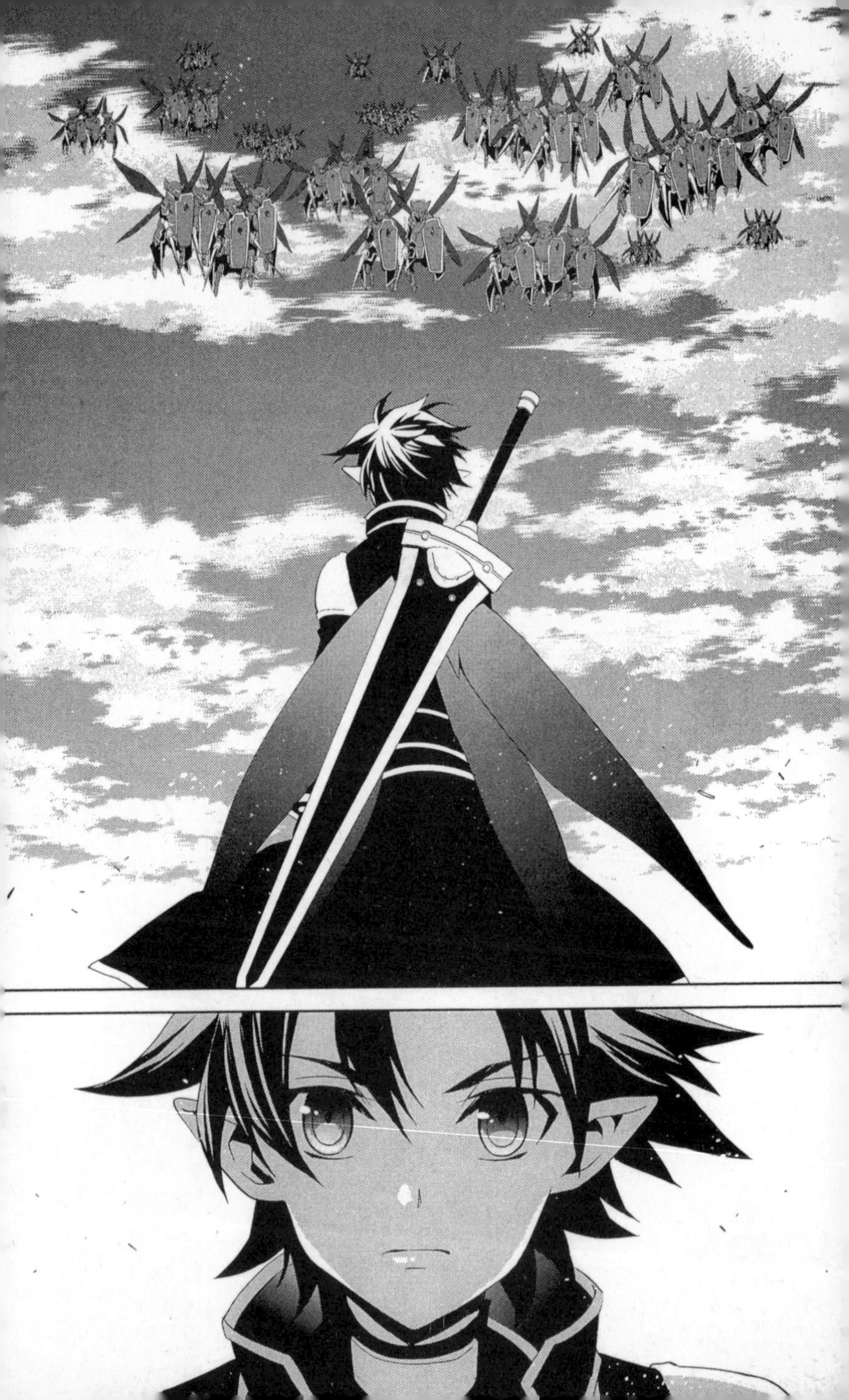

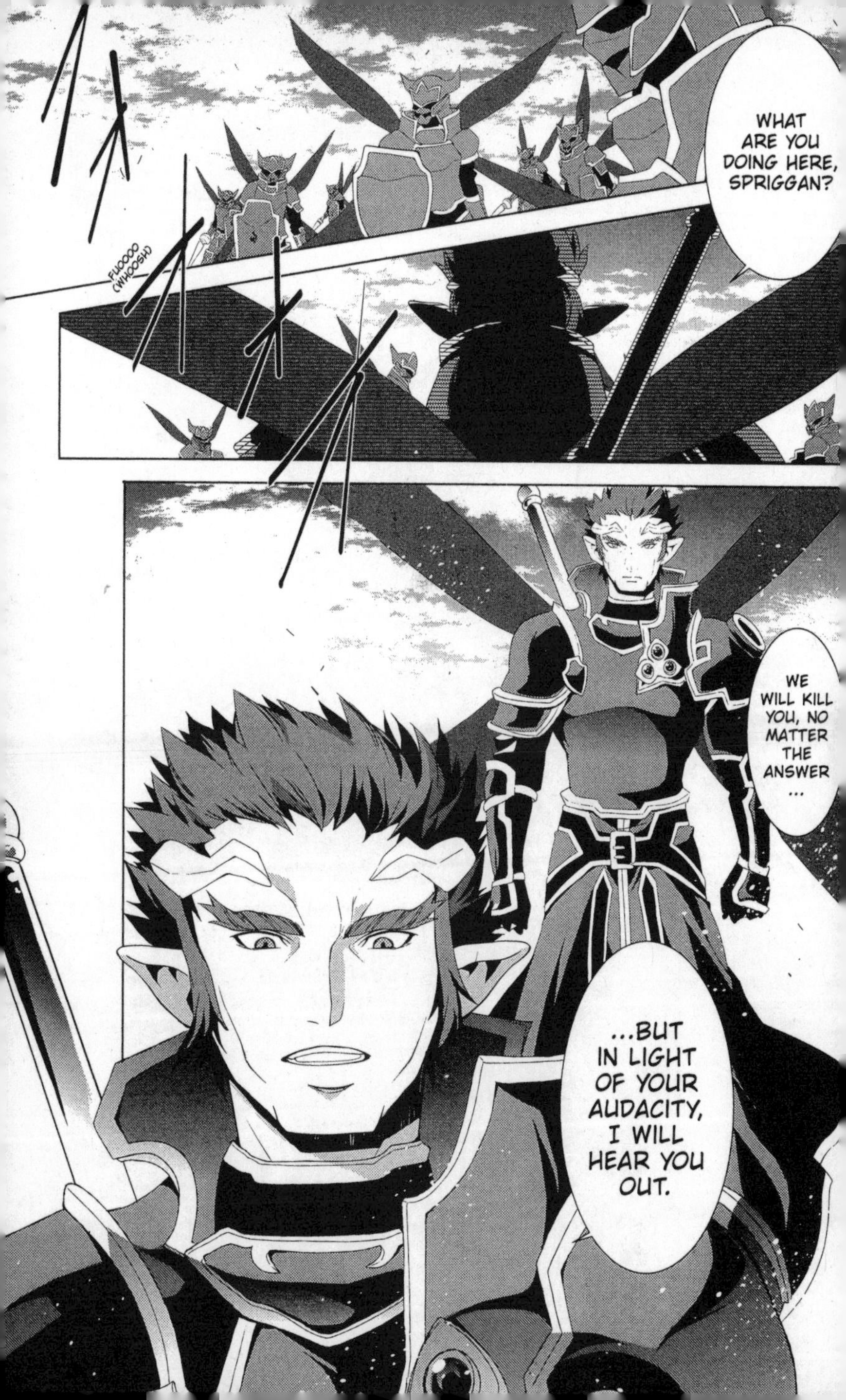
WHAT ARE YOU DOING HERE, SPRIGGAN?
FUOOOO (WHOOSH)
WE WILL KILL YOU, NO MATTER THE ANSWER ...
...BUT IN LIGHT OF YOUR AUDACITY, I WILL HEAR YOU OUT.

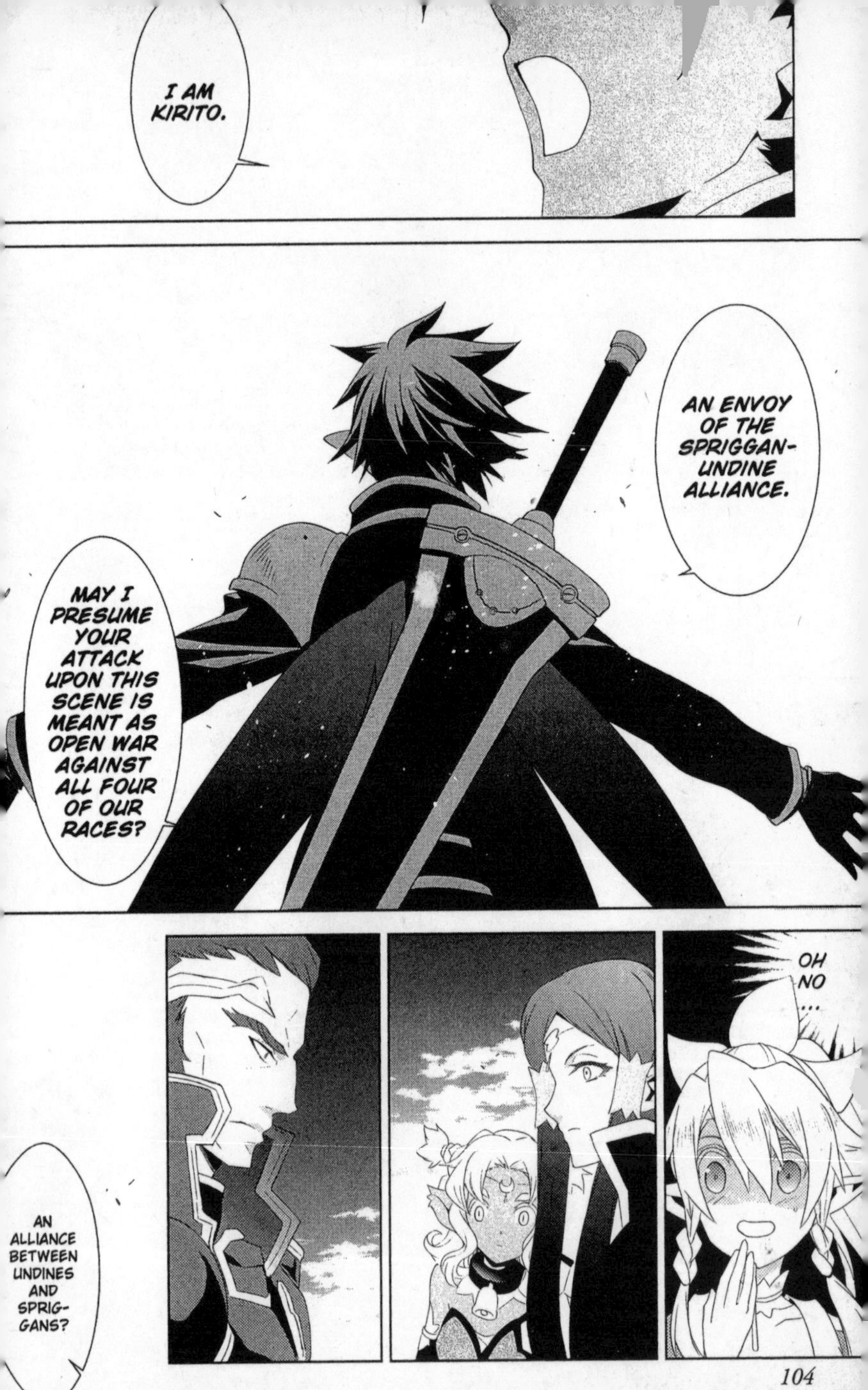
I AM KIRITO.
AN ENVOY OF THE SPRIGGAN-UNDINE ALLIANCE.
MAY I PRESUME YOUR ATTACK UPON THIS SCENE IS MEANT AS OPEN WAR AGAINST ALL FOUR OF OUR RACES?
OH NO ...
AN ALLIANCE BETWEEN UNDINES AND SPRIG-GANS?

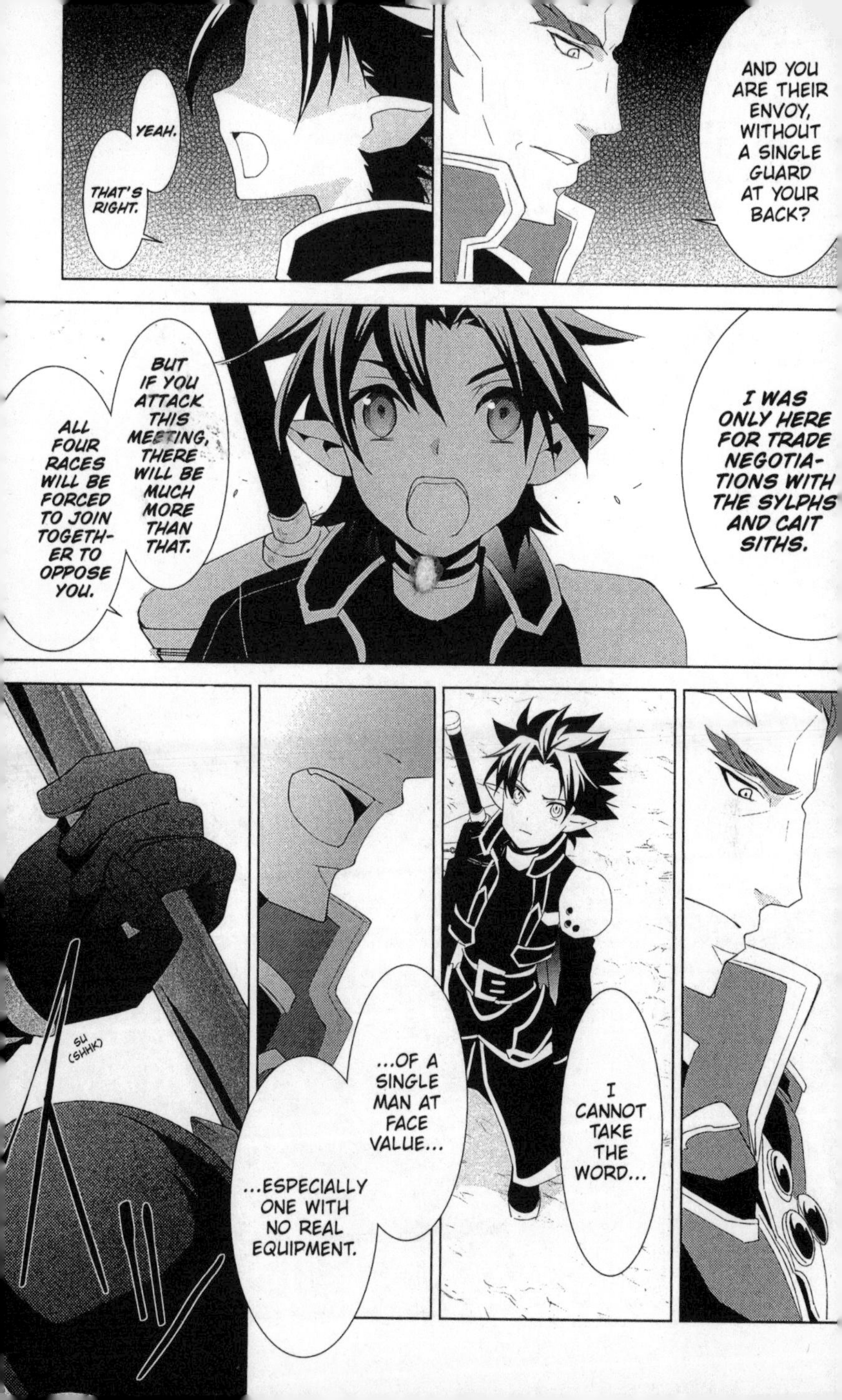
AND YOU ARE THEIR ENVOY, WITHOUT A SINGLE GUARD AT YOUR BACK?
YEAH.
THAT'S RIGHT.
I WAS ONLY HERE FOR TRADE NEGOTIATIONS WITH THE SYLPHS AND CAIT SITHS.
BUT IF YOU ATTACK THIS MEETING, THERE WILL BE MUCH MORE THAN THAT.
ALL FOUR RACES WILL BE FORCED TO JOIN TOGETHER TO OPPOSE YOU.
I CANNOT TAKE THE WORD...
...OF A SINGLE MAN AT FACE VALUE...
...ESPECIALLY ONE WITH NO REAL EQUIPMENT.
SU (SHHK)

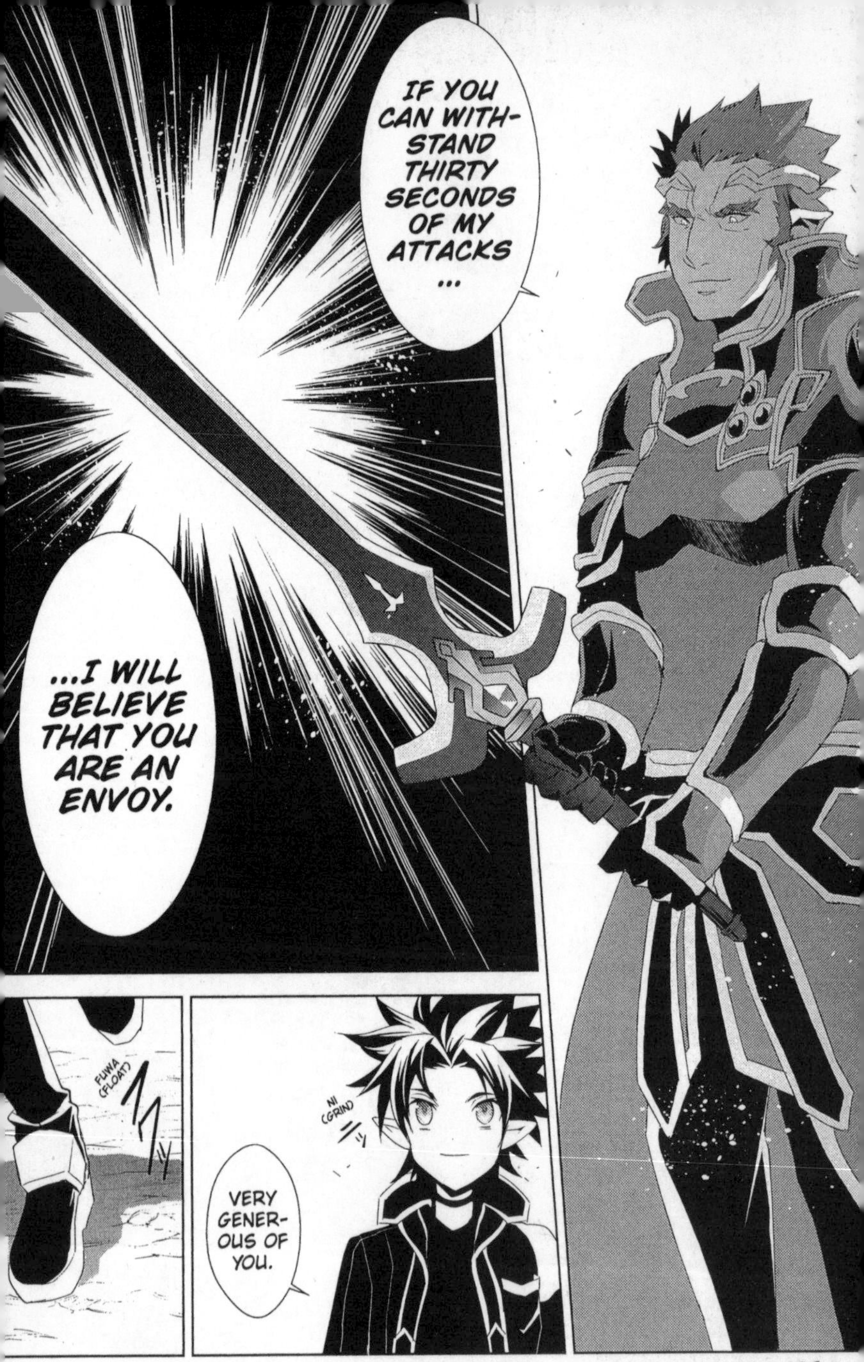
IF YOU CAN WITH-STAND THIRTY SECONDS OF MY ATTACKS ...
...I WILL BELIEVE THAT YOU ARE AN ENVOY.
NI (GRIN)
VERY GENER-OUS OF YOU.
FUWA (FLOAT)

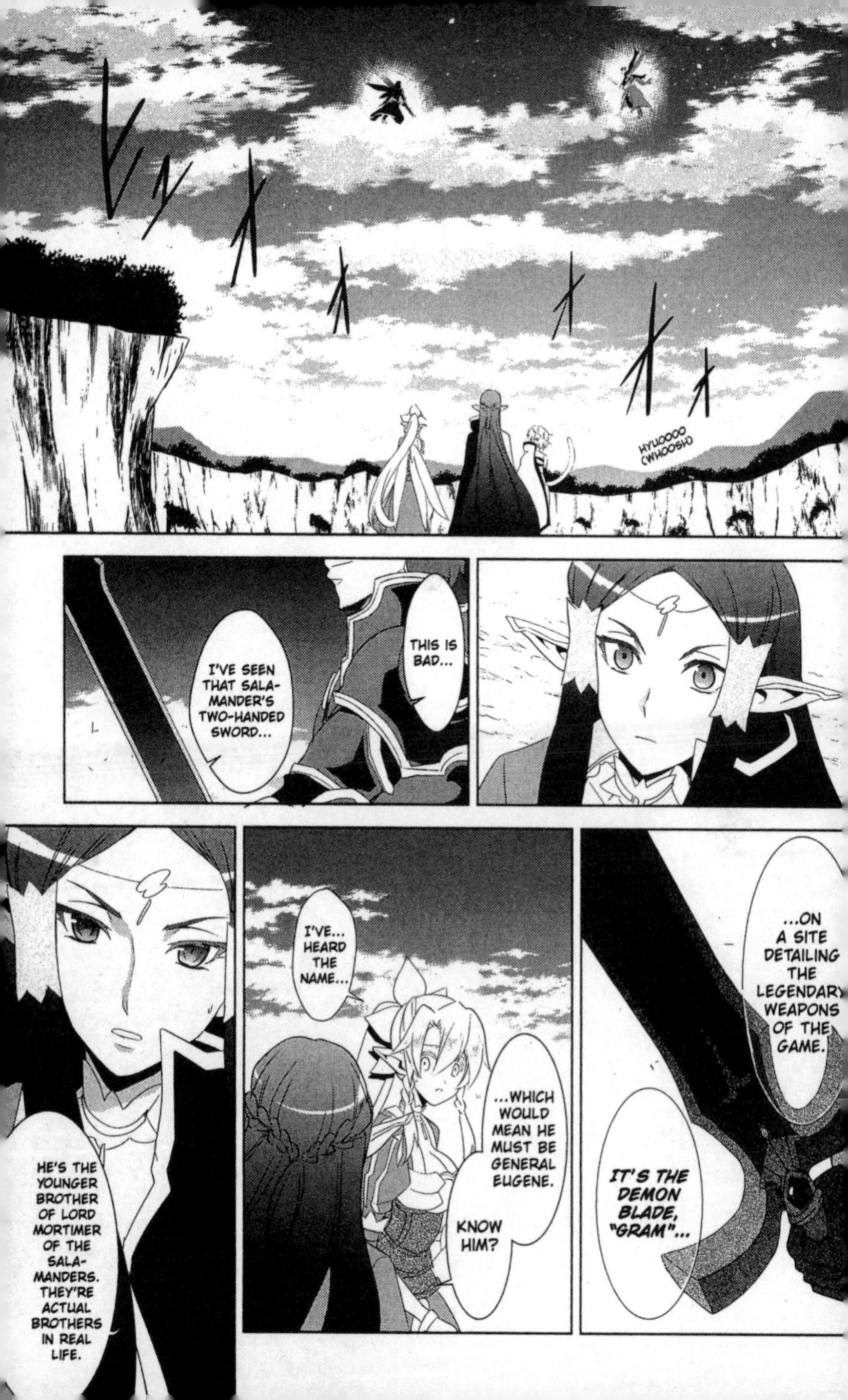
HYUOOOO (WHOOSH)
THIS IS BAD...
I'VE SEEN THAT SALAMANDER'S TWO-HANDED SWORD...
...ON A SITE DETAILING THE LEGENDARY WEAPONS OF THE GAME.
IT'S THE DEMON BLADE, "GRAM"...
I'VE... HEARD THE NAME...
...WHICH WOULD MEAN HE MUST BE GENERAL EUGENE.
KNOW HIM?
HE'S THE YOUNGER BROTHER OF LORD MORTIMER OF THE SALAMANDERS. THEY'RE ACTUAL BROTHERS IN REAL LIFE.

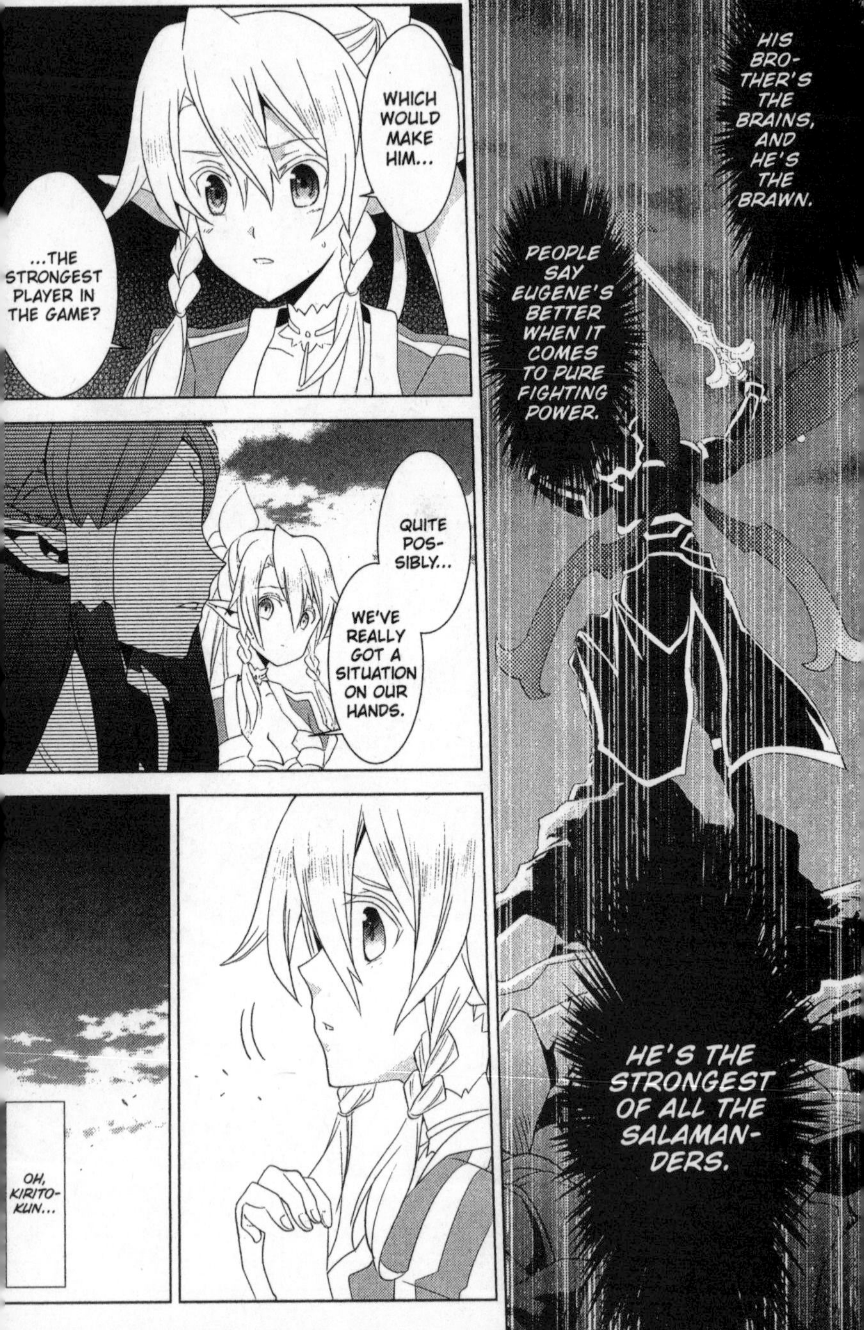
HIS BROTHER'S THE BRAINS, AND HE'S THE BRAWN.
PEOPLE SAY EUGENE'S BETTER WHEN IT COMES TO PURE FIGHTING POWER.
HE'S THE STRONGEST OF ALL THE SALAMANDERS.
WHICH WOULD MAKE HIM...
...THE STRONGEST PLAYER IN THE GAME?
QUITE POSSIBLY...
WE'VE REALLY GOT A SITUATION ON OUR HANDS.
OH, KIRITO-KUN...

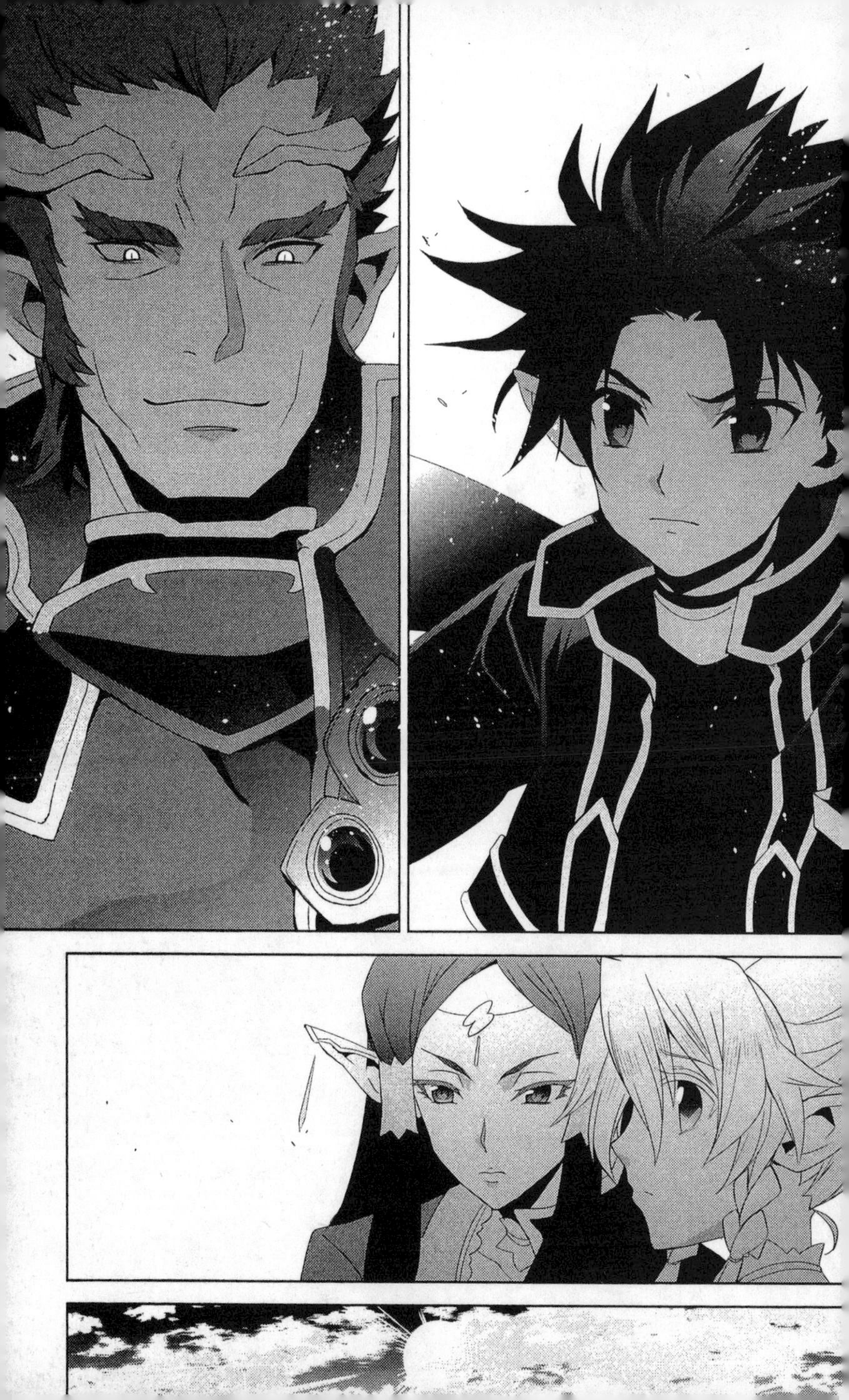

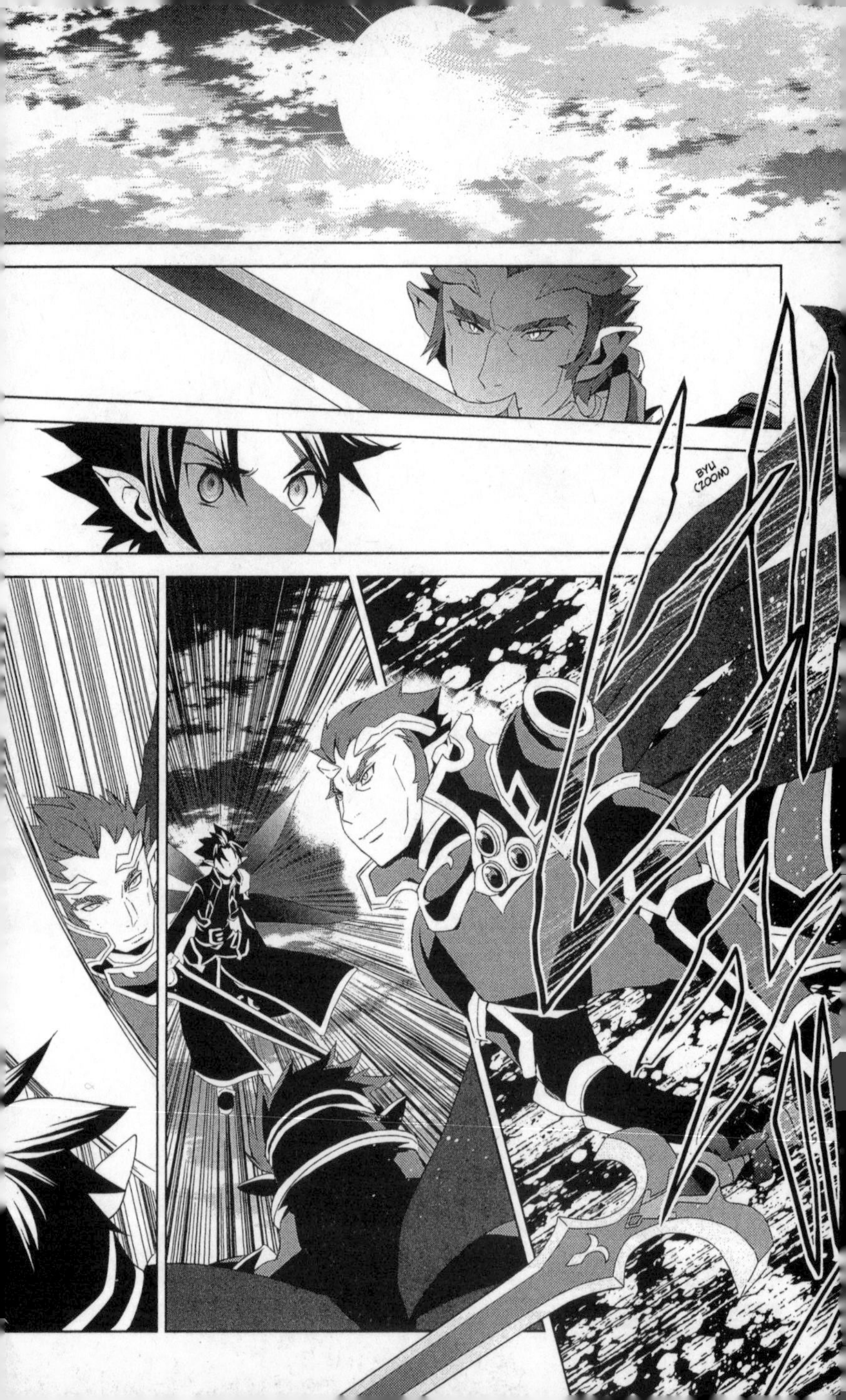
BYU
(ZOOM)

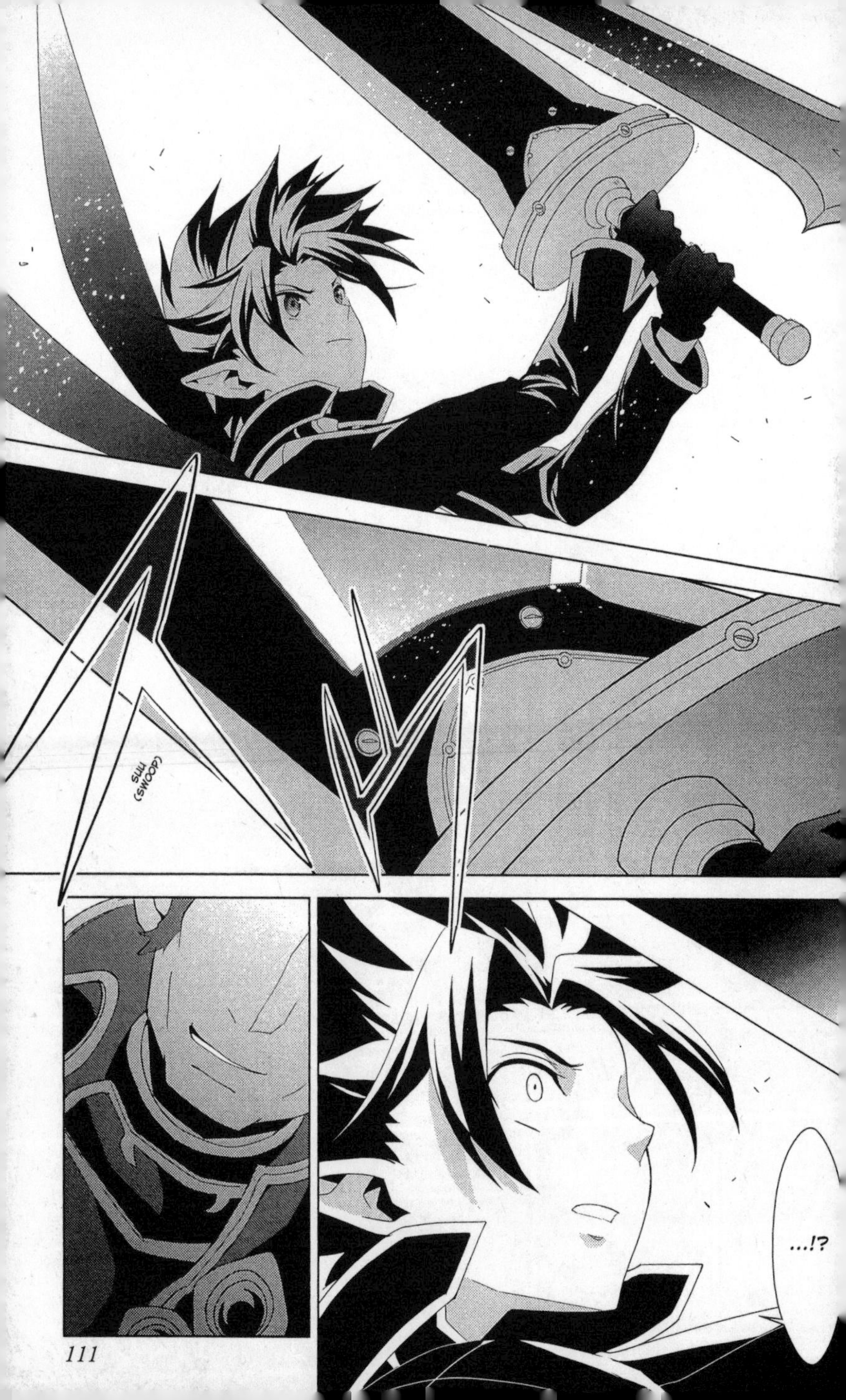
SUU
(SWOOP)
...!?

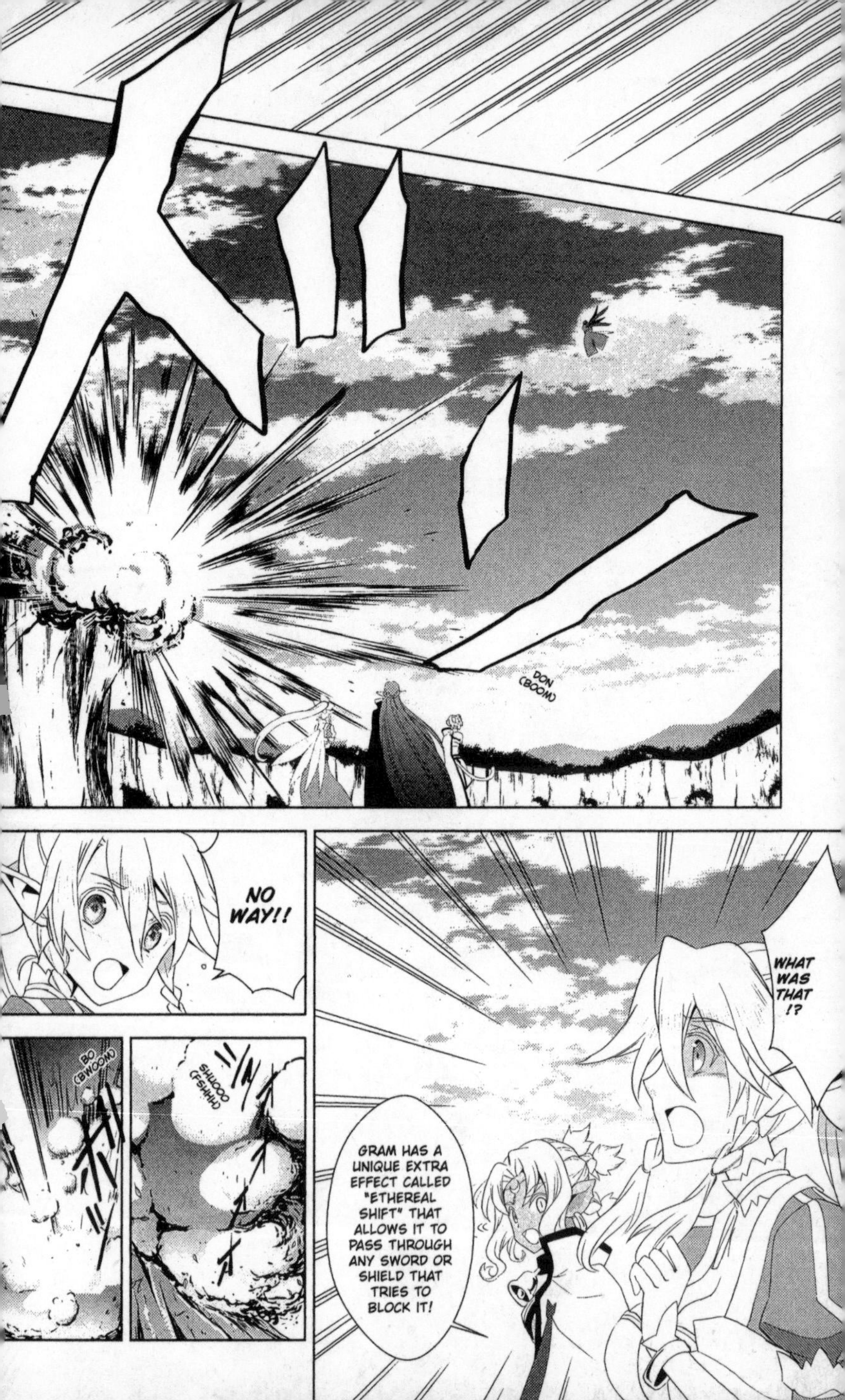
DON (BOOM)
WHAT WAS THAT!?
GRAM HAS A UNIQUE EXTRA EFFECT CALLED "ETHEREAL SHIFT" THAT ALLOWS IT TO PASS THROUGH ANY SWORD OR SHIELD THAT TRIES TO BLOCK IT!
NO WAY!!
SHUOOO (FSHHH)
BO (BWOOM)

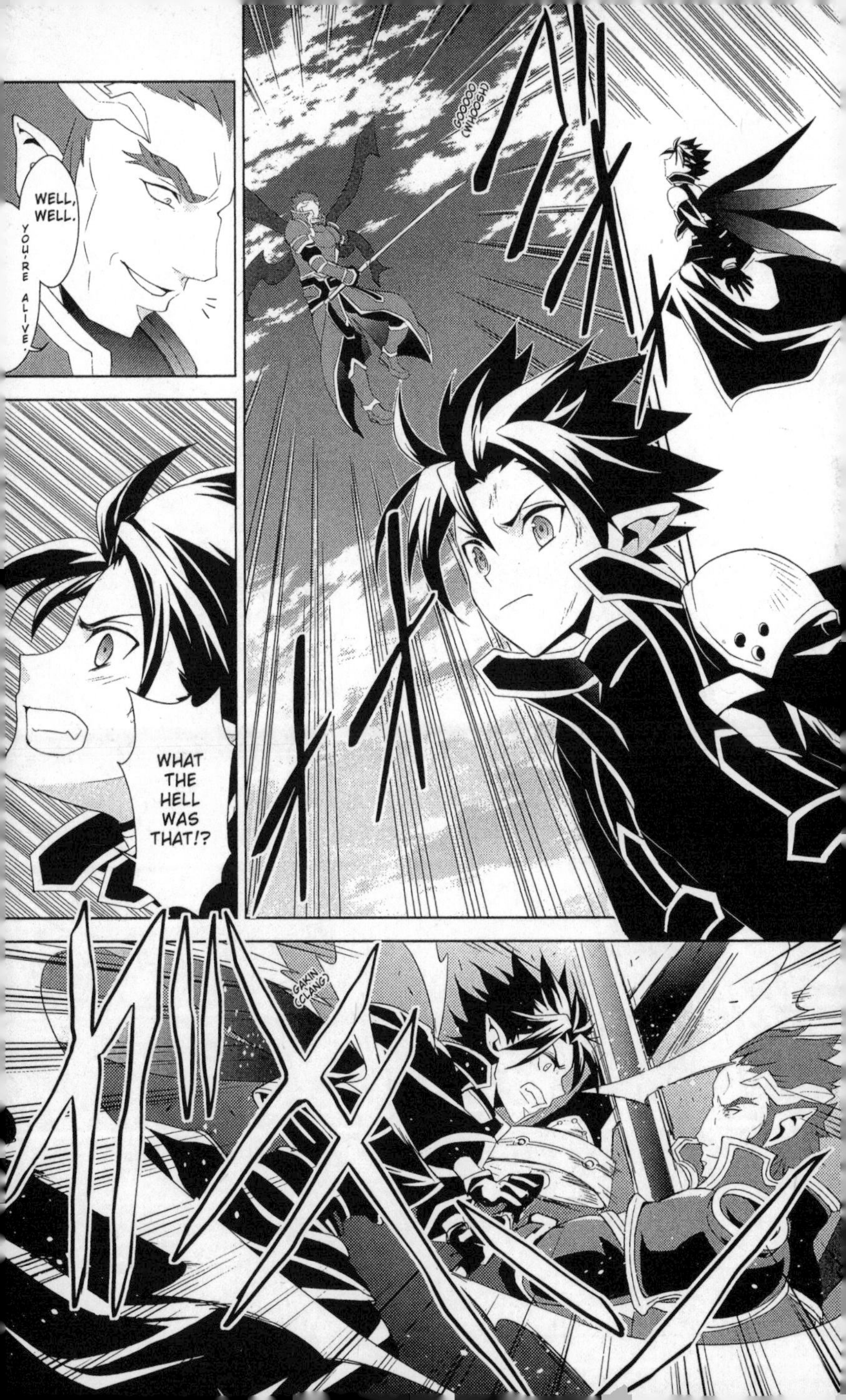
GOOOOO (WHOOSH)
WELL, WELL.
YOU'RE ALIVE.
WHAT THE HELL WAS THAT!?
GAKIN (CLANG)

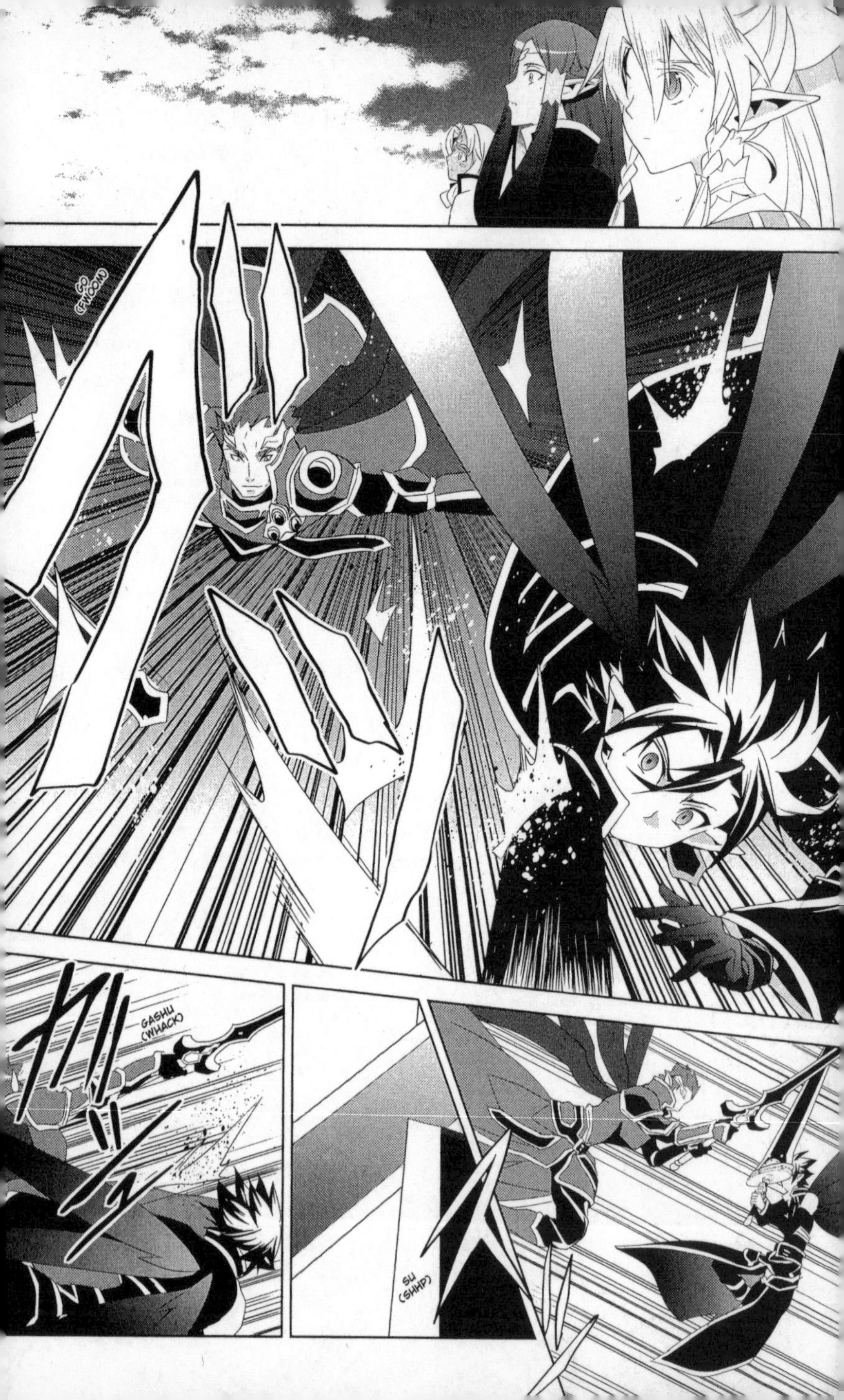
GO
(FWOOM)
SU
(SHHP)
GASHU
(WHACK)

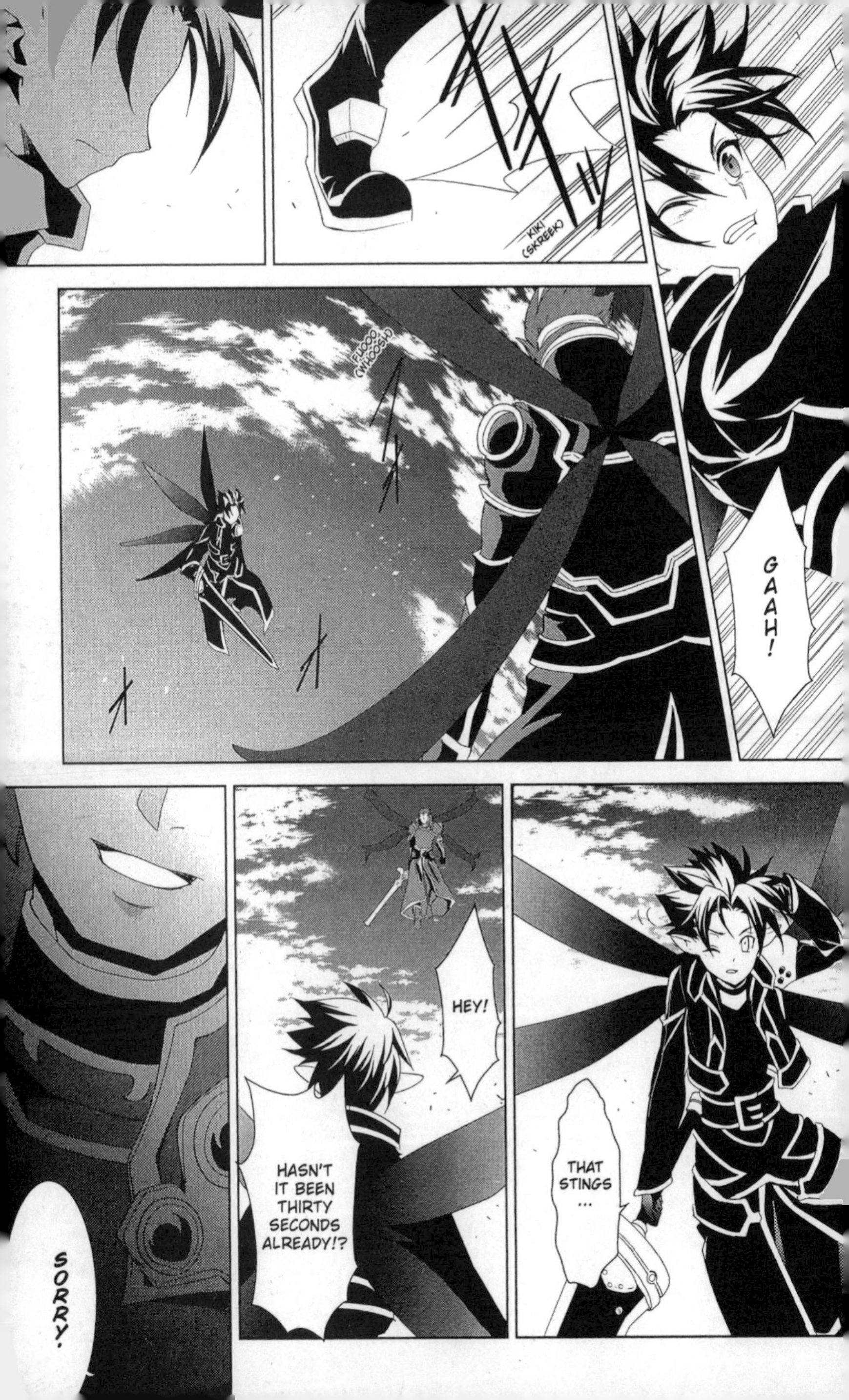
KIKI (SKREEK)
GAAH!
FUOOO (WHOOSH)
THAT STINGS ...
HEY!
HASN'T IT BEEN THIRTY SECONDS ALREADY!?
SORRY.

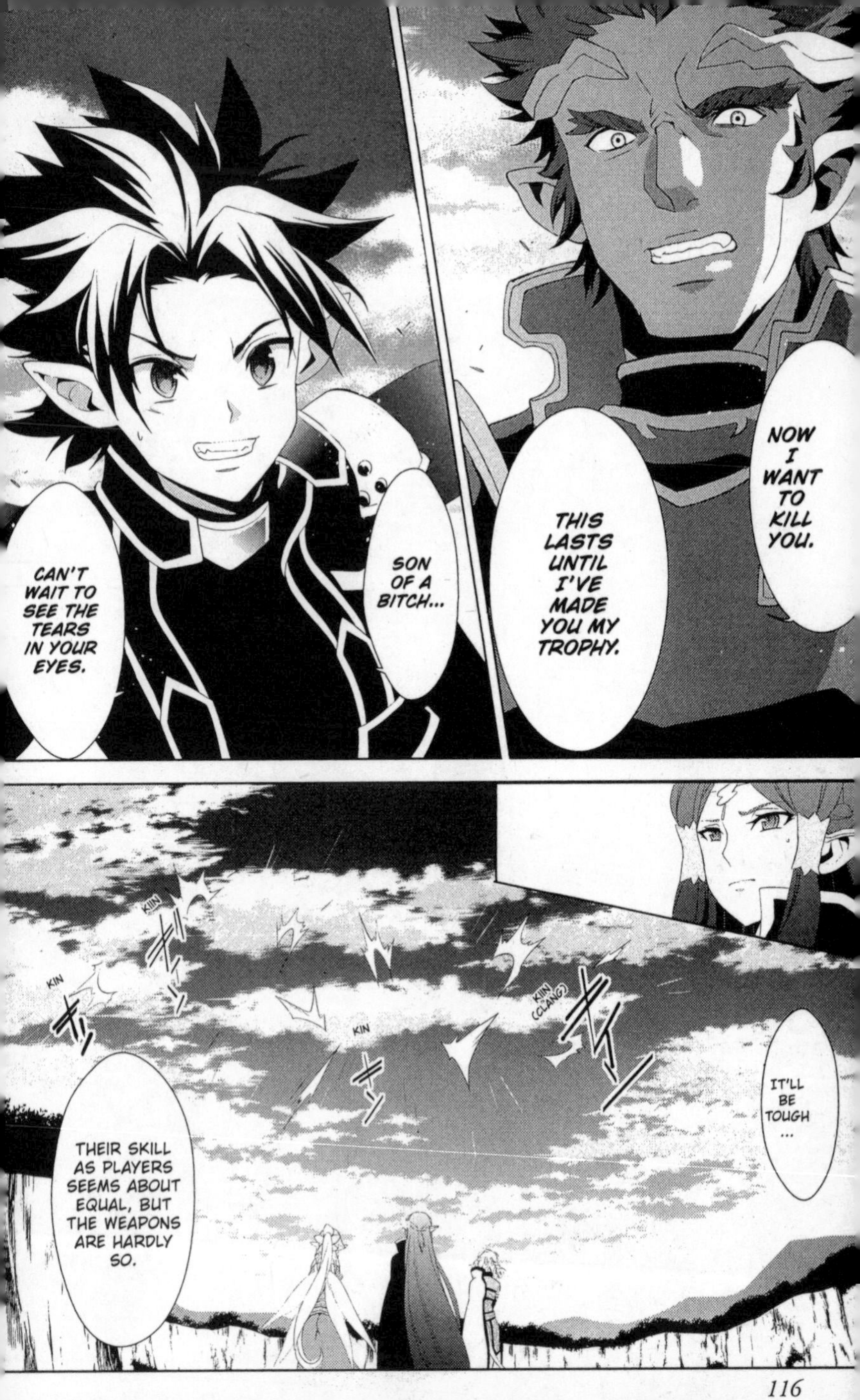
NOW I WANT TO KILL YOU.
THIS LASTS UNTIL I'VE MADE YOU MY TROPHY.
SON OF A BITCH...
CAN'T WAIT TO SEE THE TEARS IN YOUR EYES.
IT'LL BE TOUGH...
KIIN (CLANG)
KIN
KIIN
KIN
THEIR SKILL AS PLAYERS SEEMS ABOUT EQUAL, BUT THE WEAPONS ARE HARDLY SO.

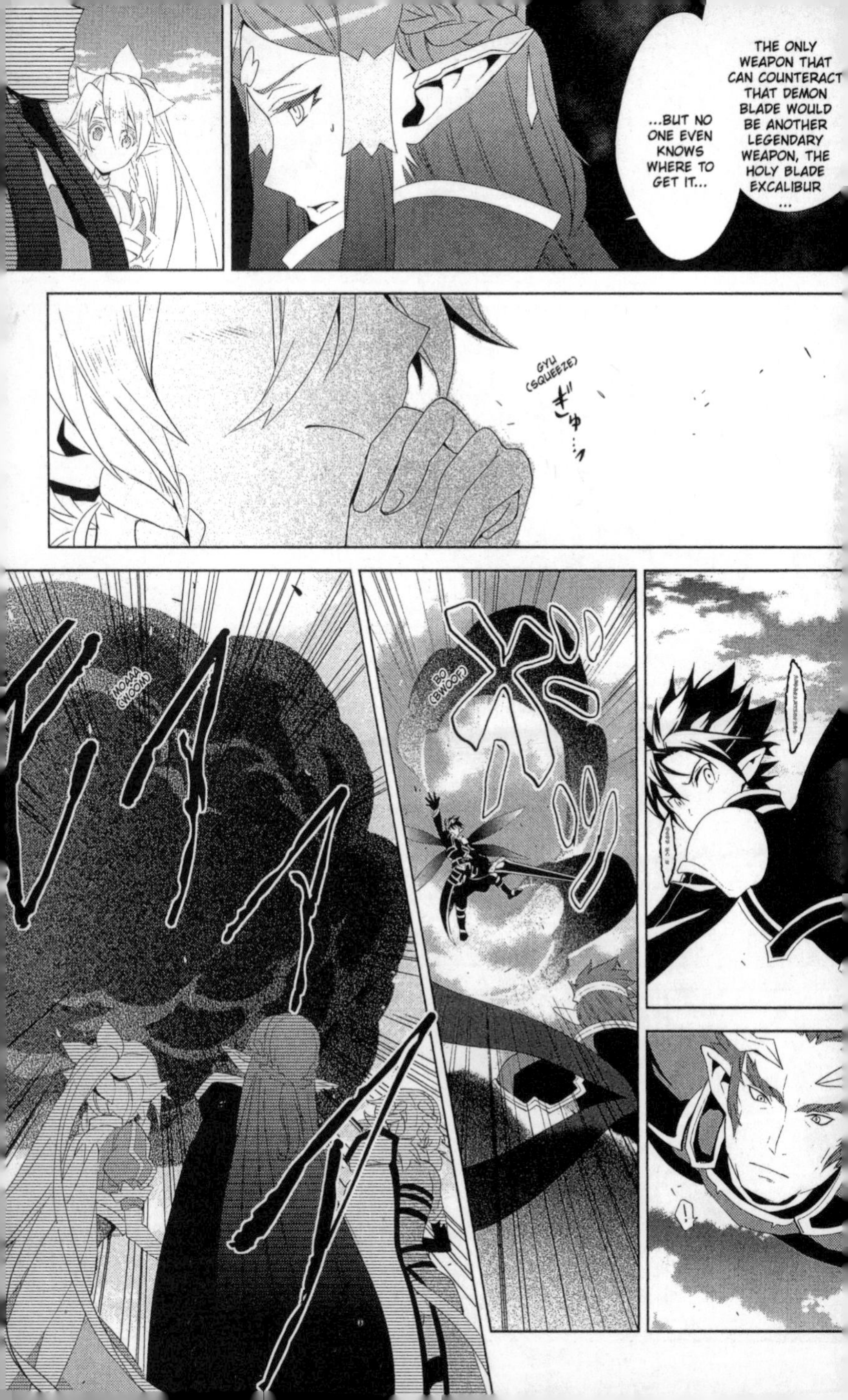
THE ONLY WEAPON THAT CAN COUNTERACT THAT DEMON BLADE WOULD BE ANOTHER LEGENDARY WEAPON, THE HOLY BLADE EXCALIBUR ...
...BUT NO ONE EVEN KNOWS WHERE TO GET IT...
GYU (SQUEEZE)
!
BO (BWOOF)

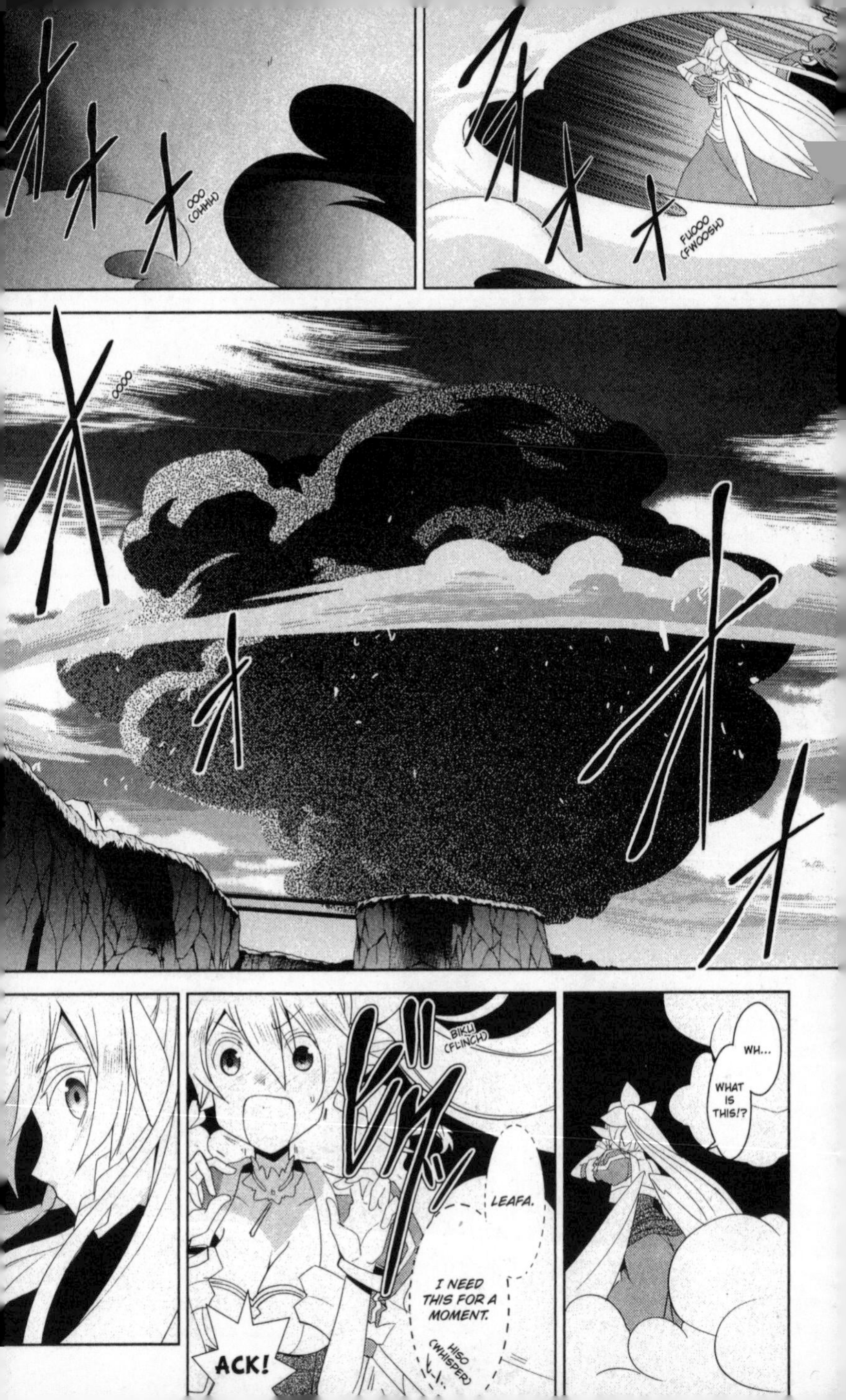
FUOOO (FWOOSH)
OOO (OHHH)
OOOO
WH... WHAT IS THIS!?
BIKU (FLINCH)
LEAFA.
I NEED THIS FOR A MOMENT.
HISO (WHISPER)
ACK!

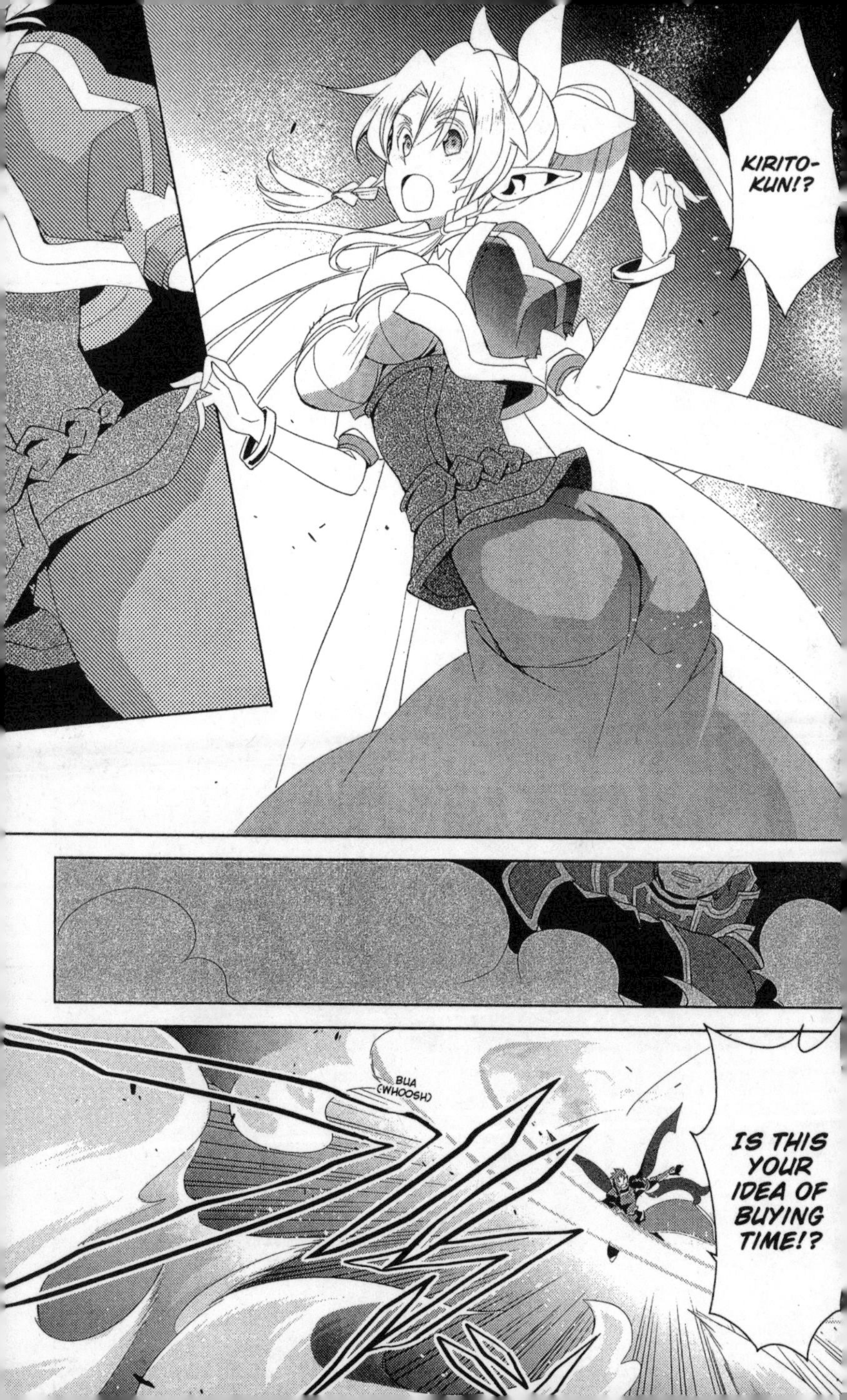
KIRITO-KUN!?
BUA (WHOOSH)
IS THIS YOUR IDEA OF BUYING TIME!?

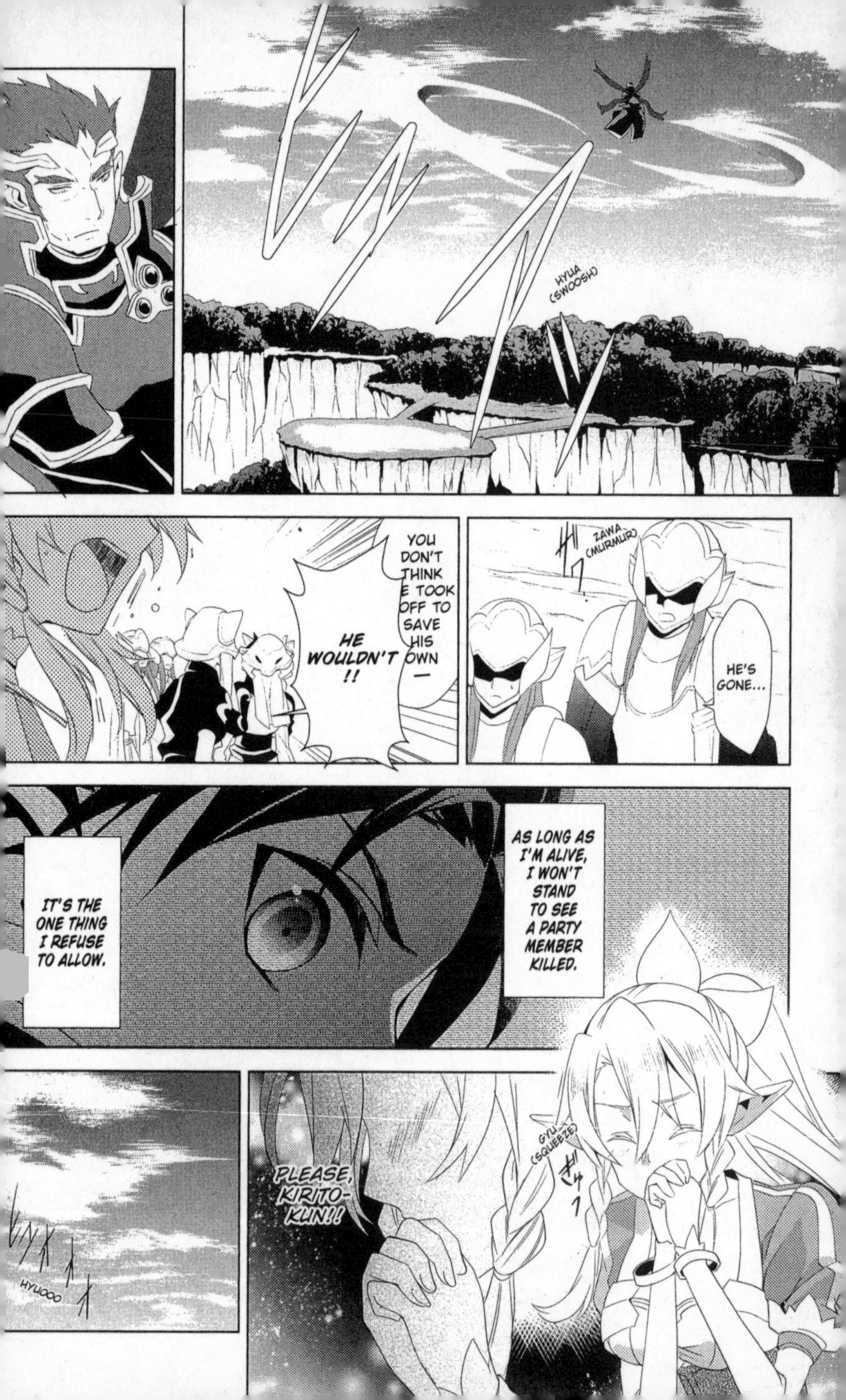
HYUA (SWOOSH)
ZAWA (MURMUR)
HE'S GONE...
YOU DON'T THINK E TOOK OFF TO SAVE HIS OWN—
HE WOULDN'T!!
AS LONG AS I'M ALIVE, I WON'T STAND TO SEE A PARTY MEMBER KILLED.
IT'S THE ONE THING I REFUSE TO ALLOW.
GYU (SQUEEZE)
PLEASE, KIRITO-KUN!!
HYUOOO

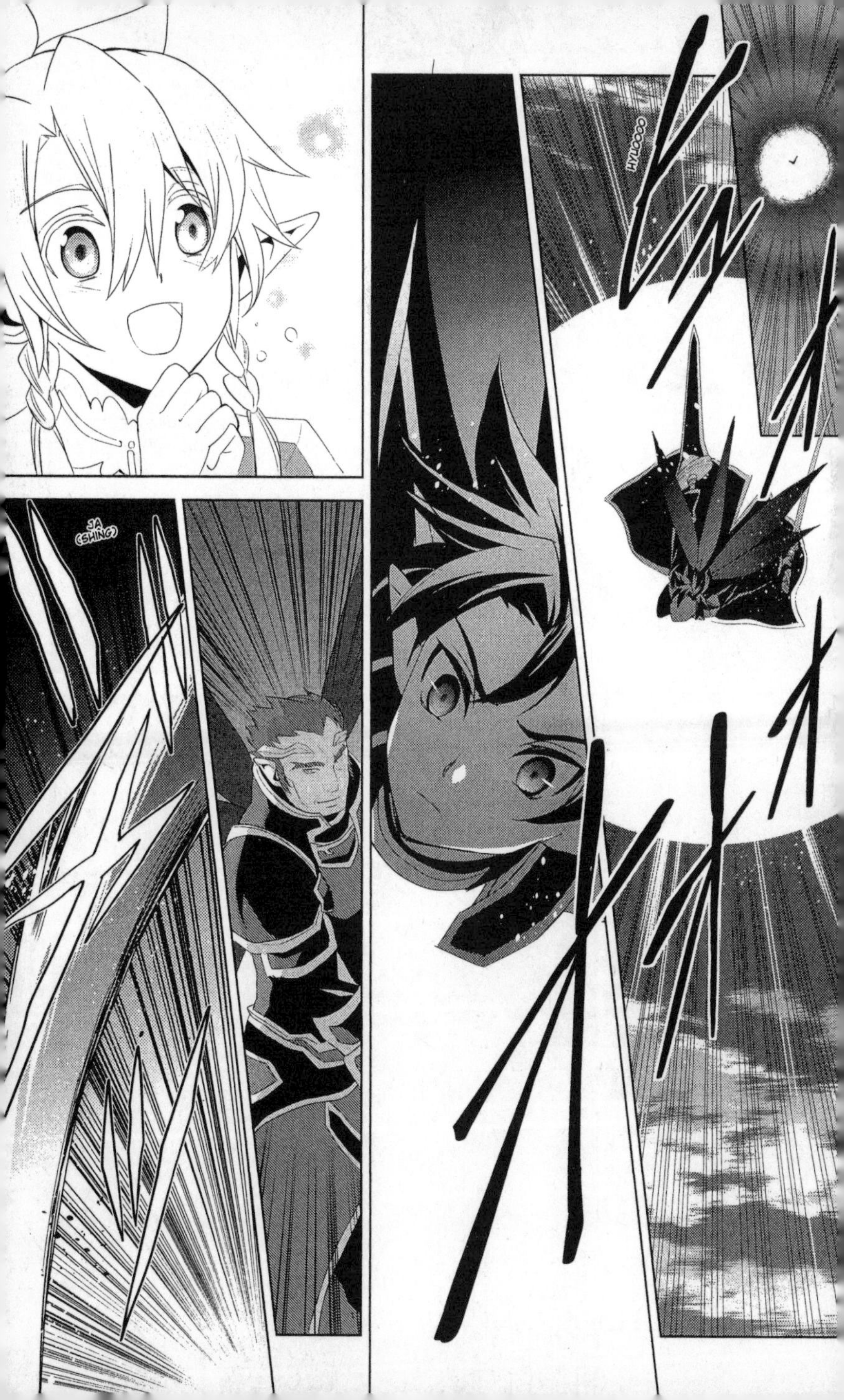
HYUOOOO
JA
(SHING)

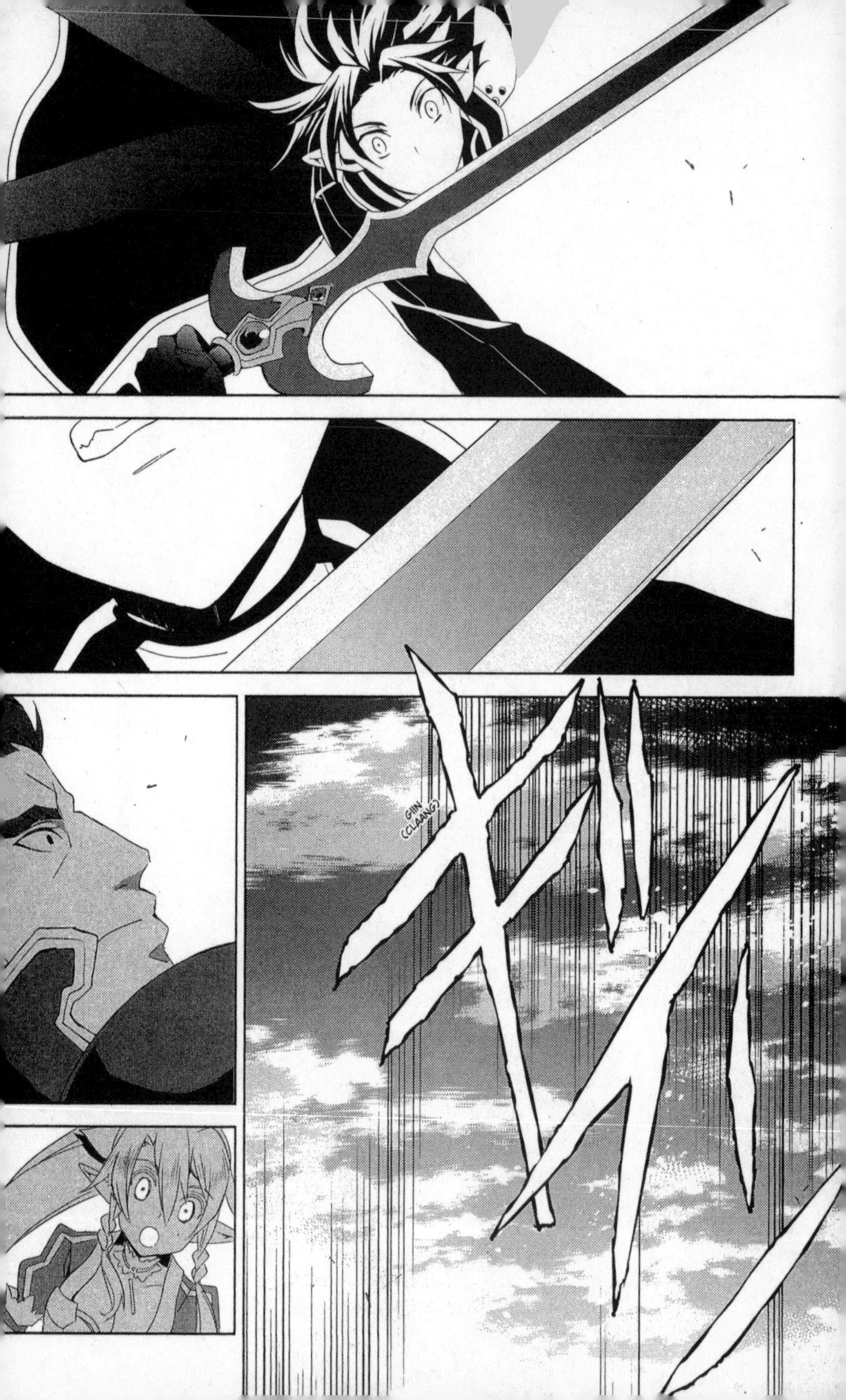
GIIN (CLAANG)

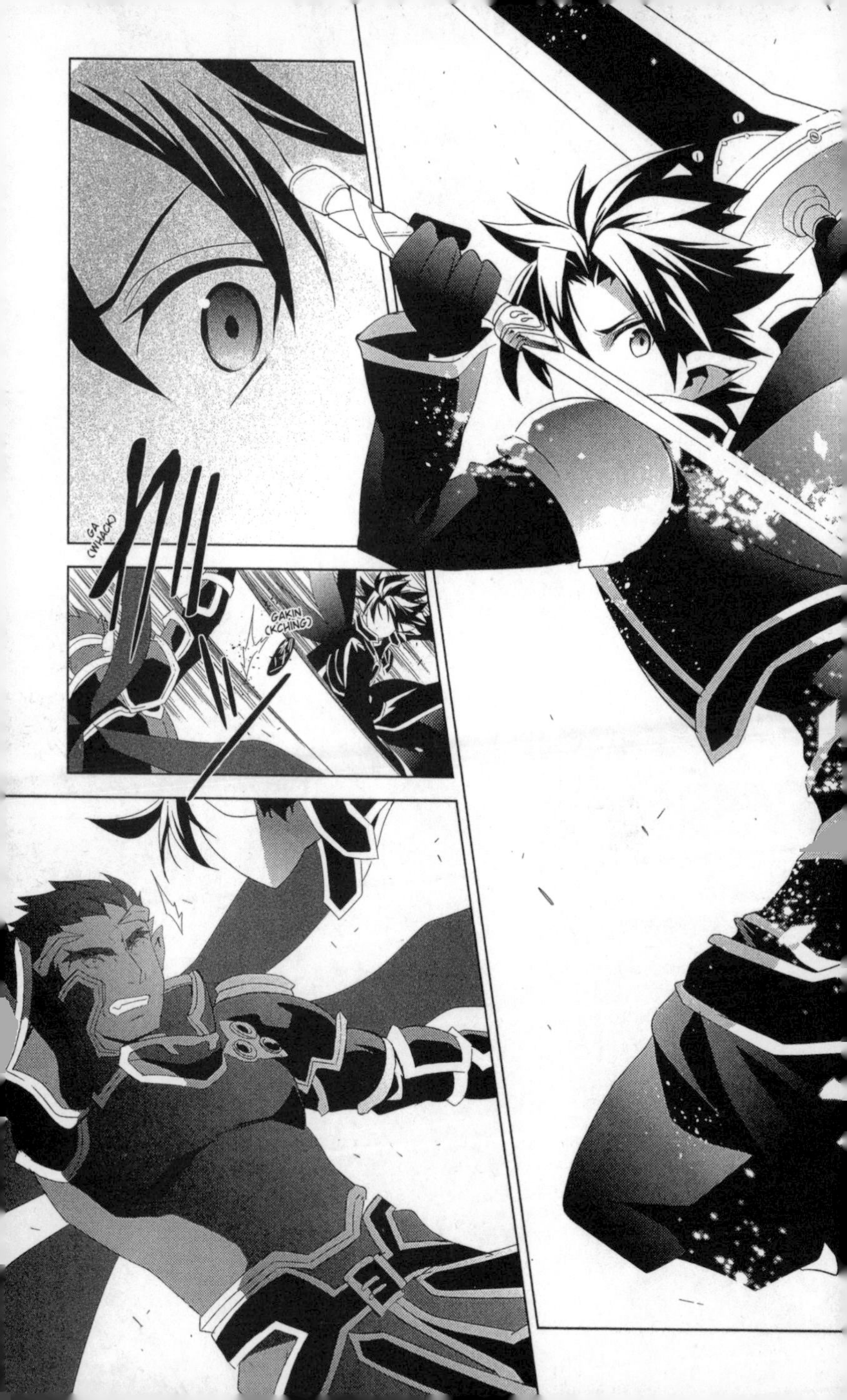
GA
(WHACK)
GAKIN
(KCHING)

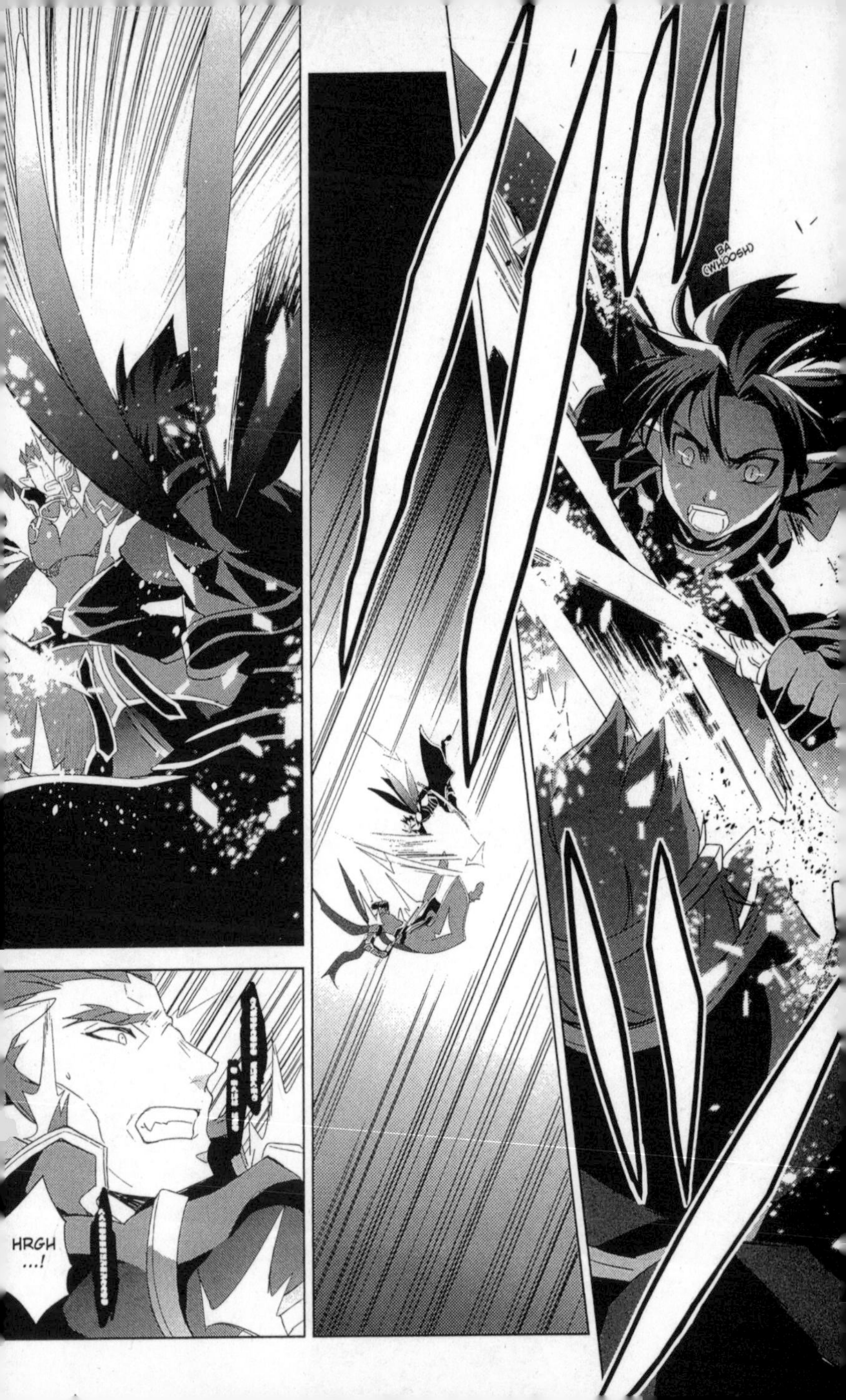
BA (WHOOSH)
HRGH ...!

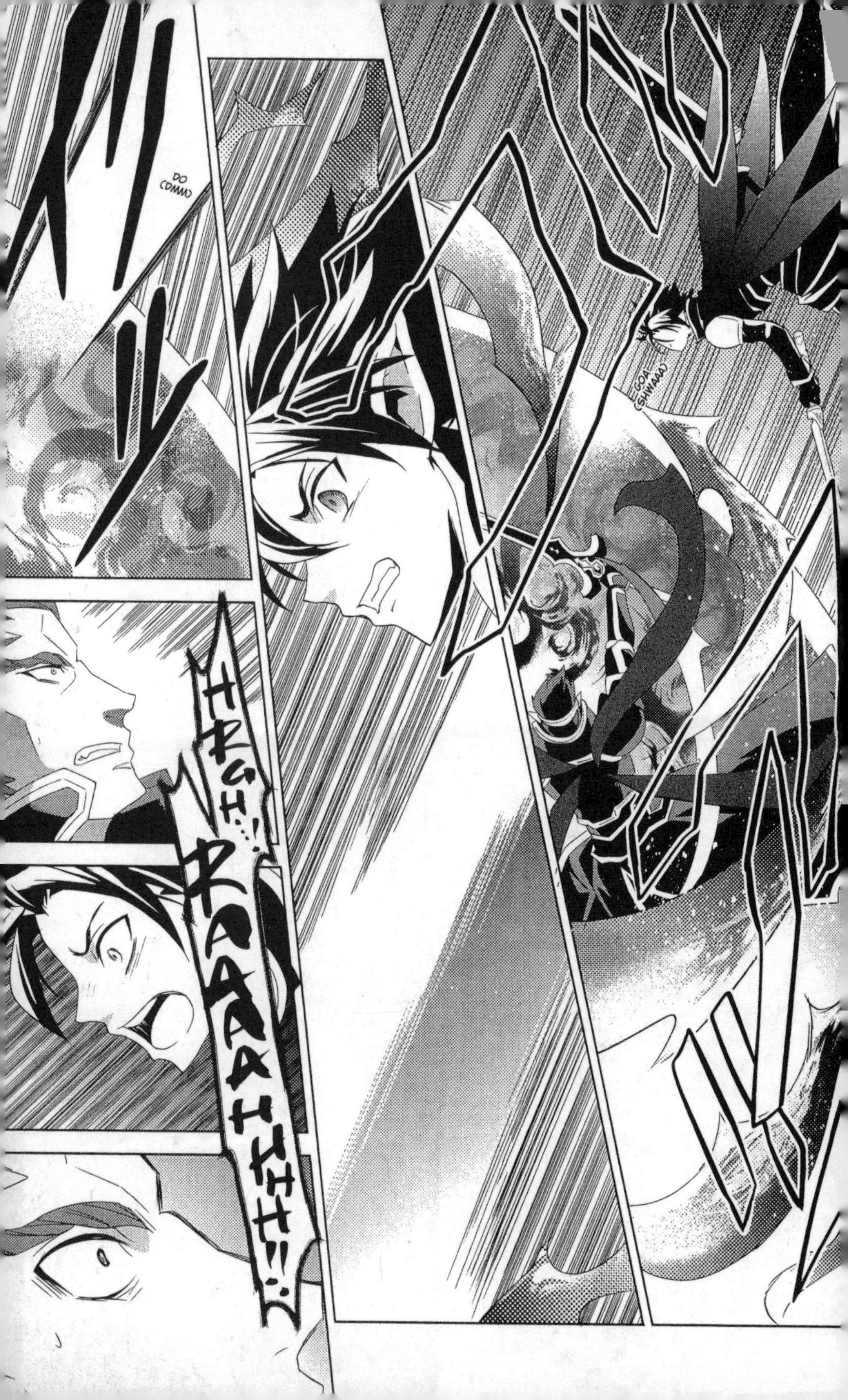
GOA (SHWAAA)
DO (DMM)
HRGH...! RAAAAHHHH!!!

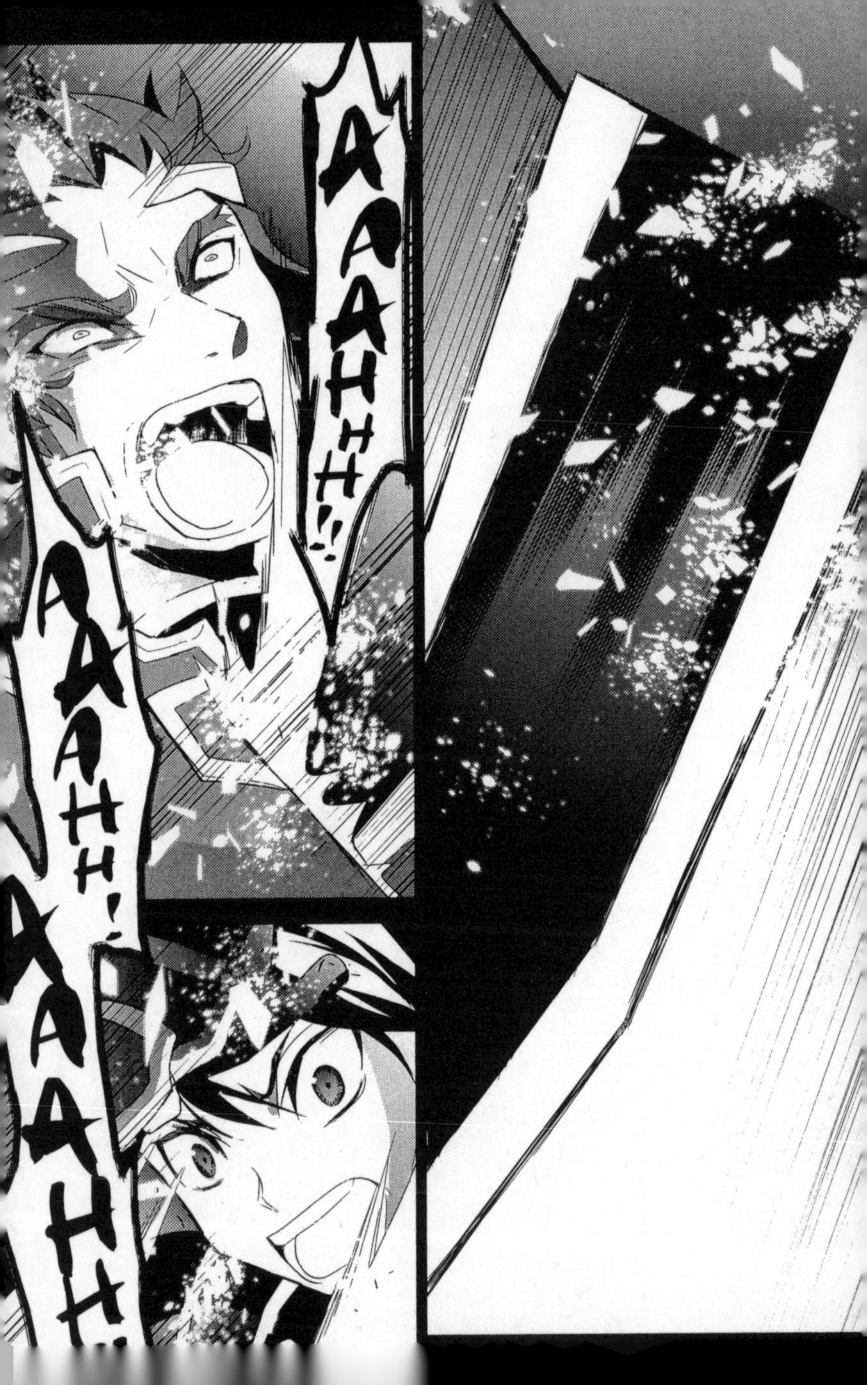
AAAHHH!!
AAAHH!
AAAAHH!

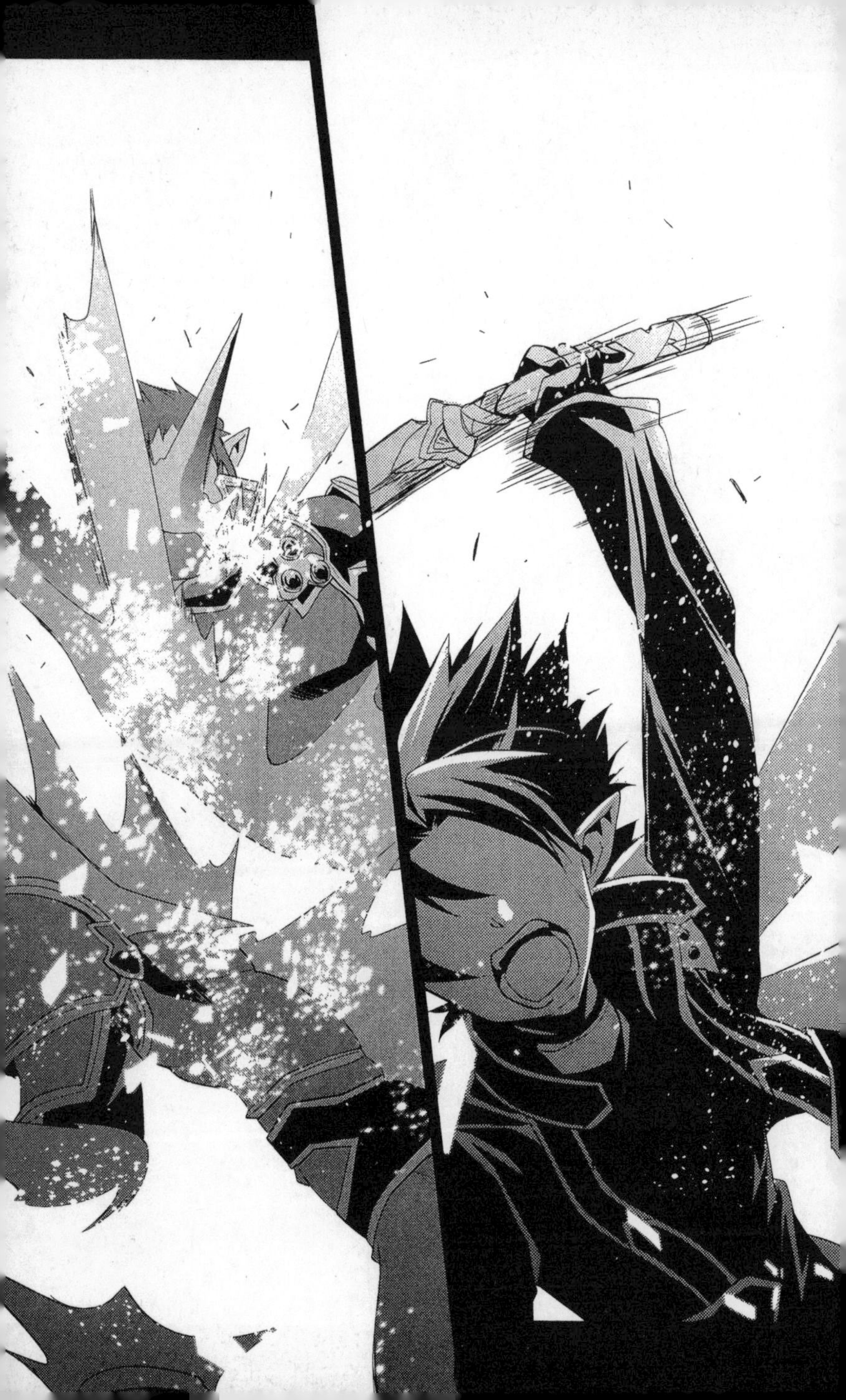

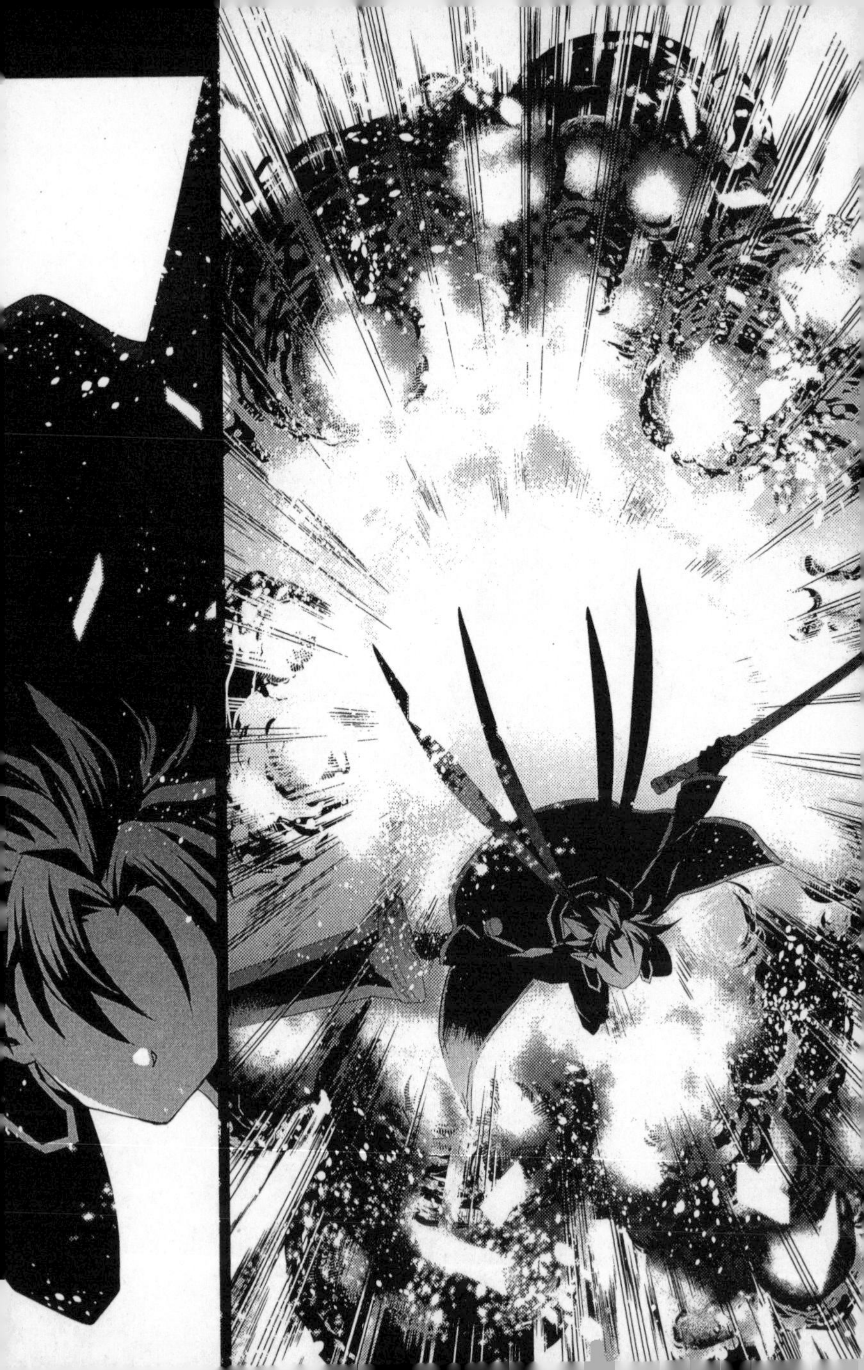

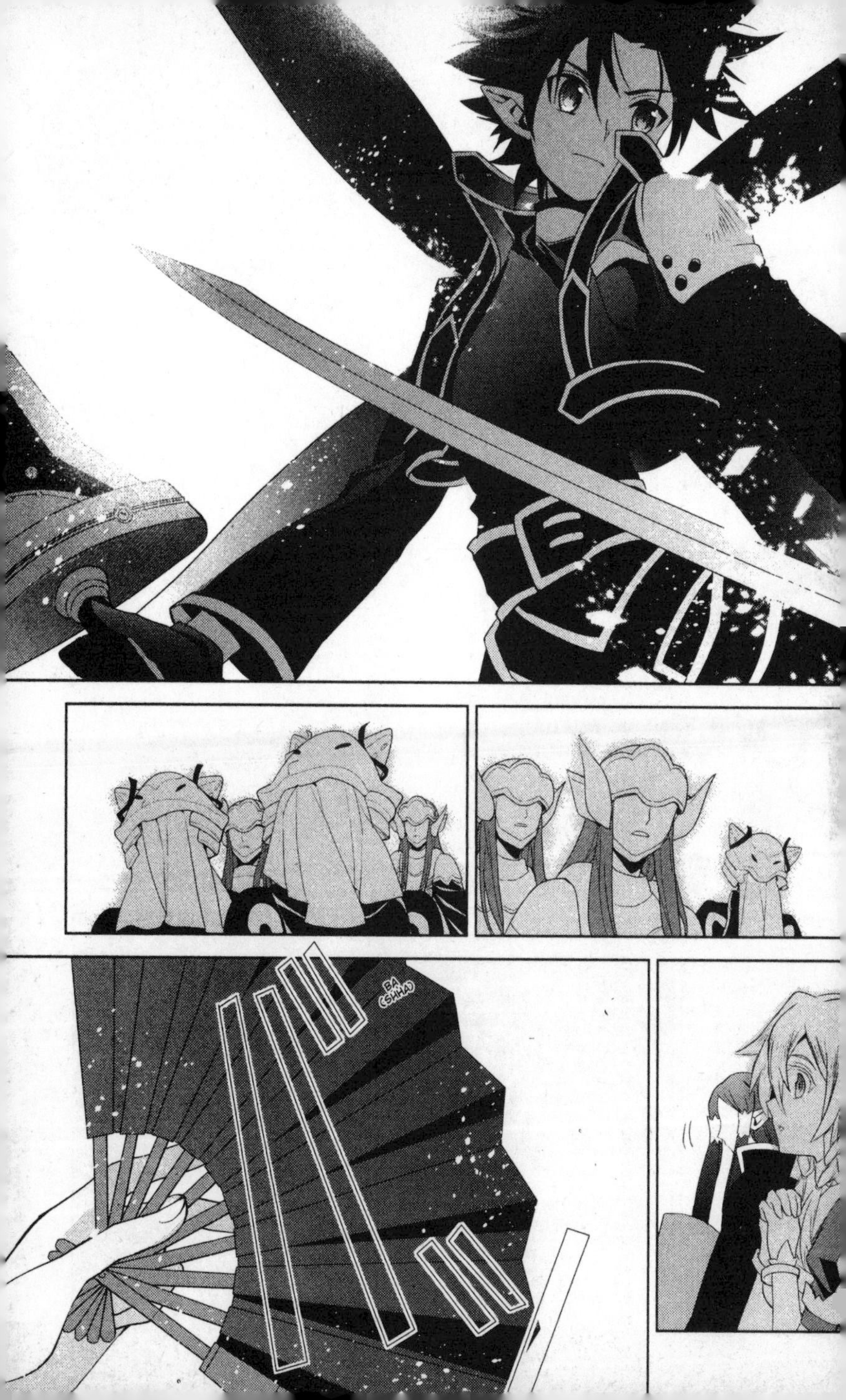
BA
(SHHA)

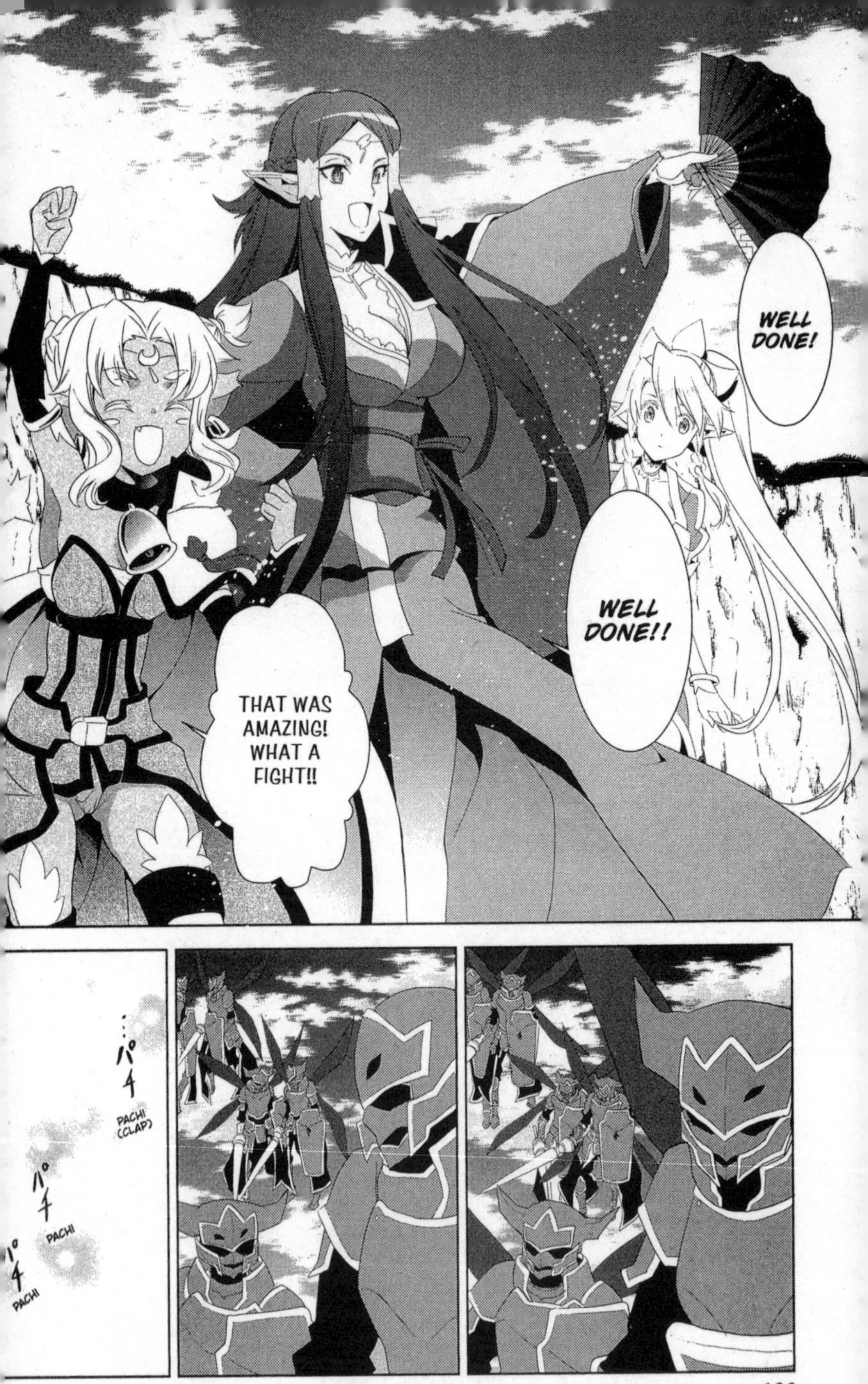
WELL DONE!
WELL DONE!!
THAT WAS AMAZING! WHAT A FIGHT!!
…パチ
PACHI (CLAP)
パチ
PACHI
パチ
PACHI

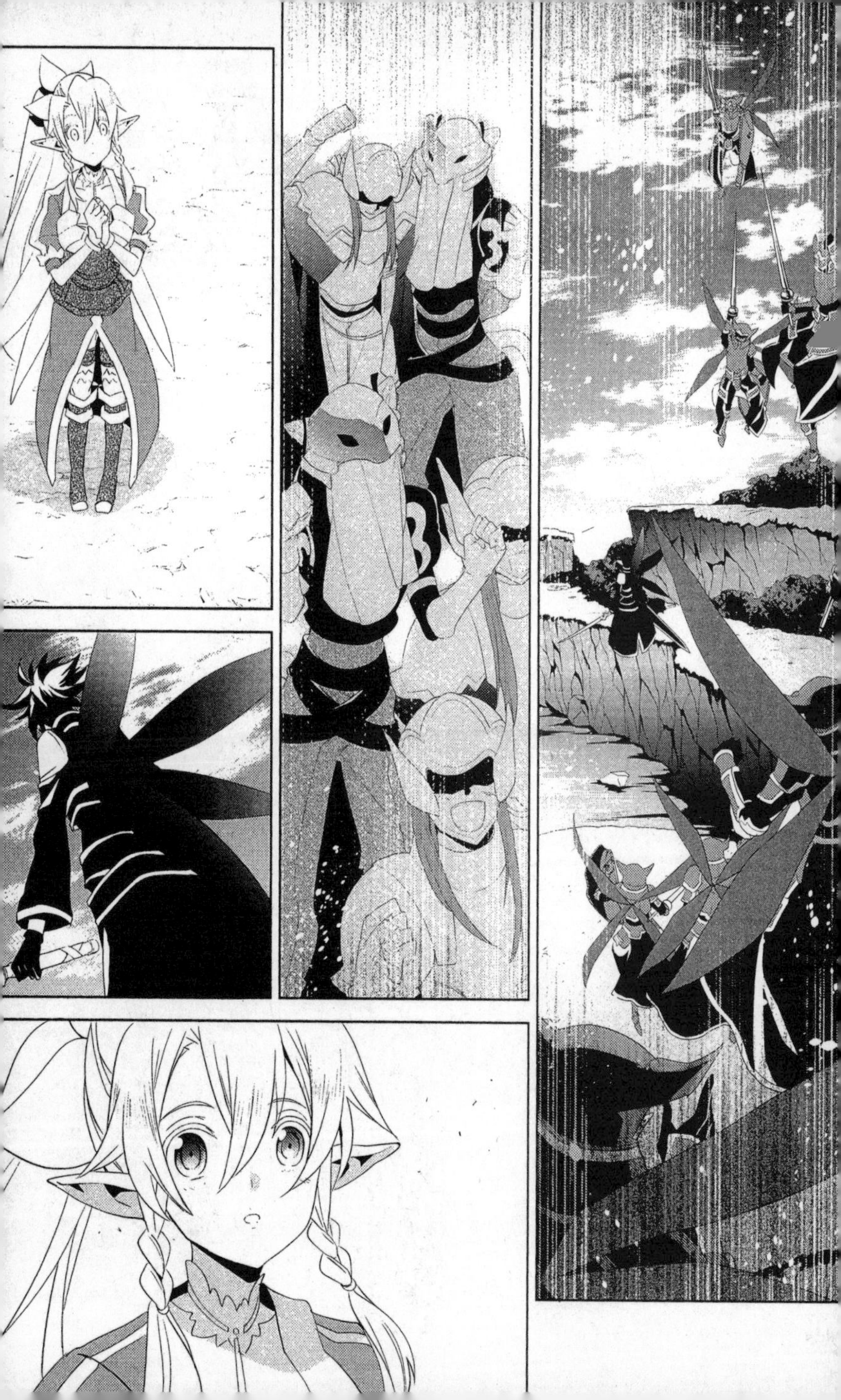

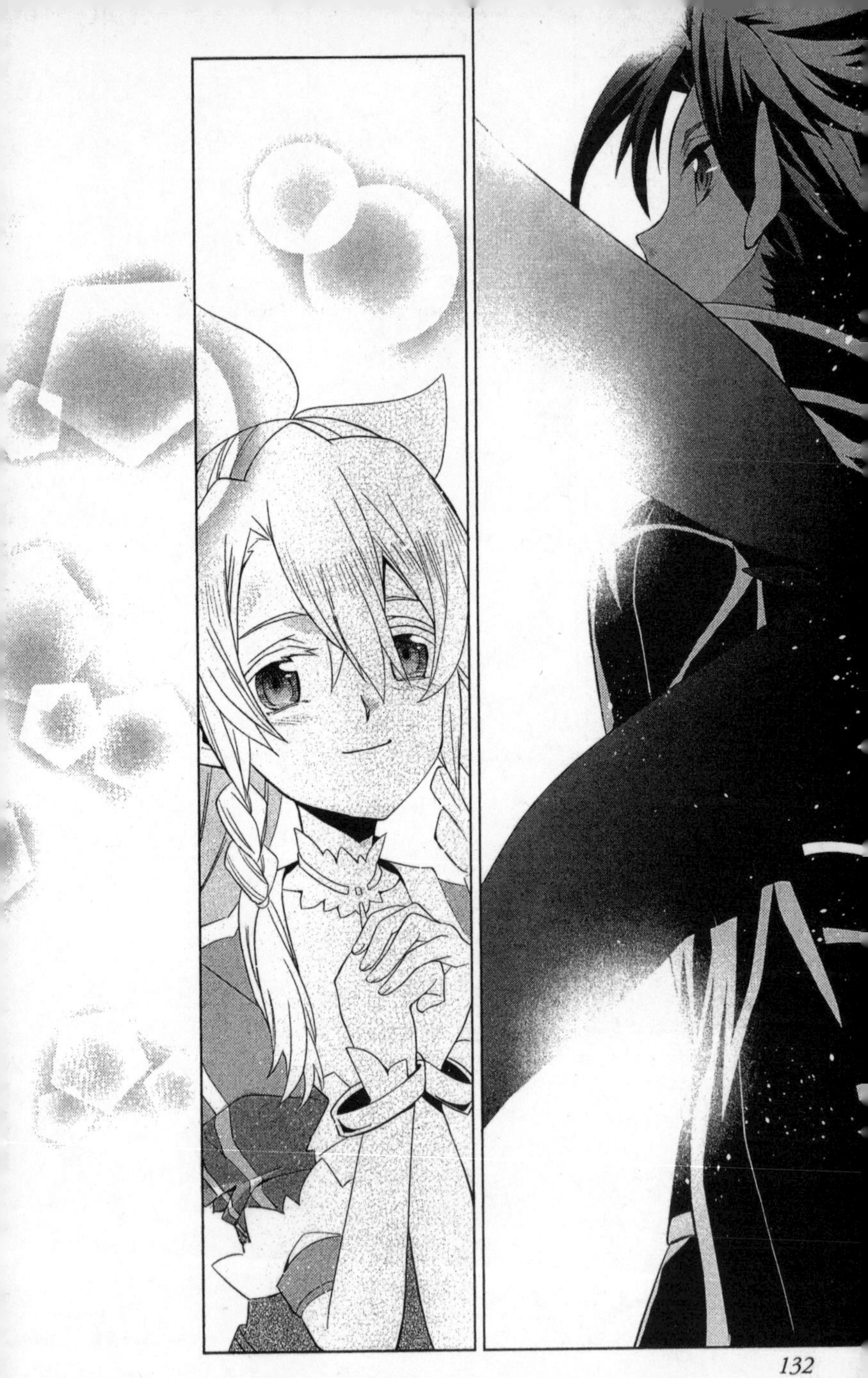

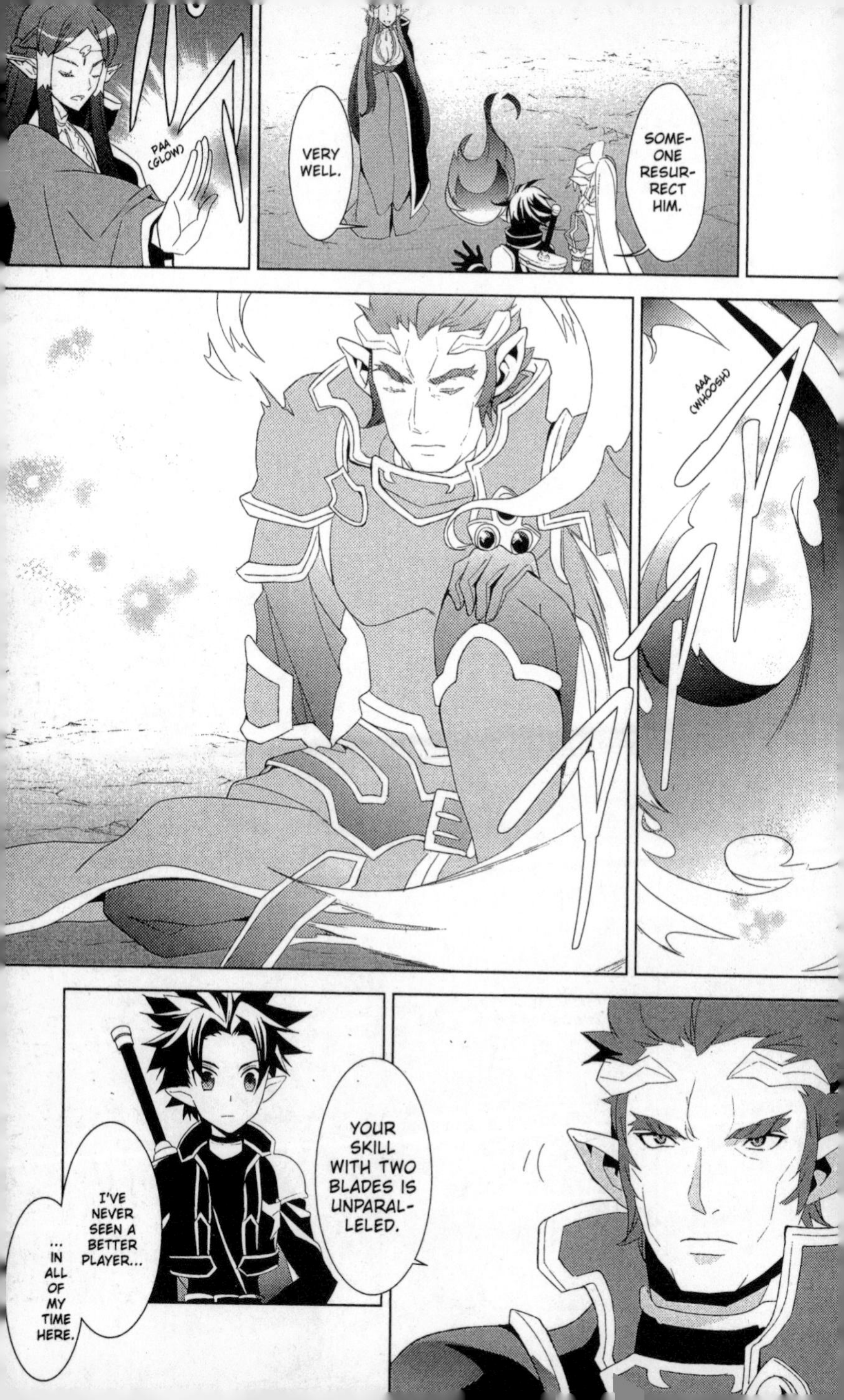
SOME-ONE RESUR-RECT HIM.
VERY WELL.
PAA (GLOW)
AAA (WHOOSH)
YOUR SKILL WITH TWO BLADES IS UNPARAL-LELED.
I'VE NEVER SEEN A BETTER PLAYER...
...IN ALL OF MY TIME HERE.

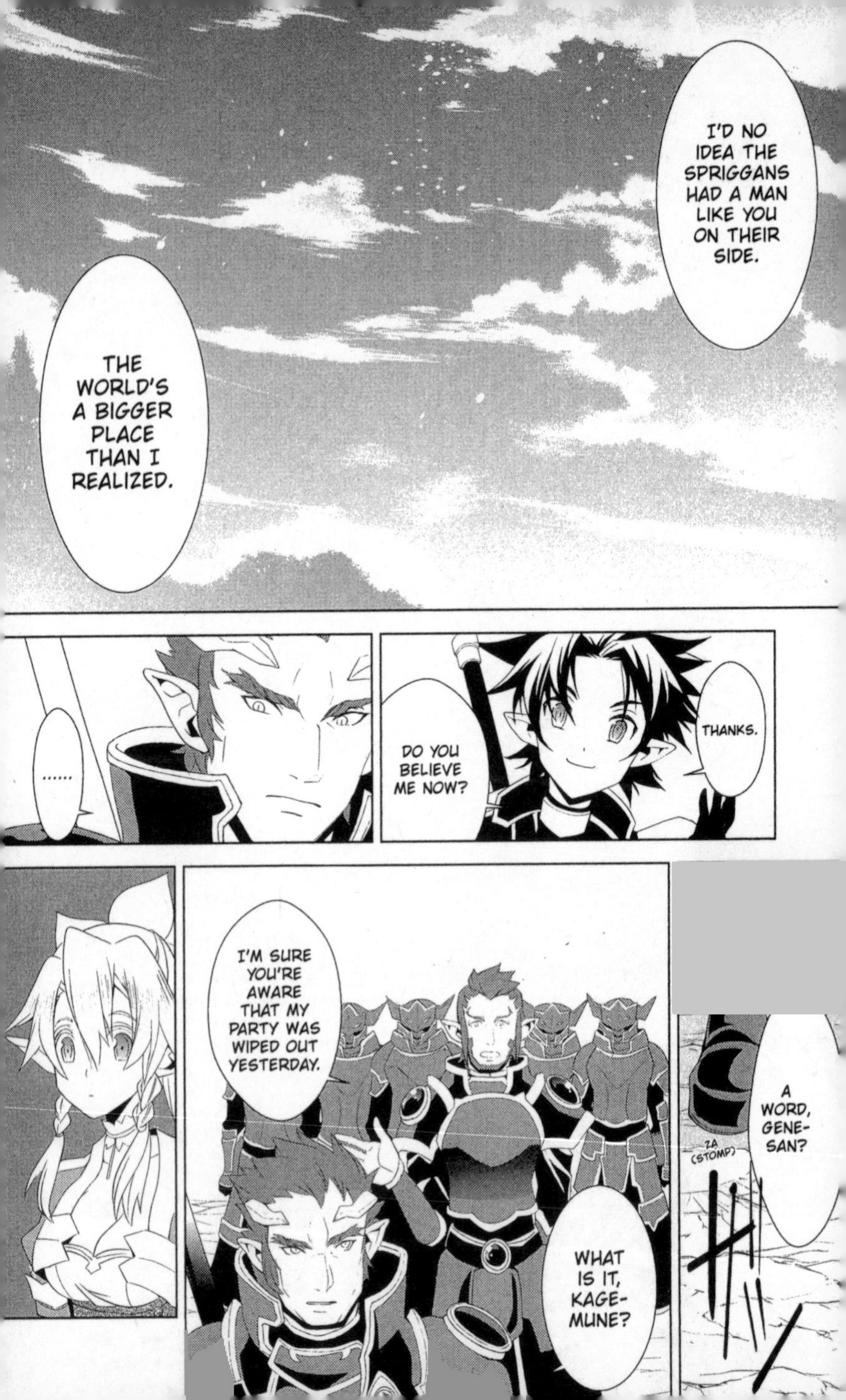
I'D NO IDEA THE SPRIGGANS HAD A MAN LIKE YOU ON THEIR SIDE.
THE WORLD'S A BIGGER PLACE THAN I REALIZED.
THANKS.
DO YOU BELIEVE ME NOW?
......
A WORD, GENE-SAN?
ZA (STOMP)
WHAT IS IT, KAGE-MUNE?
I'M SURE YOU'RE AWARE THAT MY PARTY WAS WIPED OUT YESTERDAY.

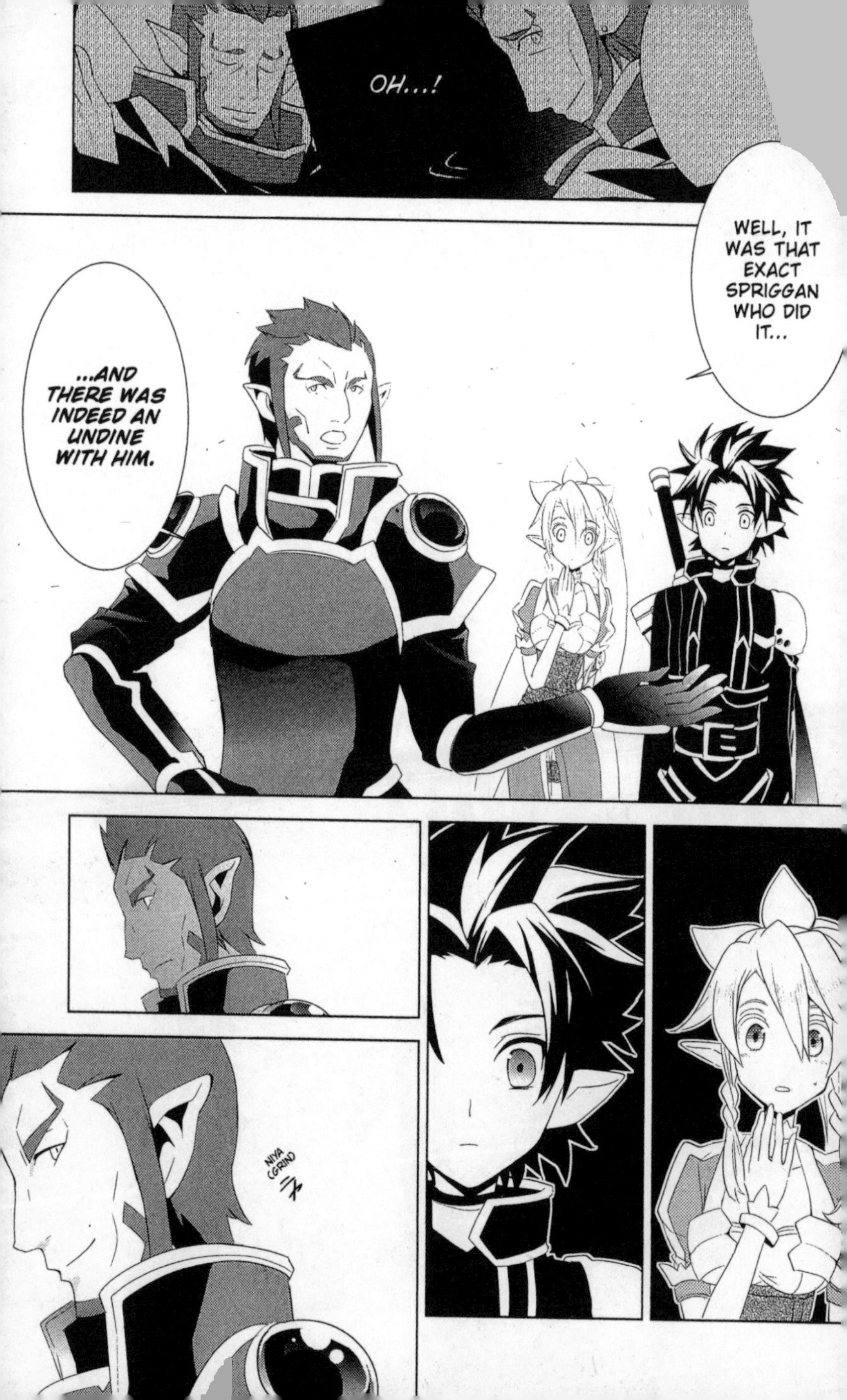
OH...!
WELL, IT WAS THAT EXACT SPRIGGAN WHO DID IT...
...AND THERE WAS INDEED AN UNDINE WITH HIM.
NIYA (GRIN)

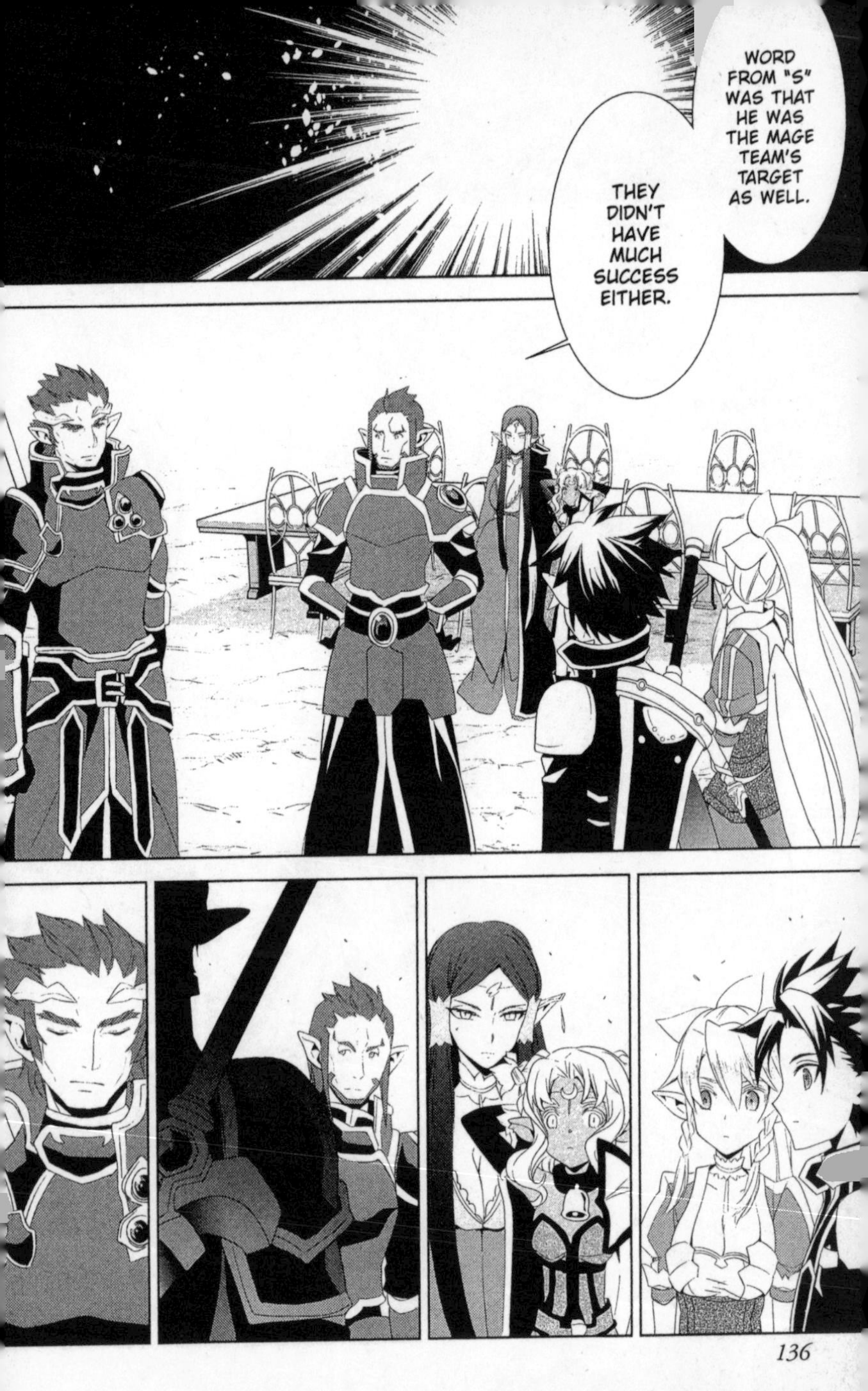
WORD FROM "S" WAS THAT HE WAS THE MAGE TEAM'S TARGET AS WELL.
THEY DIDN'T HAVE MUCH SUCCESS EITHER.

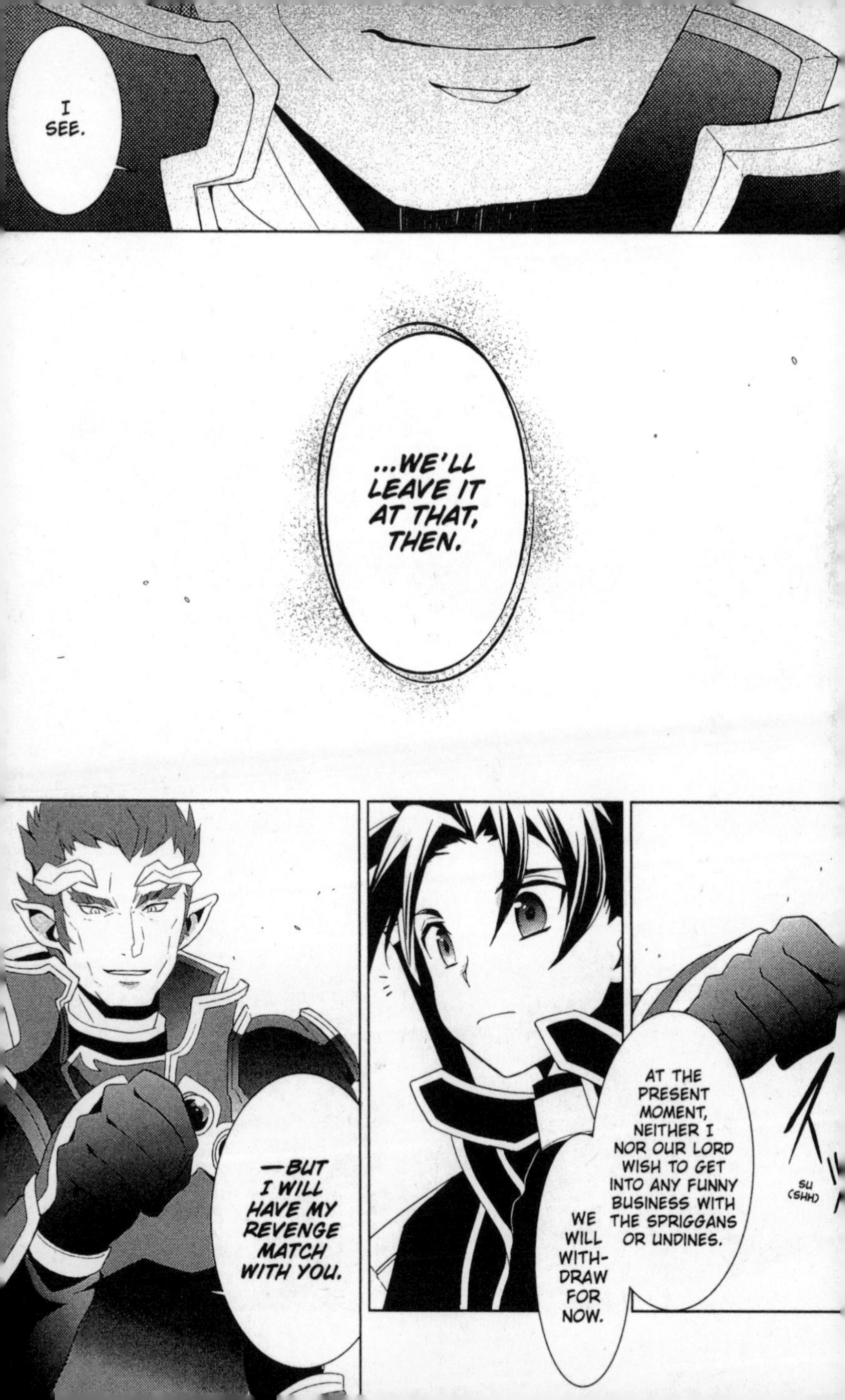

I SEE.
...WE'LL LEAVE IT AT THAT, THEN.
SU (SHH)
AT THE PRESENT MOMENT, NEITHER I NOR OUR LORD WISH TO GET INTO ANY FUNNY BUSINESS WITH THE SPRIGGANS OR UNDINES.
WE WILL WITH-DRAW FOR NOW.
—BUT I WILL HAVE MY REVENGE MATCH WITH YOU.

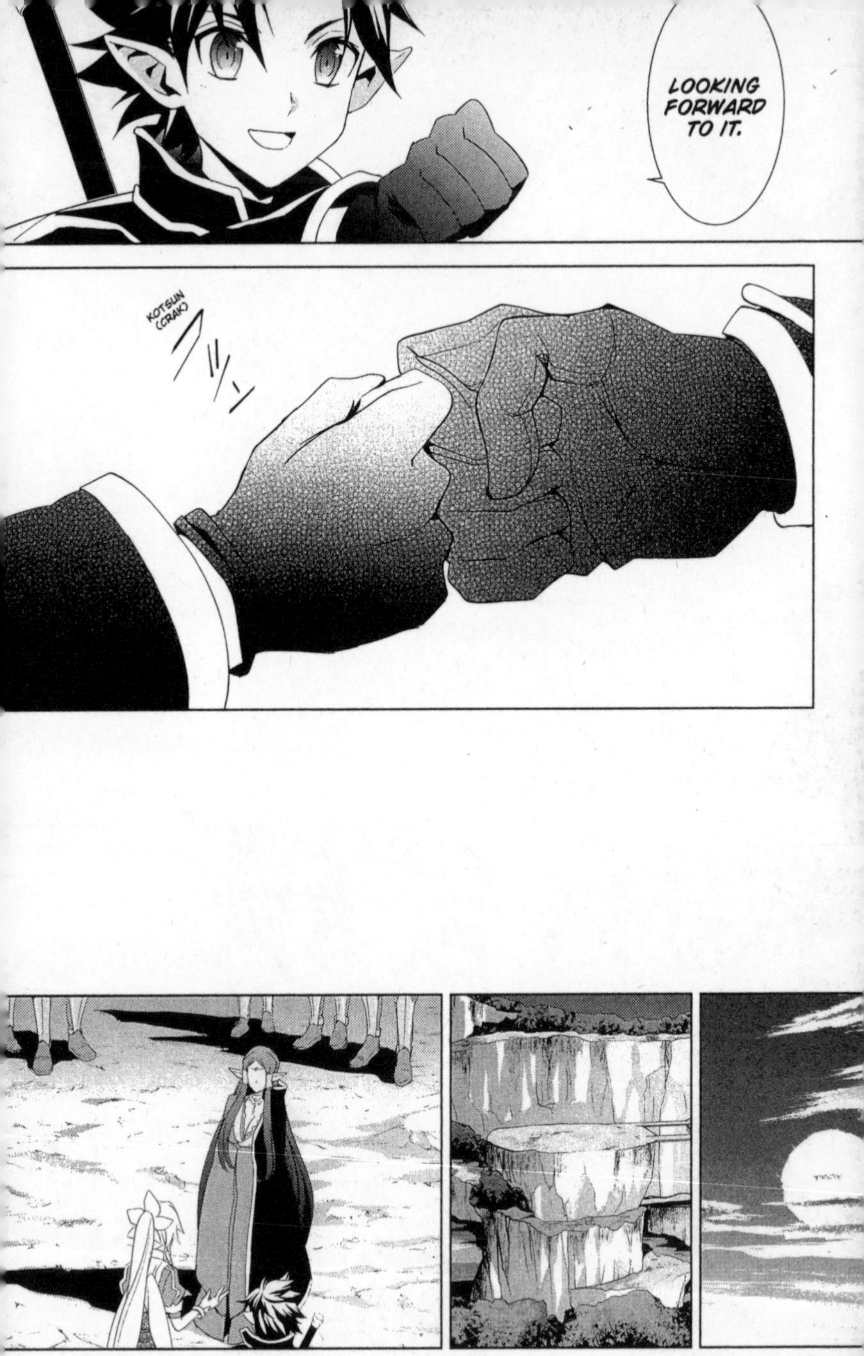
LOOKING FORWARD TO IT.
KOTSUN (CRAK)

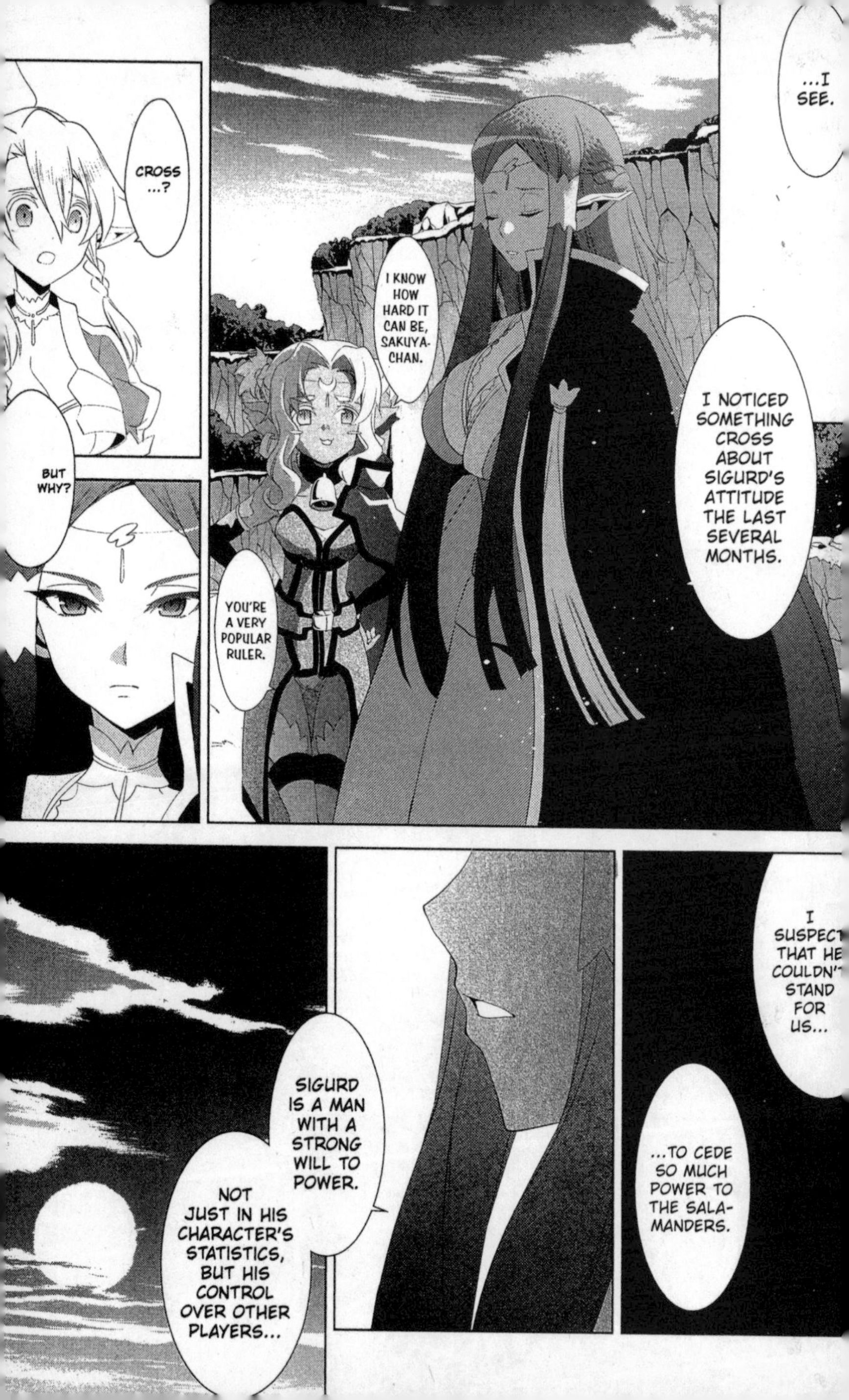
...I SEE.
I NOTICED SOMETHING CROSS ABOUT SIGURD'S ATTITUDE THE LAST SEVERAL MONTHS.
I KNOW HOW HARD IT CAN BE, SAKUYA-CHAN.
YOU'RE A VERY POPULAR RULER.
CROSS ...?
BUT WHY?
I SUSPECT THAT HE COULDN'T STAND FOR US...
...TO CEDE SO MUCH POWER TO THE SALA-MANDERS.
SIGURD IS A MAN WITH A STRONG WILL TO POWER.
NOT JUST IN HIS CHARACTER'S STATISTICS, BUT HIS CONTROL OVER OTHER PLAYERS...

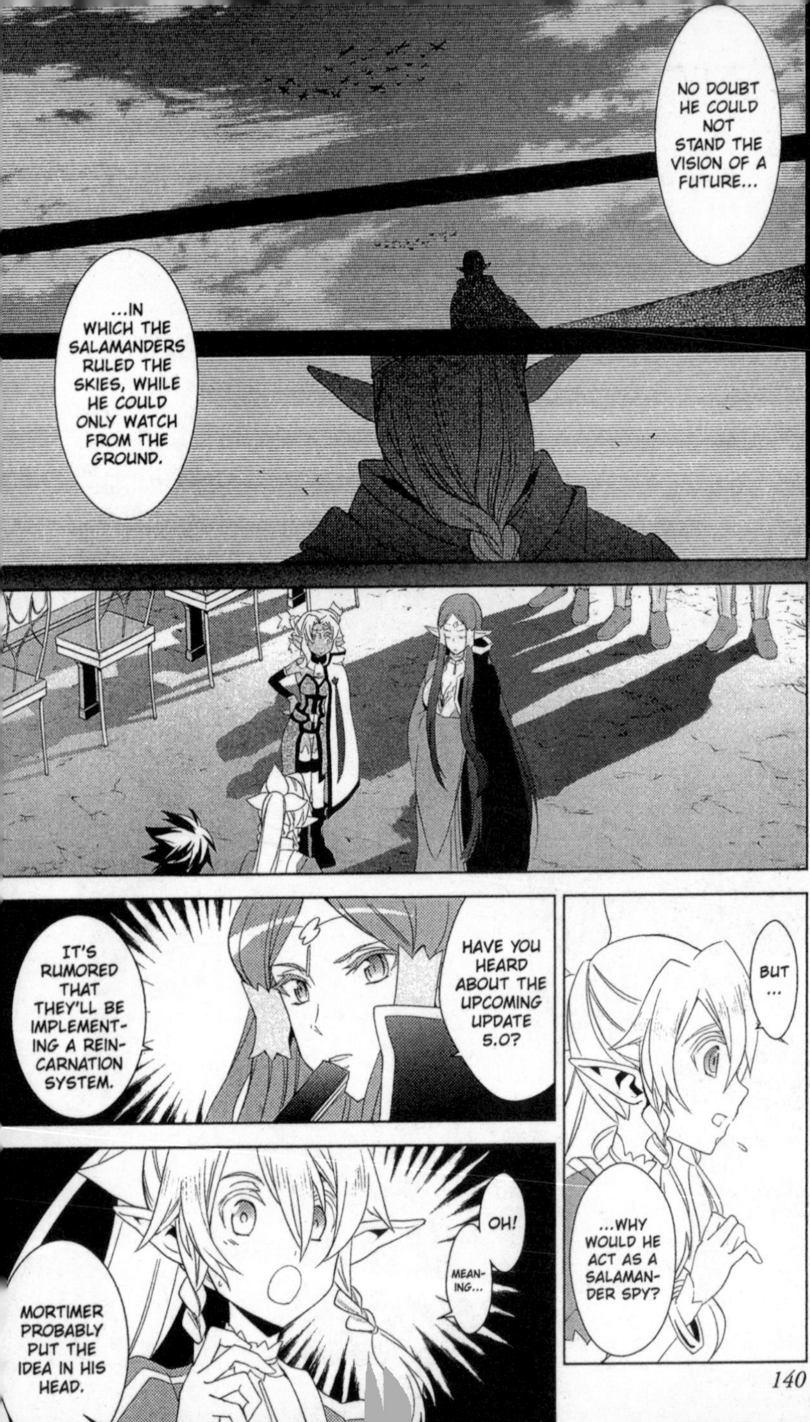
NO DOUBT HE COULD NOT STAND THE VISION OF A FUTURE...
...IN WHICH THE SALAMANDERS RULED THE SKIES, WHILE HE COULD ONLY WATCH FROM THE GROUND.
BUT...
...WHY WOULD HE ACT AS A SALAMANDER SPY?
HAVE YOU HEARD ABOUT THE UPCOMING UPDATE 5.0?
IT'S RUMORED THAT THEY'LL BE IMPLEMENTING A REINCARNATION SYSTEM.
OH!
MEANING...
MORTIMER PROBABLY PUT THE IDEA IN HIS HEAD.

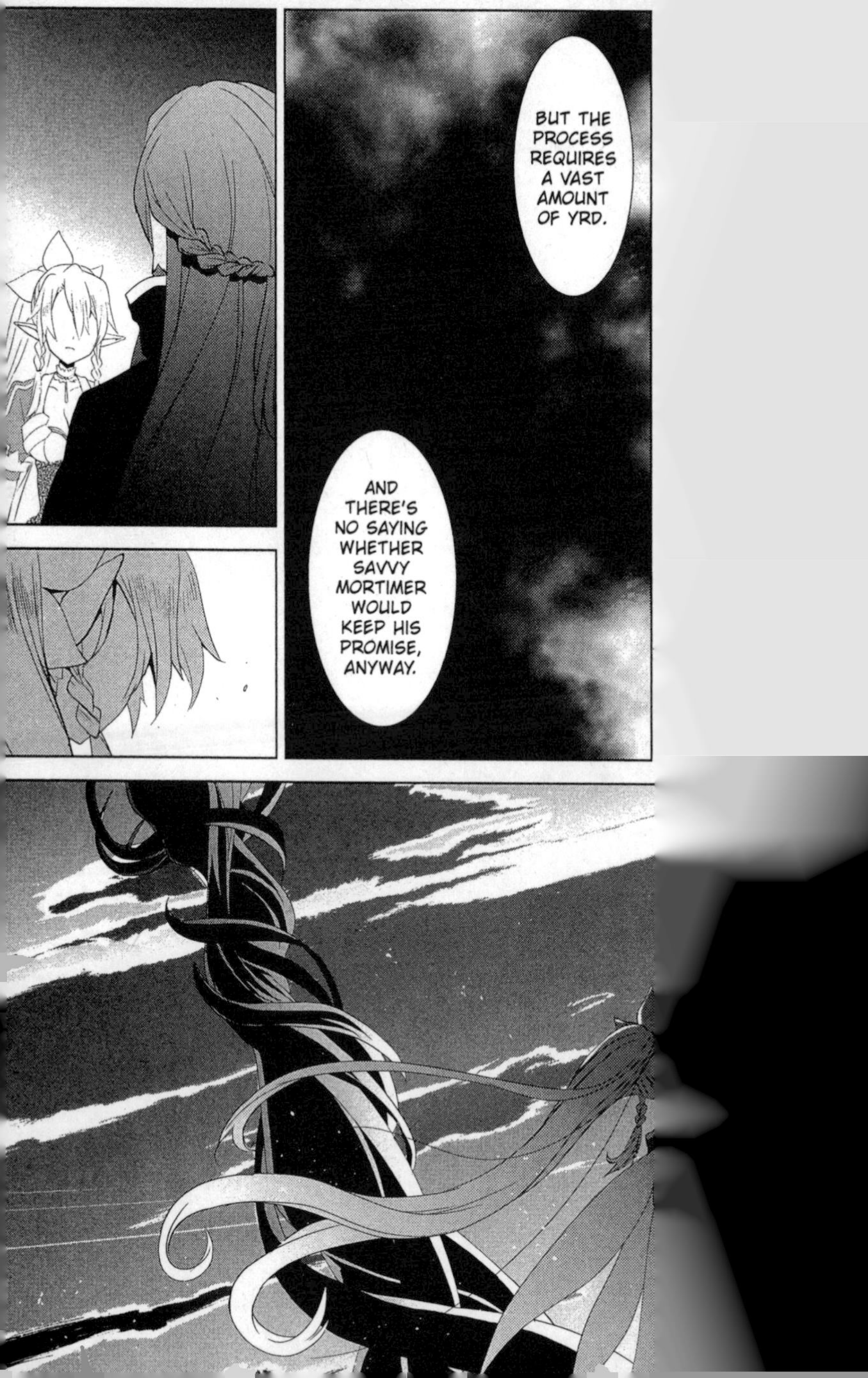
BUT THE PROCESS REQUIRES A VAST AMOUNT OF YRD.
AND THERE'S NO SAYING WHETHER SAVVY MORTIMER WOULD KEEP HIS PROMISE, ANYWAY.

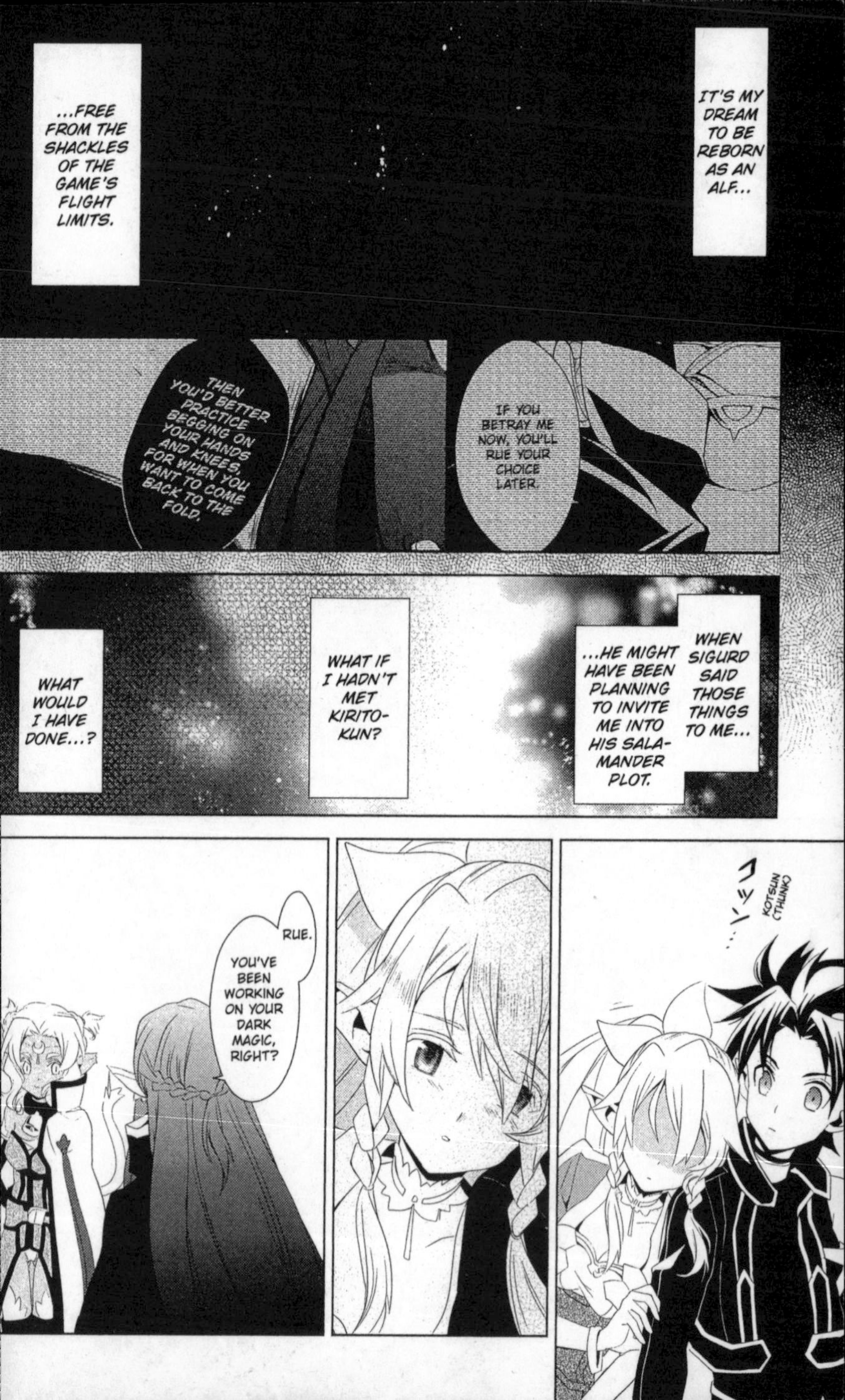
IT'S MY DREAM TO BE REBORN AS AN ALF...
...FREE FROM THE SHACKLES OF THE GAME'S FLIGHT LIMITS.
IF YOU BETRAY ME NOW, YOU'LL RUE YOUR CHOICE LATER.
THEN YOU'D BETTER PRACTICE BEGGING ON YOUR HANDS AND KNEES, FOR WHEN YOU WANT TO COME BACK TO THE FOLD.
WHEN SIGURD SAID THOSE THINGS TO ME...
...HE MIGHT HAVE BEEN PLANNING TO INVITE ME INTO HIS SALAMANDER PLOT.
WHAT IF I HADN'T MET KIRITO-KUN?
WHAT WOULD I HAVE DONE...?
コツン…
KOTSUN (THUNK)
RUE.
YOU'VE BEEN WORKING ON YOUR DARK MAGIC, RIGHT?

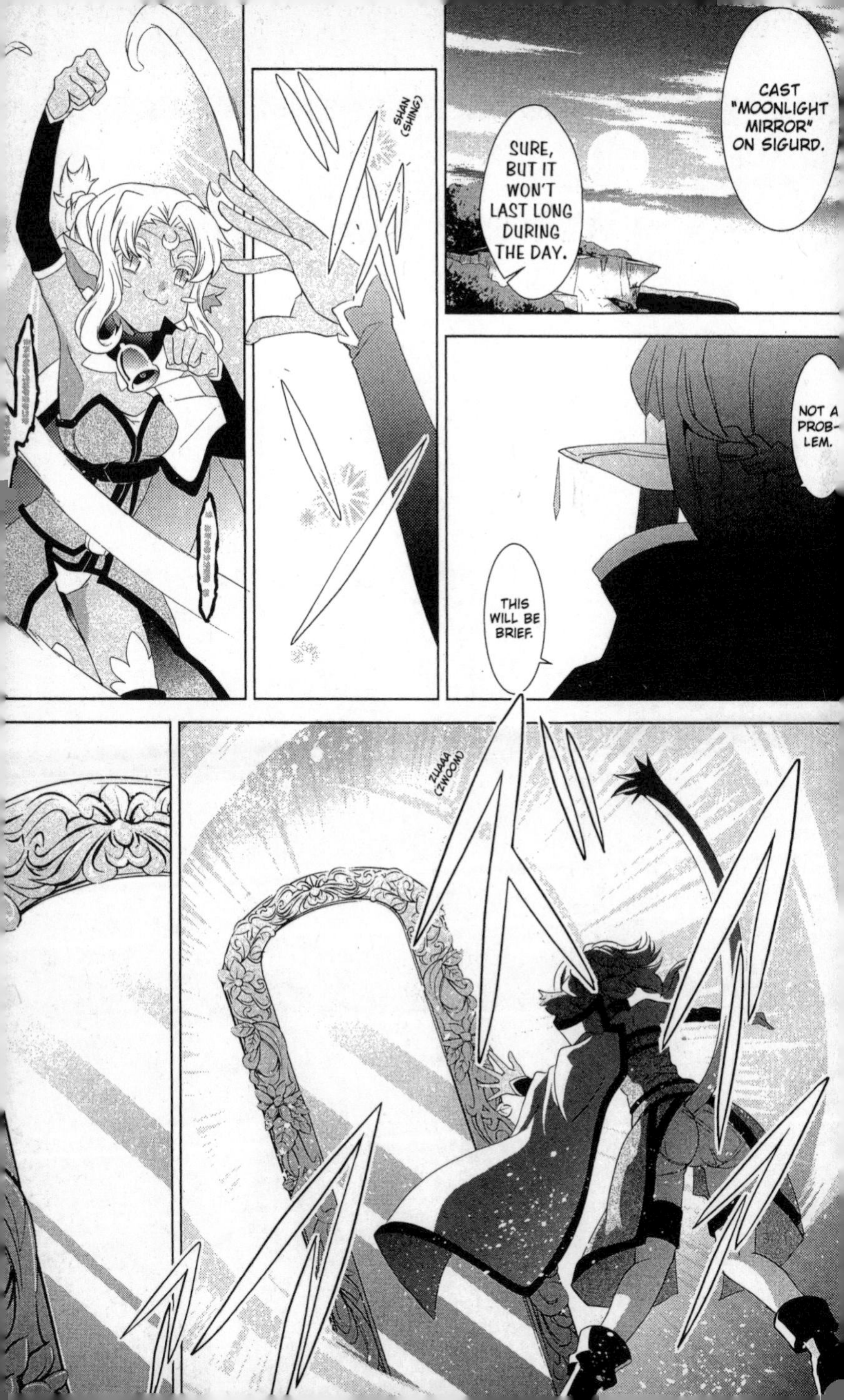
CAST "MOONLIGHT MIRROR" ON SIGURD.
SURE, BUT IT WON'T LAST LONG DURING THE DAY.
NOT A PROB-LEM.
THIS WILL BE BRIEF.
SHAN (SHING)
ZUAAA (ZWOOM)

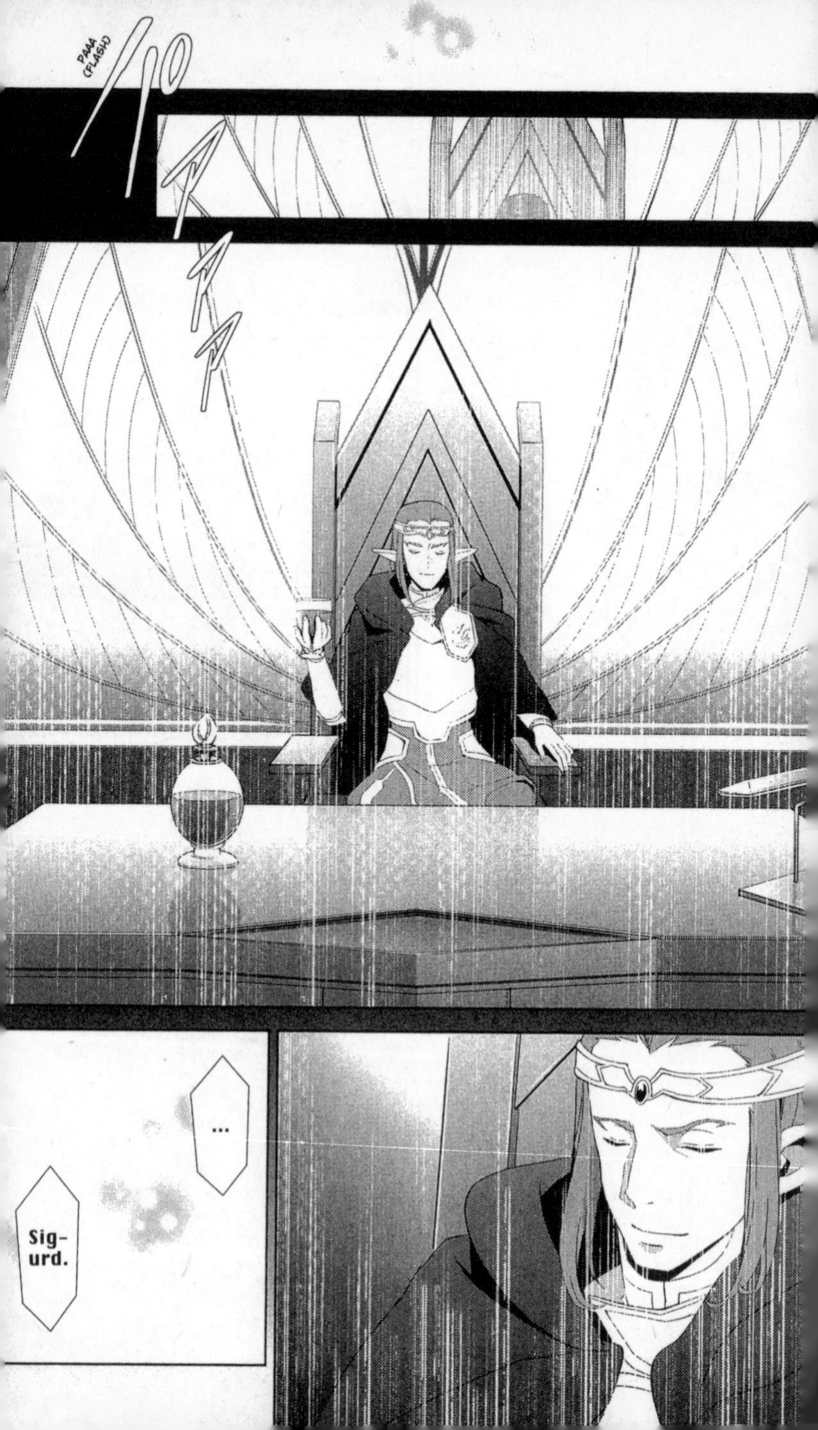
PAAA (FLASH)
...
Sig-urd.

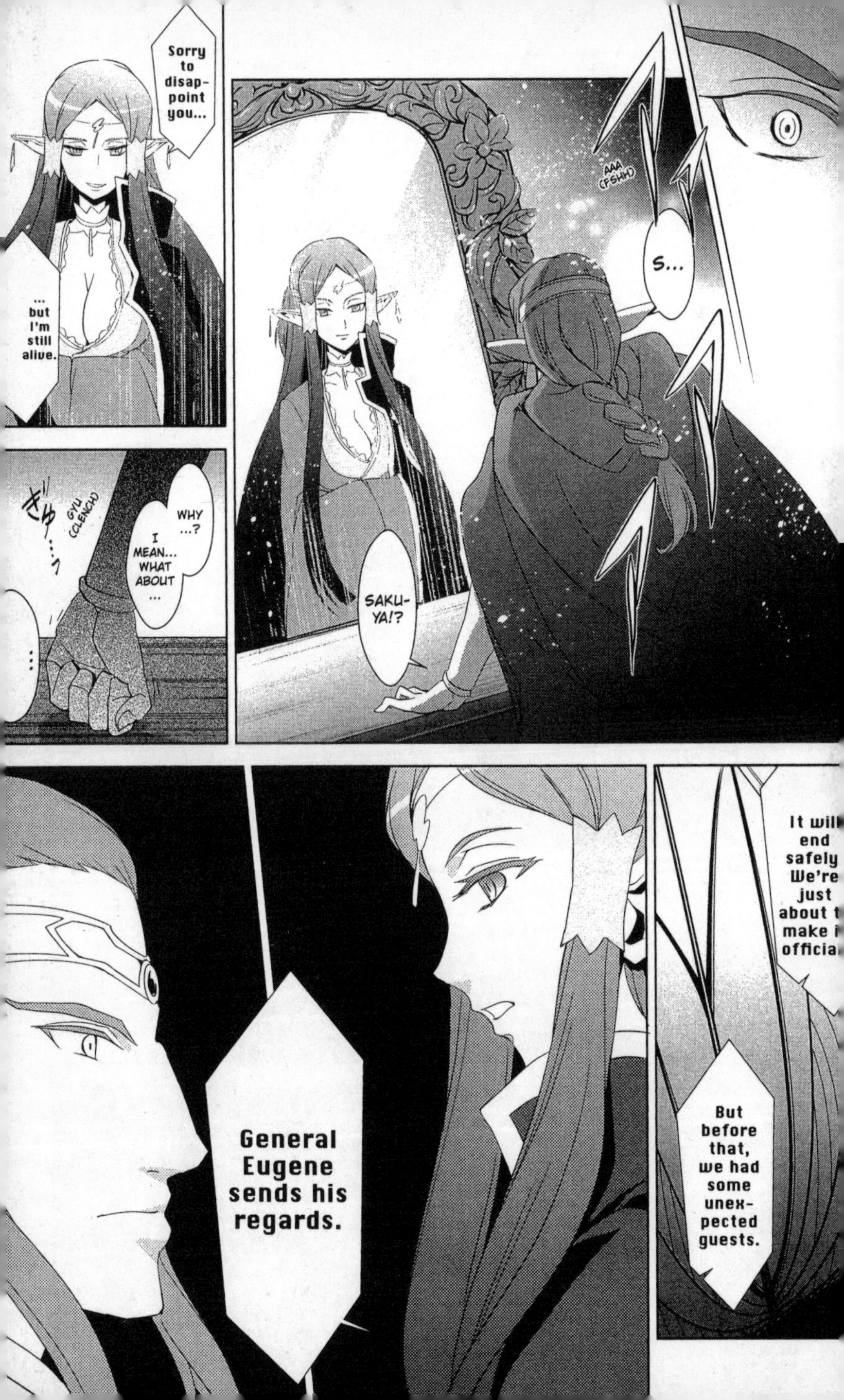
AAA (FSHH)
S...
SAKU-YA!?
Sorry to disap-point you...
... but I'm still alive.
WHY ...? I MEAN... WHAT ABOUT ...
GYU (CLENCH)
ぎゅ…っ
...
It wil end safely We're just about t make i officia
But before that, we had some unex-pected guests.
General Eugene sends his regards.

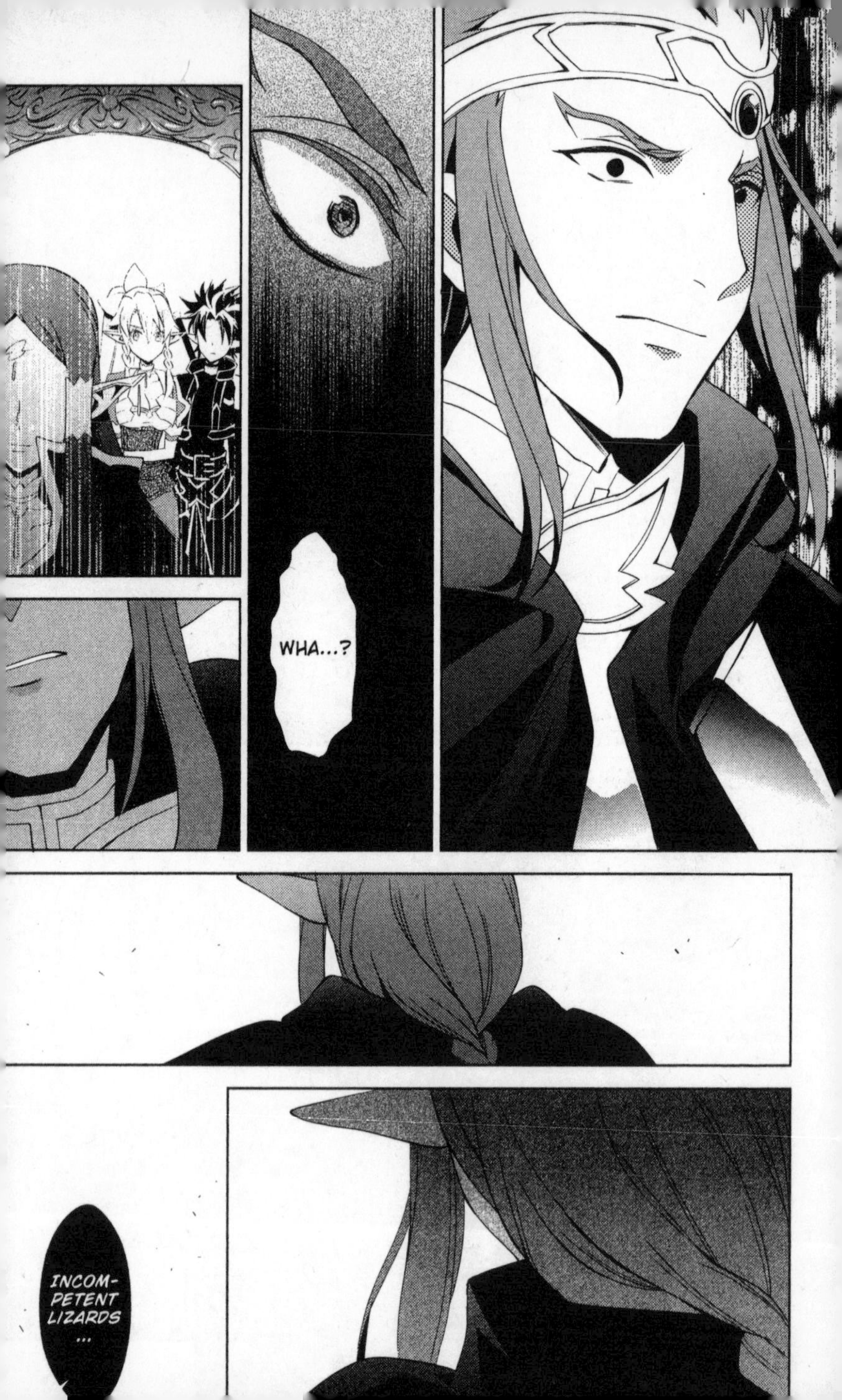
WHA...?
INCOM-PETENT LIZARDS ...

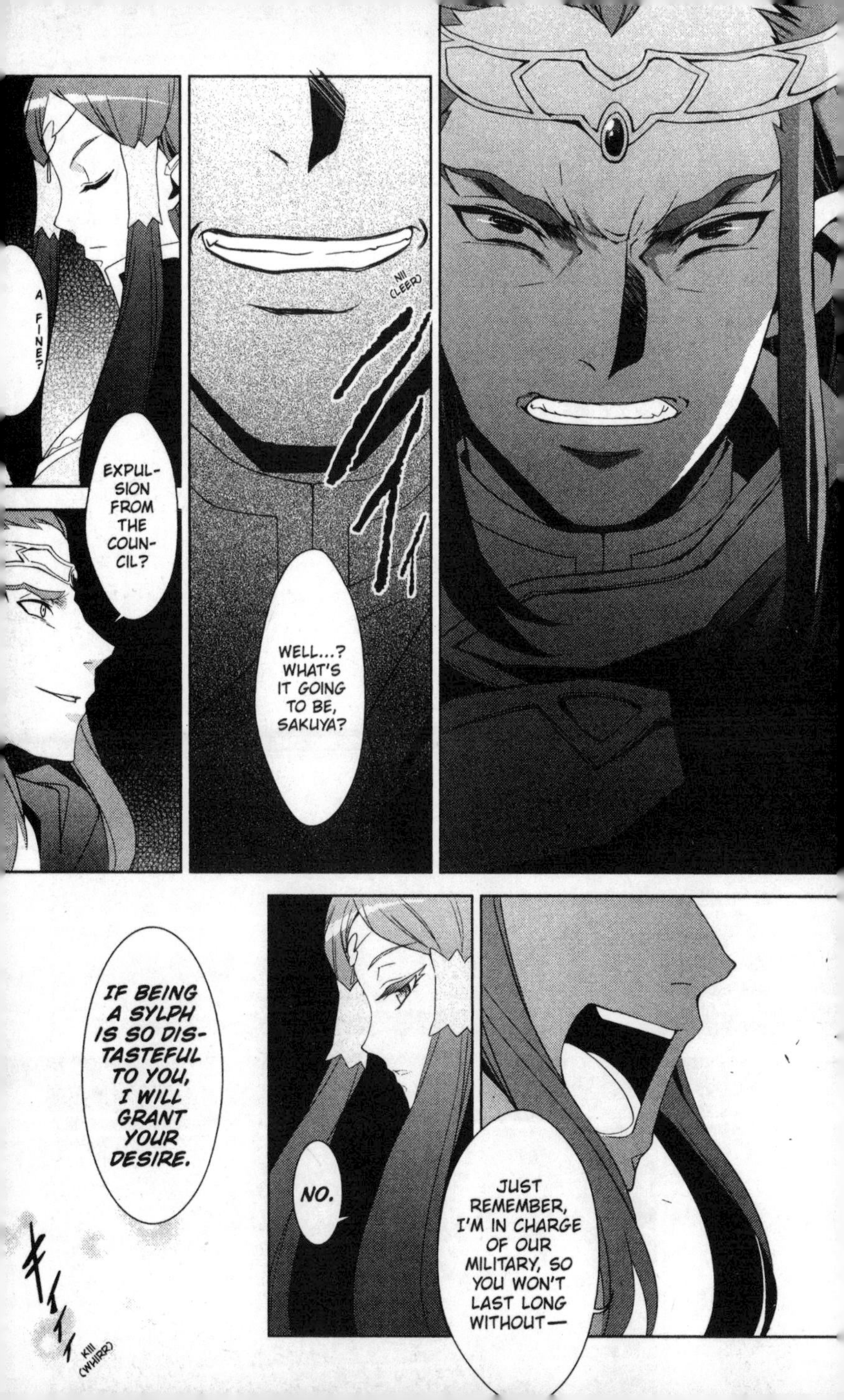
NII (LEER)
WELL...? WHAT'S IT GOING TO BE, SAKUYA?
A FINE?
EXPULSION FROM THE COUNCIL?
JUST REMEMBER, I'M IN CHARGE OF OUR MILITARY, SO YOU WON'T LAST LONG WITHOUT—
NO.
IF BEING A SYLPH IS SO DISTASTEFUL TO YOU, I WILL GRANT YOUR DESIRE.
KIII (WHIRR)

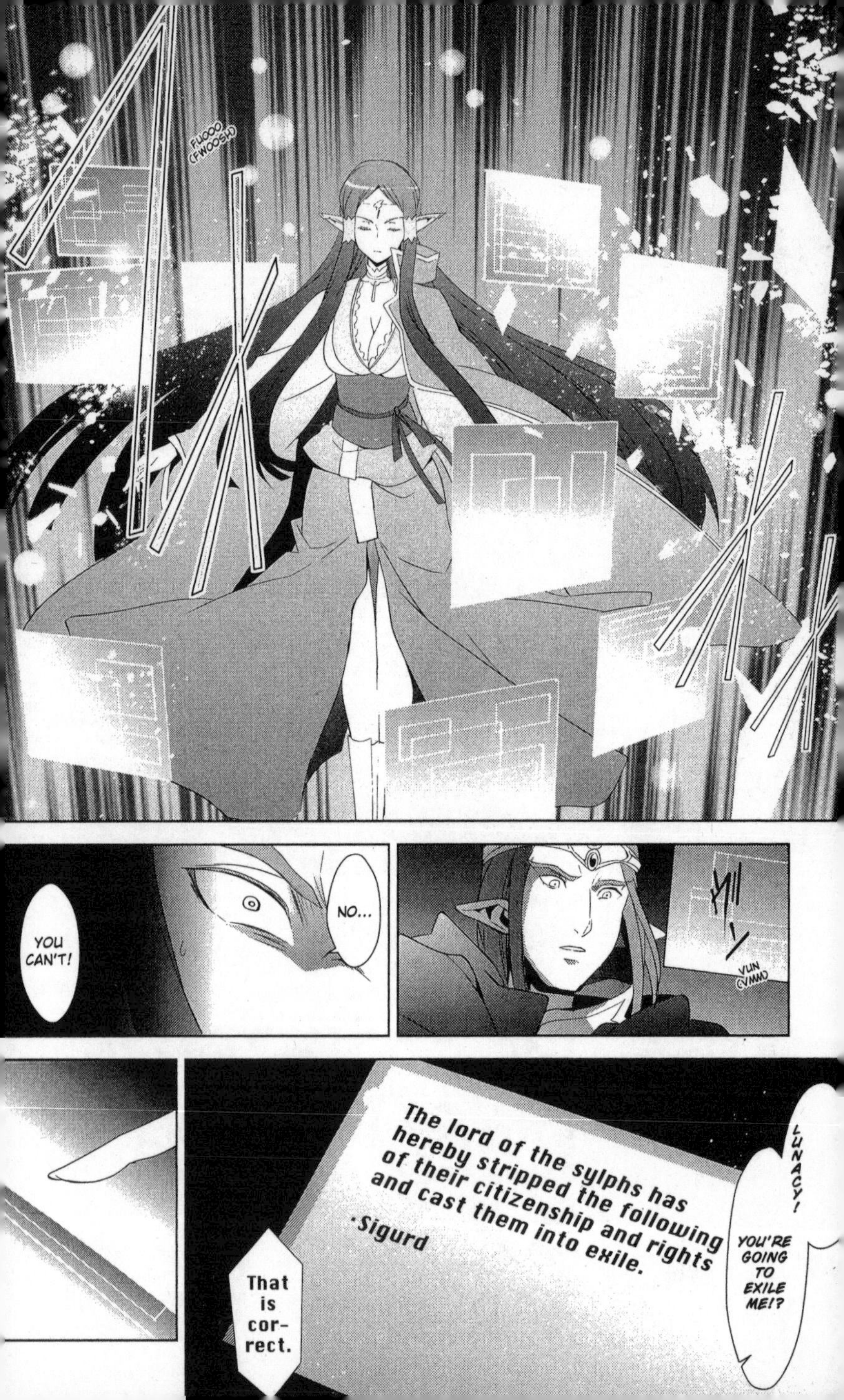
FUOOO (FWOOSH)
VUN (VMM)
NO...
YOU CAN'T!
LUNACY!
YOU'RE GOING TO EXILE ME!?
The lord of the sylphs has hereby stripped the following of their citizenship and rights and cast them into exile.
-Sigurd
That is cor-rect.

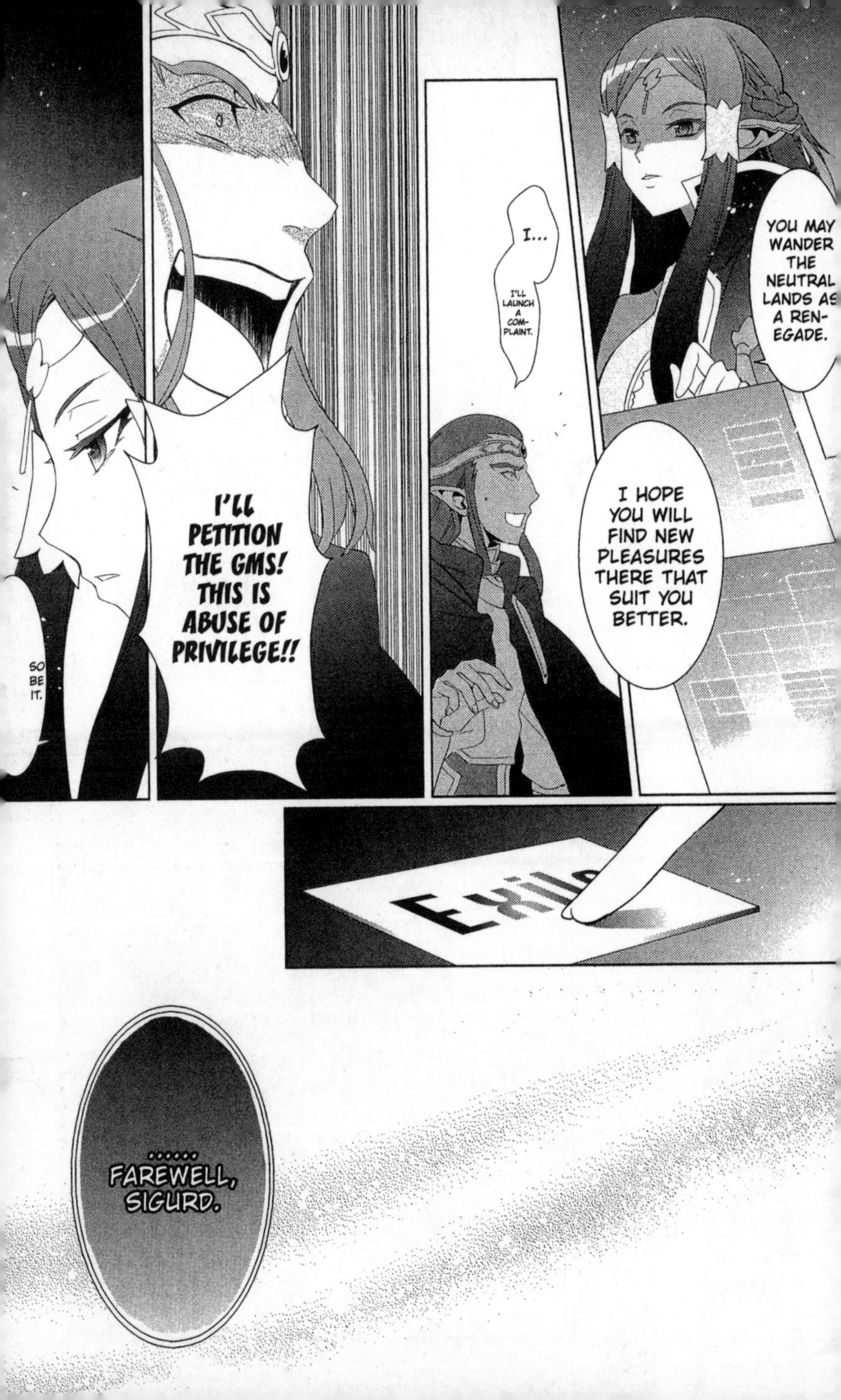
YOU MAY WANDER THE NEUTRAL LANDS AS A RENEGADE.
I HOPE YOU WILL FIND NEW PLEASURES THERE THAT SUIT YOU BETTER.
I...
I'LL LAUNCH A COMPLAINT.
I'LL PETITION THE GMS! THIS IS ABUSE OF PRIVILEGE!!
SO BE IT.
...... FAREWELL, SIGURD.

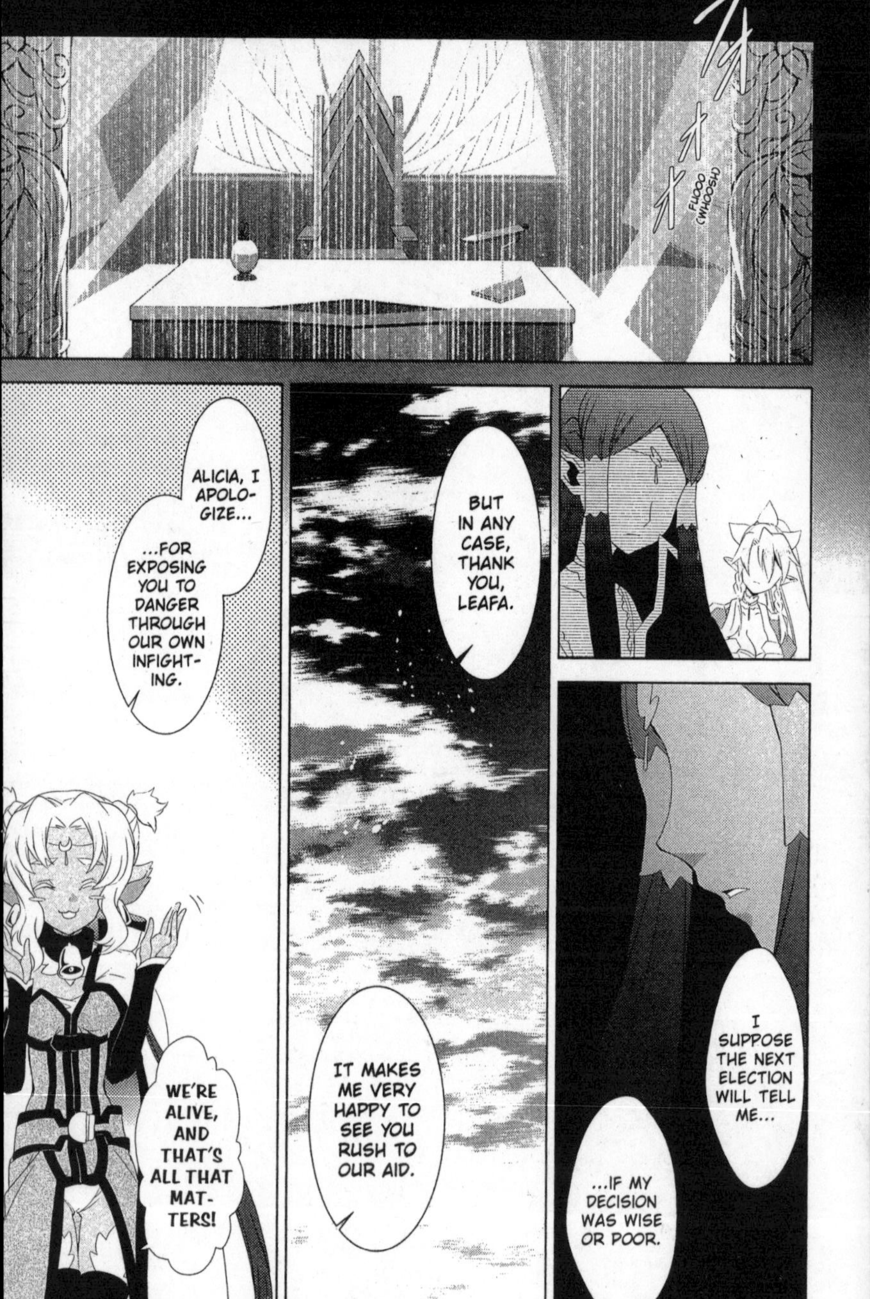
FUOOO (WHOOSH)
I SUPPOSE THE NEXT ELECTION WILL TELL ME...
...IF MY DECISION WAS WISE OR POOR.
BUT IN ANY CASE, THANK YOU, LEAFA.
IT MAKES ME VERY HAPPY TO SEE YOU RUSH TO OUR AID.
ALICIA, I APOLOGIZE...
...FOR EXPOSING YOU TO DANGER THROUGH OUR OWN INFIGHTING.
WE'RE ALIVE, AND THAT'S ALL THAT MATTERS!

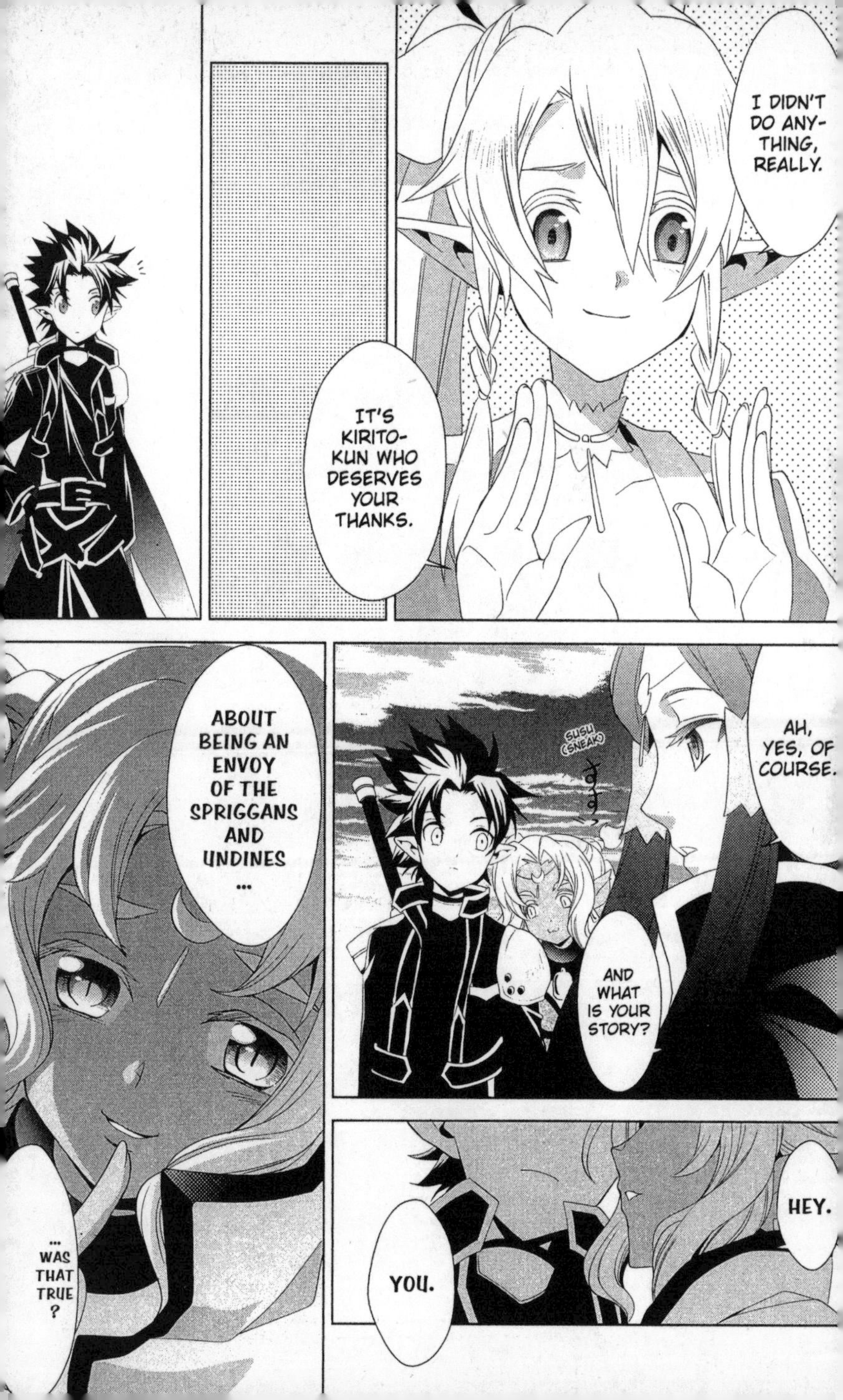
I DIDN'T DO ANYTHING, REALLY.
IT'S KIRITO-KUN WHO DESERVES YOUR THANKS.
AH, YES, OF COURSE.
SUSU (SNEAK)
AND WHAT IS YOUR STORY?
HEY.
YOU.
ABOUT BEING AN ENVOY OF THE SPRIGGANS AND UNDINES ...
... WAS THAT TRUE ?

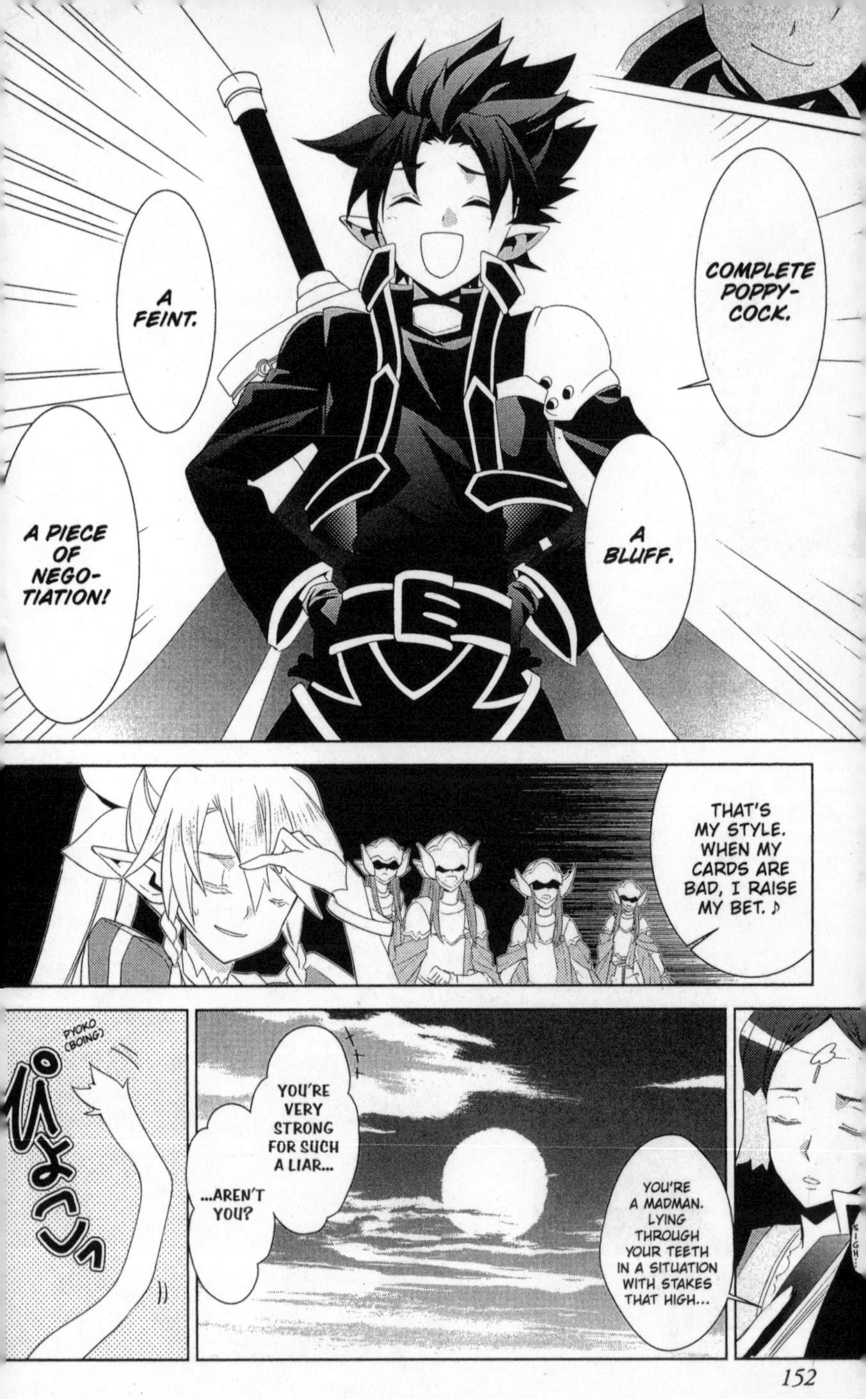
COMPLETE POPPY-COCK.
A FEINT.
A BLUFF.
A PIECE OF NEGO-TIATION!
THAT'S MY STYLE. WHEN MY CARDS ARE BAD, I RAISE MY BET. ♪
YOU'RE A MADMAN. LYING THROUGH YOUR TEETH IN A SITUATION WITH STAKES THAT HIGH...
SIGH...
YOU'RE VERY STRONG FOR SUCH A LIAR...
...AREN'T YOU?
PYOKO (BOING)

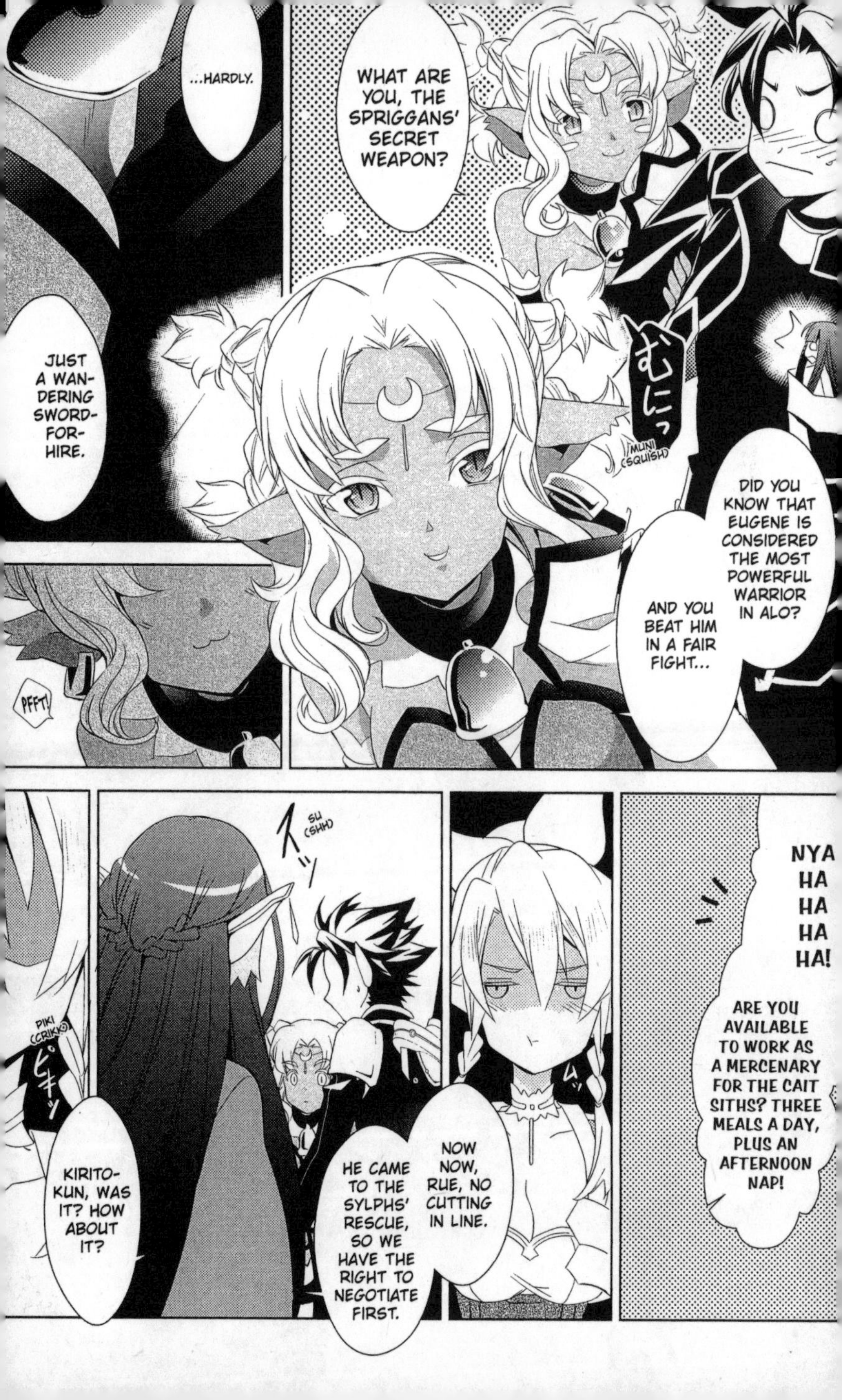
WHAT ARE YOU, THE SPRIGGANS' SECRET WEAPON?
むにっ
MUNI (SQUISH)
DID YOU KNOW THAT EUGENE IS CONSIDERED THE MOST POWERFUL WARRIOR IN ALO?
AND YOU BEAT HIM IN A FAIR FIGHT...
...HARDLY.
JUST A WANDERING SWORD-FOR-HIRE.
PFFT!
NYA HA HA HA HA!
ARE YOU AVAILABLE TO WORK AS A MERCENARY FOR THE CAIT SITHS? THREE MEALS A DAY, PLUS AN AFTERNOON NAP!
NOW NOW, RUE, NO CUTTING IN LINE.
HE CAME TO THE SYLPHS' RESCUE, SO WE HAVE THE RIGHT TO NEGOTIATE FIRST.
SU (SHH)
PIKI (CRIKK)
KIRITO-KUN, WAS IT? HOW ABOUT IT?

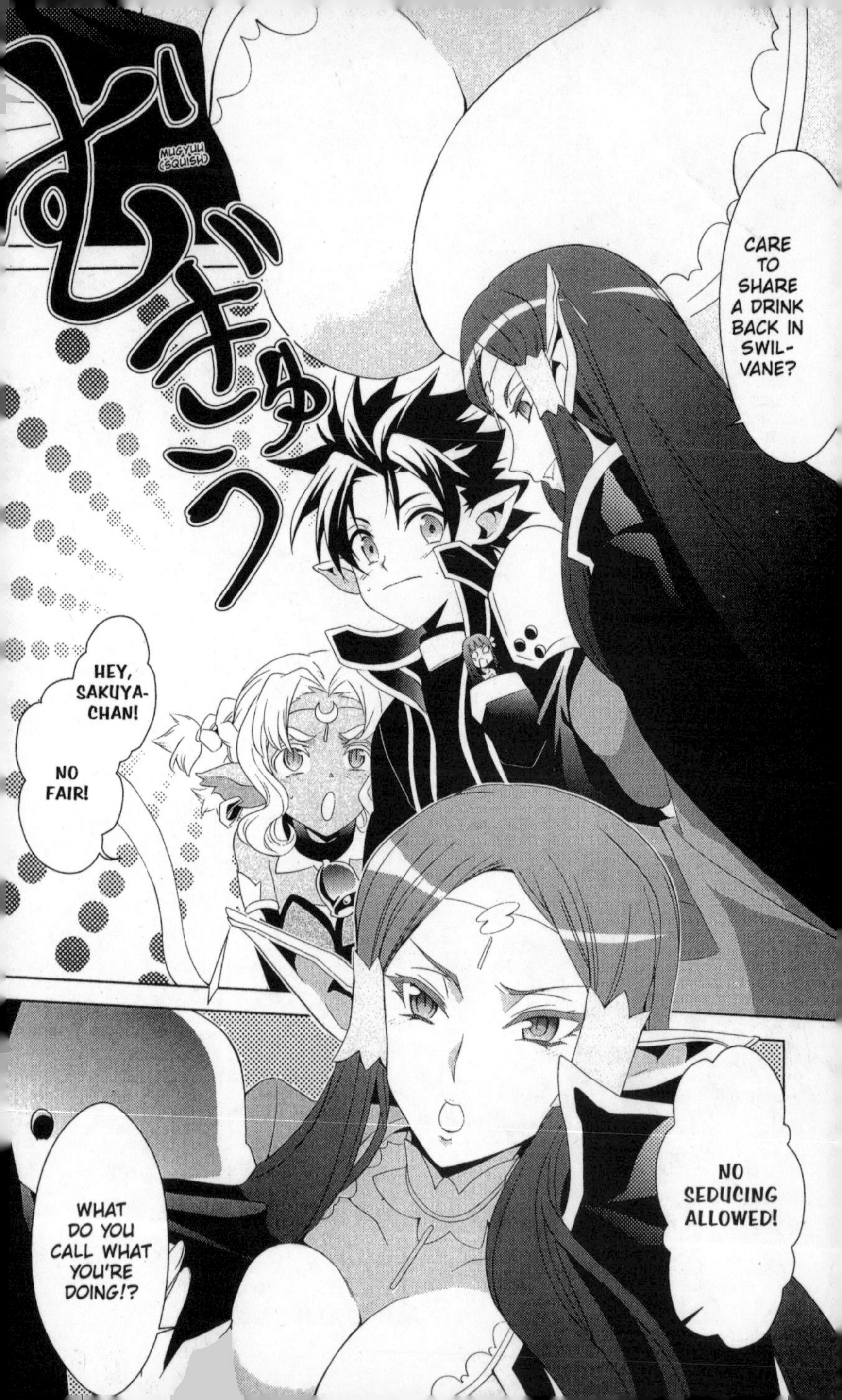
CARE TO SHARE A DRINK BACK IN SWIL-VANE?
むぎゅう
MUGYUU (SQUISH)
HEY, SAKUYA-CHAN!
NO FAIR!
NO SEDUCING ALLOWED!
WHAT DO YOU CALL WHAT YOU'RE DOING!?

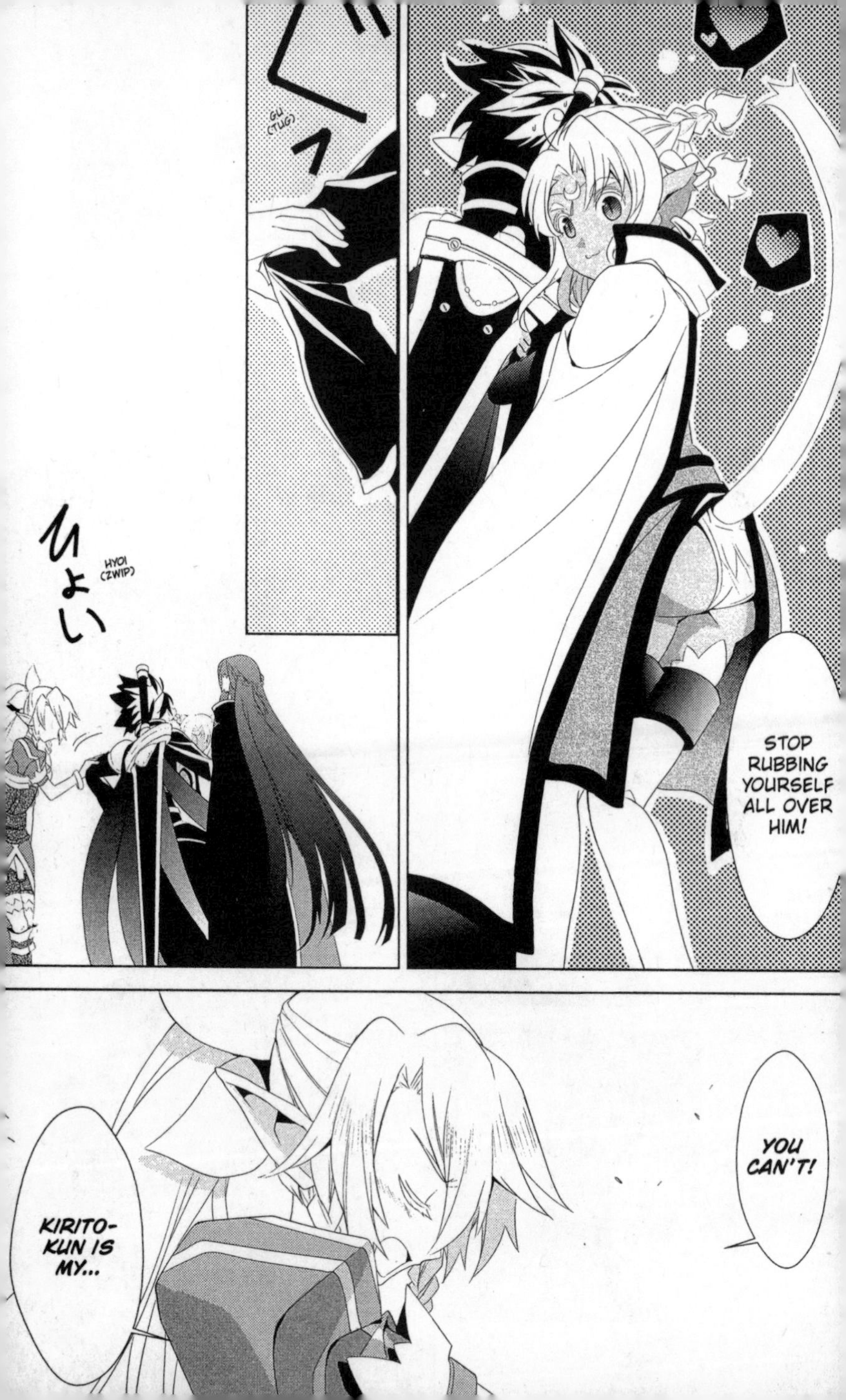
STOP RUBBING YOURSELF ALL OVER HIM!
GU (TUG)
ひょい
HYOI (ZWIP)
YOU CAN'T!
KIRITO-KUN IS MY...

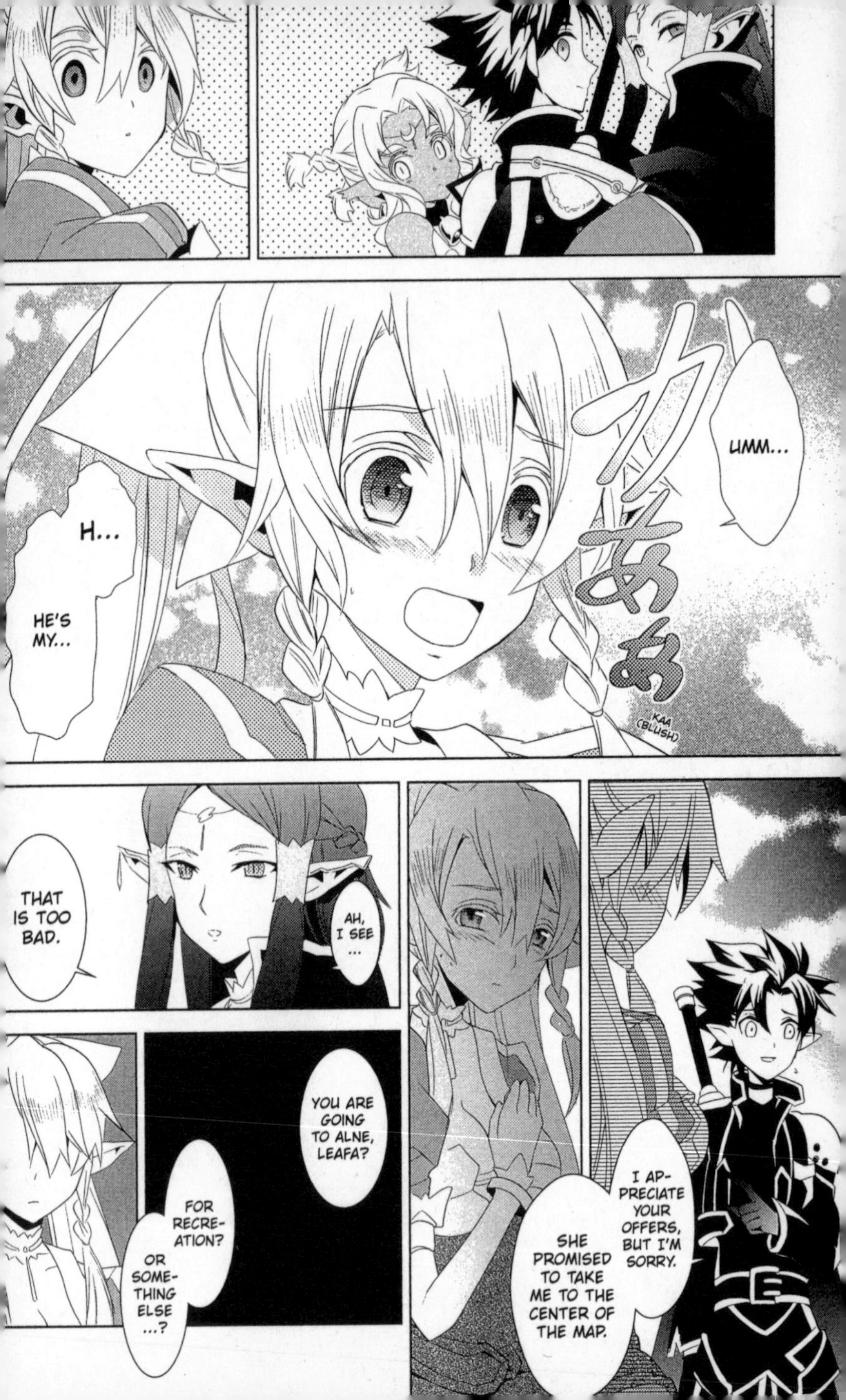
UMM...
カぁぁ
KAA (BLUSH)
H...
HE'S MY...
I APPRECIATE YOUR OFFERS, BUT I'M SORRY.
SHE PROMISED TO TAKE ME TO THE CENTER OF THE MAP.
AH, I SEE...
THAT IS TOO BAD.
YOU ARE GOING TO ALNE, LEAFA?
FOR RECREATION?
OR SOMETHING ELSE...?

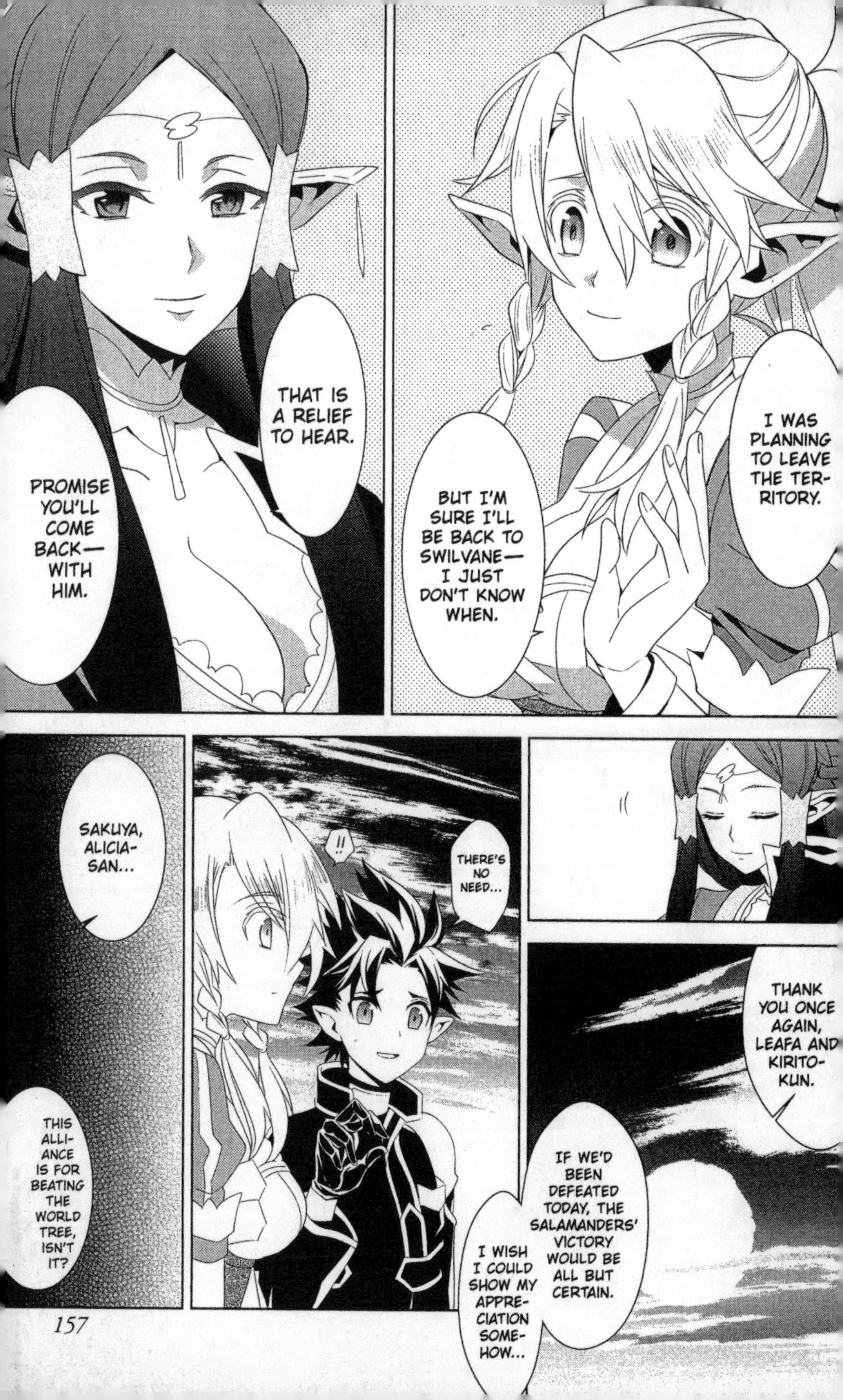
I WAS PLANNING TO LEAVE THE TER-RITORY.
BUT I'M SURE I'LL BE BACK TO SWILVANE— I JUST DON'T KNOW WHEN.
THAT IS A RELIEF TO HEAR.
PROMISE YOU'LL COME BACK— WITH HIM.
THANK YOU ONCE AGAIN, LEAFA AND KIRITO-KUN.
IF WE'D BEEN DEFEATED TODAY, THE SALAMANDERS' VICTORY WOULD BE ALL BUT CERTAIN.
I WISH I COULD SHOW MY APPRECIATION SOME-HOW...
!!
THERE'S NO NEED...
SAKUYA, ALICIA-SAN...
THIS ALLI-ANCE IS FOR BEATING THE WORLD TREE, ISN'T IT?

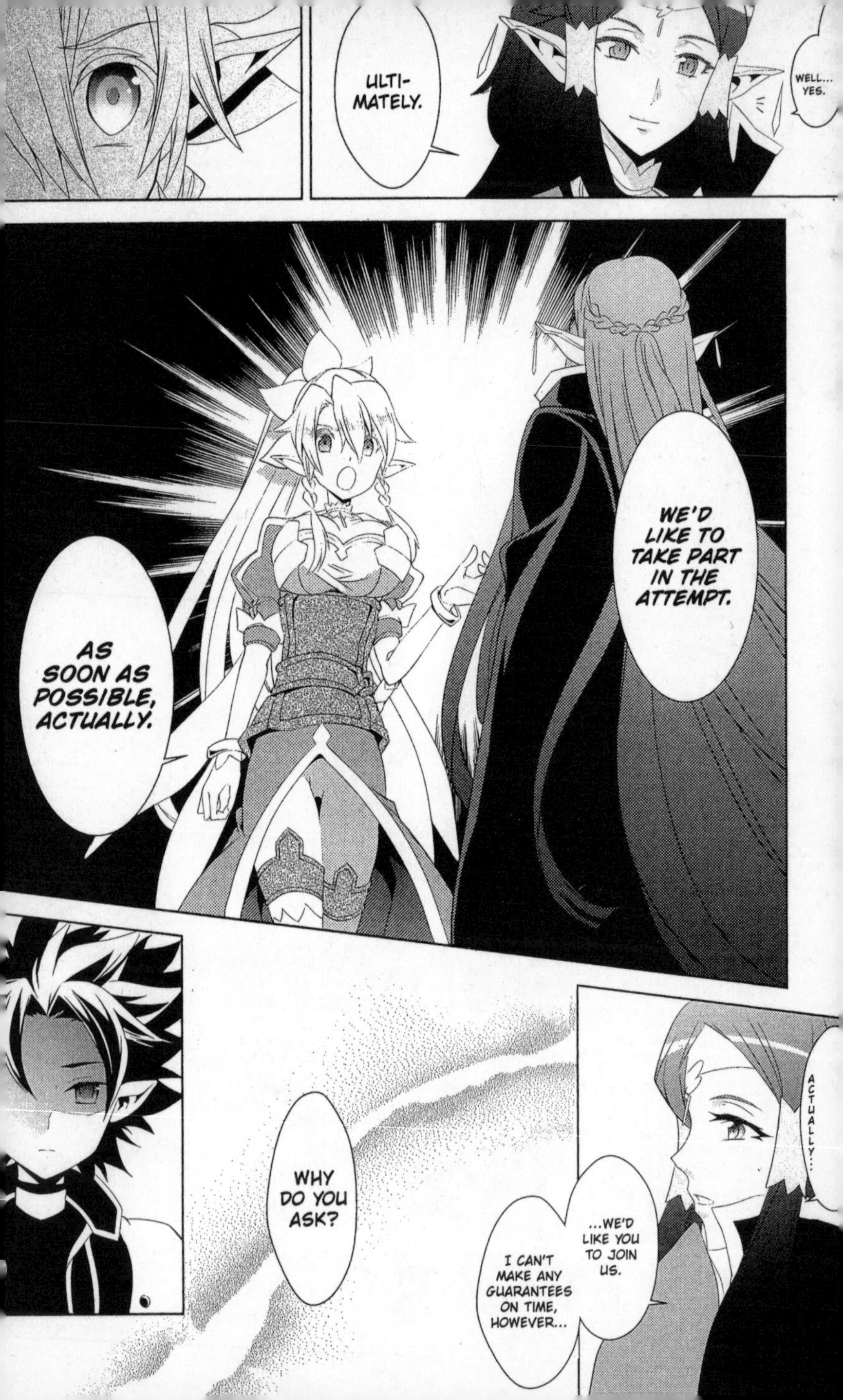
WELL... YES.
ULTI-MATELY.
WE'D LIKE TO TAKE PART IN THE ATTEMPT.
AS SOON AS POSSIBLE, ACTUALLY.
WHY DO YOU ASK?
ACTUALLY...
...WE'D LIKE YOU TO JOIN US.
I CAN'T MAKE ANY GUARANTEES ON TIME, HOWEVER...

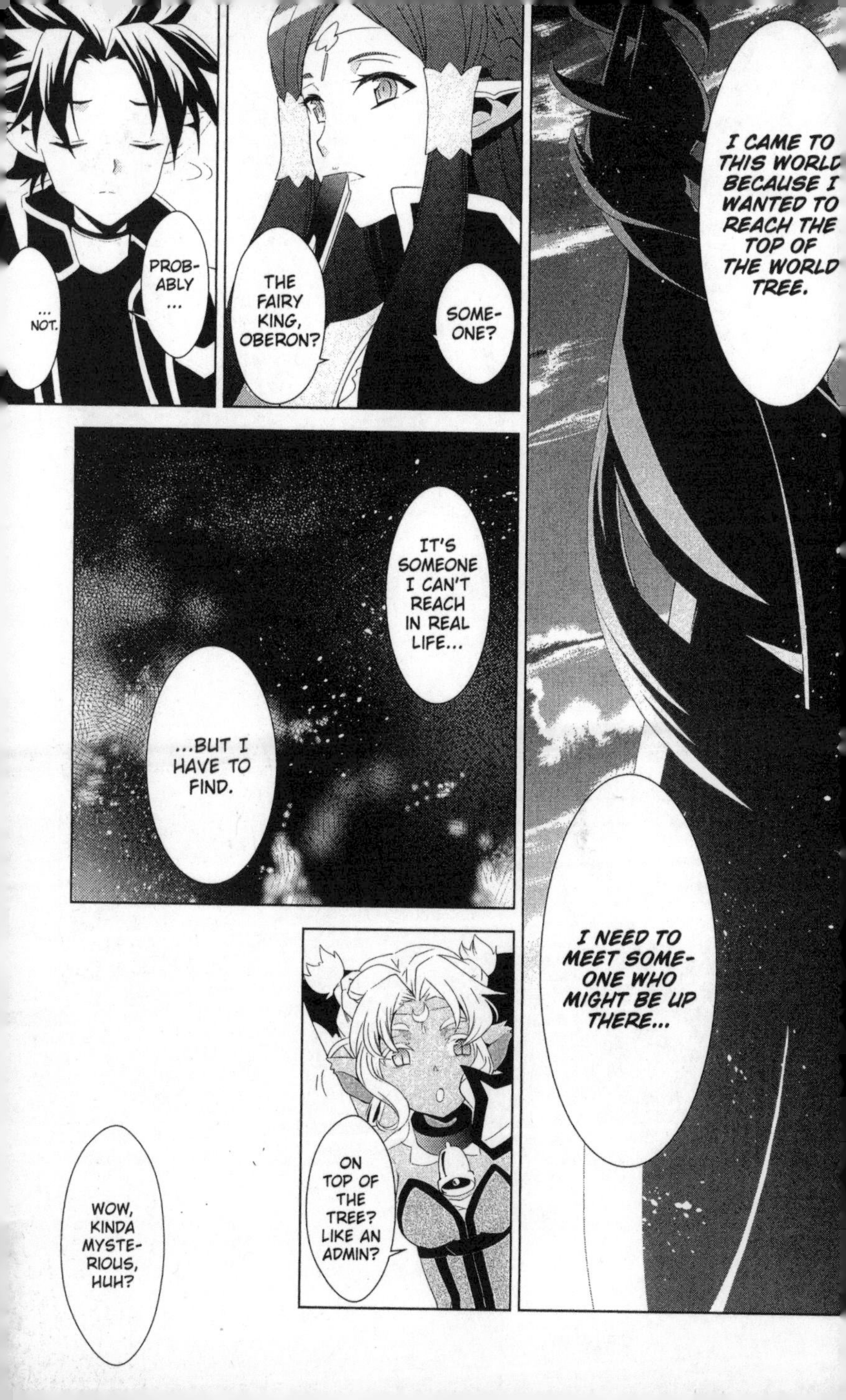
I CAME TO THIS WORLD BECAUSE I WANTED TO REACH THE TOP OF THE WORLD TREE.
I NEED TO MEET SOME-ONE WHO MIGHT BE UP THERE...
SOME-ONE?
THE FAIRY KING, OBERON?
PROB-ABLY...
...NOT.
IT'S SOMEONE I CAN'T REACH IN REAL LIFE...
...BUT I HAVE TO FIND.
ON TOP OF THE TREE? LIKE AN ADMIN?
WOW, KINDA MYSTE-RIOUS, HUH?

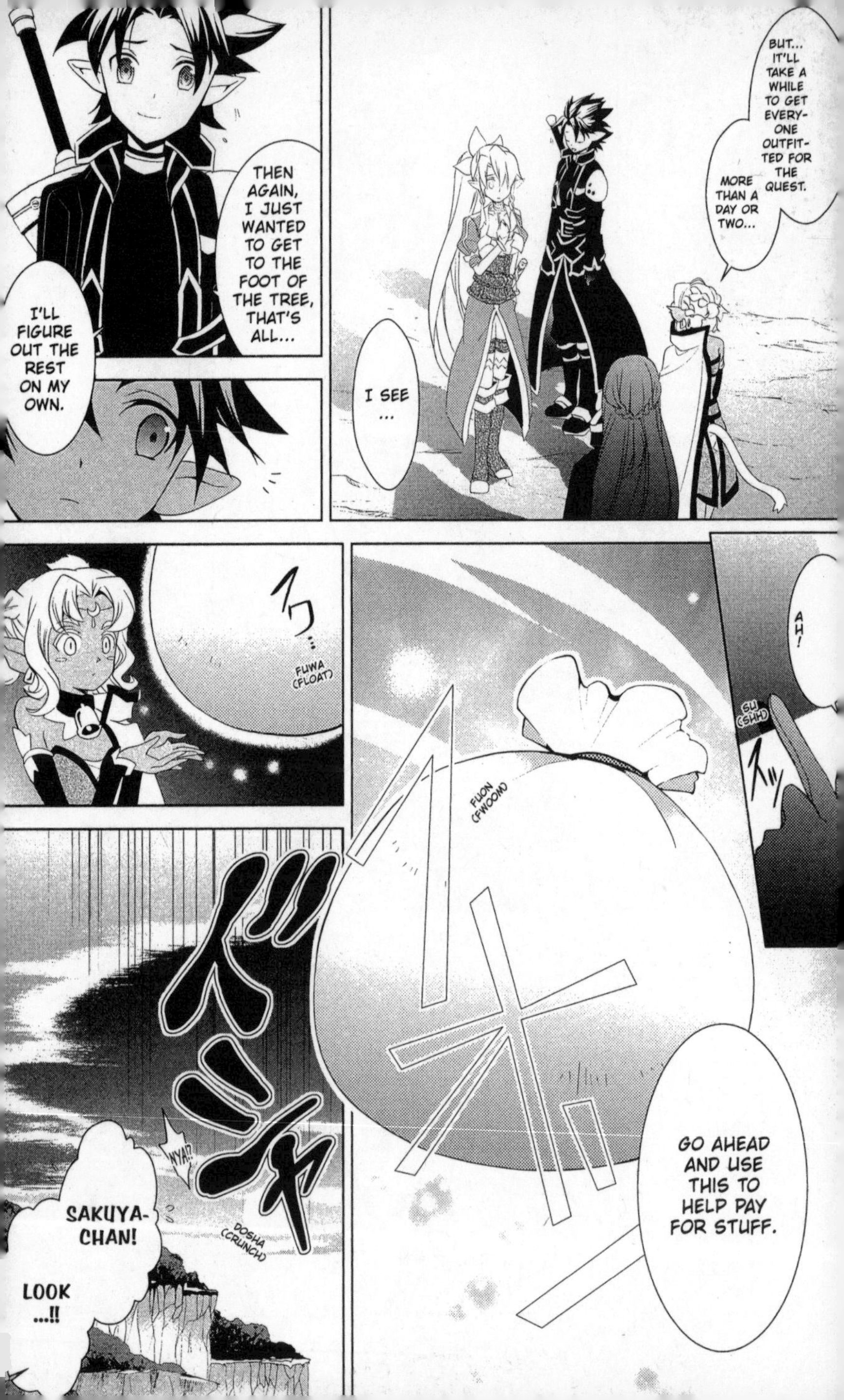
BUT... IT'LL TAKE A WHILE TO GET EVERY-ONE OUTFIT-TED FOR THE QUEST.
MORE THAN A DAY OR TWO...
I SEE...
THEN AGAIN, I JUST WANTED TO GET TO THE FOOT OF THE TREE, THAT'S ALL...
I'LL FIGURE OUT THE REST ON MY OWN.
AH!
SU (SHH)
FUON (FWOOM)
GO AHEAD AND USE THIS TO HELP PAY FOR STUFF.
FUWA (FLOAT)
NYA!?
DOSHA (CRUNCH)
SAKUYA-CHAN!
LOOK ...!!

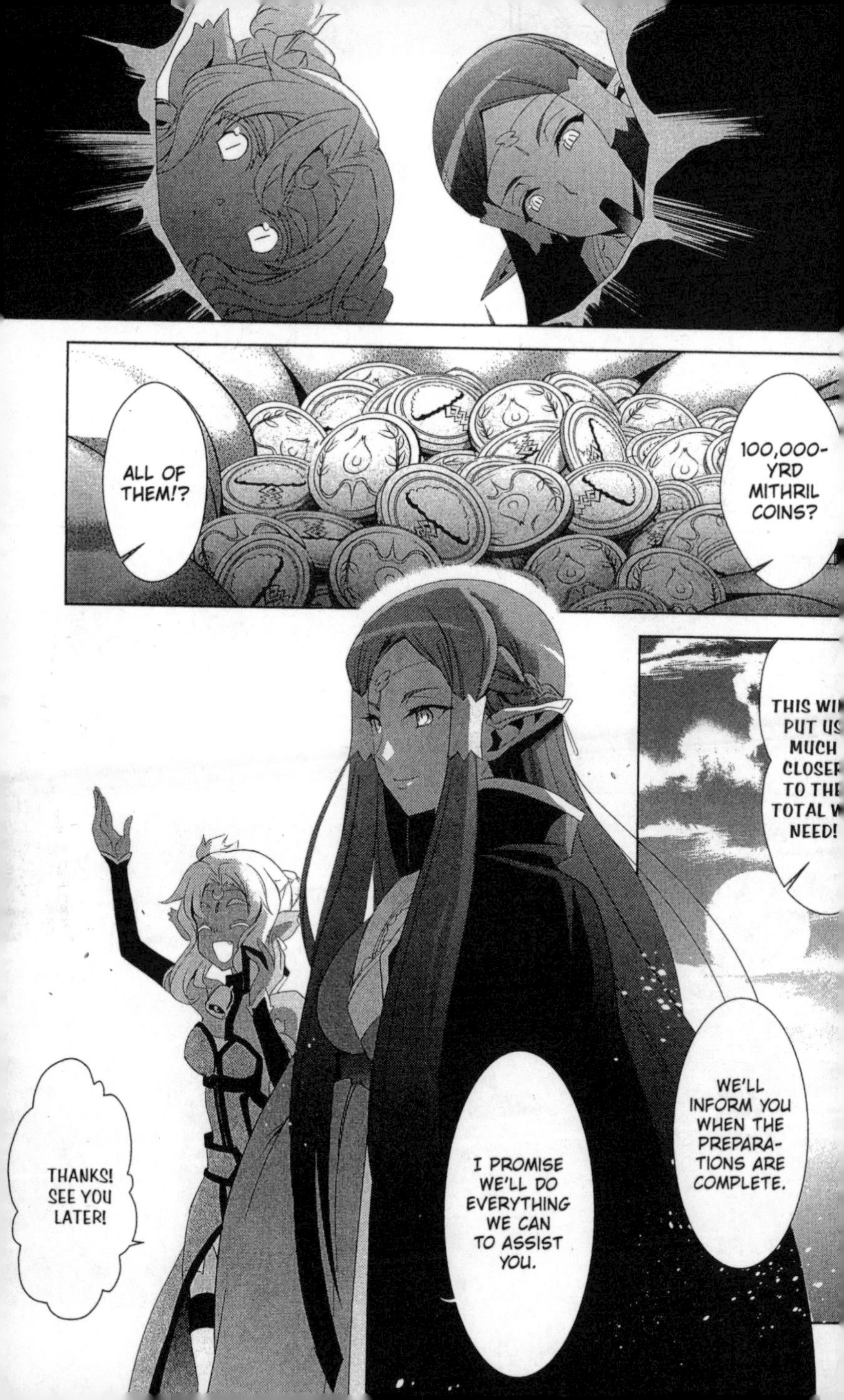
100,000-YRD MITHRIL COINS?
ALL OF THEM!?
THIS WI PUT US MUCH CLOSE TO THE TOTAL W NEED!
WE'LL INFORM YOU WHEN THE PREPARATIONS ARE COMPLETE.
I PROMISE WE'LL DO EVERYTHING WE CAN TO ASSIST YOU.
THANKS! SEE YOU LATER!

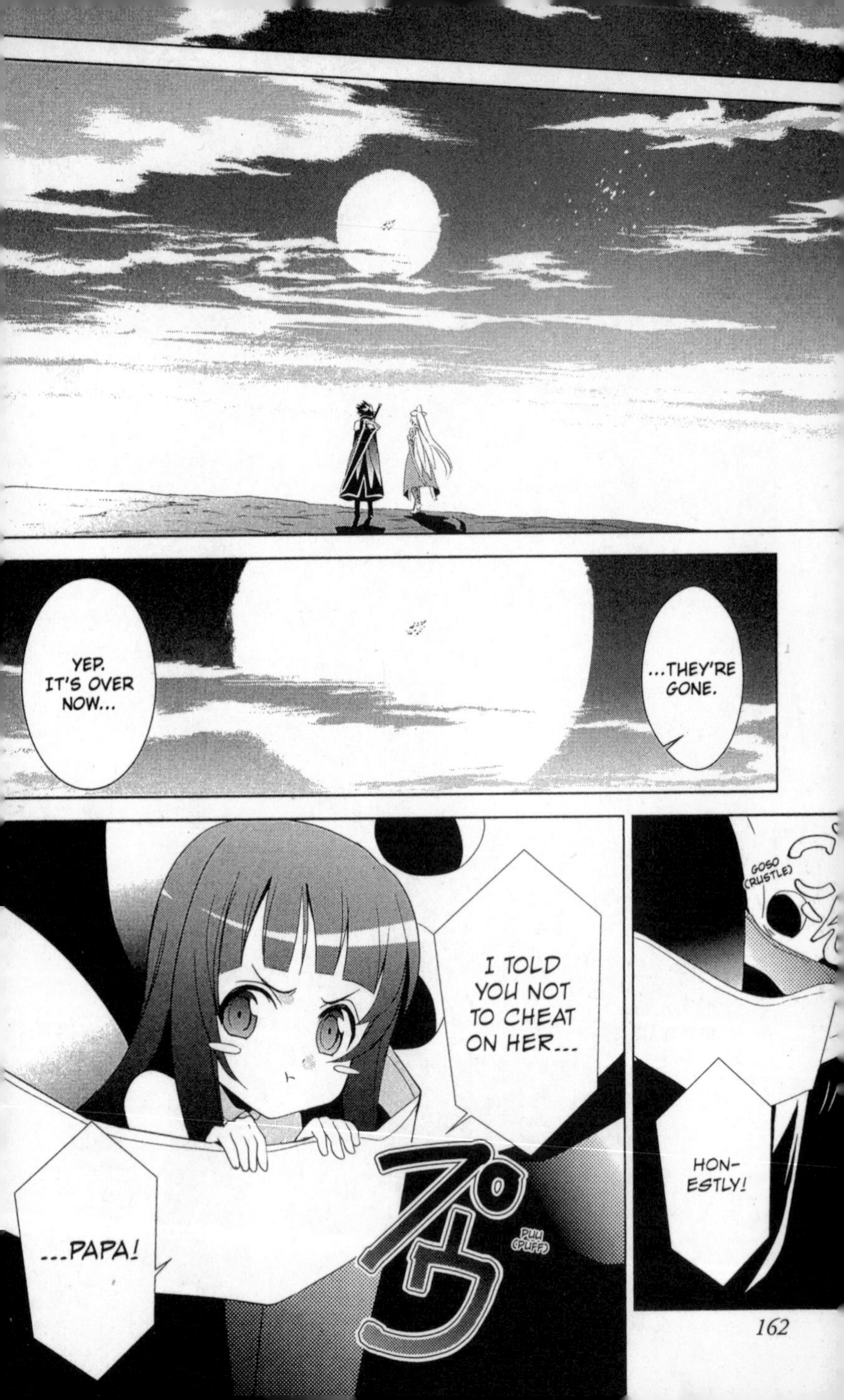
...THEY'RE GONE.
YEP. IT'S OVER NOW...
GOSO (RUSTLE)
HON-ESTLY!
I TOLD YOU NOT TO CHEAT ON HER...
PUU (PUFF)
...PAPA!

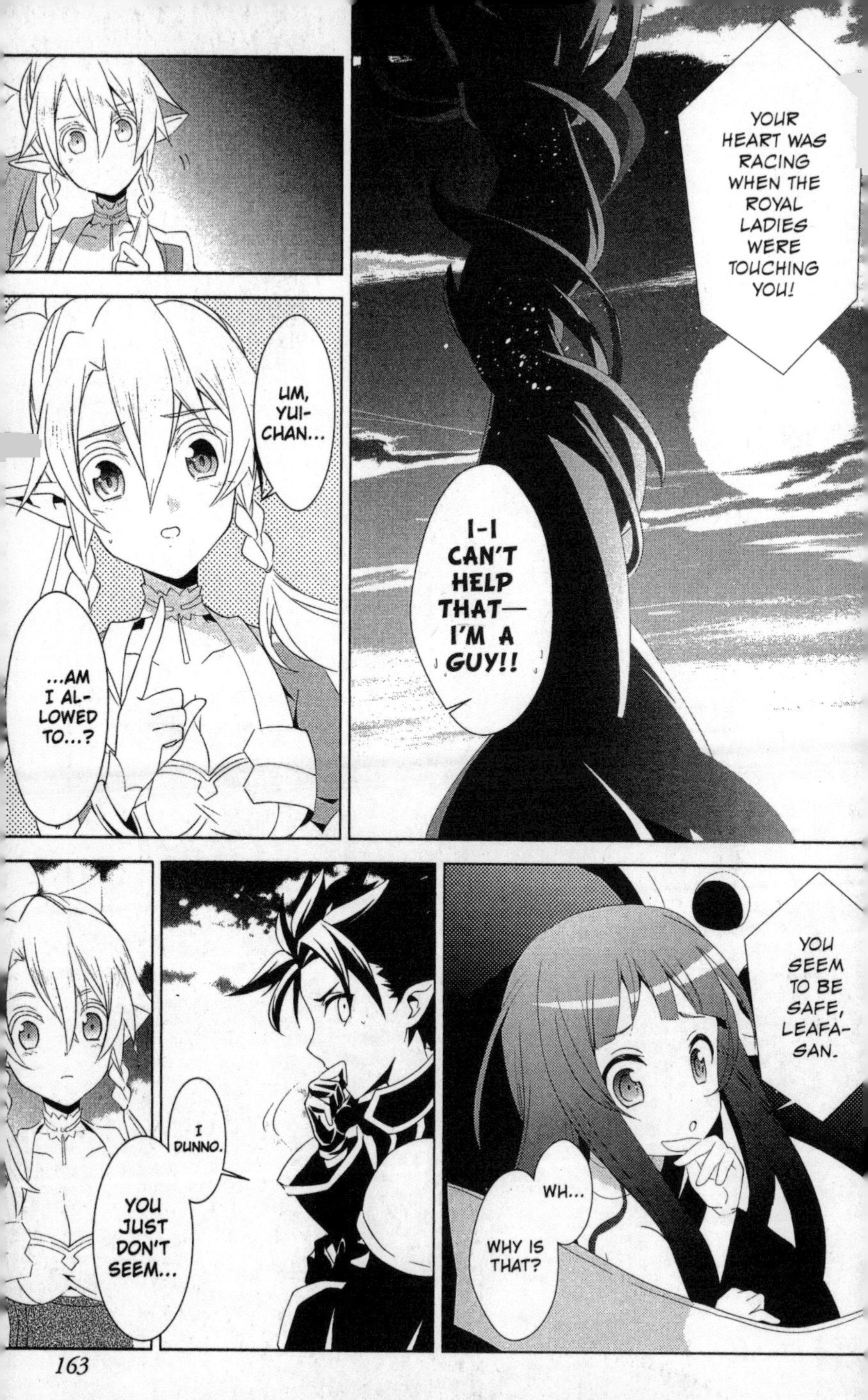
YOUR HEART WAS RACING WHEN THE ROYAL LADIES WERE TOUCHING YOU!
I-I CAN'T HELP THAT— I'M A GUY!!
UM, YUI-CHAN...
...AM I AL-LOWED TO...?
YOU SEEM TO BE SAFE, LEAFA-SAN.
WH...
WHY IS THAT?
I DUNNO.
YOU JUST DON'T SEEM...

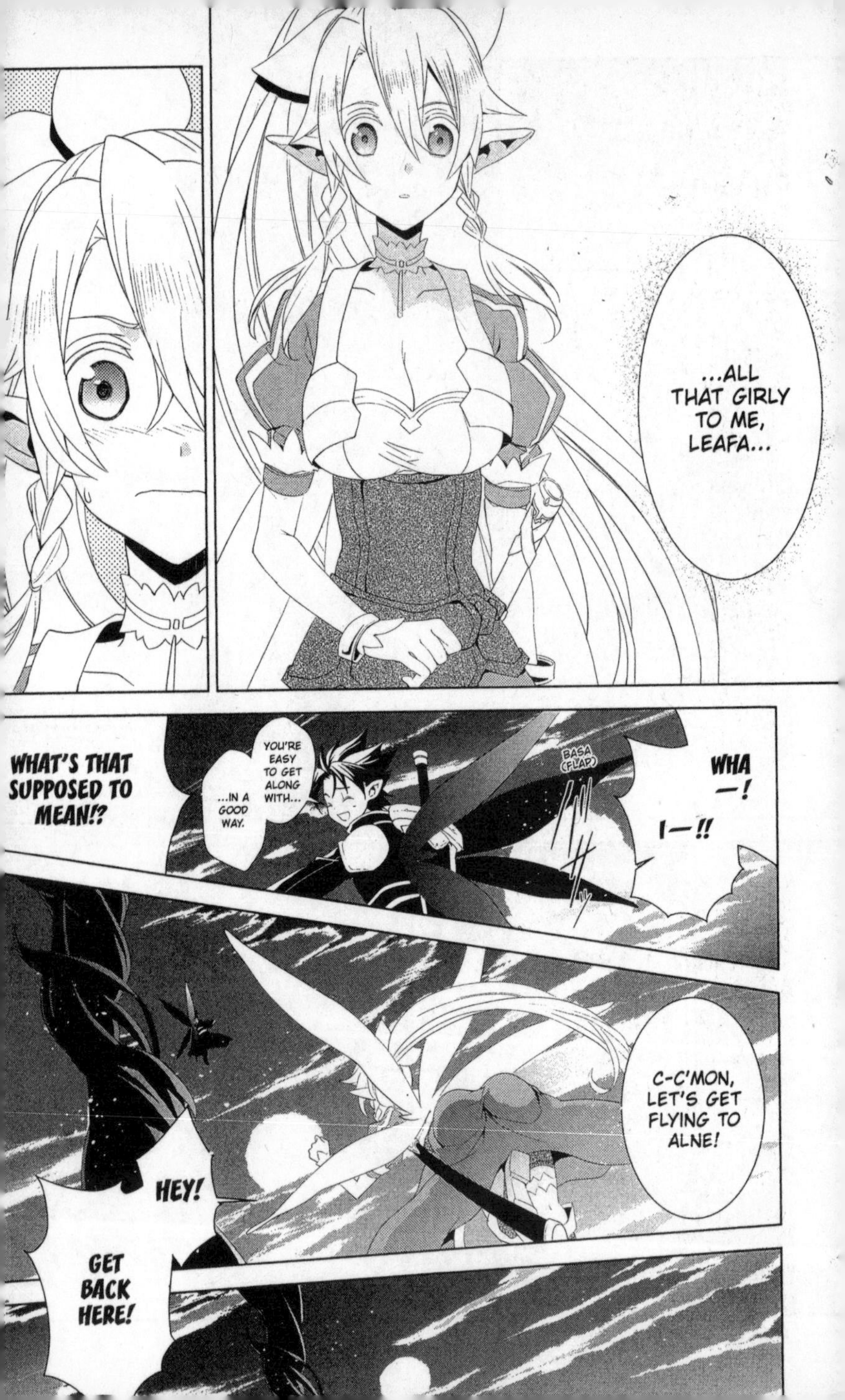
...ALL THAT GIRLY TO ME, LEAFA...
WHA—!
I—!!
BASA (FLAP)
YOU'RE EASY TO GET ALONG WITH...
...IN A GOOD WAY.
WHAT'S THAT SUPPOSED TO MEAN!?
C-C'MON, LET'S GET FLYING TO ALNE!
HEY!
GET BACK HERE!

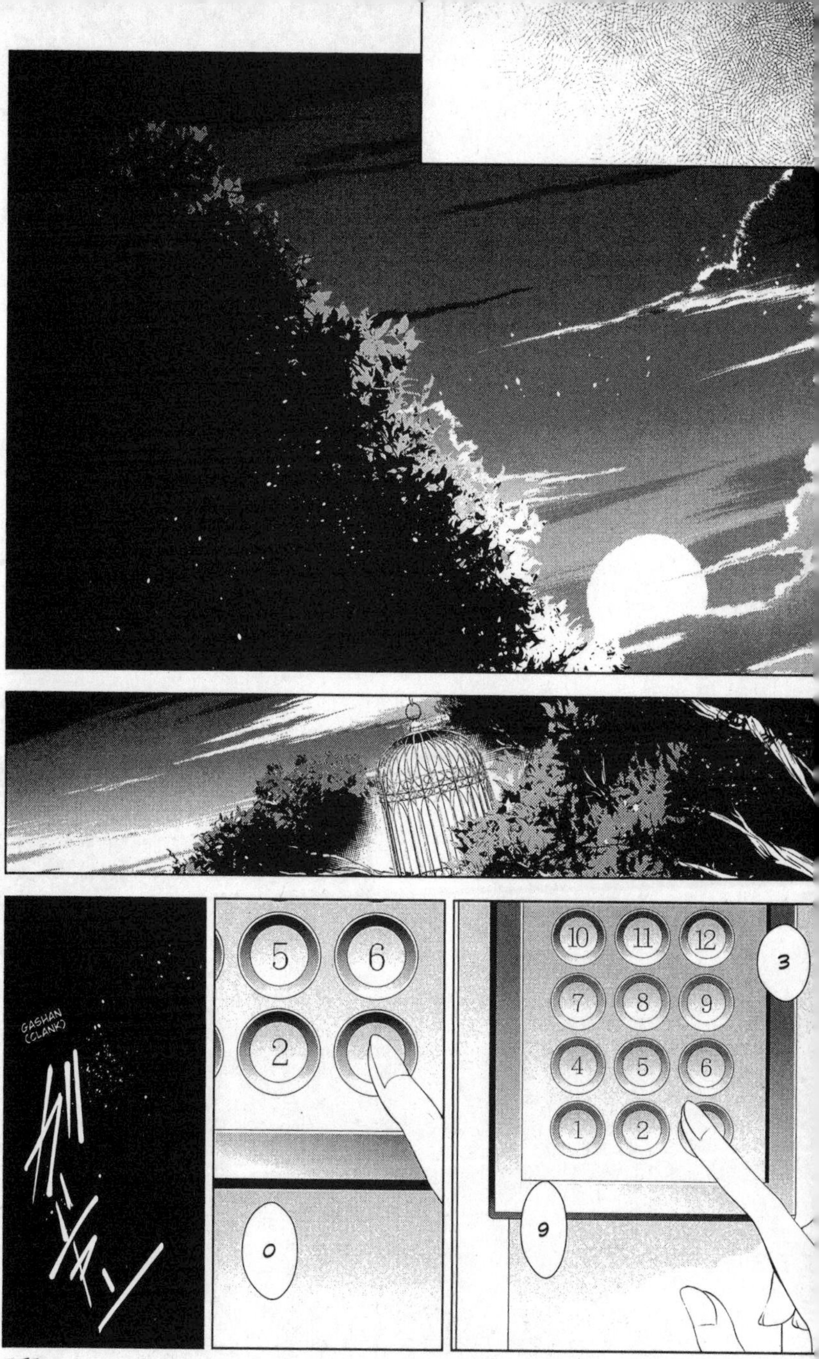
3
9
0
GASHAN (CLANK)

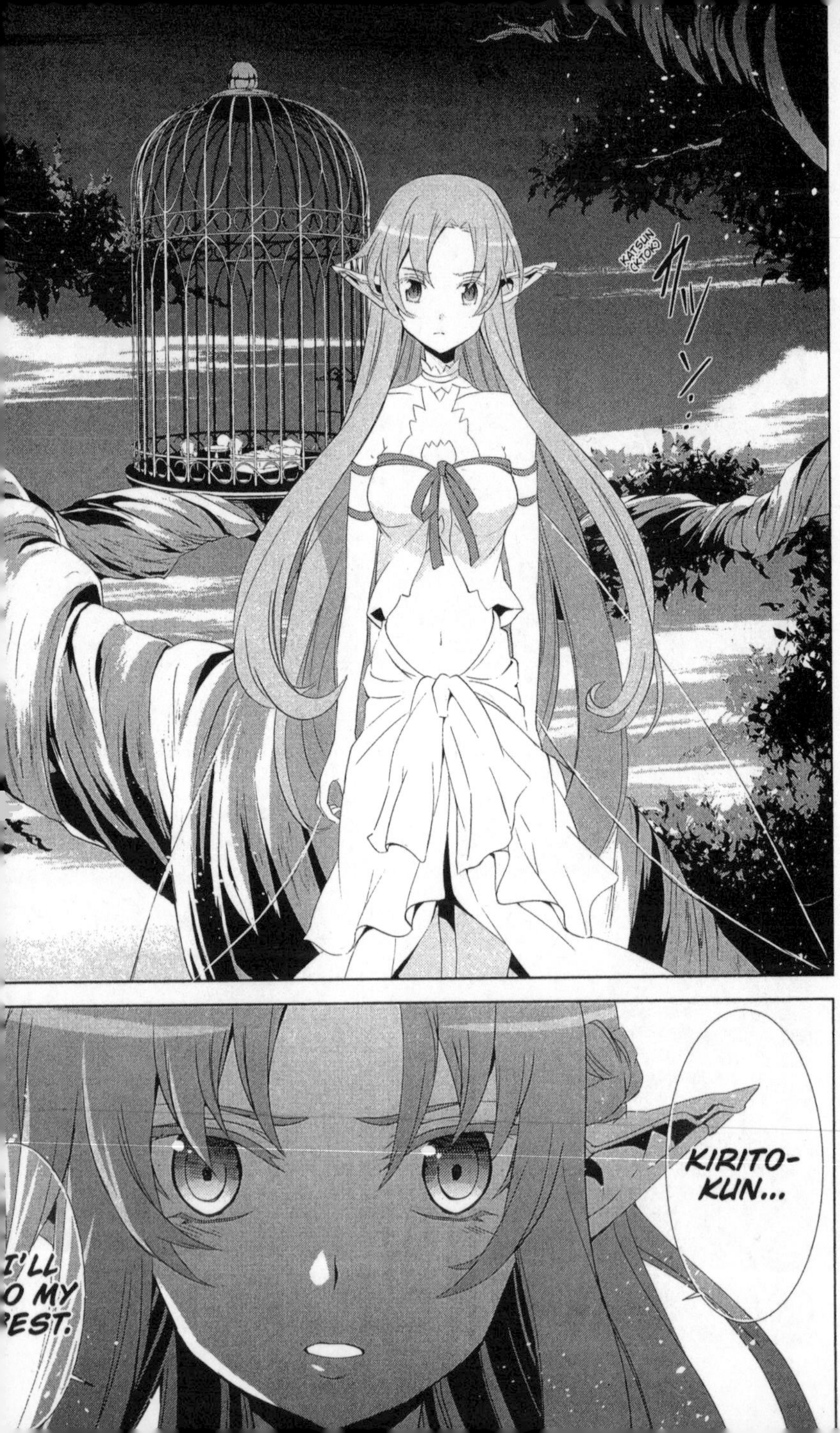KATSUN (KICK)
カツン…
KIRITO-KUN...
I'LL
O MY
EST.

SWORD ART ONLINE
fairy dance

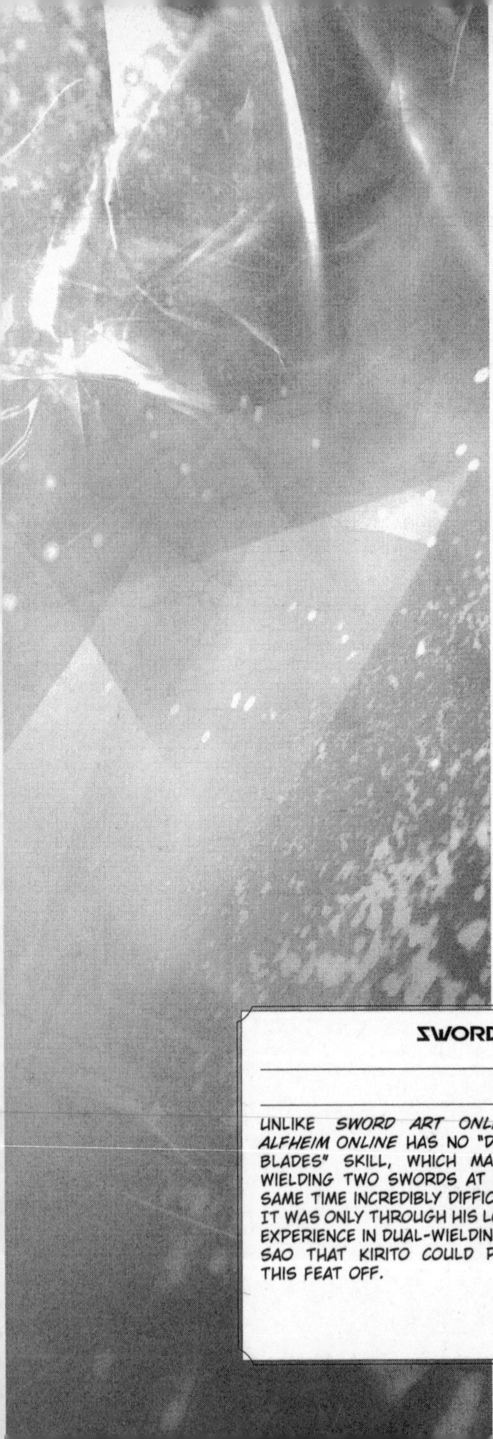

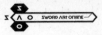

SWORD ART ONLINE fairy dance 03
BACKGROUND GUIDE

DUAL BLADES IN ALO

UNLIKE *SWORD ART ONLINE*, *ALFHEIM ONLINE* HAS NO "DUAL BLADES" SKILL, WHICH MAKES WIELDING TWO SWORDS AT THE SAME TIME INCREDIBLY DIFFICULT. IT WAS ONLY THROUGH HIS LONG EXPERIENCE IN DUAL-WIELDING IN SAO THAT KIRITO COULD PULL THIS FEAT OFF.

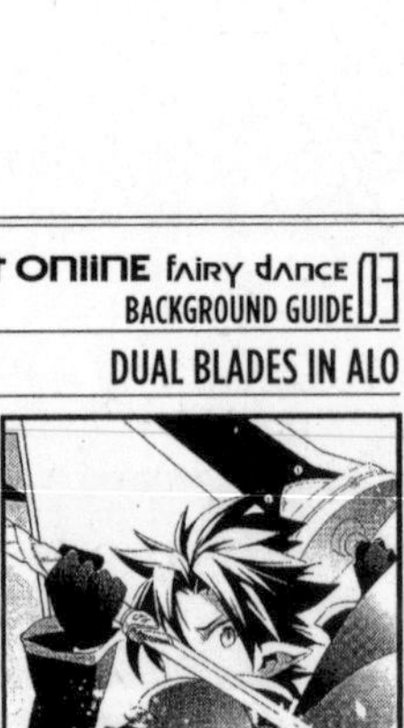

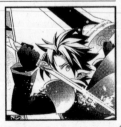

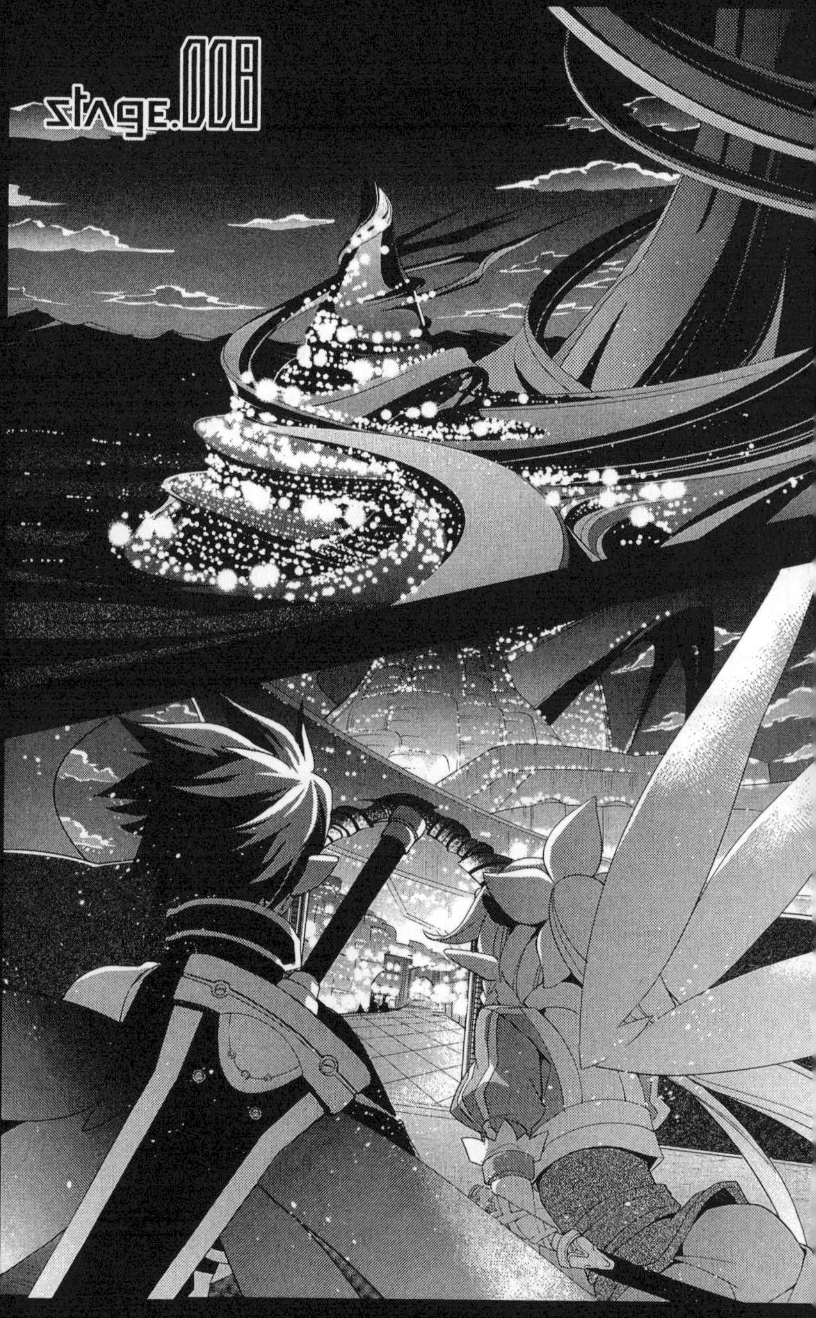
stage.008

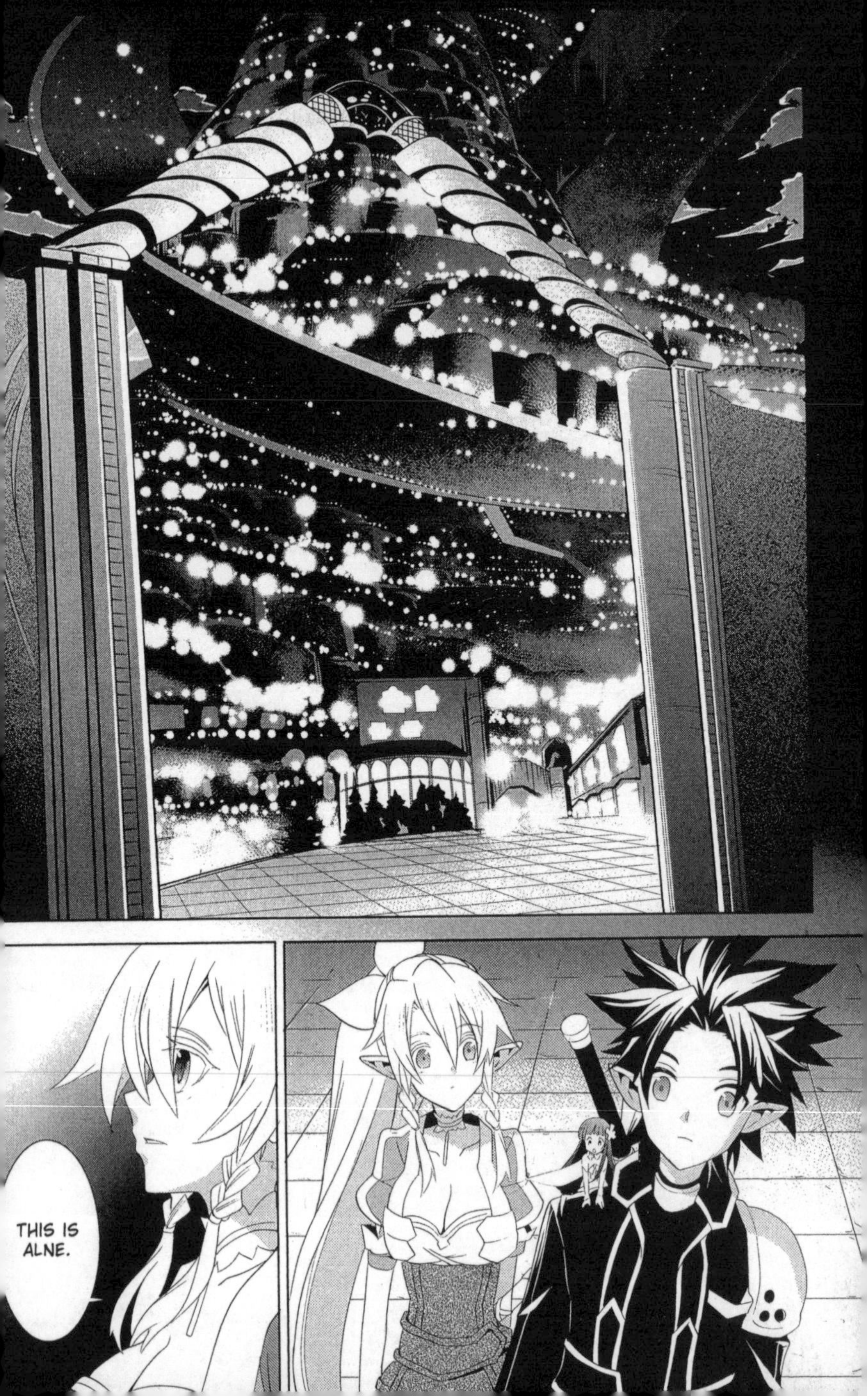
THIS IS ALNE.

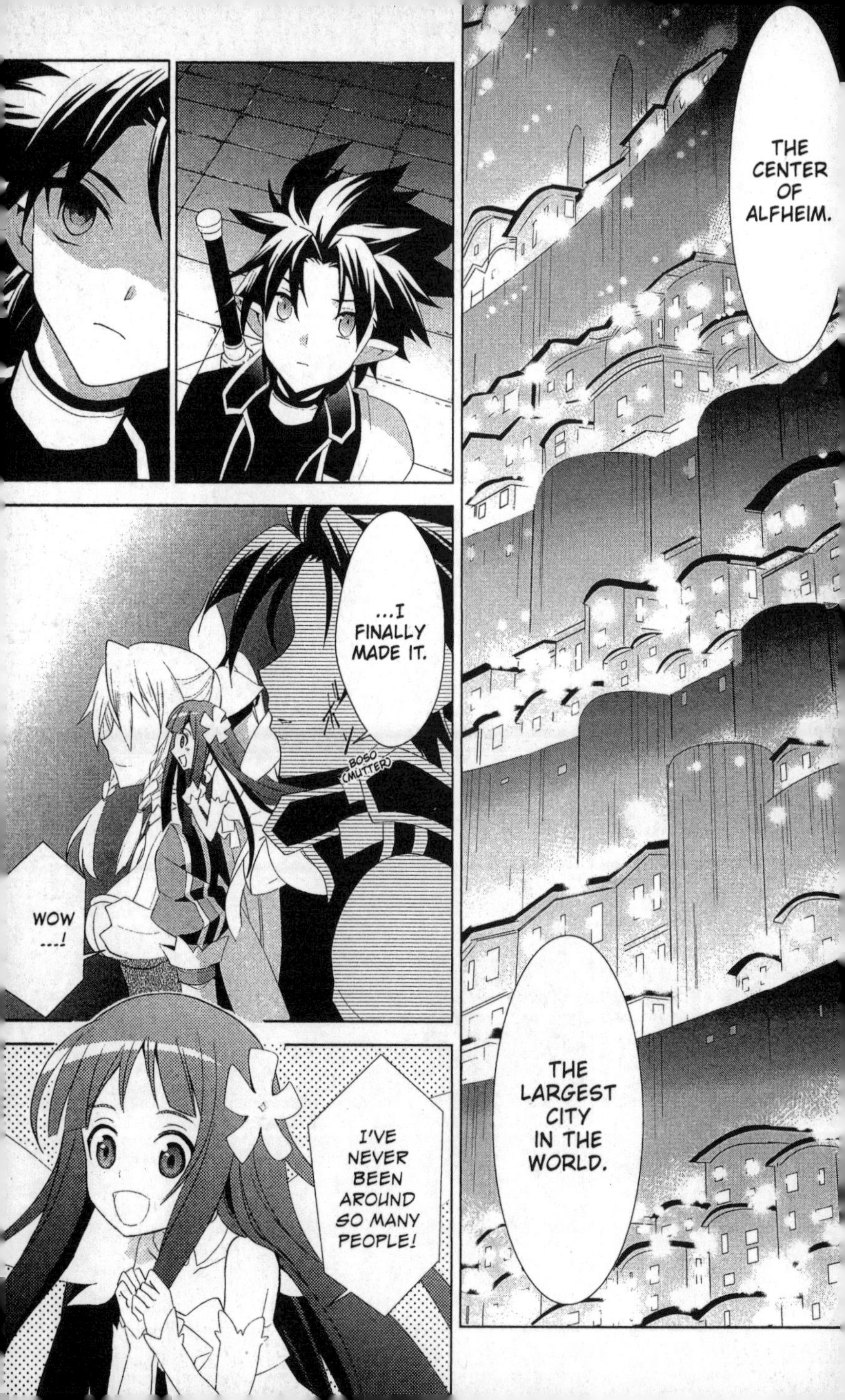
THE CENTER OF ALFHEIM.
THE LARGEST CITY IN THE WORLD.
...I FINALLY MADE IT.
BOSO (MUTTER)
WOW ...!
I'VE NEVER BEEN AROUND SO MANY PEOPLE!

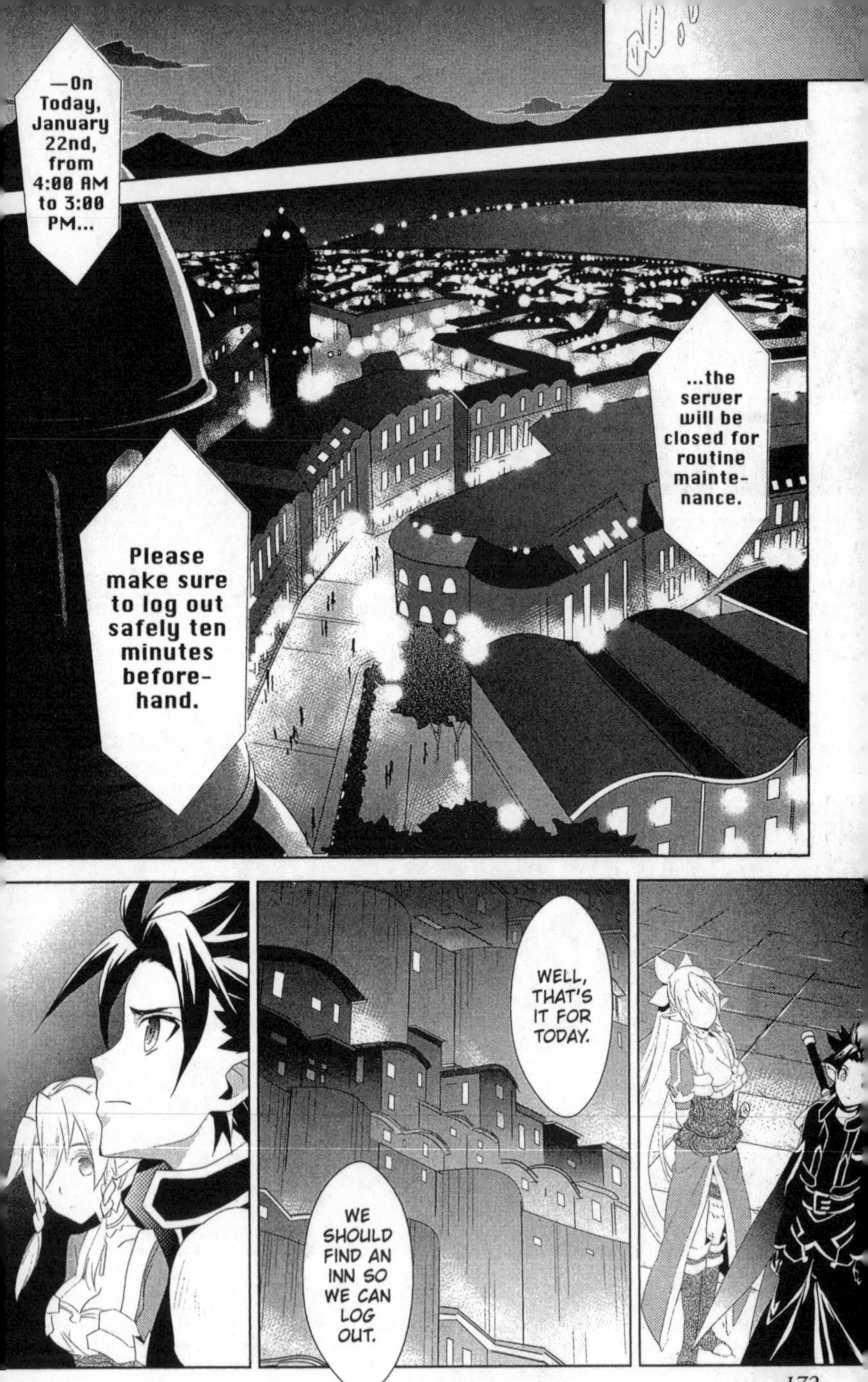
—On Today, January 22nd, from 4:00 AM to 3:00 PM...
...the server will be closed for routine maintenance.
Please make sure to log out safely ten minutes beforehand.
WELL, THAT'S IT FOR TODAY.
WE SHOULD FIND AN INN SO WE CAN LOG OUT.

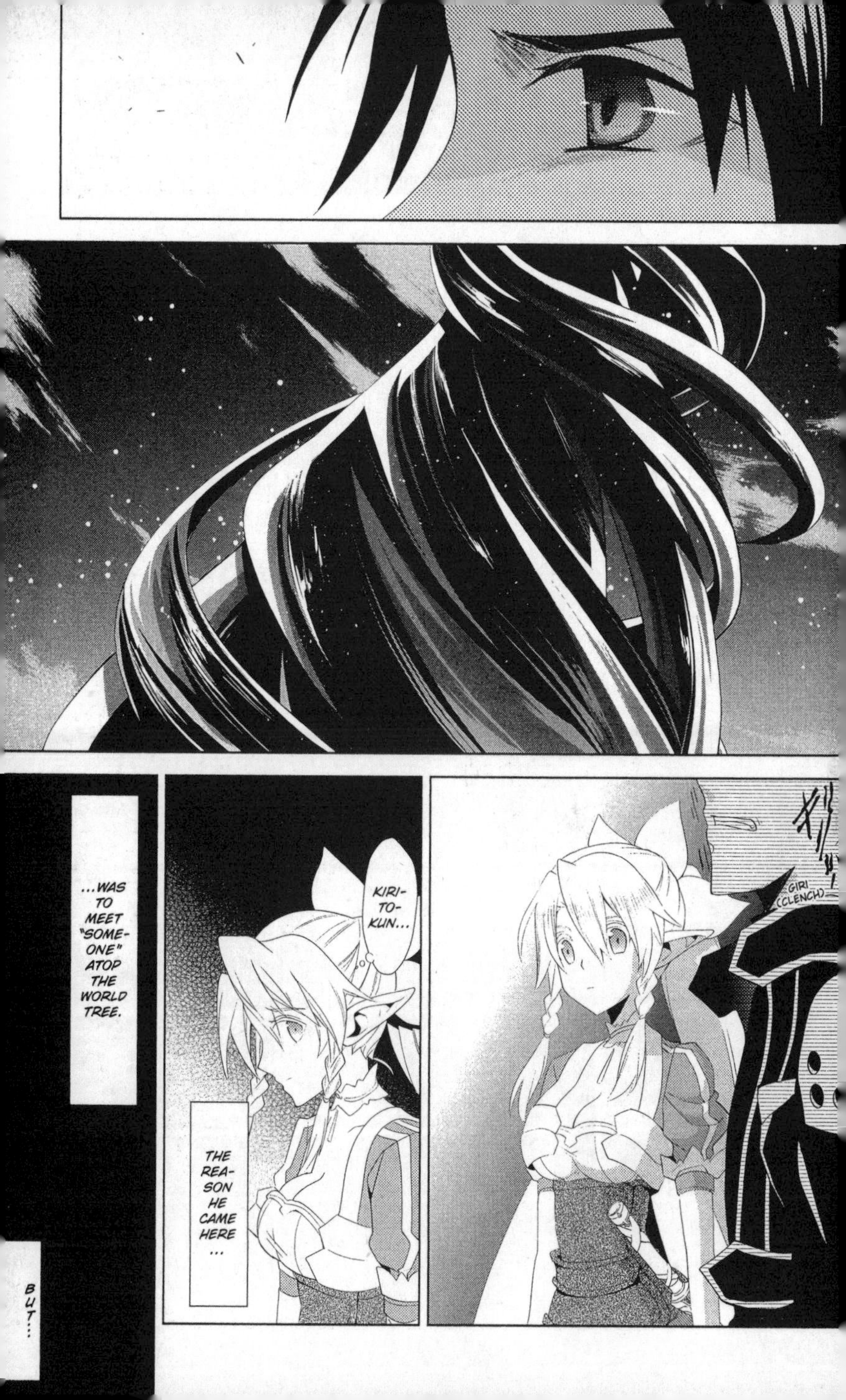
GIRI (CLENCH)
KIRI-TO-KUN...
THE REASON HE CAME HERE...
...WAS TO MEET "SOMEONE" ATOP THE WORLD TREE.
BUT...

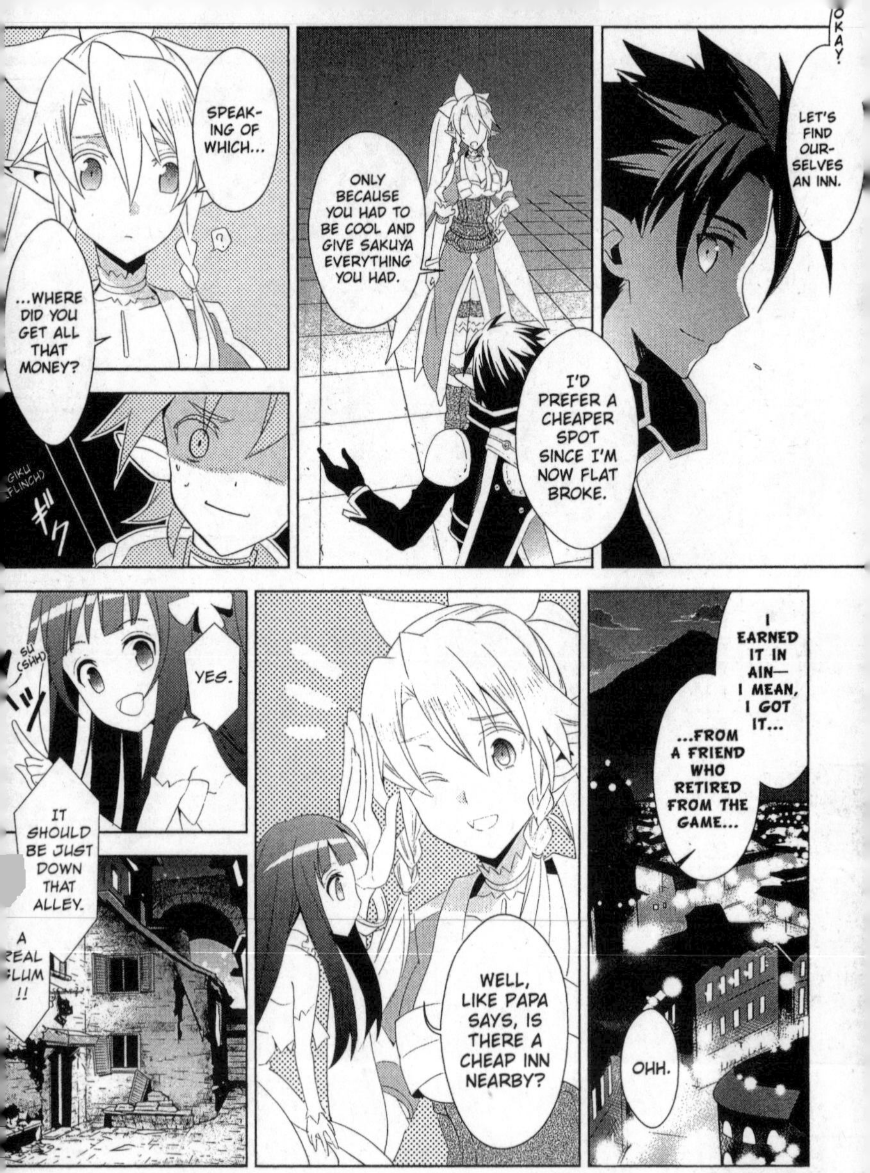
OKAY.
LET'S FIND OURSELVES AN INN.
I'D PREFER A CHEAPER SPOT SINCE I'M NOW FLAT BROKE.
ONLY BECAUSE YOU HAD TO BE COOL AND GIVE SAKUYA EVERYTHING YOU HAD.
SPEAK-ING OF WHICH...
?
...WHERE DID YOU GET ALL THAT MONEY?
GIKU (FLINCH)
I EARNED IT IN AIN— I MEAN, I GOT IT...
...FROM A FRIEND WHO RETIRED FROM THE GAME...
OHH.
WELL, LIKE PAPA SAYS, IS THERE A CHEAP INN NEARBY?
SU (SHH)
YES.
IT SHOULD BE JUST DOWN THAT ALLEY.
A REAL SLUM!!

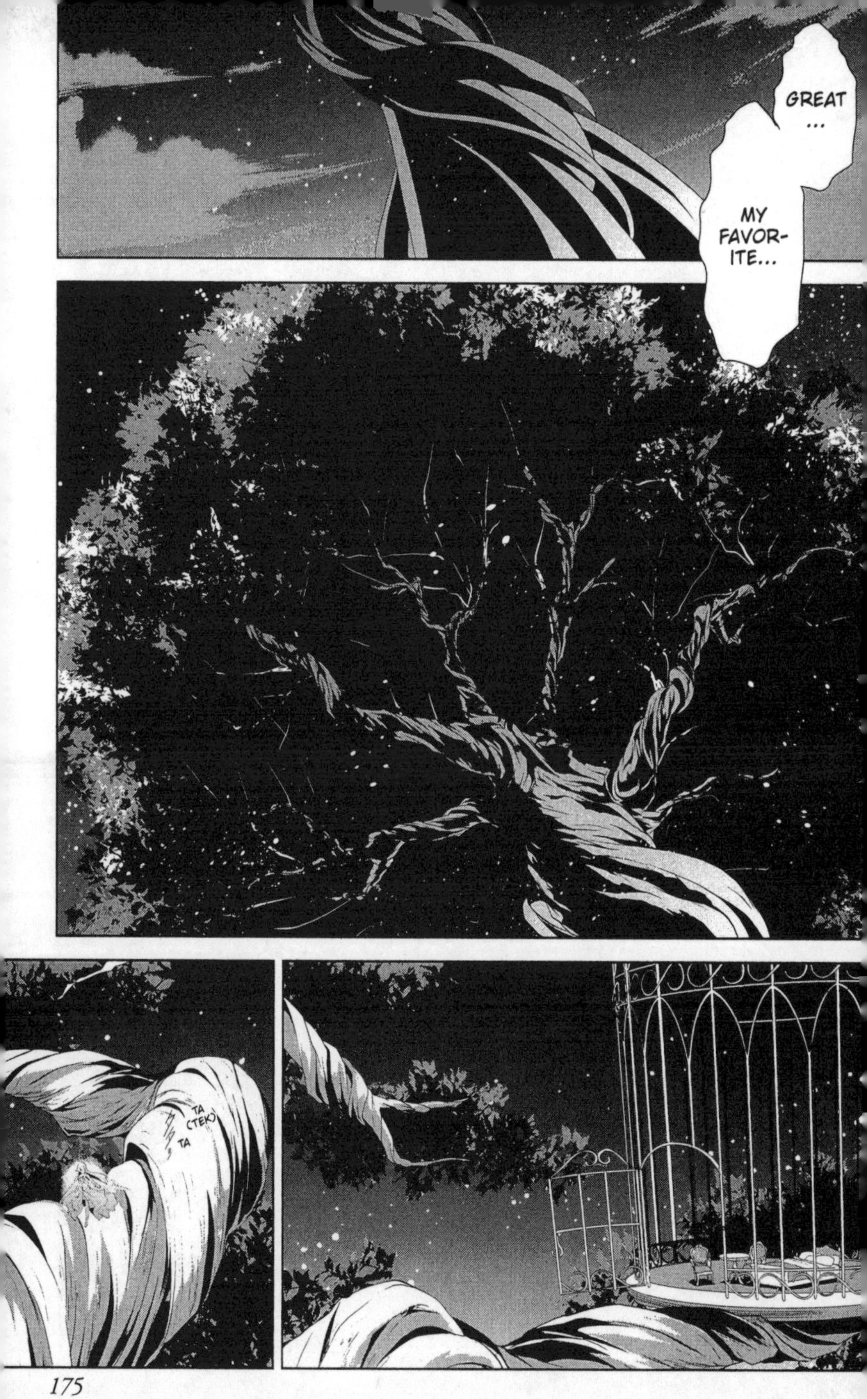
GREAT...
MY FAVOR-ITE...
TA (TEK) TA

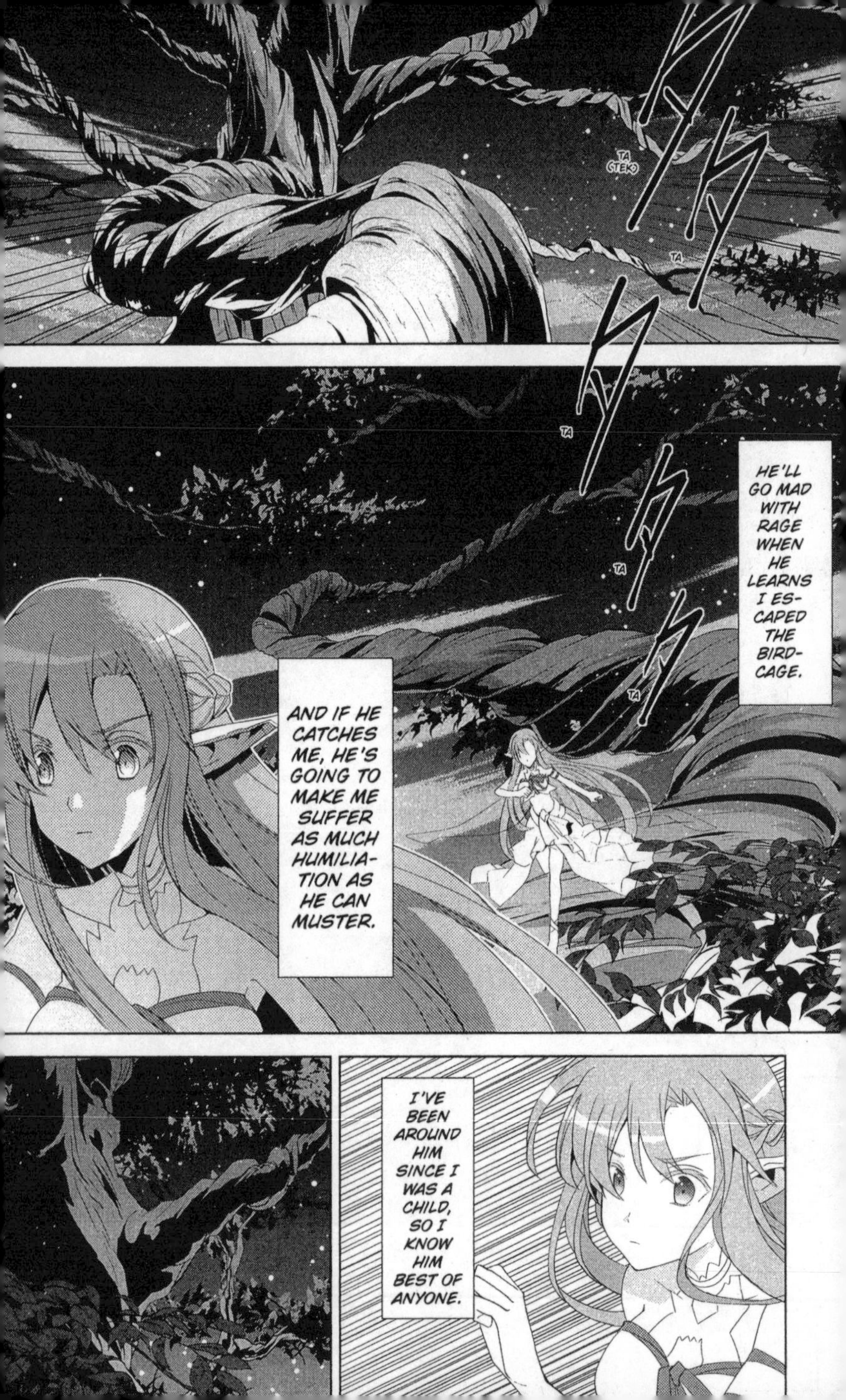
TA (TEK)
TA
HE'LL GO MAD WITH RAGE WHEN HE LEARNS I ESCAPED THE BIRDCAGE.
TA
TA
TA
AND IF HE CATCHES ME, HE'S GOING TO MAKE ME SUFFER AS MUCH HUMILIATION AS HE CAN MUSTER.
I'VE BEEN AROUND HIM SINCE I WAS A CHILD, SO I KNOW HIM BEST OF ANYONE.

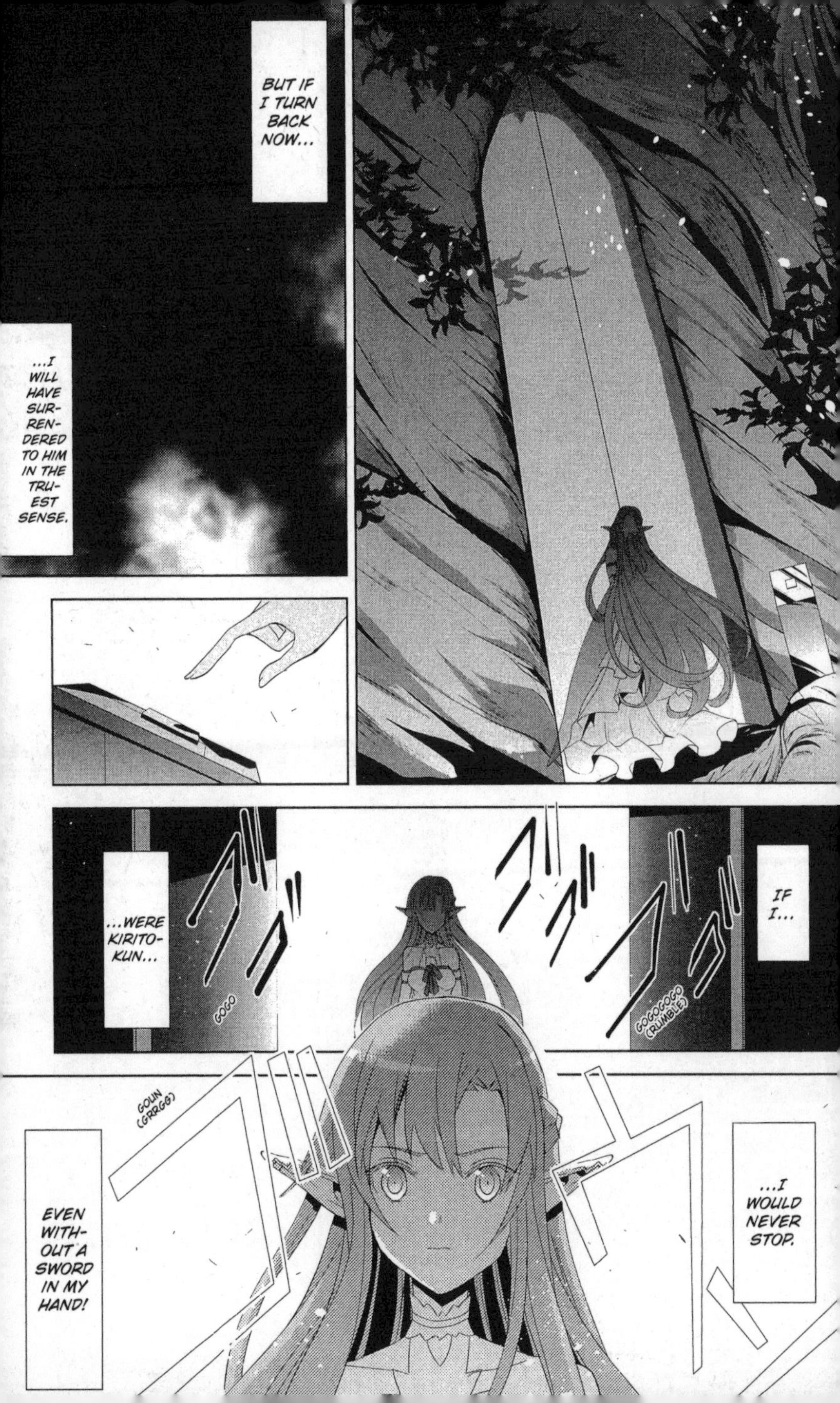
BUT IF I TURN BACK NOW...
...I WILL HAVE SURRENDERED TO HIM IN THE TRUEST SENSE.
IF I...
GOGOGOGO (RUMBLE)
...WERE KIRITO-KUN...
GOGO
...I WOULD NEVER STOP.
GOUN (GRRGG)
EVEN WITHOUT A SWORD IN MY HAND!

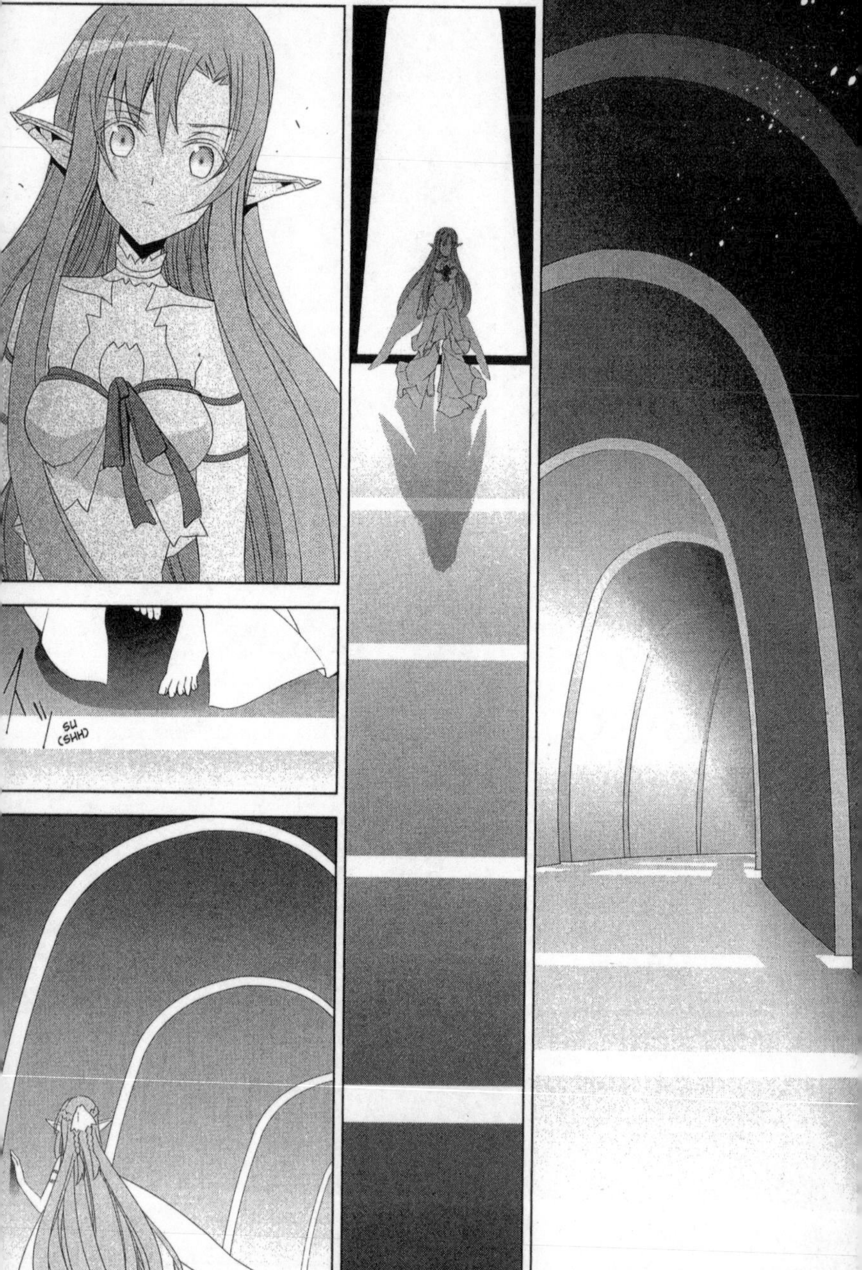
SU
(SHH)

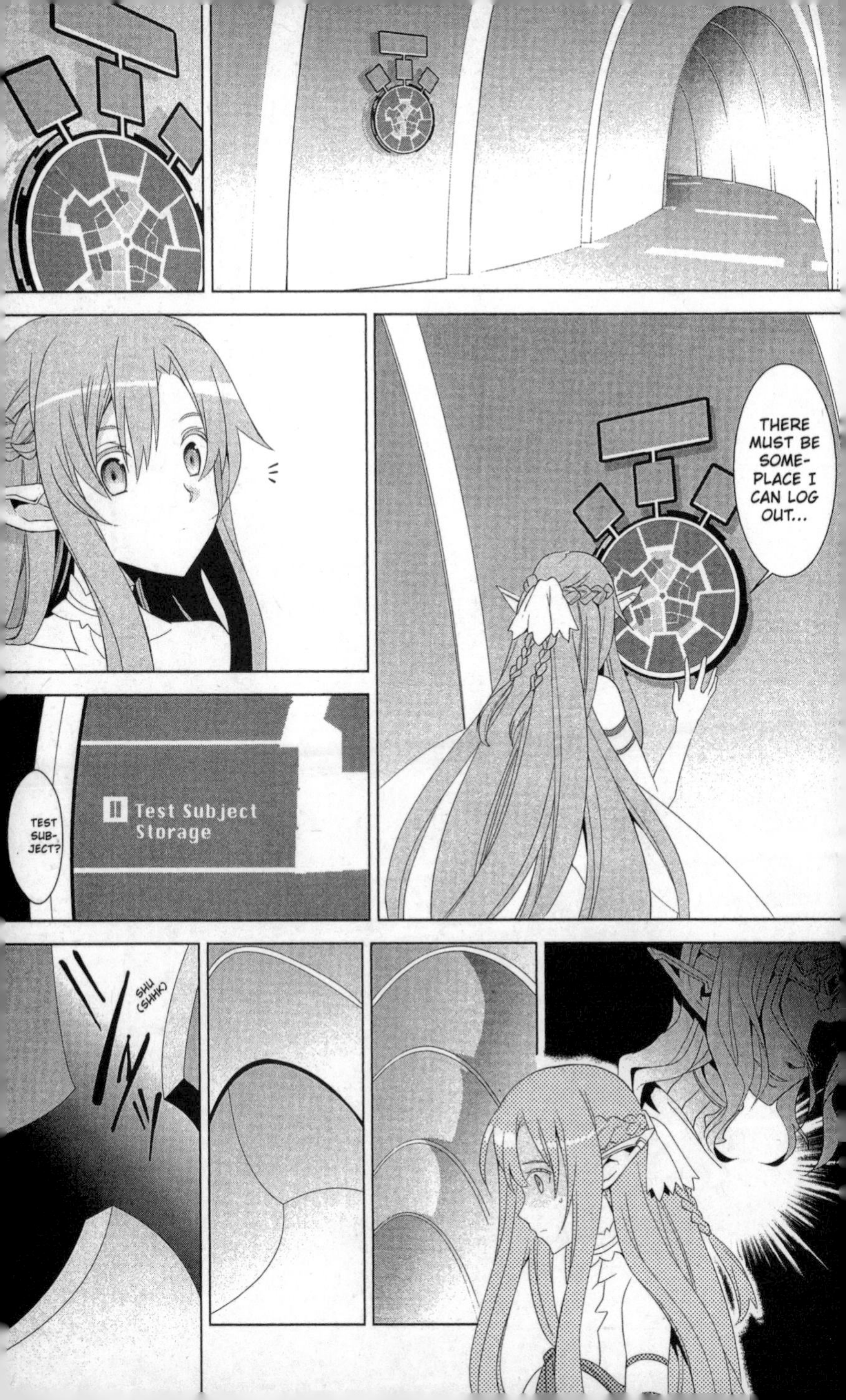
THERE MUST BE SOME-PLACE I CAN LOG OUT...
Test Subject Storage
TEST SUB-JECT?
SHU (SHHK)

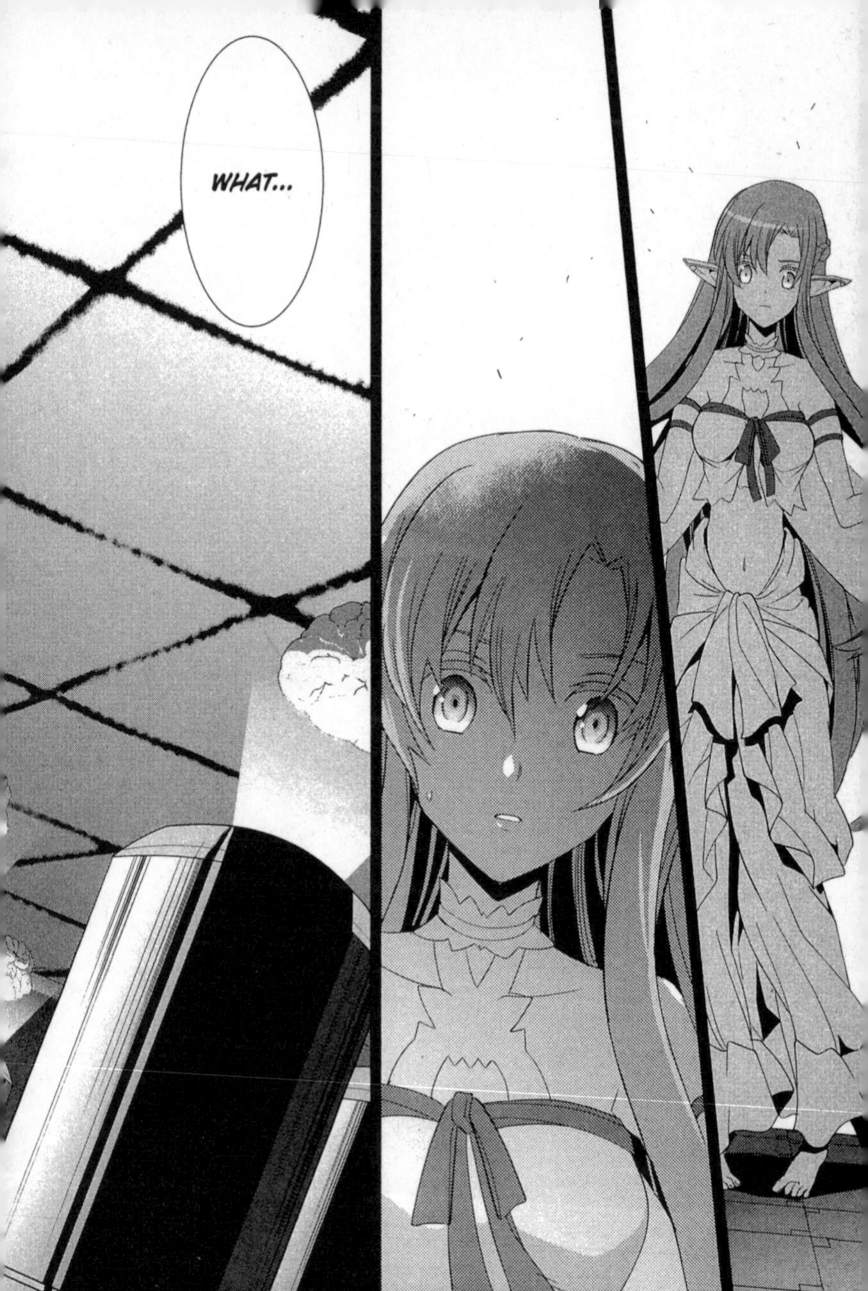
WHAT...

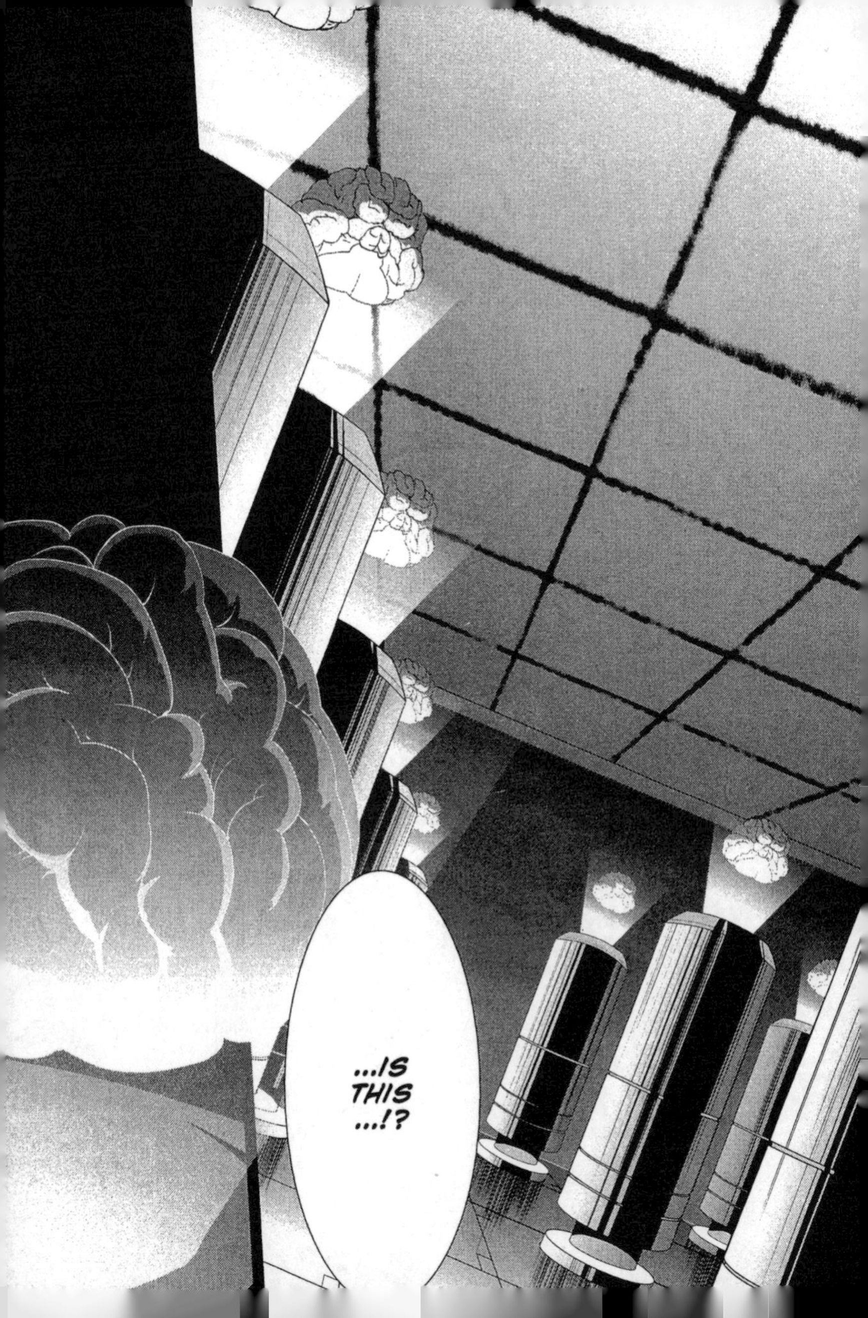
...IS THIS ...!?

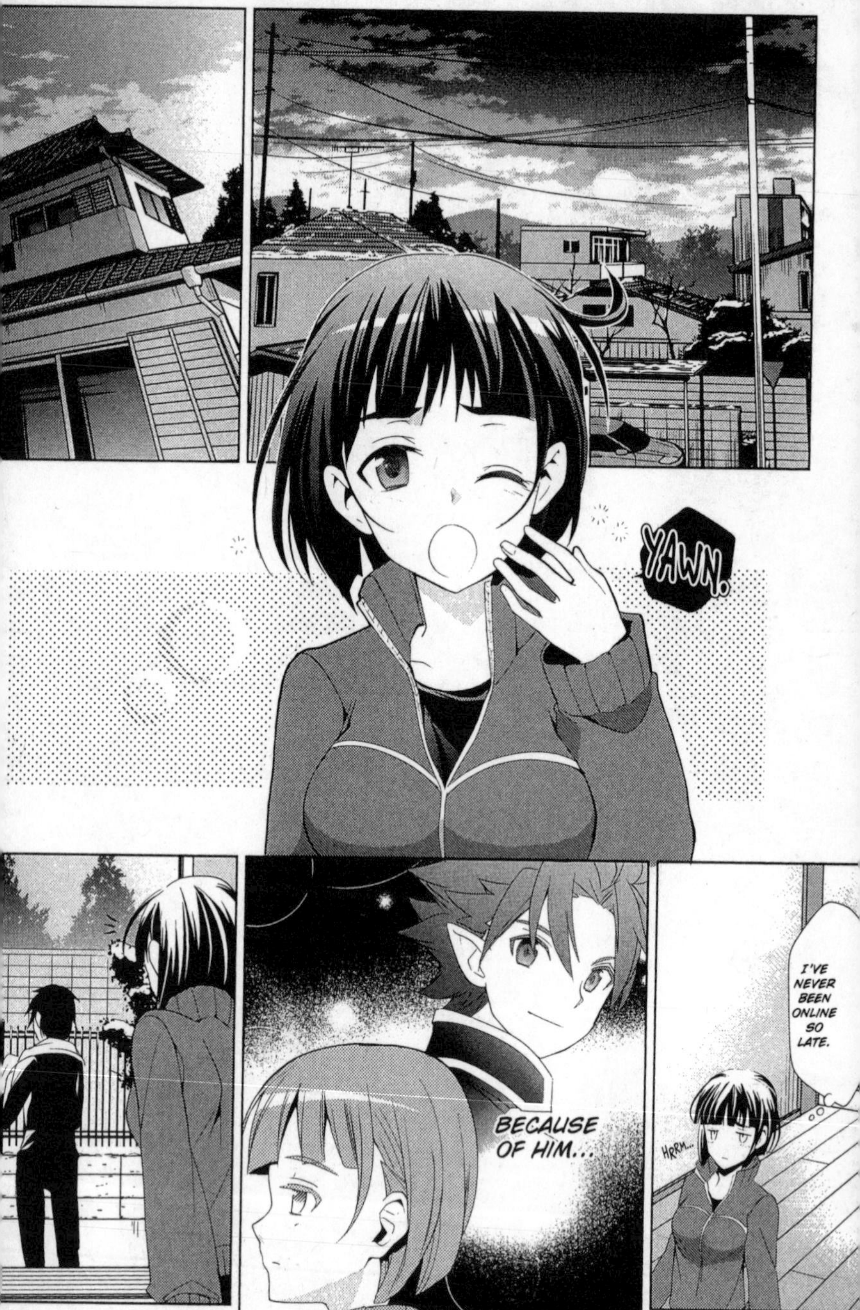
YAWN.
I'VE NEVER BEEN ONLINE SO LATE.
HRRM...
BECAUSE OF HIM...

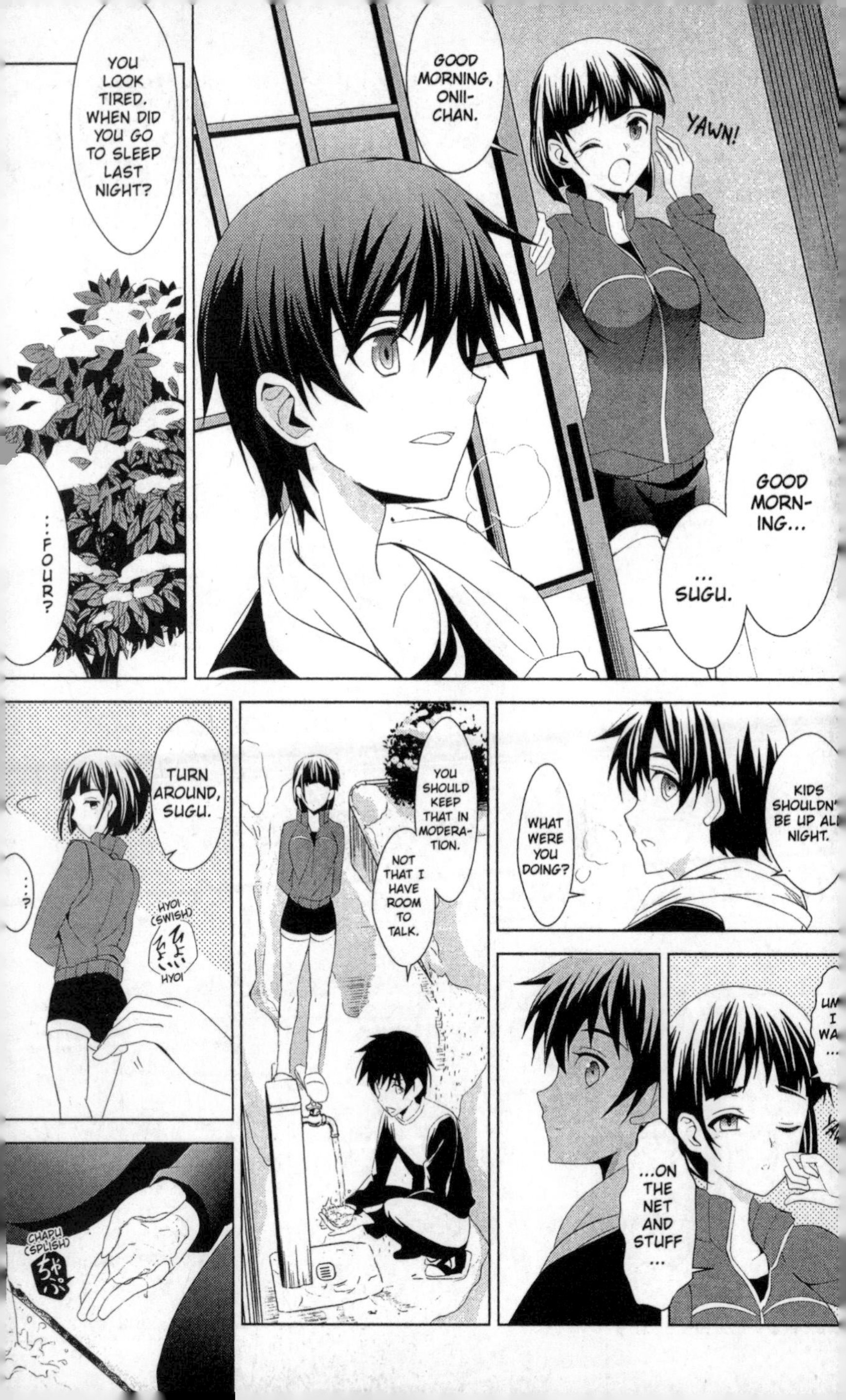
GOOD MORNING, ONII-CHAN.
YAWN!
GOOD MORNING...
... SUGU.
YOU LOOK TIRED. WHEN DID YOU GO TO SLEEP LAST NIGHT?
...FOUR?
KIDS SHOULDN' BE UP AL NIGHT.
WHAT WERE YOU DOING?
UM I WA ...
...ON THE NET AND STUFF ...
YOU SHOULD KEEP THAT IN MODERATION.
NOT THAT I HAVE ROOM TO TALK.
TURN AROUND, SUGU.
...?
HYOI (SWISH)
ひょい
HYOI
CHAPU (SPLISH)
ちゃぷ

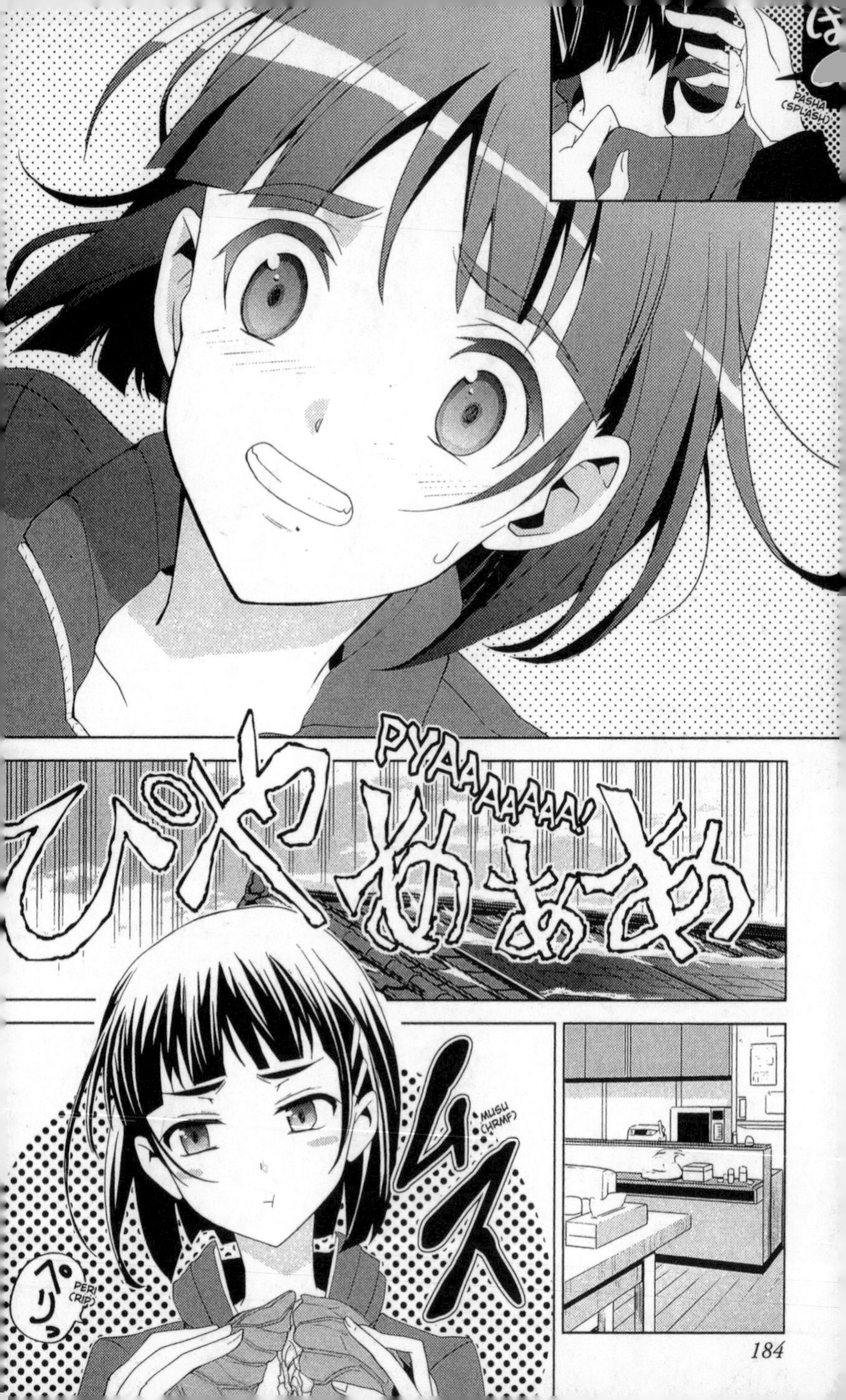
PASHA (SPLASH)
ぴゃあああ
PYAAAAAAA!
MUSU (HRMF)
ムス
PERI (RIP)
ぺりっ

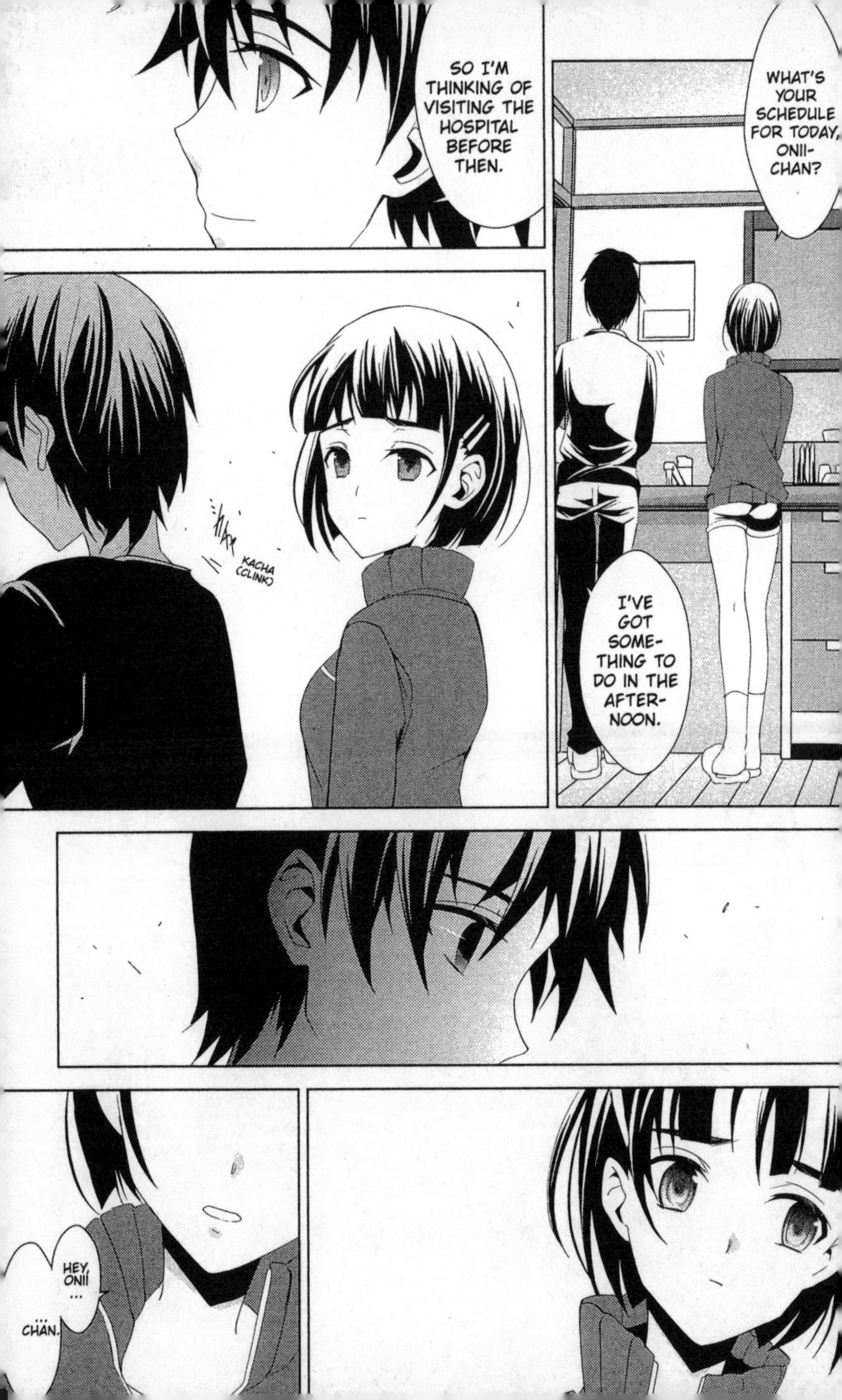
WHAT'S YOUR SCHEDULE FOR TODAY, ONII-CHAN?
I'VE GOT SOMETHING TO DO IN THE AFTERNOON.
SO I'M THINKING OF VISITING THE HOSPITAL BEFORE THEN.
KACHA (CLINK)
HEY, ONII ...
... CHAN.

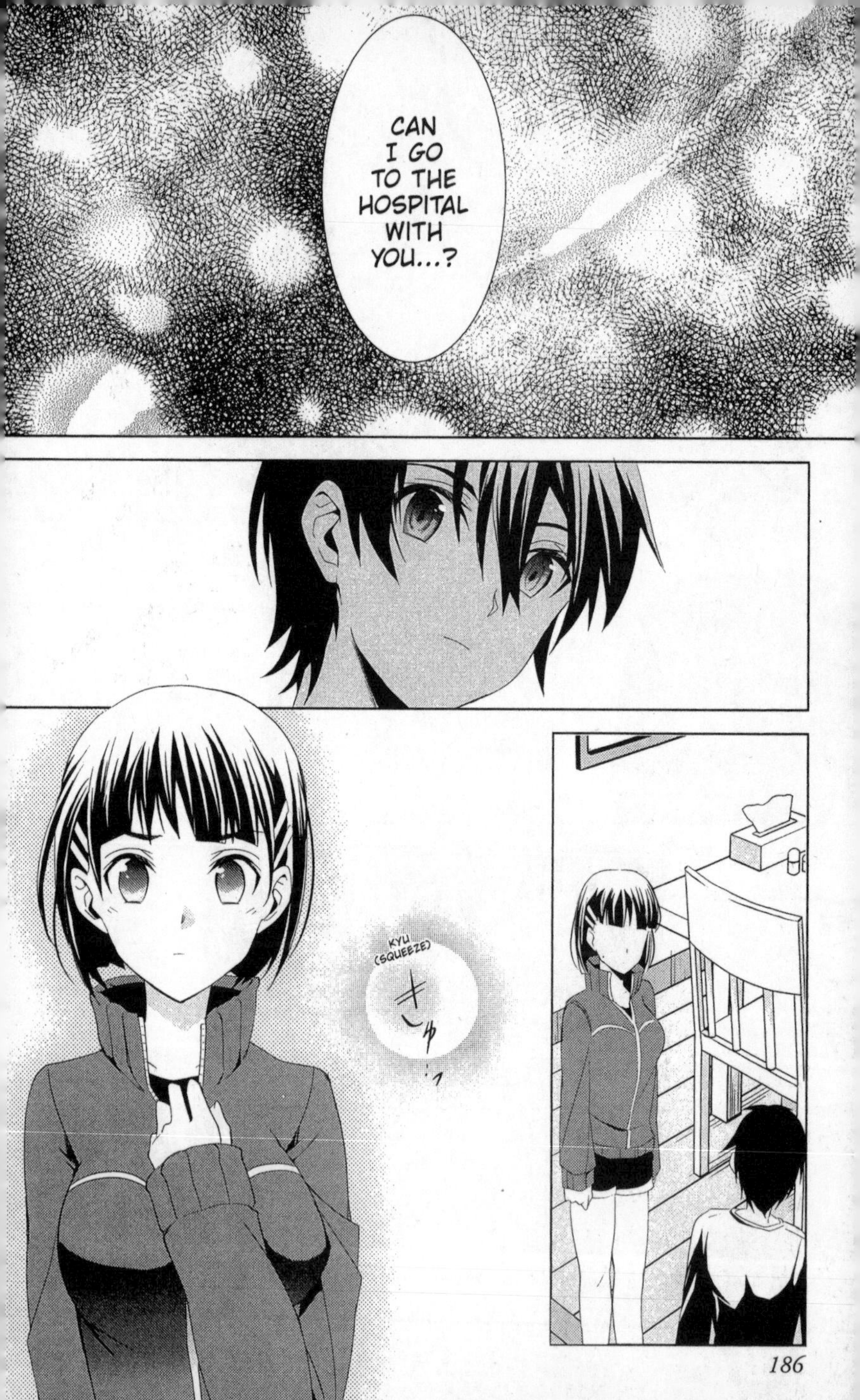
CAN I GO TO THE HOSPITAL WITH YOU...?
KYU (SQUEEZE)
きゅっ

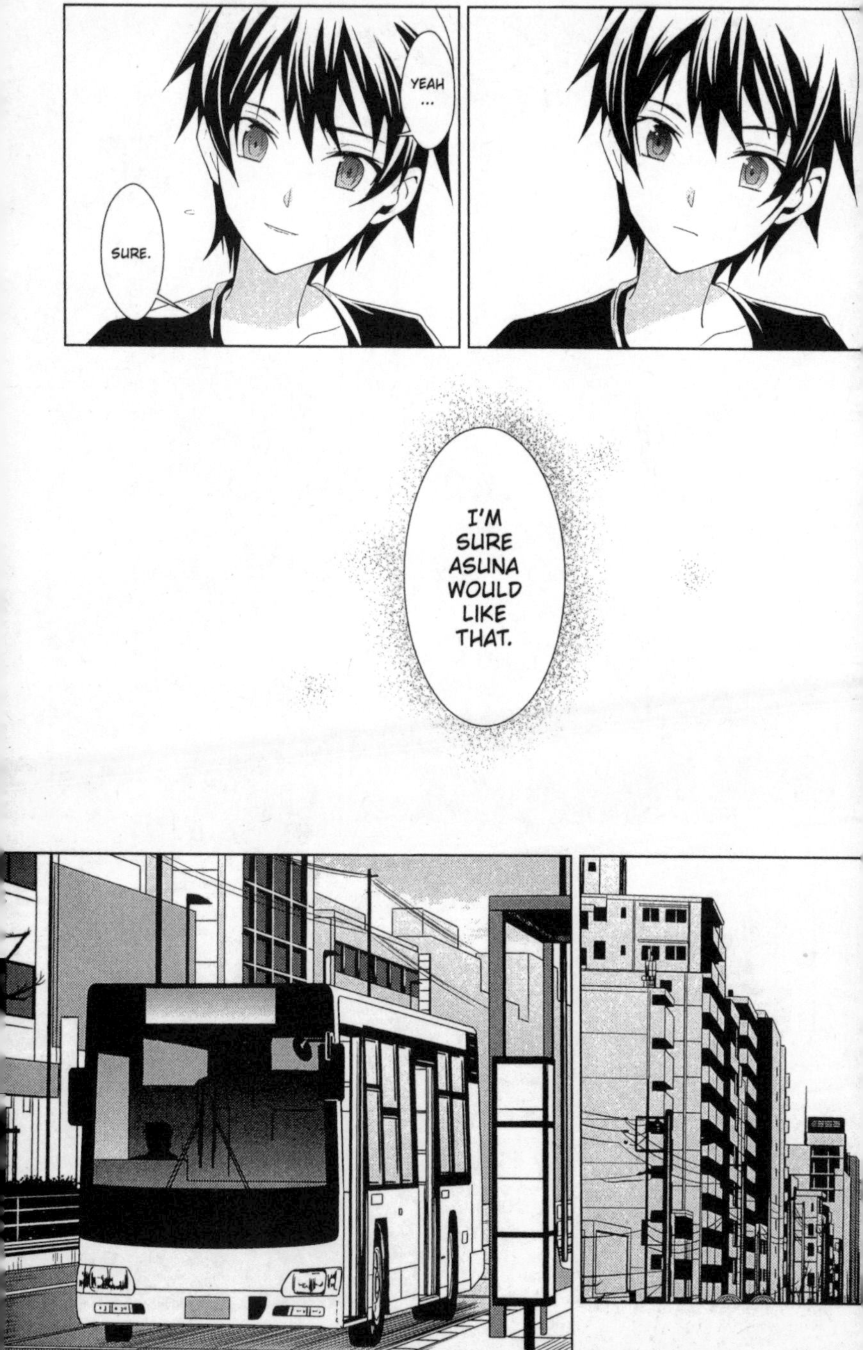
YEAH ...
SURE.
I'M SURE ASUNA WOULD LIKE THAT.

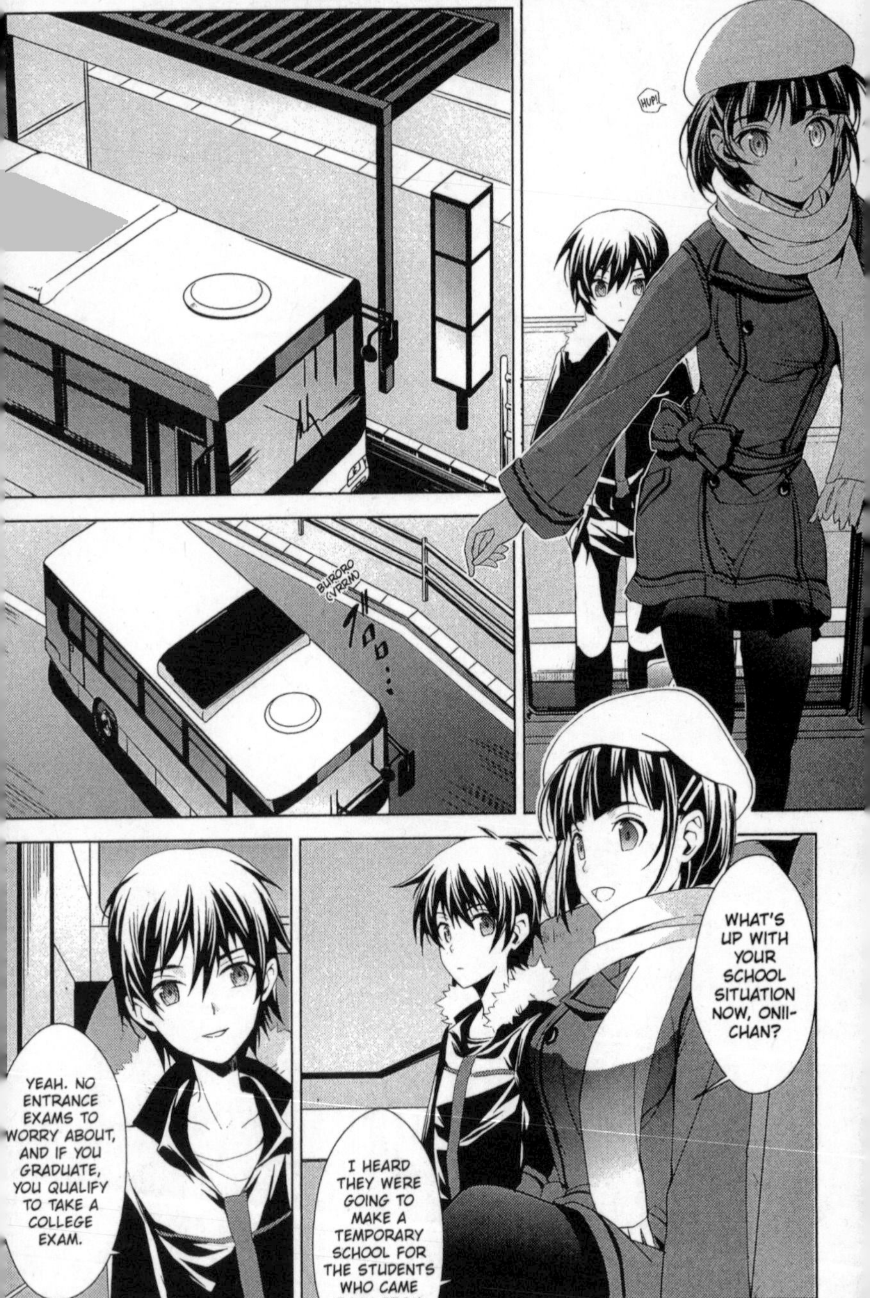
HUP!
BURORO (VRRM)
WHAT'S UP WITH YOUR SCHOOL SITUATION NOW, ONII-CHAN?
I HEARD THEY WERE GOING TO MAKE A TEMPORARY SCHOOL FOR THE STUDENTS WHO CAME BACK FROM SAO.
YEAH. NO ENTRANCE EXAMS TO WORRY ABOUT, AND IF YOU GRADUATE, YOU QUALIFY TO TAKE A COLLEGE EXAM.

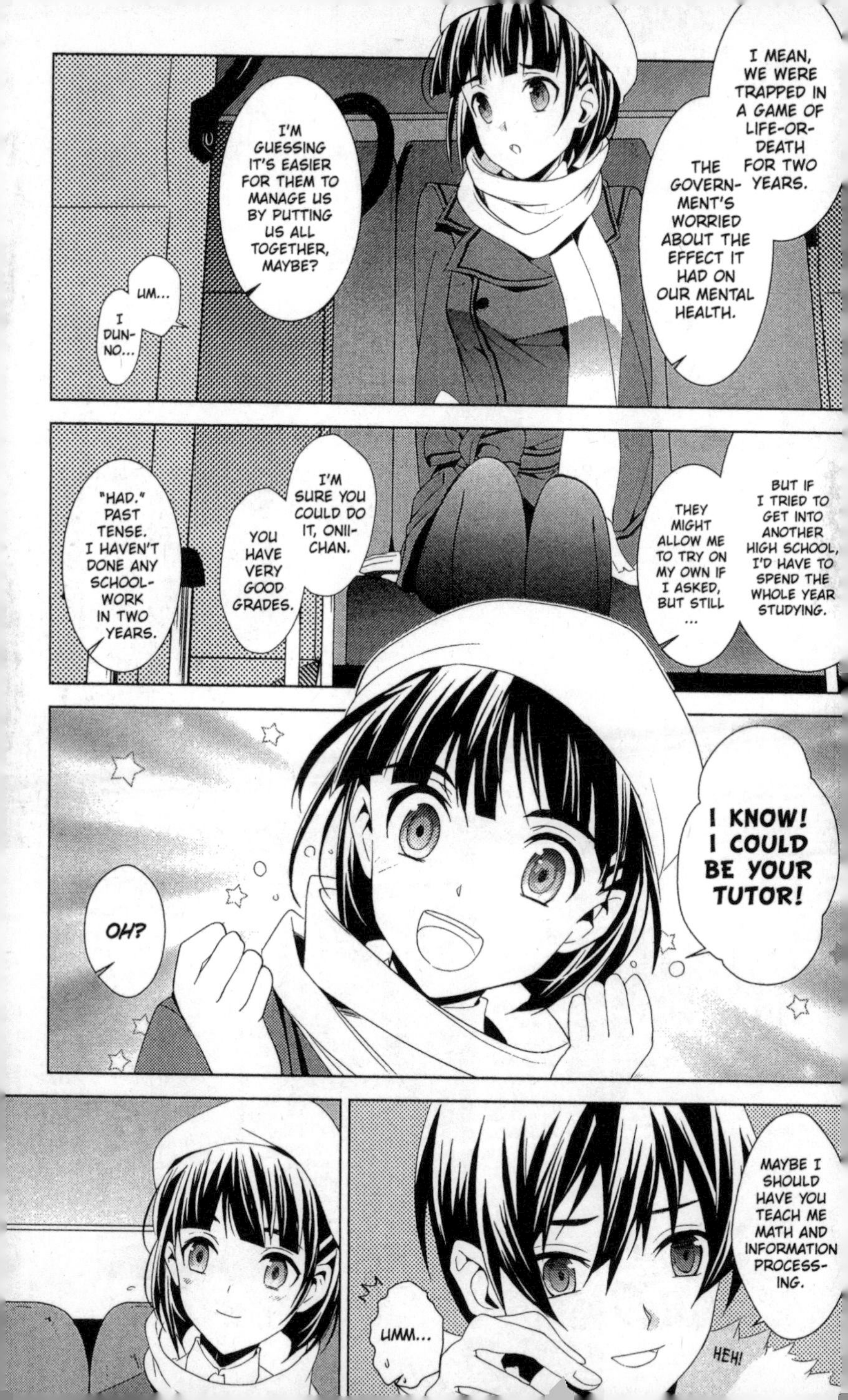
I MEAN, WE WERE TRAPPED IN A GAME OF LIFE-OR-DEATH FOR TWO YEARS.
THE GOVERN-MENT'S WORRIED ABOUT THE EFFECT IT HAD ON OUR MENTAL HEALTH.
I'M GUESSING IT'S EASIER FOR THEM TO MANAGE US BY PUTTING US ALL TOGETHER, MAYBE?
UM... I DUN-NO...
BUT IF I TRIED TO GET INTO ANOTHER HIGH SCHOOL, I'D HAVE TO SPEND THE WHOLE YEAR STUDYING.
THEY MIGHT ALLOW ME TO TRY ON MY OWN IF I ASKED, BUT STILL ...
I'M SURE YOU COULD DO IT, ONII-CHAN.
YOU HAVE VERY GOOD GRADES.
"HAD." PAST TENSE. I HAVEN'T DONE ANY SCHOOL-WORK IN TWO YEARS.
I KNOW! I COULD BE YOUR TUTOR!
OH?
MAYBE I SHOULD HAVE YOU TEACH ME MATH AND INFORMATION PROCESS-ING.
HEH!
UMM...

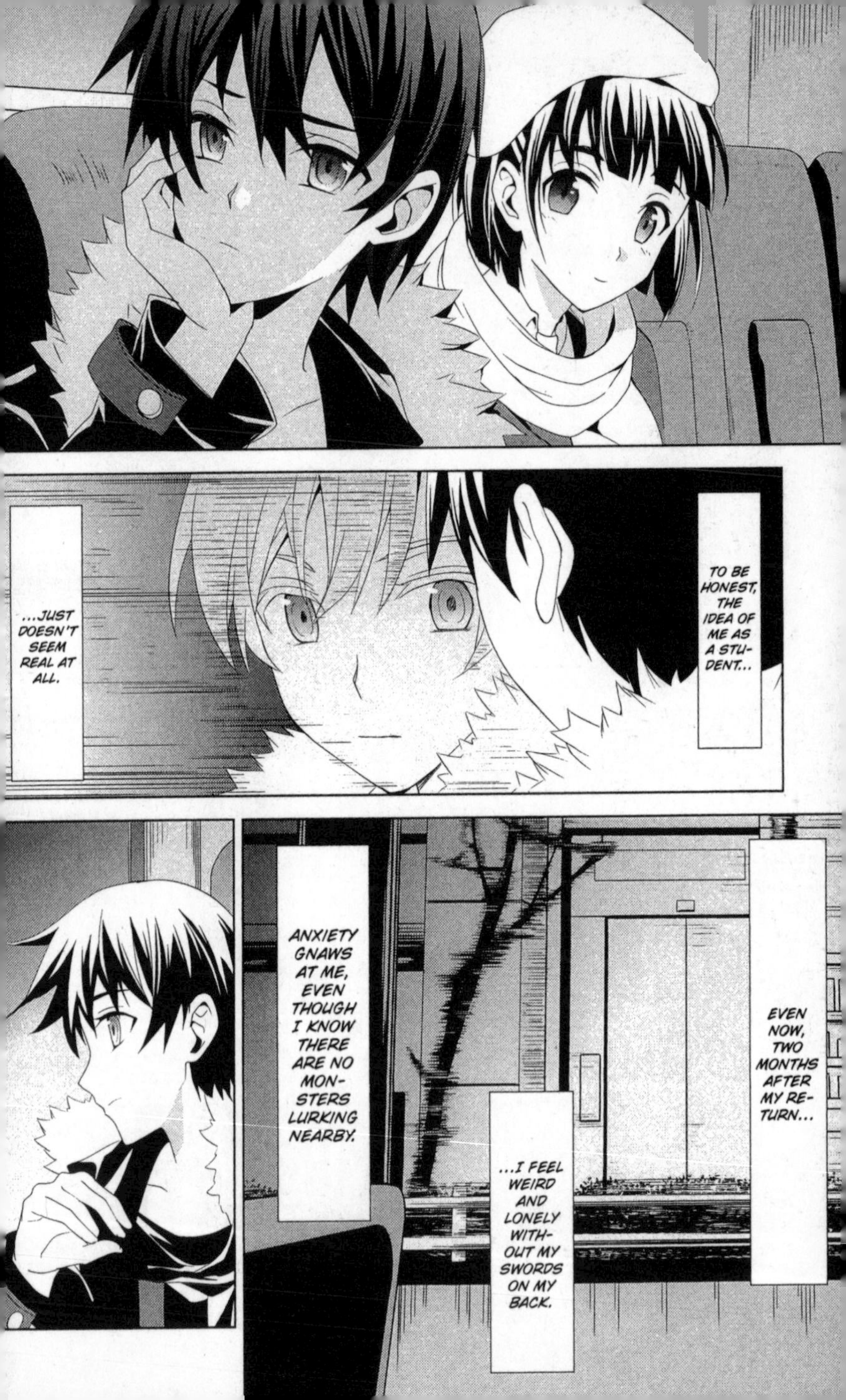

TO BE HONEST, THE IDEA OF ME AS A STUDENT...
...JUST DOESN'T SEEM REAL AT ALL.
EVEN NOW, TWO MONTHS AFTER MY RETURN...
...I FEEL WEIRD AND LONELY WITHOUT MY SWORDS ON MY BACK.
ANXIETY GNAWS AT ME, EVEN THOUGH I KNOW THERE ARE NO MONSTERS LURKING NEARBY.

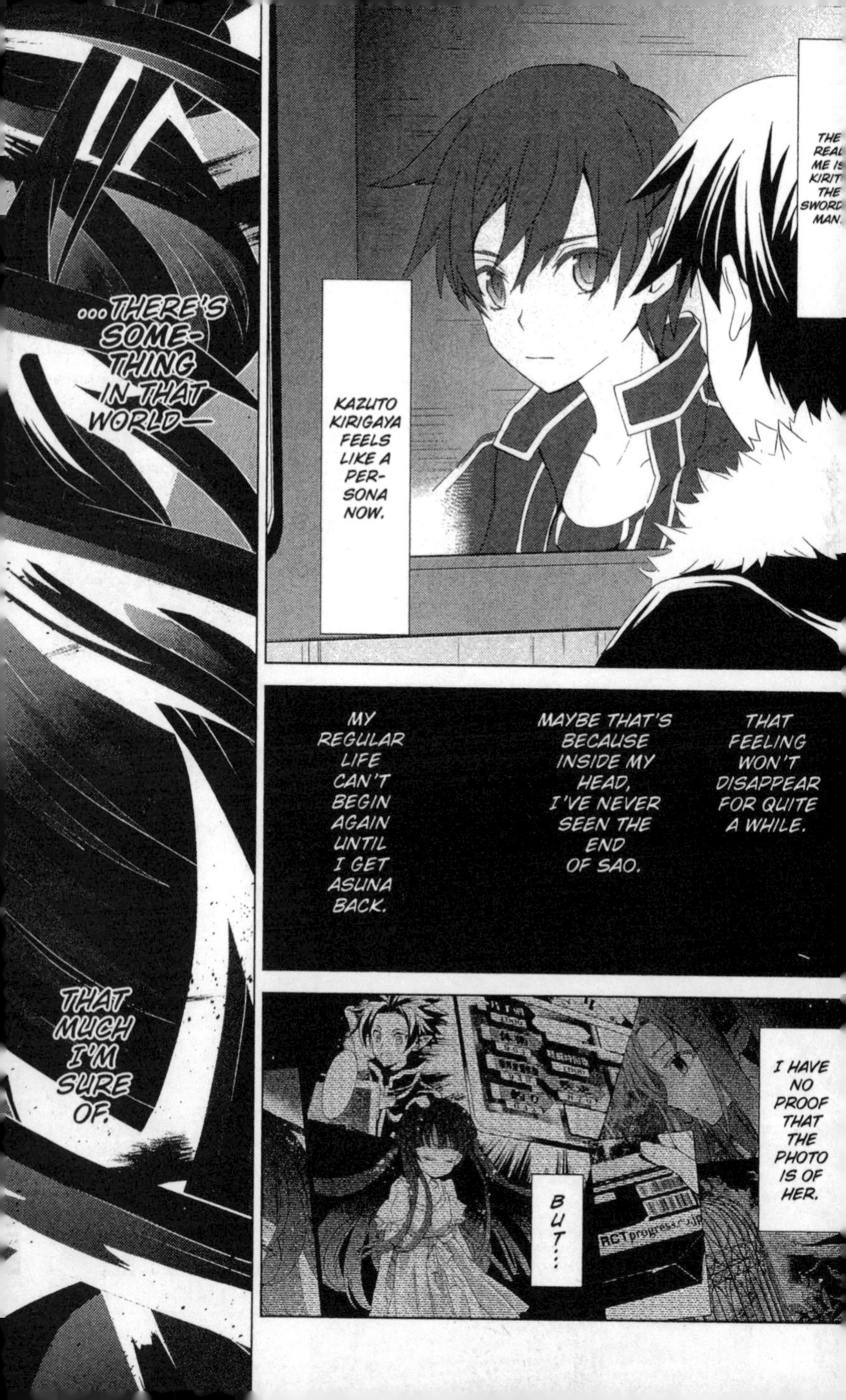
THE REAL ME IS KIRIT THE SWORD MAN.
KAZUTO KIRIGAYA FEELS LIKE A PER-SONA NOW.
THAT FEELING WON'T DISAPPEAR FOR QUITE A WHILE.
MAYBE THAT'S BECAUSE INSIDE MY HEAD, I'VE NEVER SEEN THE END OF SAO.
MY REGULAR LIFE CAN'T BEGIN AGAIN UNTIL I GET ASUNA BACK.
I HAVE NO PROOF THAT THE PHOTO IS OF HER.
BUT...
...THERE'S SOME-THING IN THAT WORLD—
THAT MUCH I'M SURE OF.

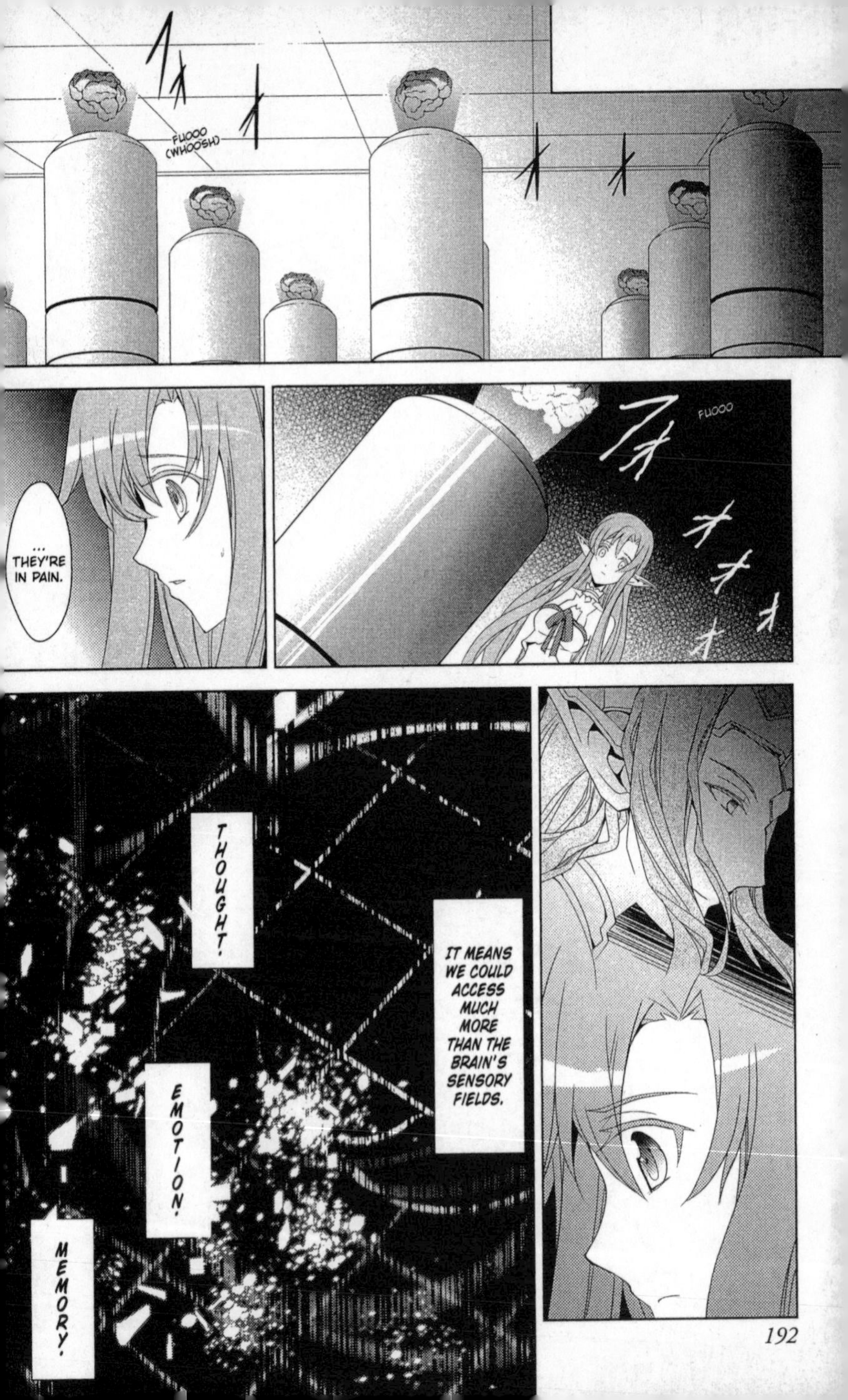
FUOOO (WHOOSH)
FUOOO
... THEY'RE IN PAIN.
IT MEANS WE COULD ACCESS MUCH MORE THAN THE BRAIN'S SENSORY FIELDS.
THOUGHT.
EMOTION.
MEMORY.

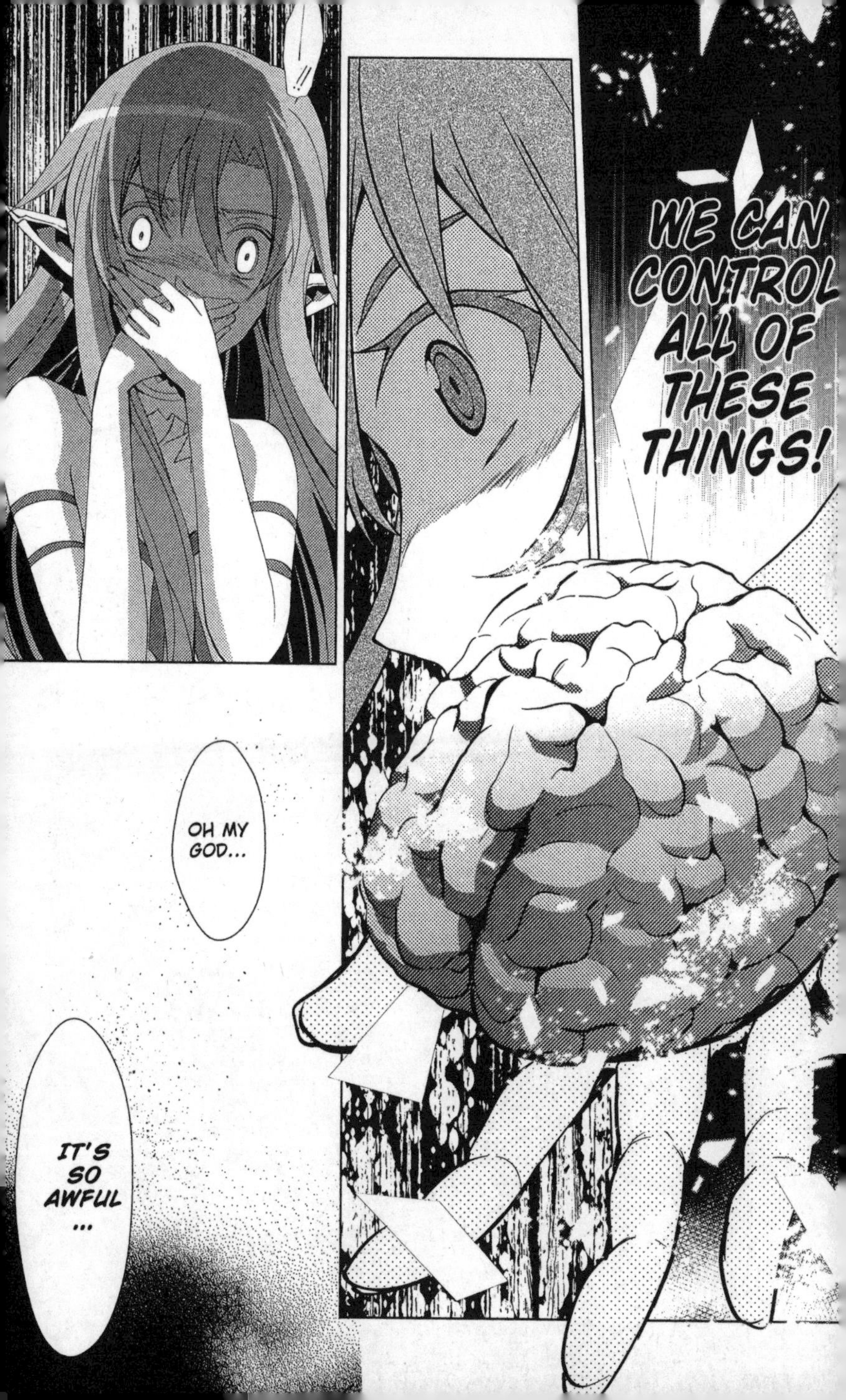
WE CAN CONTROL ALL OF THESE THINGS!
OH MY GOD...
IT'S SO AWFUL ...

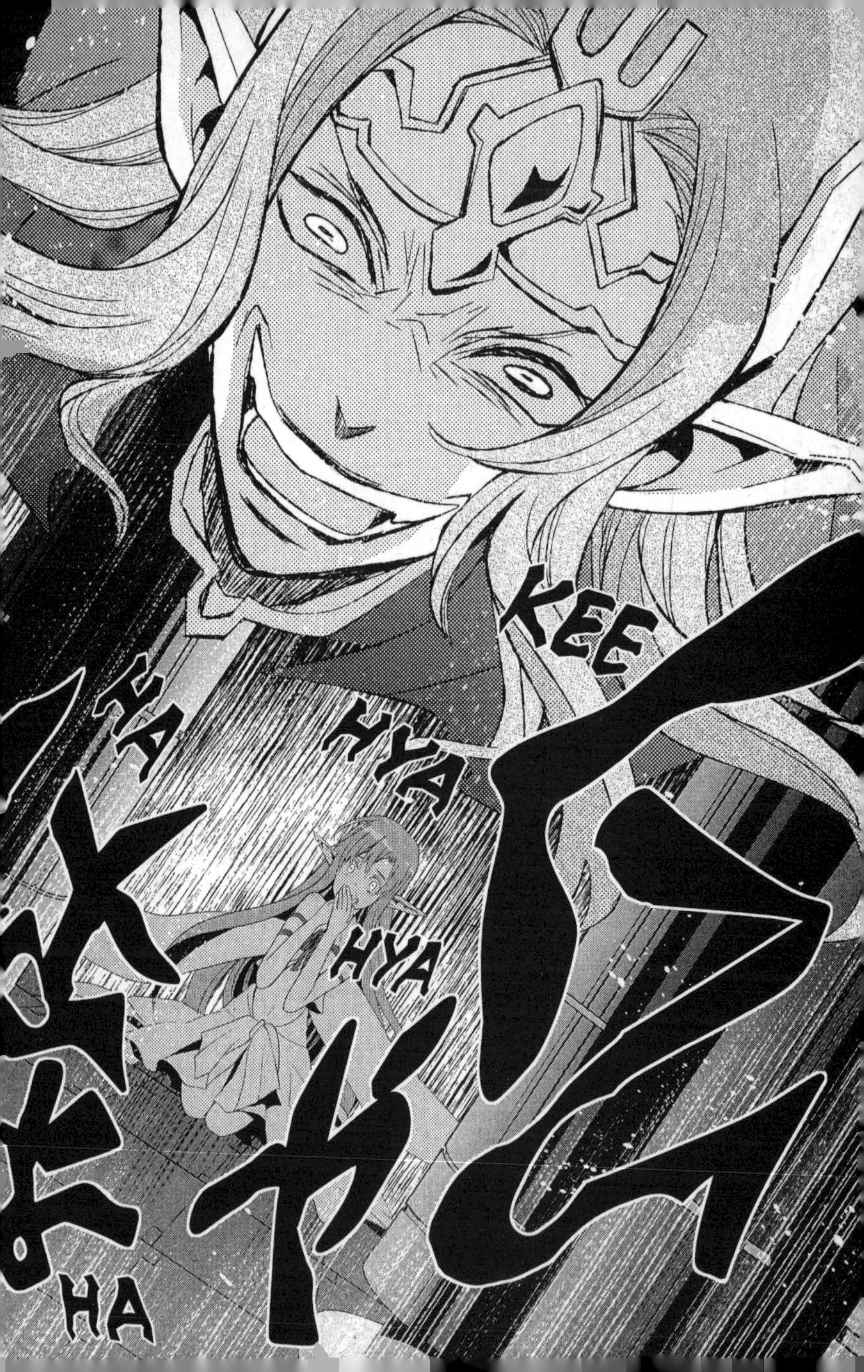
KEE
HYA
HA
HYA
HA

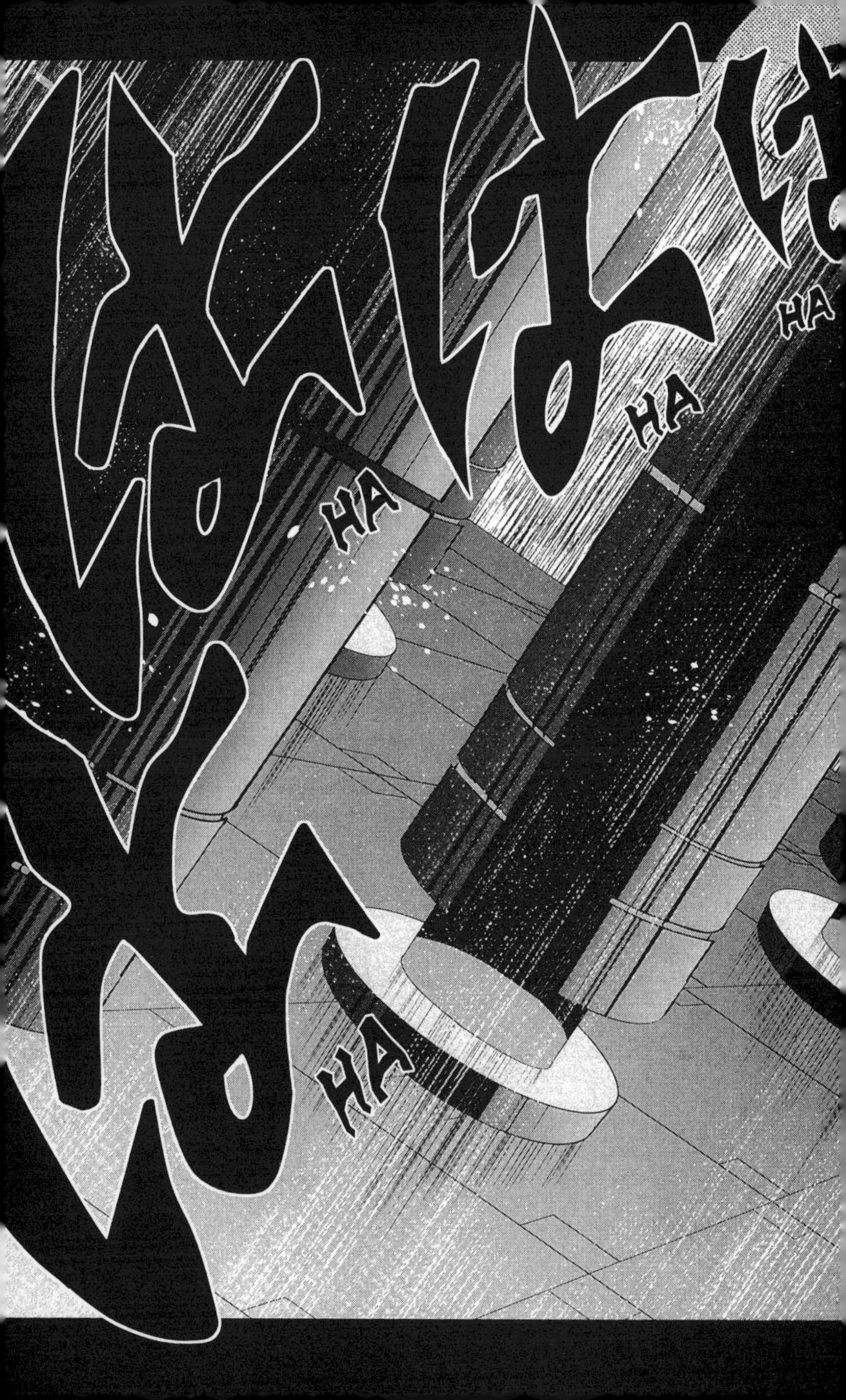
HA
HA
HA
HA

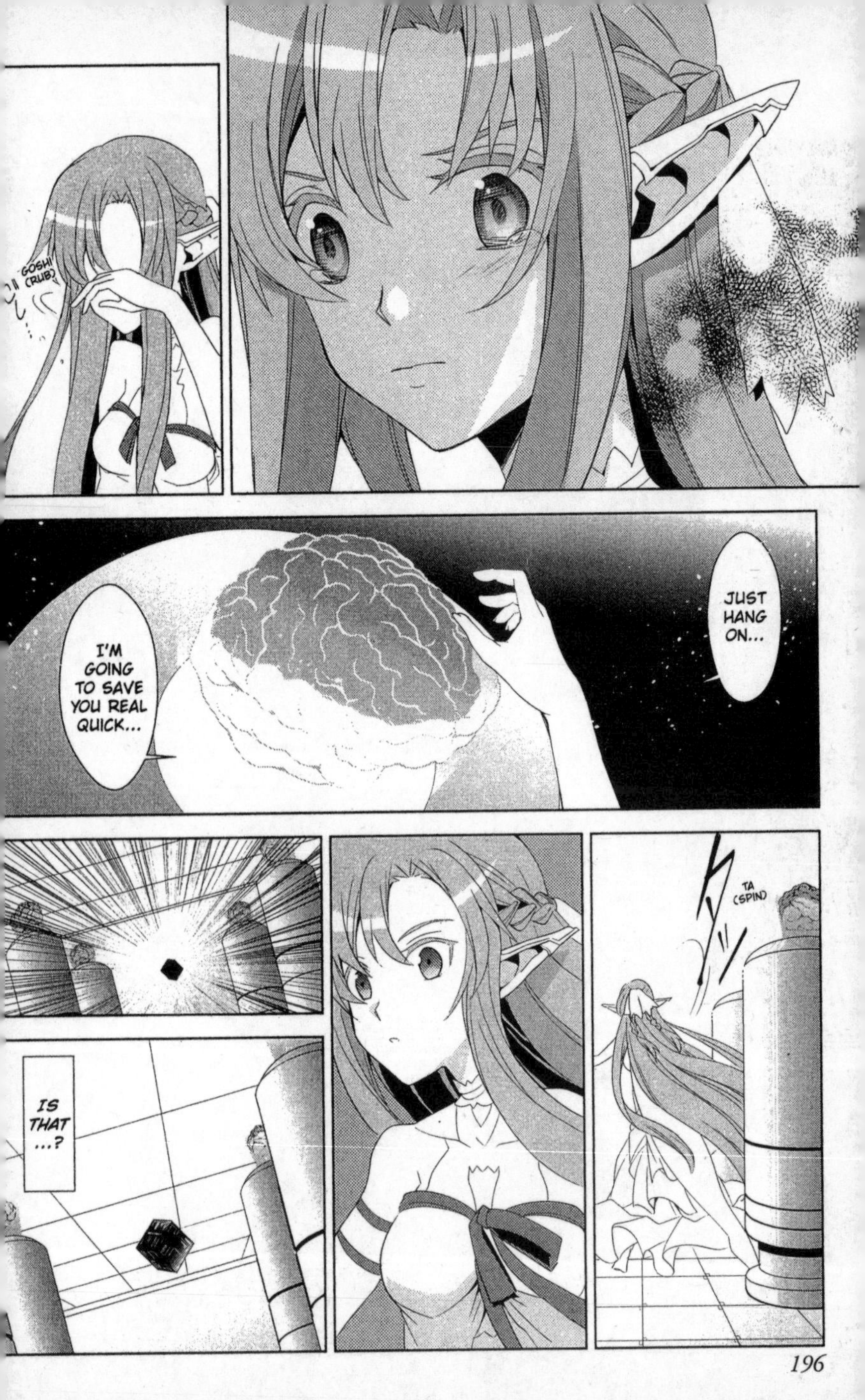
GOSHI (RUB)
JUST HANG ON...
I'M GOING TO SAVE YOU REAL QUICK...
TA (SPIN)
IS THAT ...?

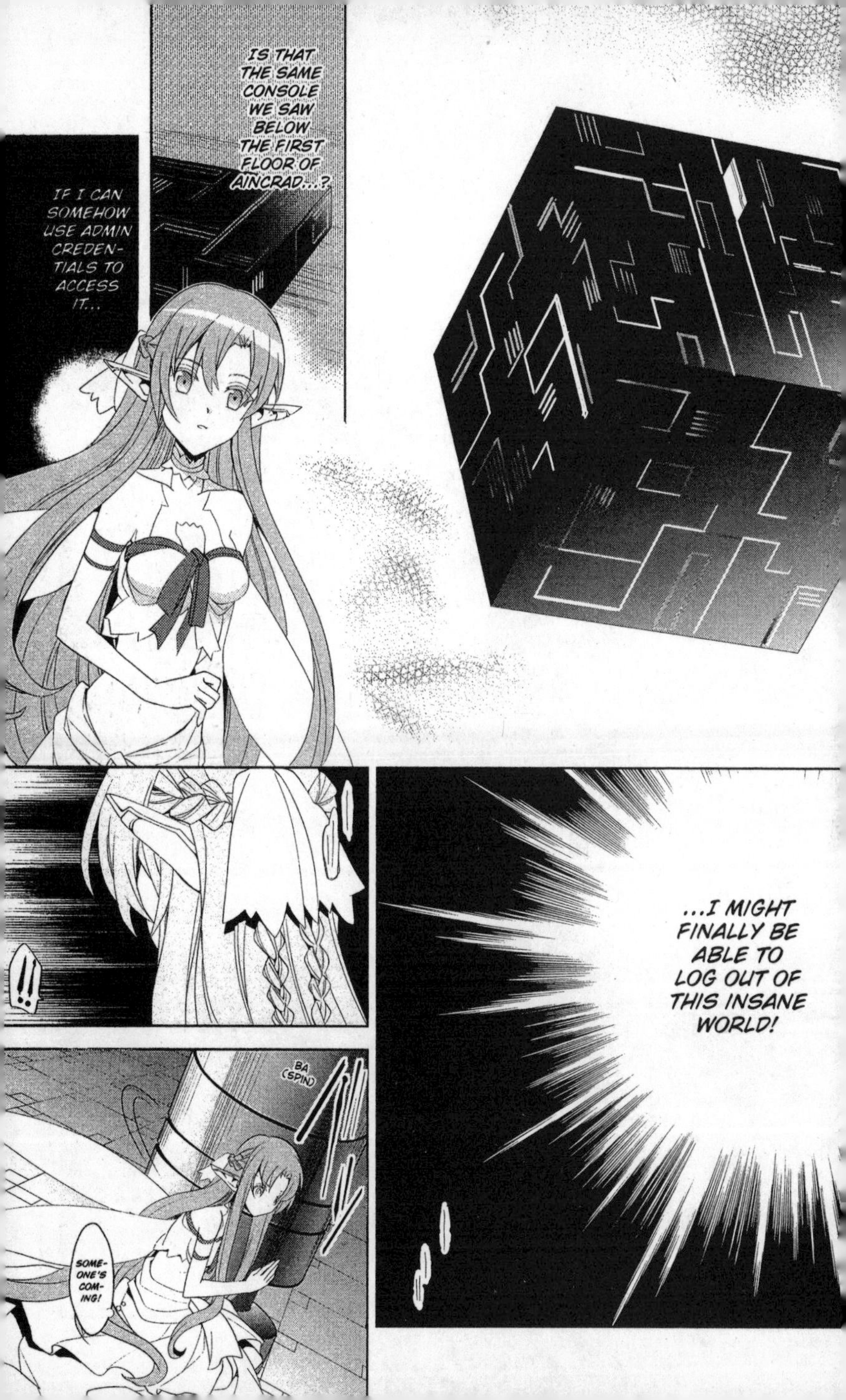
IS THAT THE SAME CONSOLE WE SAW BELOW THE FIRST FLOOR OF AINCRAD...?
IF I CAN SOMEHOW USE ADMIN CREDEN-TIALS TO ACCESS IT...
...I MIGHT FINALLY BE ABLE TO LOG OUT OF THIS INSANE WORLD!
!!
BA (SPIN)
SOME-ONE'S COM-ING!

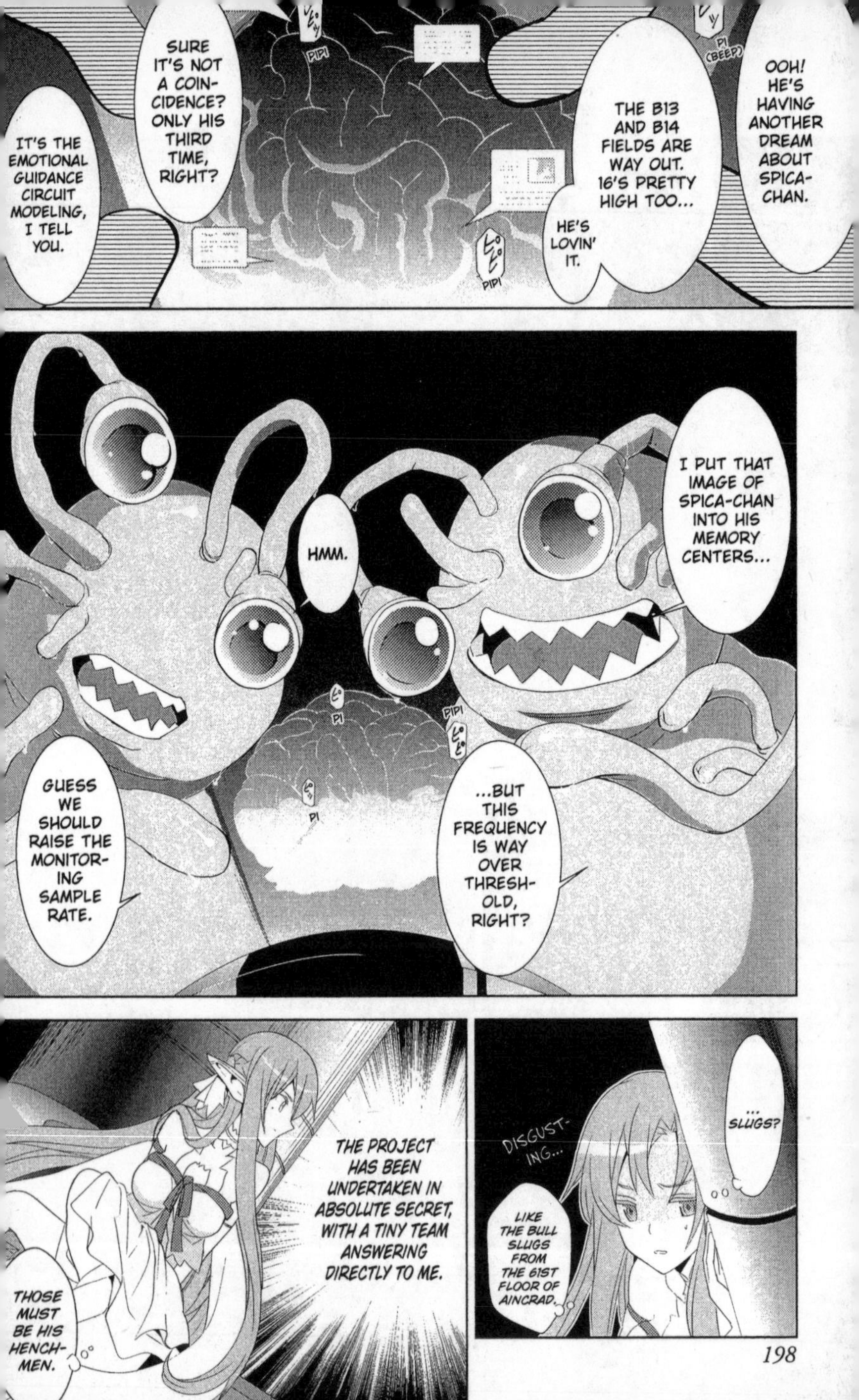
OOH! HE'S HAVING ANOTHER DREAM ABOUT SPICA-CHAN.
PI (BEEP)
THE B13 AND B14 FIELDS ARE WAY OUT. 16'S PRETTY HIGH TOO...
HE'S LOVIN' IT.
PIPI
PIPI
SURE IT'S NOT A COINCIDENCE? ONLY HIS THIRD TIME, RIGHT?
IT'S THE EMOTIONAL GUIDANCE CIRCUIT MODELING, I TELL YOU.
I PUT THAT IMAGE OF SPICA-CHAN INTO HIS MEMORY CENTERS...
HMM.
PIPI
PI
...BUT THIS FREQUENCY IS WAY OVER THRESHOLD, RIGHT?
PI
GUESS WE SHOULD RAISE THE MONITORING SAMPLE RATE.
...SLUGS?
DISGUSTING...
LIKE THE BULL SLUGS FROM THE 61ST FLOOR OF AINCRAD.
THE PROJECT HAS BEEN UNDERTAKEN IN ABSOLUTE SECRET, WITH A TINY TEAM ANSWERING DIRECTLY TO ME.
THOSE MUST BE HIS HENCHMEN.

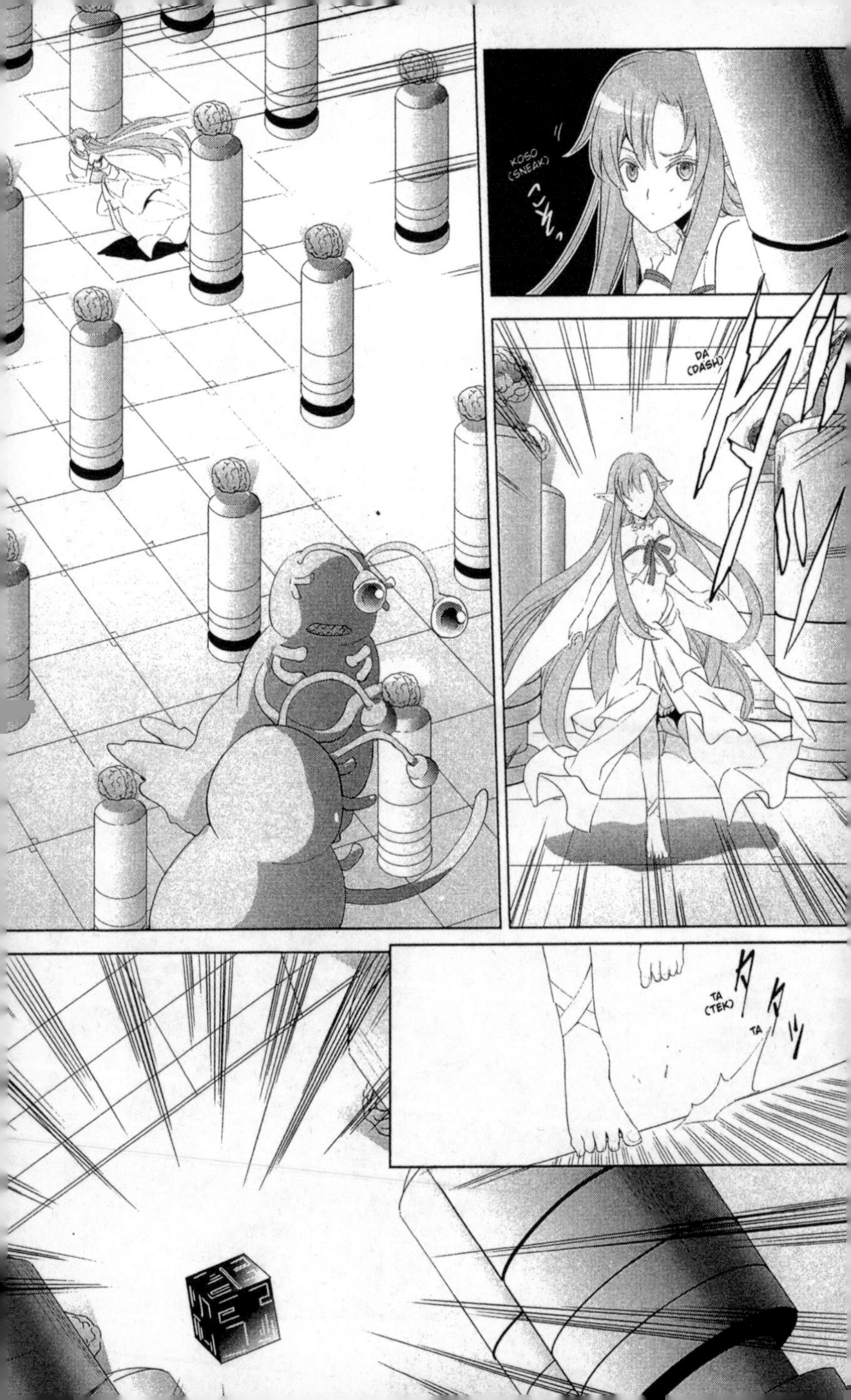
KOSO (SNEAK)
DA (DASH)
TA (TEK)
TA

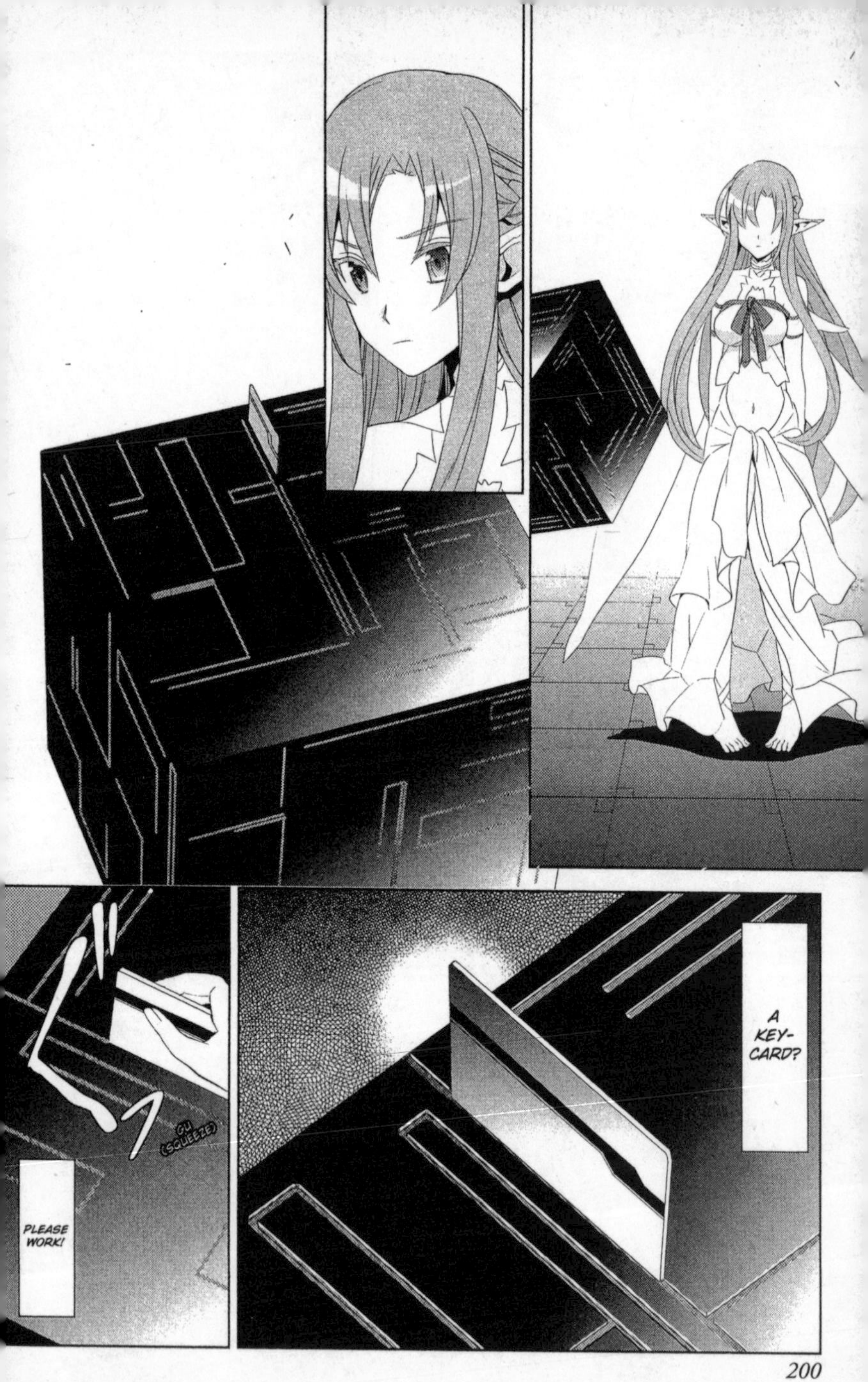
A KEY-CARD?
GU (SQUEEZE)
PLEASE WORK!

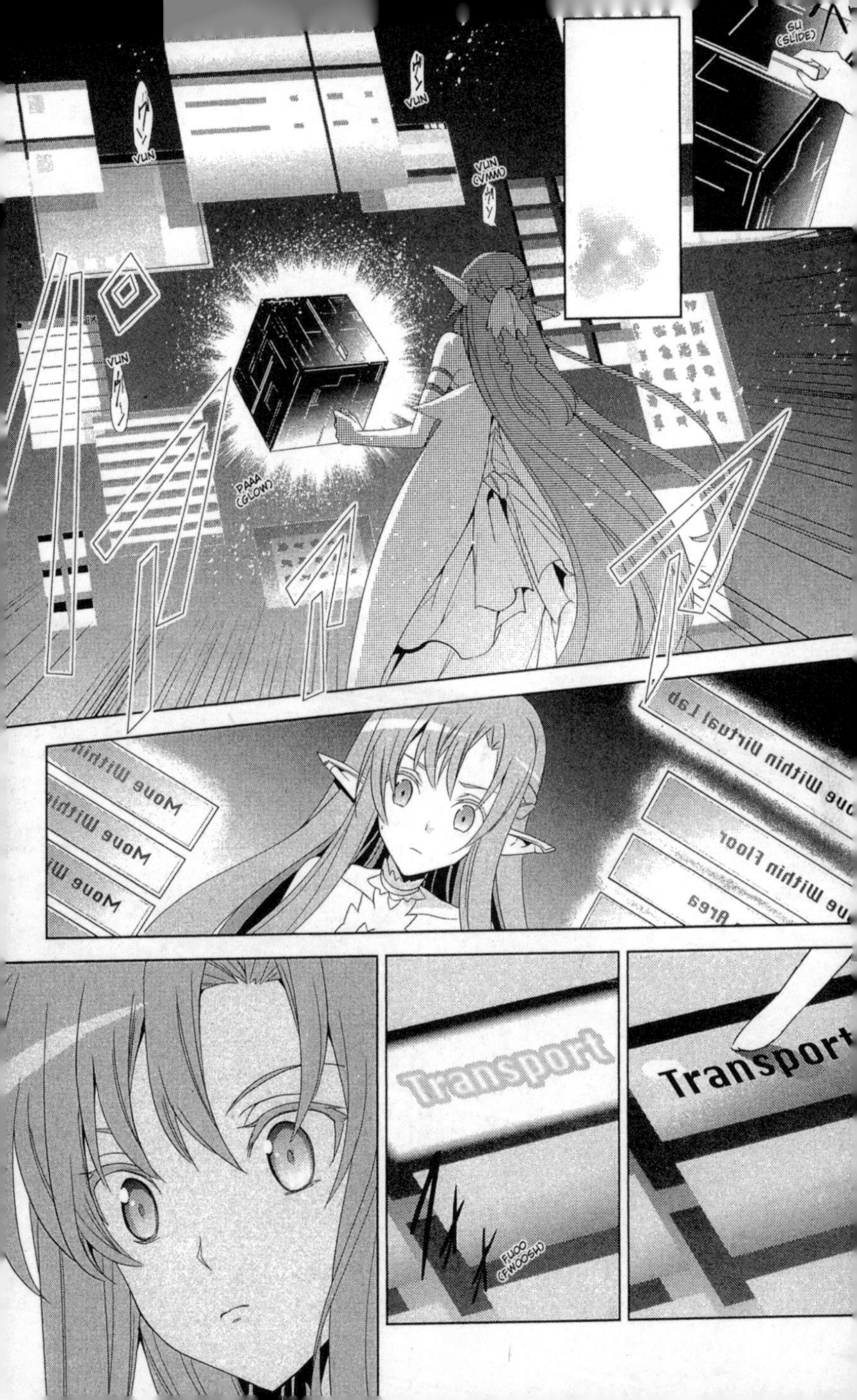
SU (SLIDE)
VUN
VUN
VUN (VWM)
VUN
PAAA (GLOW)
oue Within Virtual Lab
oue Within Floor
Area
Moue Withi
Moue Withi
Moue W
Transport
Transport
FUOO (FWOOSH)

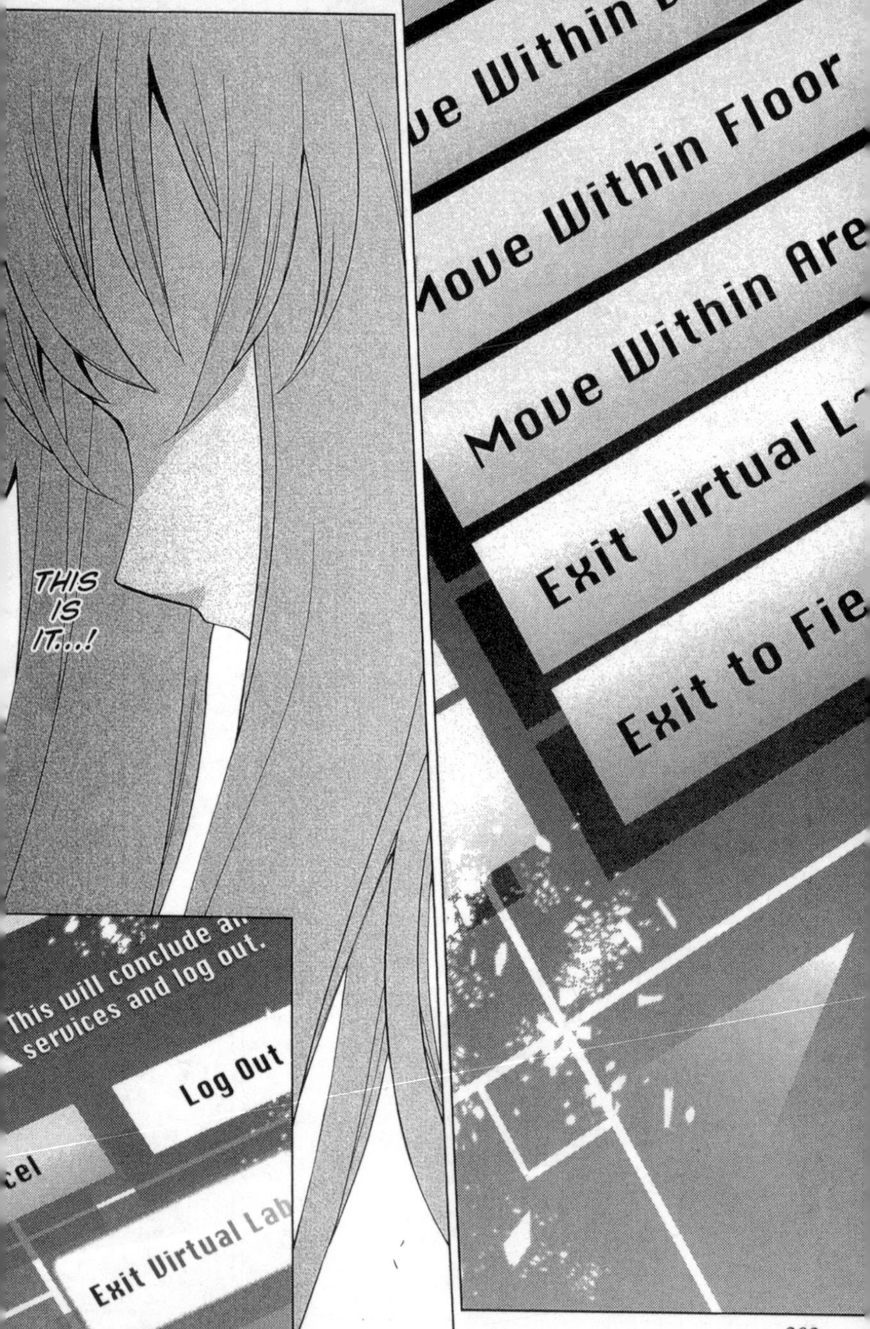
Move Within Floor
Move Within Are
Exit Virtual L
Exit to Fie
THIS IS IT...!
This will conclude al
services and log out.
Log Out
cel
Exit Virtual Lab

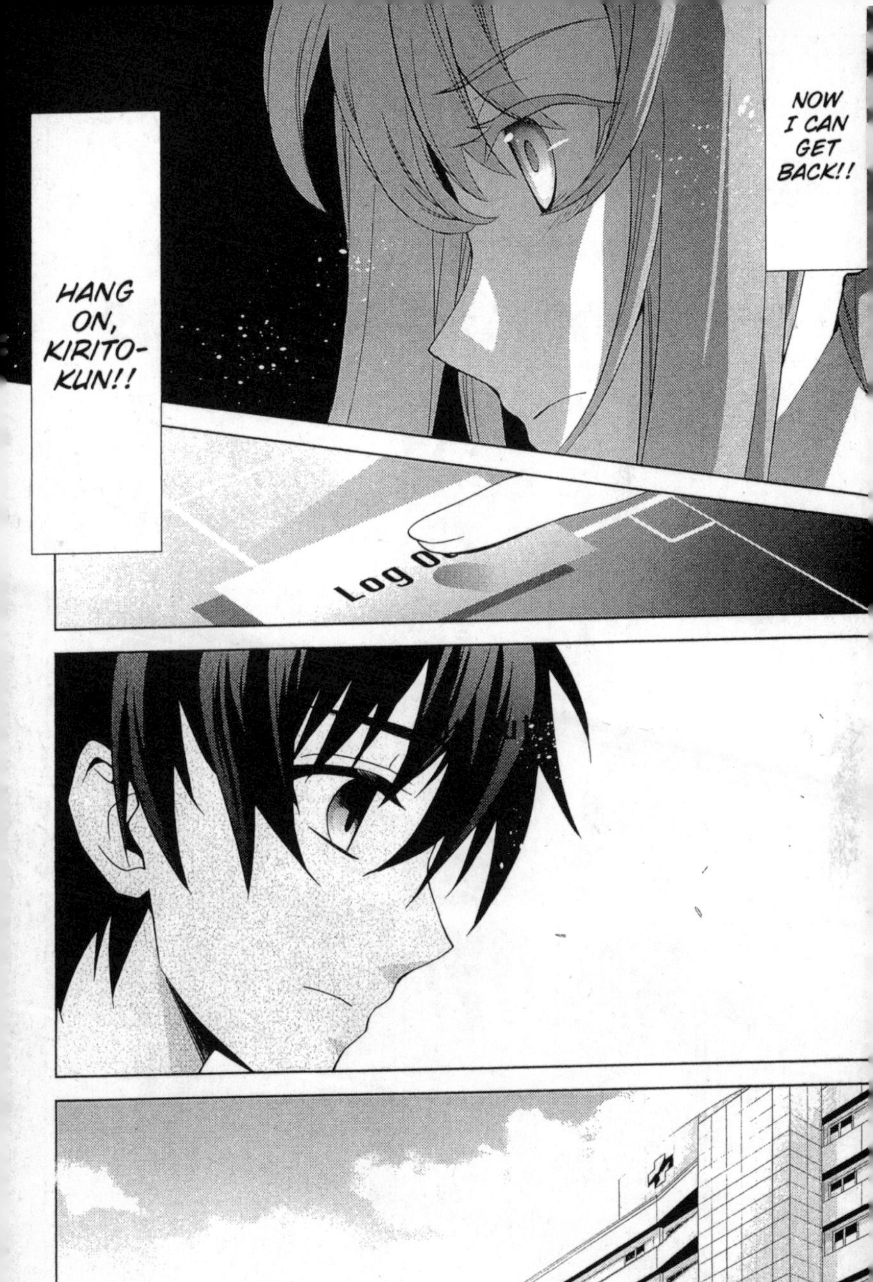
NOW I CAN GET BACK!!
HANG ON, KIRITO-KUN!!

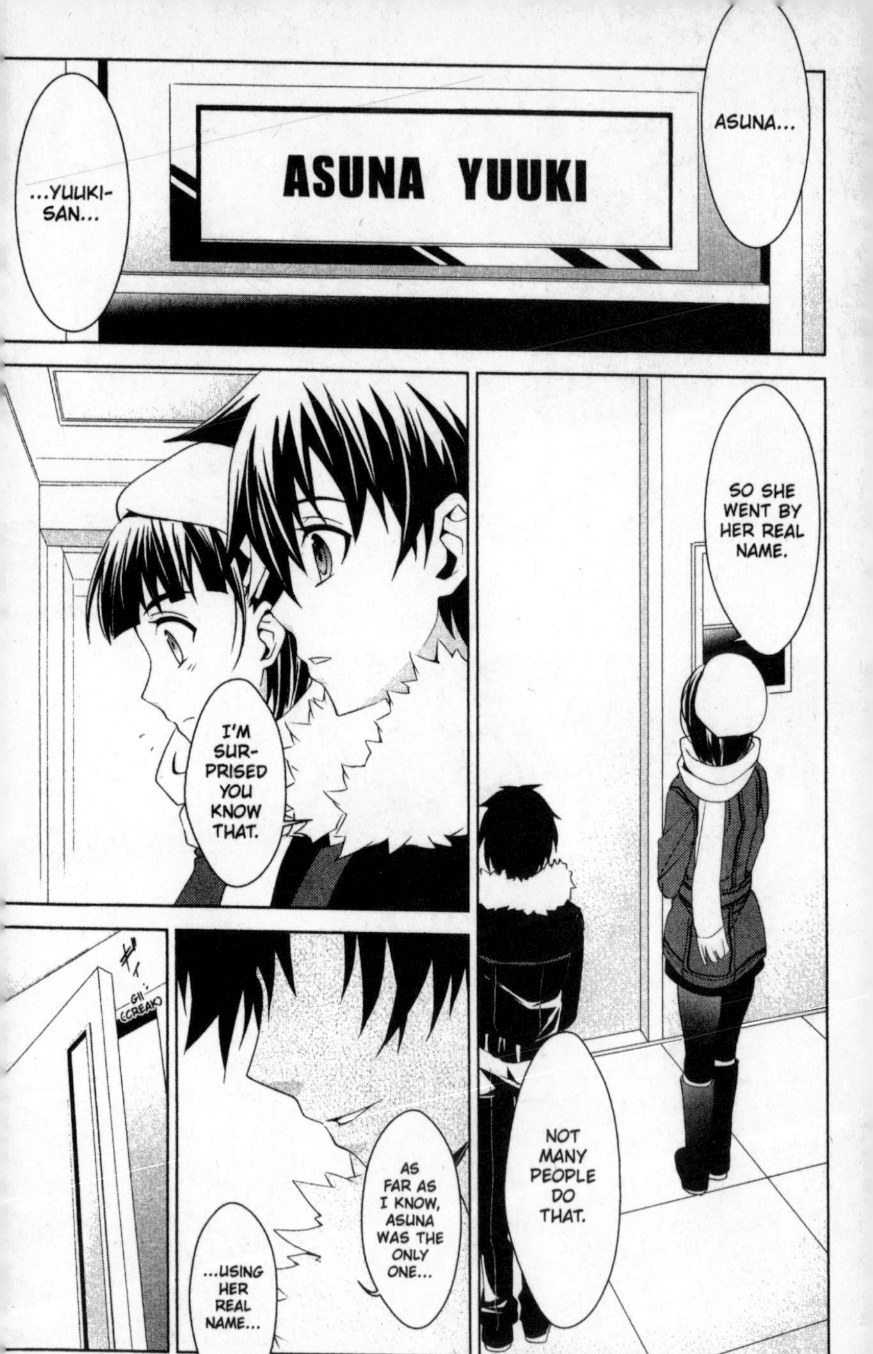
ASUNA...
ASUNA YUUKI
...YUUKI-SAN...
SO SHE WENT BY HER REAL NAME.
NOT MANY PEOPLE DO THAT.
I'M SURPRISED YOU KNOW THAT.
AS FAR AS I KNOW, ASUNA WAS THE ONLY ONE...
...USING HER REAL NAME...
GII (CREAK)

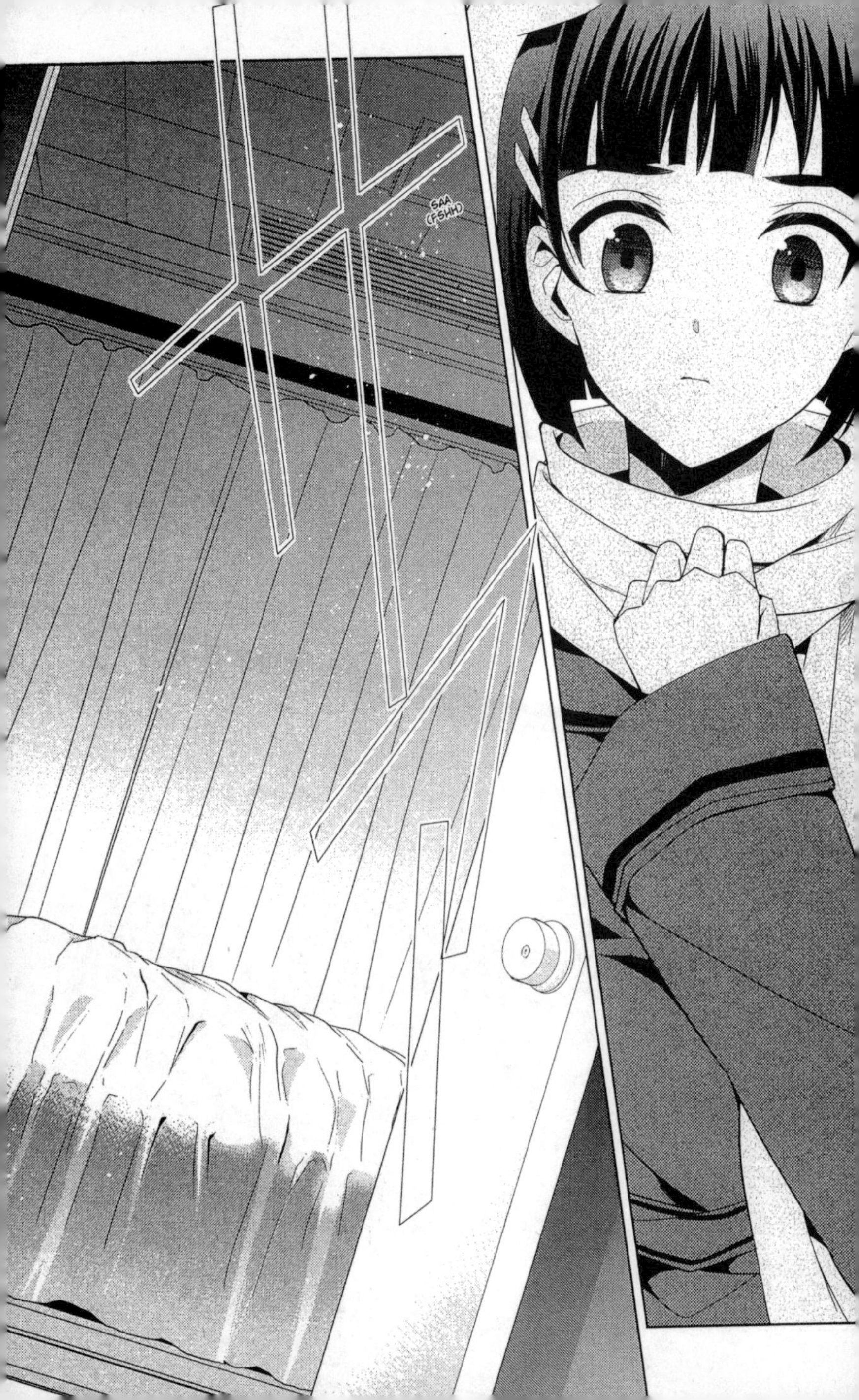
SAA
(FSHH)

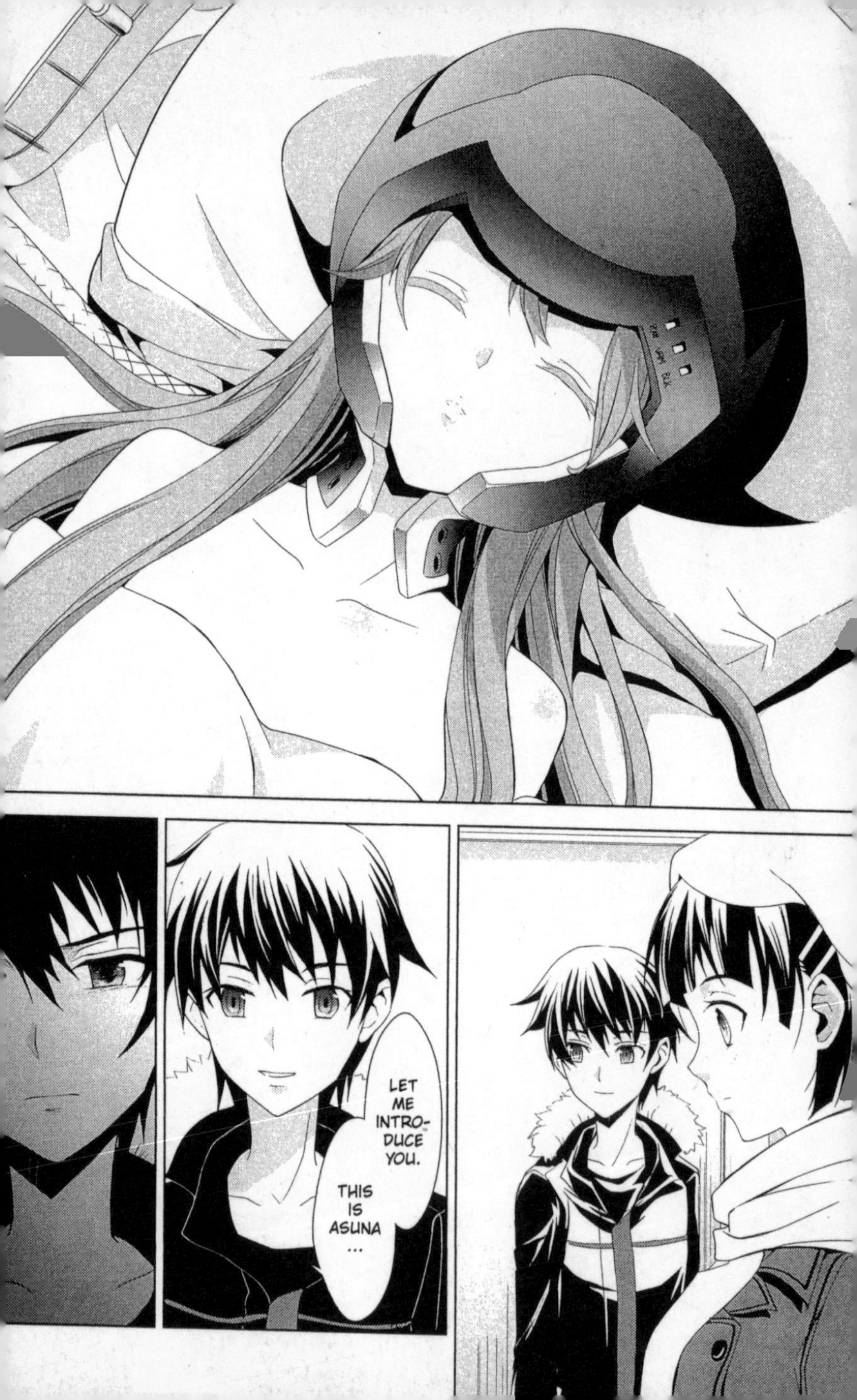
LET ME INTRO-DUCE YOU.
THIS IS ASUNA ...

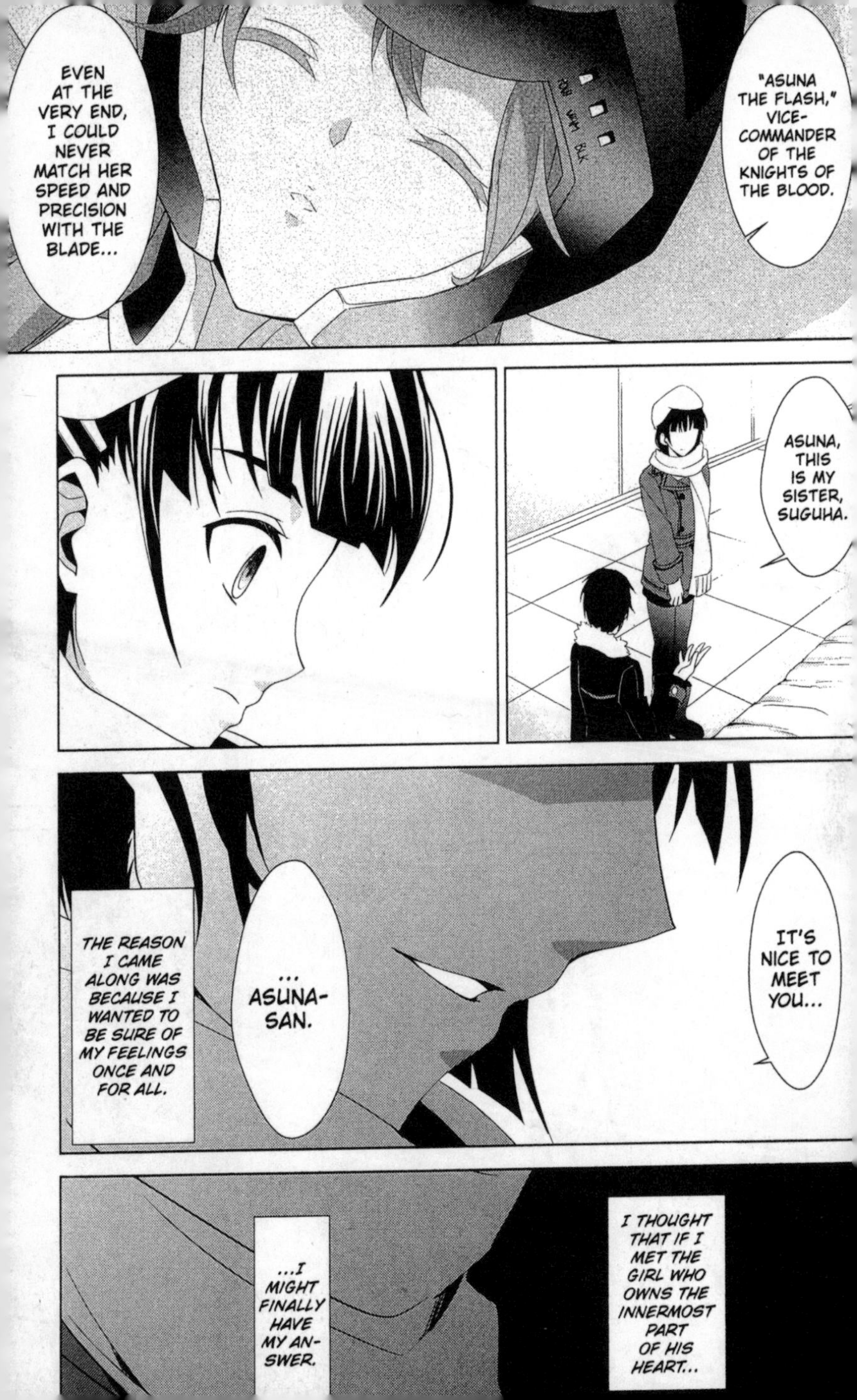
"ASUNA THE FLASH," VICE-COMMANDER OF THE KNIGHTS OF THE BLOOD.
EVEN AT THE VERY END, I COULD NEVER MATCH HER SPEED AND PRECISION WITH THE BLADE...
ASUNA, THIS IS MY SISTER, SUGUHA.
IT'S NICE TO MEET YOU...
...ASUNA-SAN.
THE REASON I CAME ALONG WAS BECAUSE I WANTED TO BE SURE OF MY FEELINGS ONCE AND FOR ALL.
I THOUGHT THAT IF I MET THE GIRL WHO OWNS THE INNERMOST PART OF HIS HEART...
...I MIGHT FINALLY HAVE MY AN-SWER.

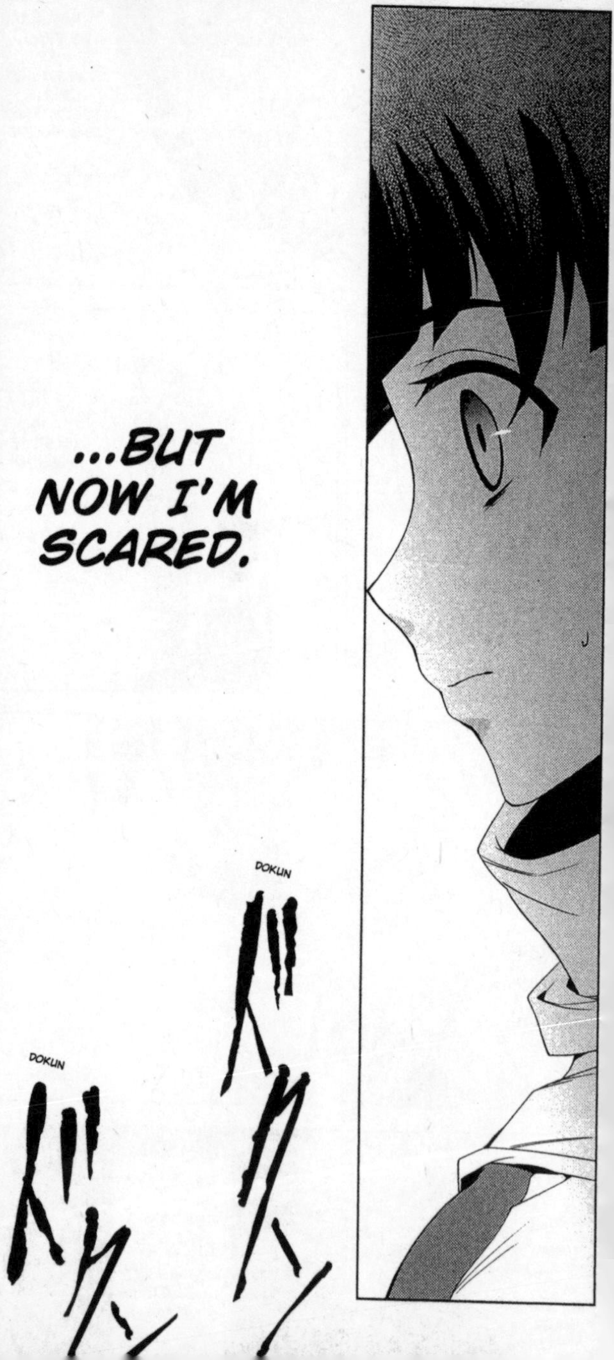
...BUT NOW I'M SCARED.
DOKUN
DOKUN

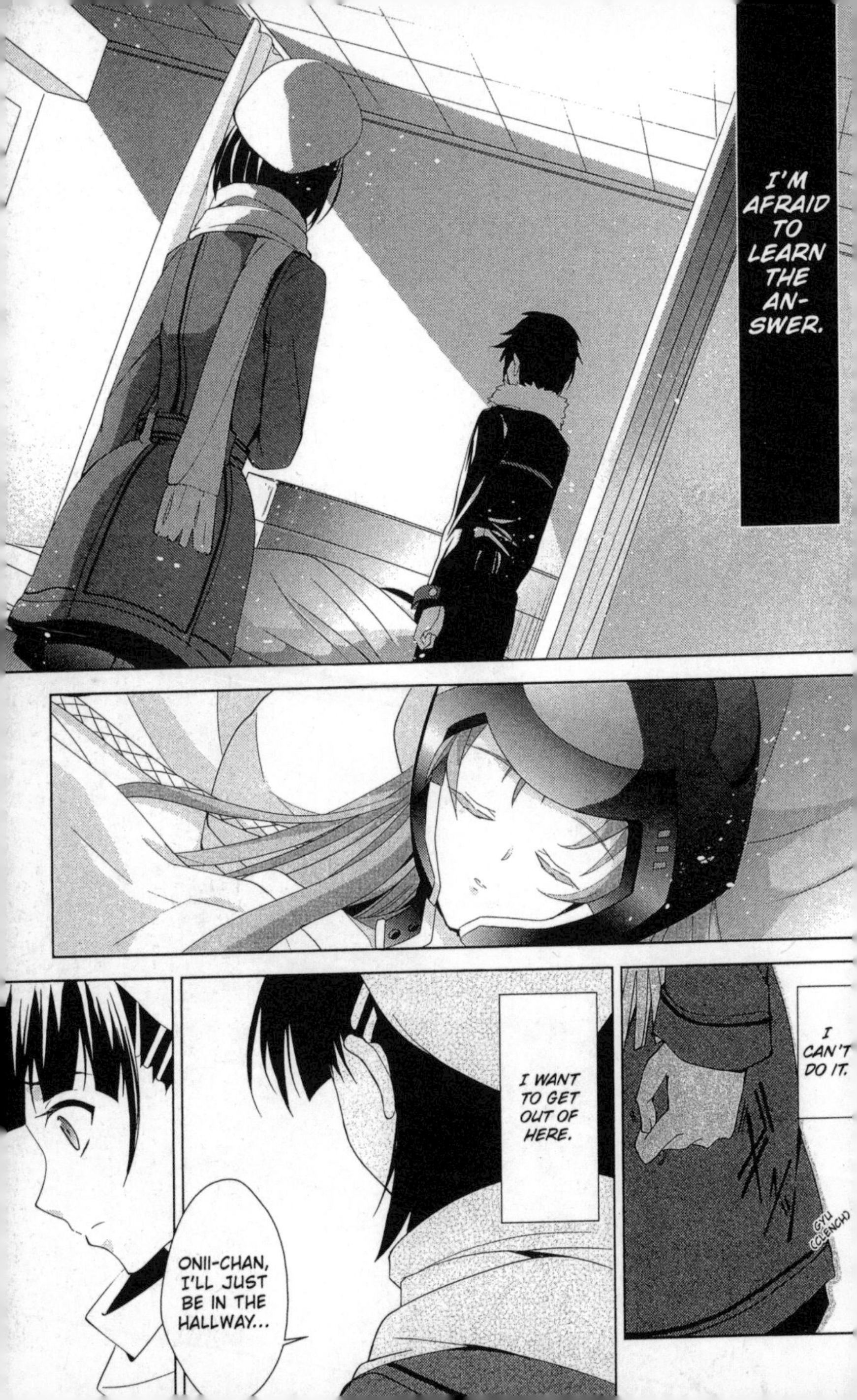
I'M AFRAID TO LEARN THE AN-SWER.
I CAN'T DO IT.
GYU (CLENCH)
I WANT TO GET OUT OF HERE.
ONII-CHAN, I'LL JUST BE IN THE HALLWAY...

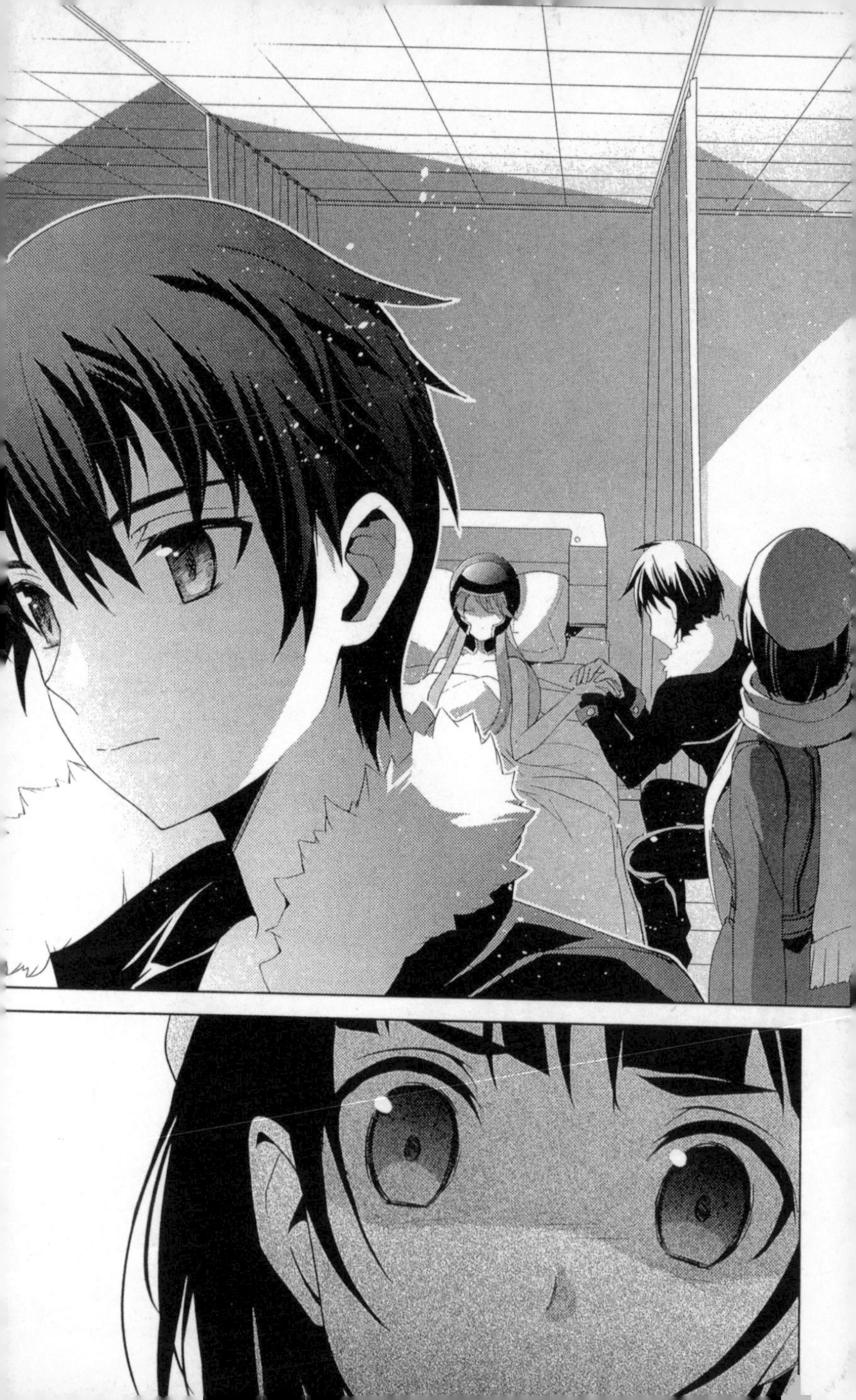

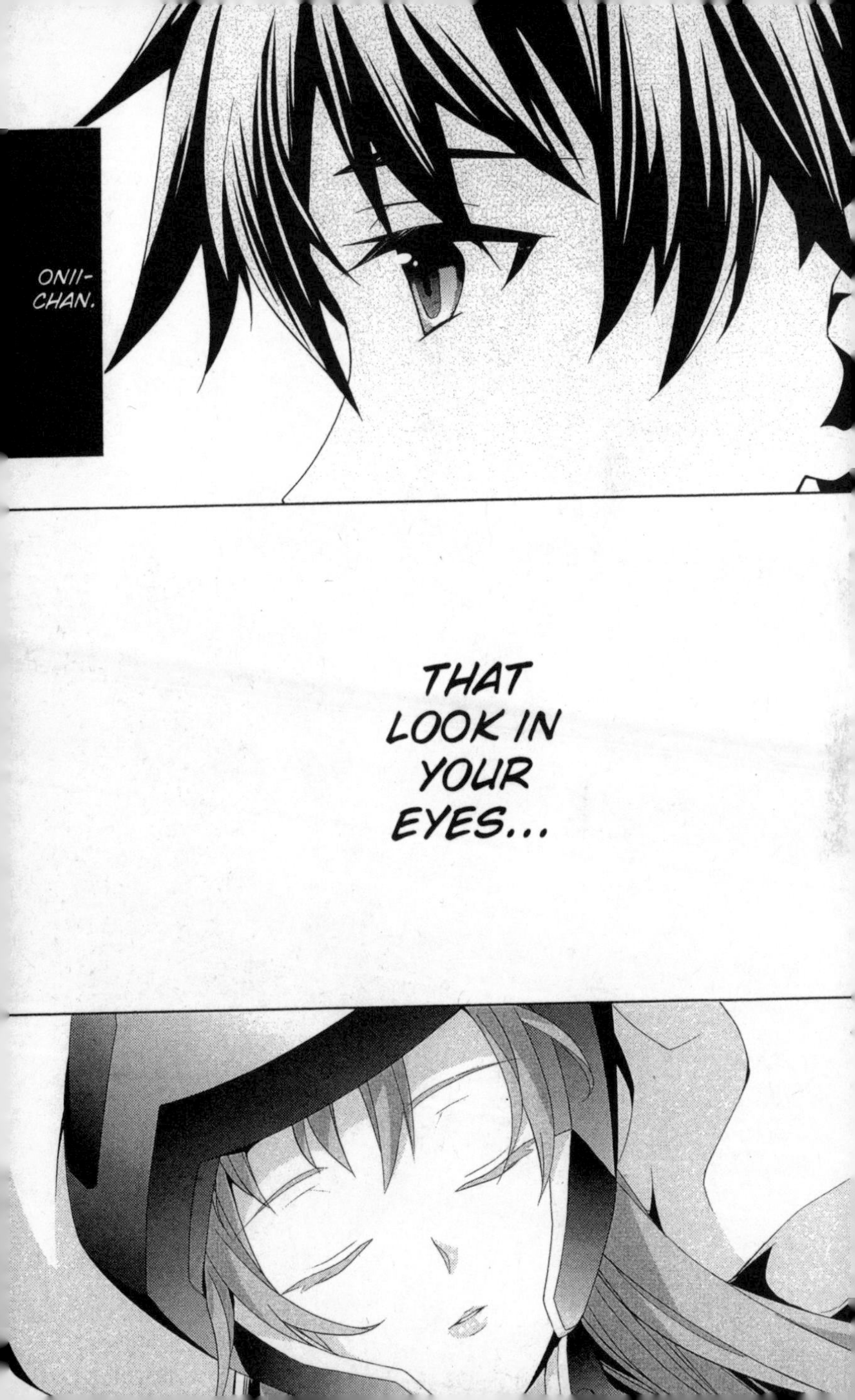
ONII-CHAN.
THAT LOOK IN YOUR EYES...

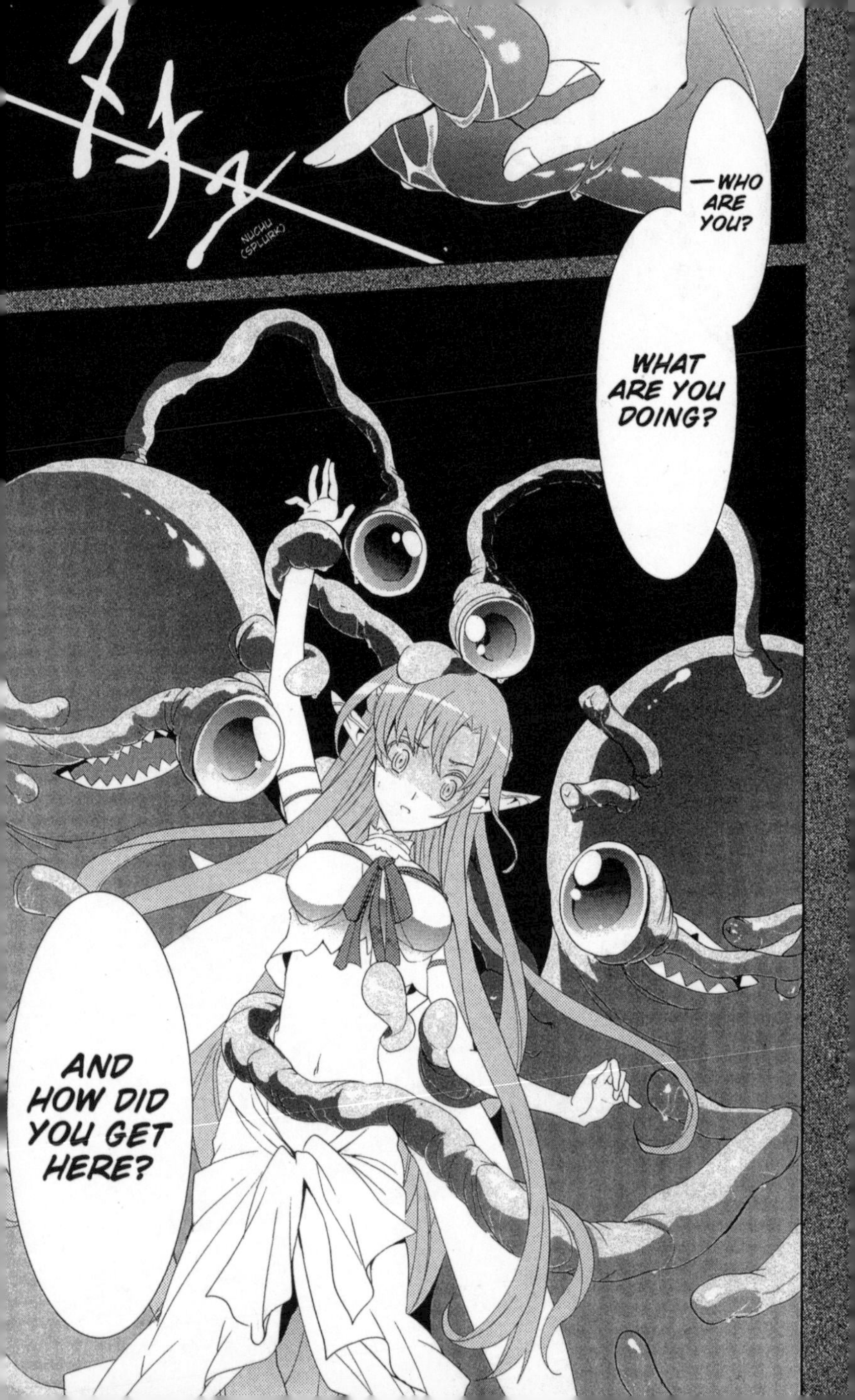
—WHO ARE YOU?
NUCHU (SPLURK)
WHAT ARE YOU DOING?
AND HOW DID YOU GET HERE?

SWORD ART ONLINE
fairy dance

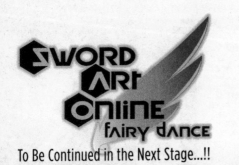

To Be Continued in the Next Stage...!!

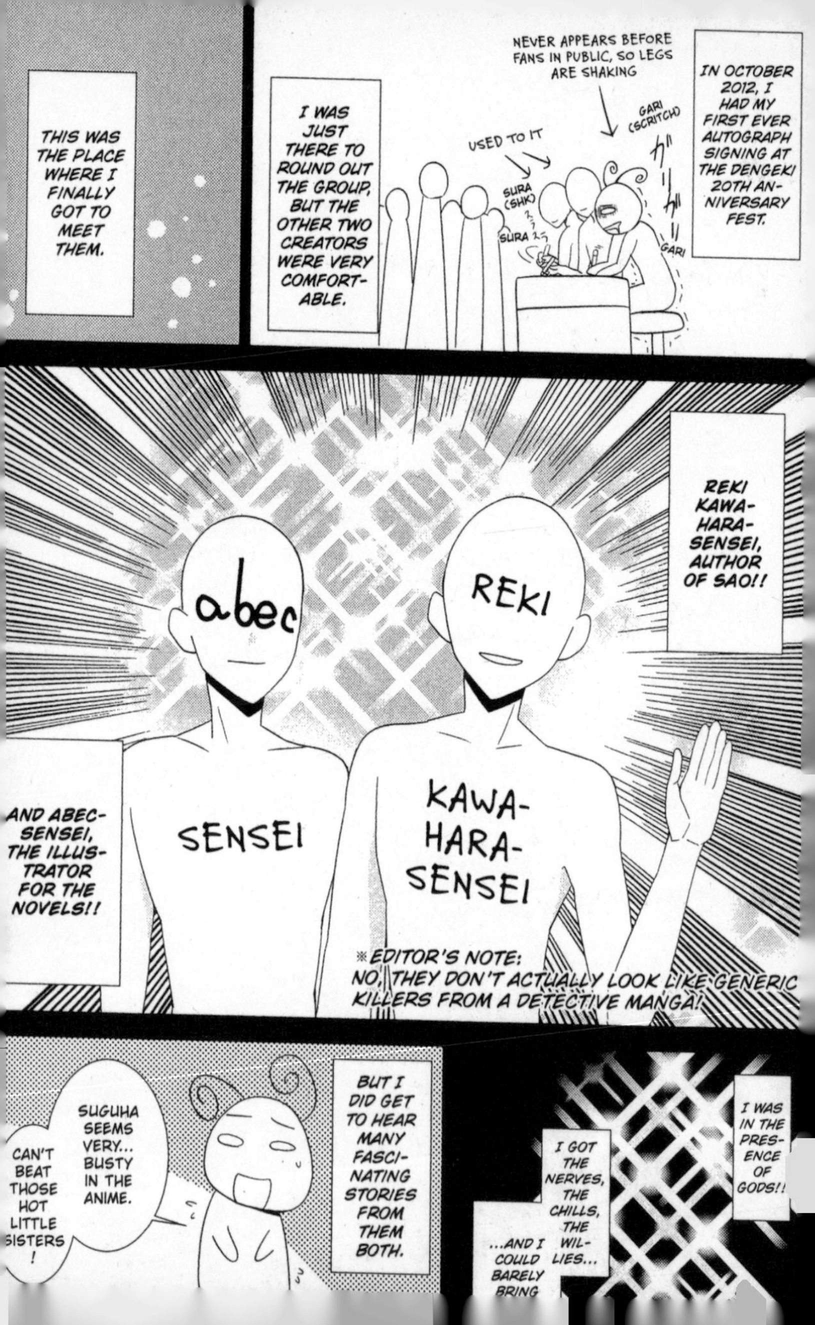
IN OCTOBER 2012, I HAD MY FIRST EVER AUTOGRAPH SIGNING AT THE DENGEKI 20TH ANNIVERSARY FEST.
NEVER APPEARS BEFORE FANS IN PUBLIC, SO LEGS ARE SHAKING
GARI (SCRITCH)
GARI
USED TO IT
SURA (SHK)
SURA
I WAS JUST THERE TO ROUND OUT THE GROUP, BUT THE OTHER TWO CREATORS WERE VERY COMFORTABLE.
THIS WAS THE PLACE WHERE I FINALLY GOT TO MEET THEM.
REKI KAWAHARA-SENSEI, AUTHOR OF SAO!!
REKI KAWAHARA-SENSEI
abec SENSEI
AND ABEC-SENSEI, THE ILLUSTRATOR FOR THE NOVELS!!
※EDITOR'S NOTE: NO, THEY DON'T ACTUALLY LOOK LIKE GENERIC KILLERS FROM A DETECTIVE MANGA!
I WAS IN THE PRESENCE OF GODS!!
I GOT THE NERVES, THE CHILLS, THE WILLIES...
...AND I COULD BARELY BRING
BUT I DID GET TO HEAR MANY FASCINATING STORIES FROM THEM BOTH.
SUGUHA SEEMS VERY... BUSTY IN THE ANIME.
CAN'T BEAT THOSE HOT LITTLE SISTERS!

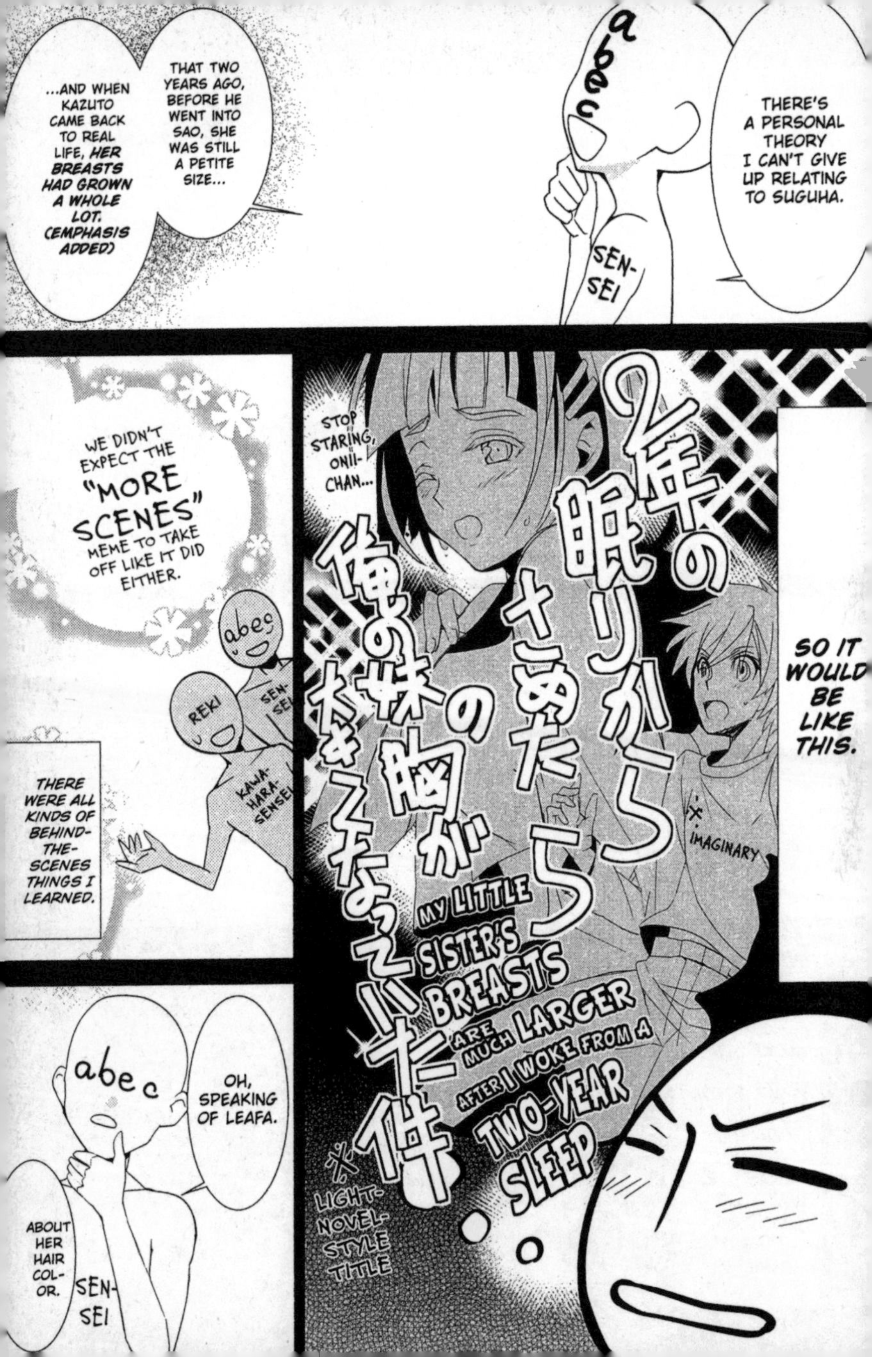
THERE'S A PERSONAL THEORY I CAN'T GIVE UP RELATING TO SUGUHA.
abec
SEN-SEI
THAT TWO YEARS AGO, BEFORE HE WENT INTO SAO, SHE WAS STILL A PETITE SIZE...
...AND WHEN KAZUTO CAME BACK TO REAL LIFE, HER BREASTS HAD GROWN A WHOLE LOT. (EMPHASIS ADDED)
SO IT WOULD BE LIKE THIS.
2年の眠りからさめたら俺の妹の胸が大きくなってた件。
MY LITTLE SISTER'S BREASTS ARE MUCH LARGER AFTER I WOKE FROM A TWO-YEAR SLEEP
※LIGHT-NOVEL-STYLE TITLE
STOP STARING, ONII-CHAN...
※IMAGINARY
WE DIDN'T EXPECT THE "MORE SCENES" MEME TO TAKE OFF LIKE IT DID EITHER.
abec
SEN-SEI
REKI
KAWA-HARA-SENSEI
THERE WERE ALL KINDS OF BEHIND-THE-SCENES THINGS I LEARNED.
OH, SPEAKING OF LEAFA.
abec
ABOUT HER HAIR COL-OR.
SEN-SEI

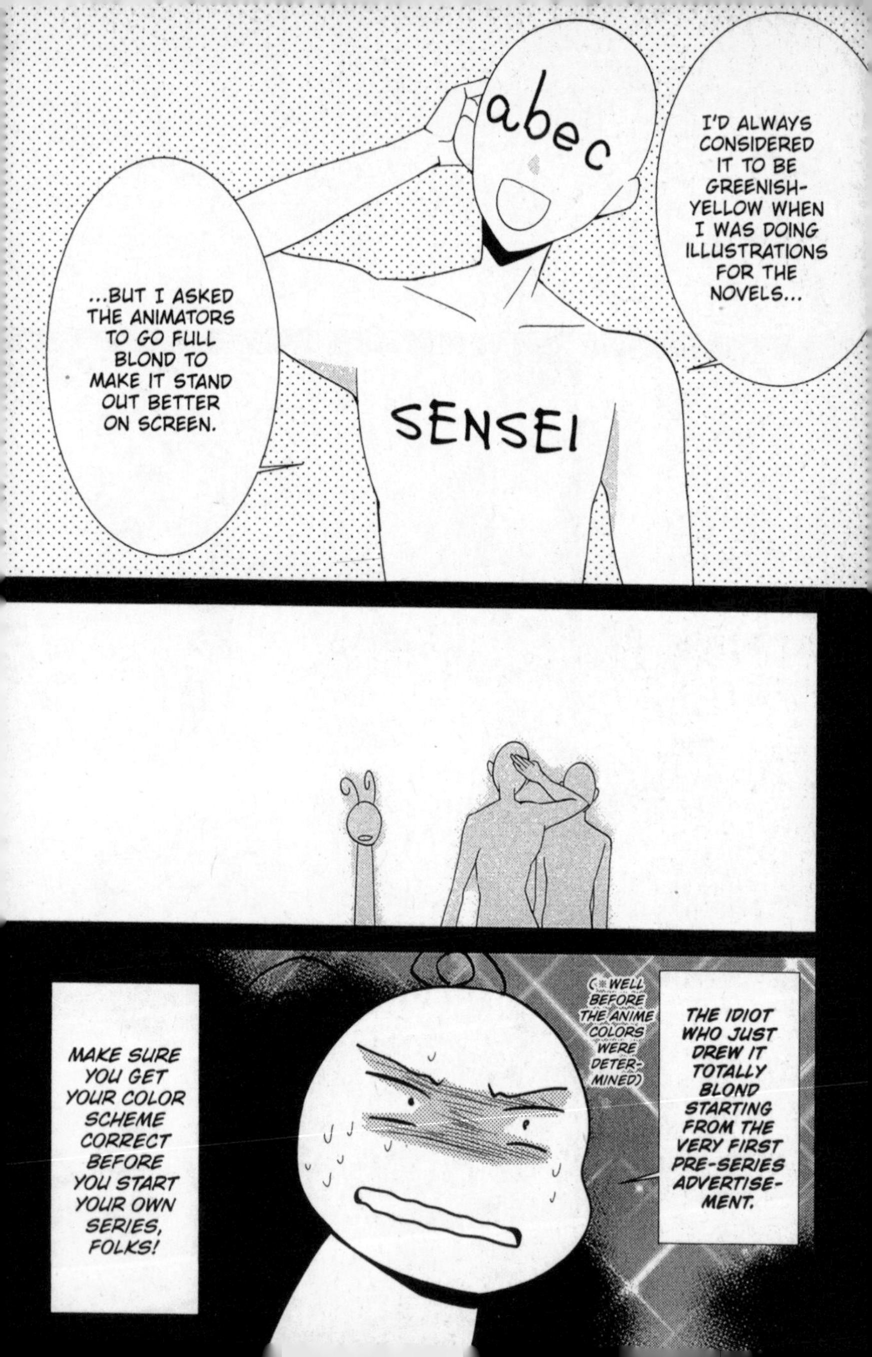
I'D ALWAYS CONSIDERED IT TO BE GREENISH-YELLOW WHEN I WAS DOING ILLUSTRATIONS FOR THE NOVELS...
abec
...BUT I ASKED THE ANIMATORS TO GO FULL BLOND TO MAKE IT STAND OUT BETTER ON SCREEN.
SENSEI
THE IDIOT WHO JUST DREW IT TOTALLY BLOND STARTING FROM THE VERY FIRST PRE-SERIES ADVERTISEMENT.
(※WELL BEFORE THE ANIME COLORS WERE DETERMINED)
MAKE SURE YOU GET YOUR COLOR SCHEME CORRECT BEFORE YOU START YOUR OWN SERIES, FOLKS!

SPECIAL THANKS

RIONA
CORAL

TOMOAKI IKEDA
MITSUHIRO ONODA
SAORI MIYAMOTO
TAKASHI SAKAI

EMIRI NIHEI
MASAOMI ITO

REKI KAWAHARA
ABEC

KAZUMA MIKI
TOMOYUKI TSUCHIYA

THE STAFF OF THE SWORD ART ONLINE
ANIME SERIES

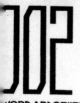

002

WORD ART ONLINE fairy dance

t: tsubasa haduki
riginal story: reki kawahara
aracter design: abec

special comment

original story: reki kawahara

UNLIKE AINCRAD, WHICH WAS TOLD FROM KIRITO'S PERSPECTIVE, THERE ARE THREE PROTAGONISTS IN THE FAIRY DANCE ARC: KIRITO, WHO SEEKS TO FREE HIS DEAR LOVE. ASUNA, WHO ATTEMPTS TO ESCAPE HER PRISON. AND LEAFA, WHO IS CAUGHT BETWEEN KAZUTO AND KIRITO. BECAUSE OF THIS, THE NATURAL BREADTH OF THE STORY'S ATMOSPHERE—THE DIFFERENCE BETWEEN THE SERIOUS AND COMICAL SCENES—IS QUITE LARGER THAN BEFORE. THE PART OF THE STORY CONTAINED IN THIS SECOND VOLUME IS ESPECIALLY NOTABLE FOR THIS, AND I BELIEVE IT MUST HAVE BEEN QUITE DIFFICULT TO CAPTURE IN MANGA FORM. BUT HADUKI-SAN'S POWERFUL YET DELICATE LINEWORK PLUNGED ME INTO THIS ALTERNATE WORLD AND WRAPPED ME UP IN A STORY THAT I SHOULD ALREADY KNOW QUITE WELL. NOW I'M REALLY EXCITED TO READ WHAT COMES NEXT!

CONGRATULATIONS ON THE RELEASE OF YOUR SECOND BOOK. I CAN'T WAIT FOR THE CLIMAX OF THE STORY IN THE NEXT VOLUME!

REKI KAWAHARA

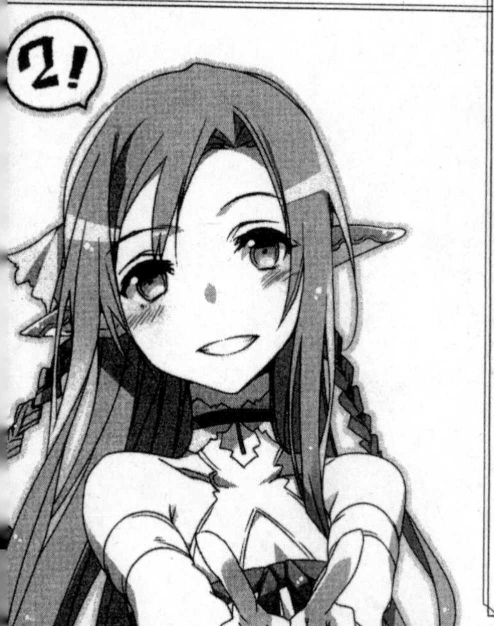
2!

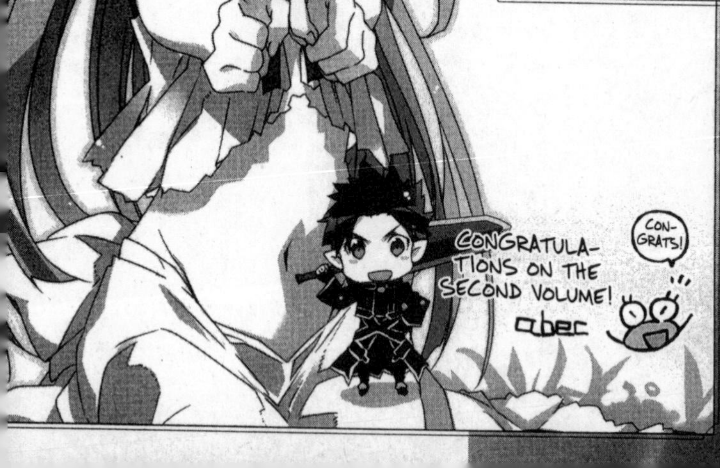
CON-GRATS!
CONGRATULATIONS ON THE SECOND VOLUME!
abec

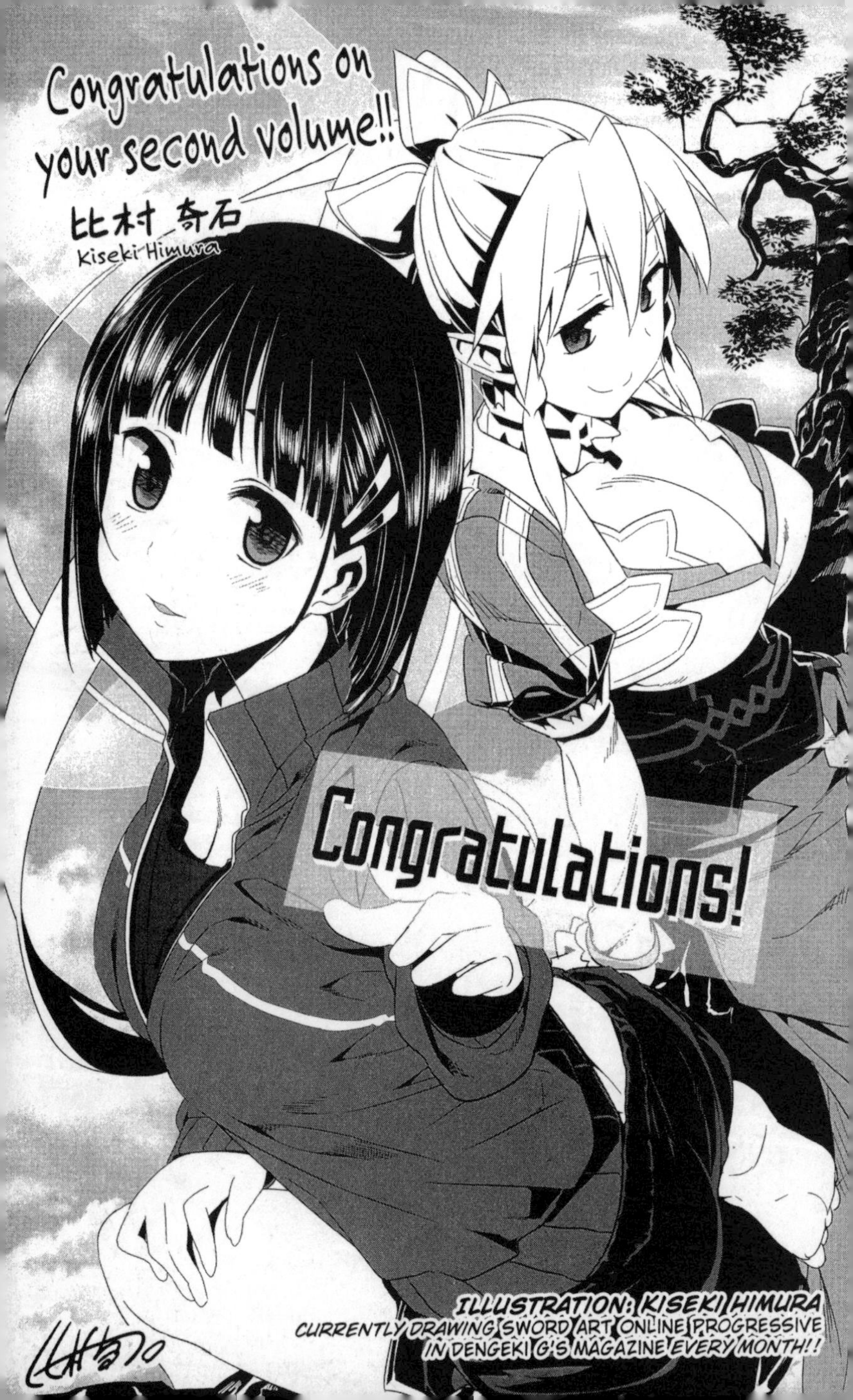
Congratulations on your second volume!!
比村 奇石
Kiseki Himura
Congratulations!
ILLUSTRATION: KISEKI HIMURA
CURRENTLY DRAWING SWORD ART ONLINE PROGRESSIVE
IN DENGEKI G'S MAGAZINE EVERY MONTH!!

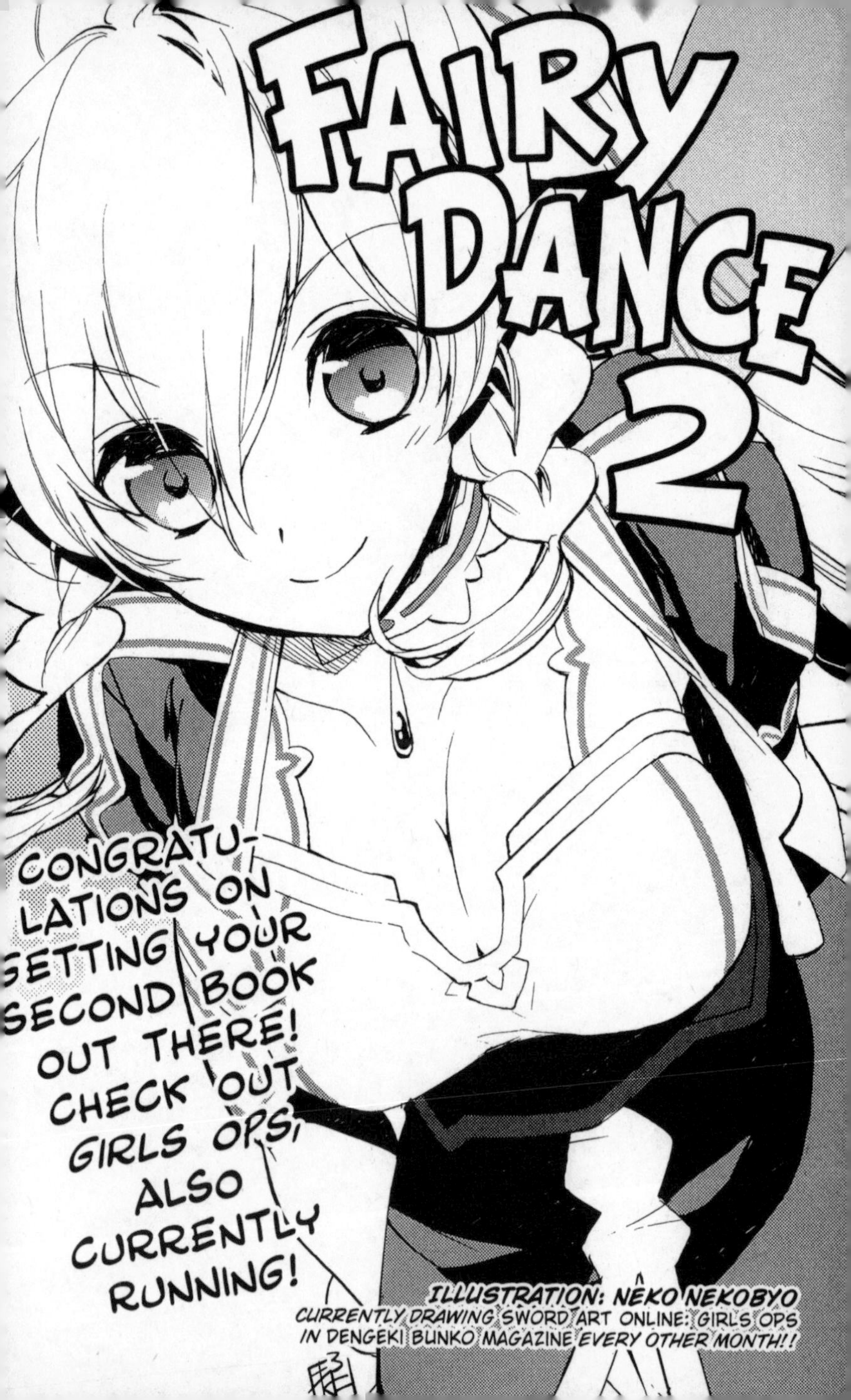
FAIRY DANCE 2
CONGRATU-LATIONS ON GETTING YOUR SECOND BOOK OUT THERE! CHECK OUT GIRLS OPS, ALSO CURRENTLY RUNNING!
ILLUSTRATION: NEKO NEKOBYO
CURRENTLY DRAWING SWORD ART ONLINE: GIRLS OPS IN DENGEKI BUNKO MAGAZINE EVERY OTHER MONTH!!

SWORD ART ONLINE
FAIRY DANCE

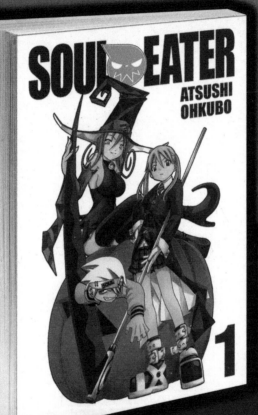

Date: 2/25/16

GRA 741.5 SWO V.2
Kawahara, Reki,
Sword art online. Fairy dance /

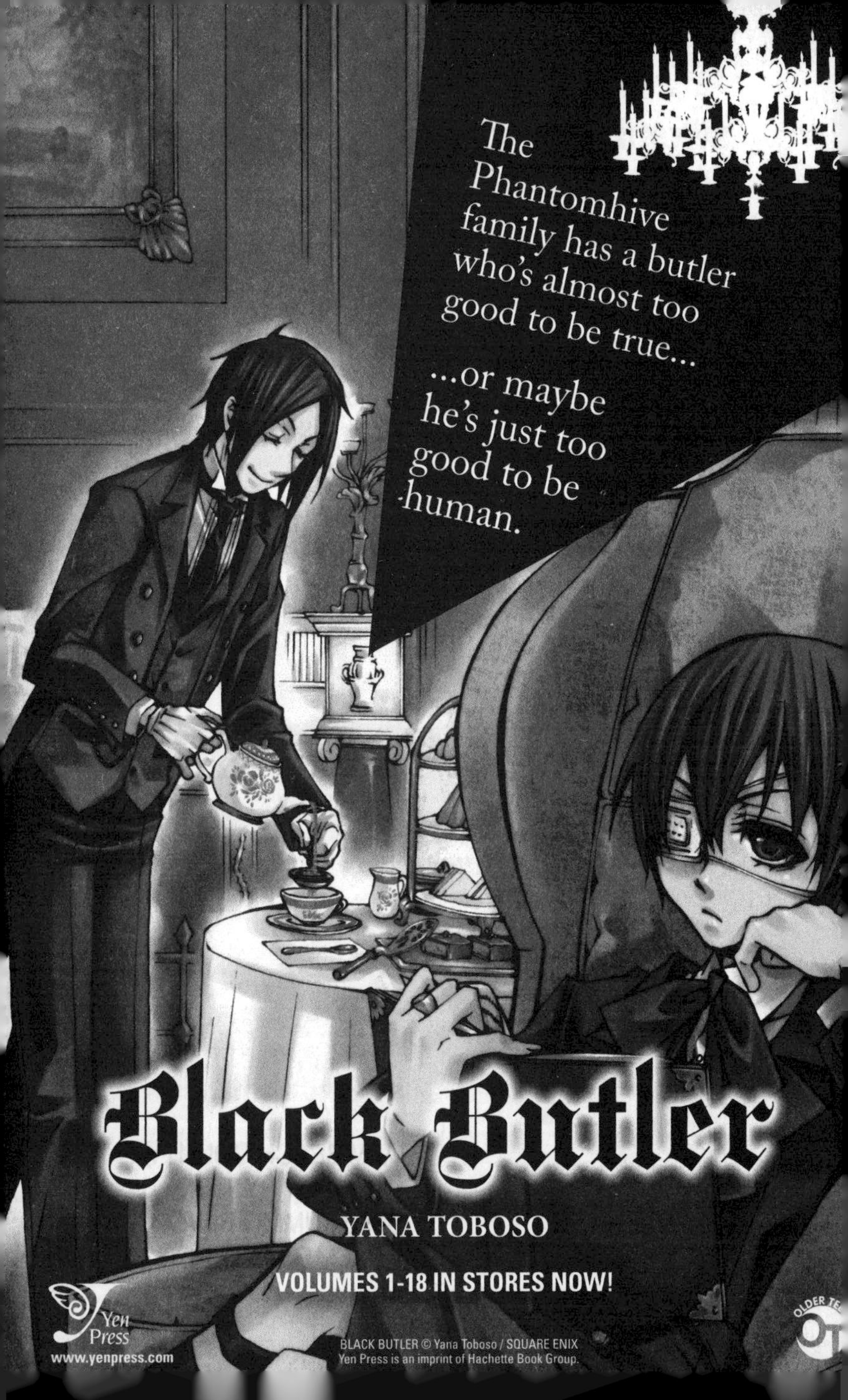
The Phantomhive family has a butler who's almost too good to be true...
...or maybe he's just too good to be human.
Black Butler
YANA TOBOSO
VOLUMES 1-18 IN STORES NOW!
Yen Press
www.yenpress.com
BLACK BUTLER © Yana Toboso / SQUARE ENIX
Yen Press is an imprint of Hachette Book Group.
OLDER TEEN
OT

SWORD ART ONLINE: FAIRY DANCE ②

ART: TSUBASA HADUKI
ORIGINAL STORY: REKI KAWAHARA
CHARACTER DESIGN: ABEC

Translation: Stephen Paul • **Lettering: Lys Blakeslee**

SWORD ART ONLINE: FAIRY DANCE
© REKI KAWAHARA/TSUBASA HADUKI 2013
All rights reserved.
Edited by ASCII MEDIA WORKS
First published in Japan in 2013 by KADOKAWA CORPORATION, Tokyo.
English translation rights arranged with KADOKAWA CORPORATION, Tokyo, through Tuttle-Mori Agency, Inc., Tokyo.

English translation © 2014 by Hachette Book Group, Inc.

Yen Press
Hachette Book Group
1290 Avenue of the Americas
New York, NY 10104

www.HachetteBookGroup.com
www.YenPress.com

Yen Press is an imprint of Hachette Book Group, Inc. The Yen Press name and logo are trademarks of Hachette Book Group, Inc.

First Yen Press Edition: November 2014

ISBN: 978-0-316-33655-0

10 9 8 7 6 5 4 3

BVG

Printed in the United States of America